PRAISE FOR

"In a career and life full of [...] raphy makes clear—was often as mind-boggling. . . . Hip-hop writer S.H. Fernando Jr. benefits from an insider's understanding of the milieu and provides generous context." —Kitty Empire, *The Guardian*

"Trying to focus on the tale of the eccentric, enigmatic, and anonymous rapper-producer Dumile Daniel Thompson—a.k.a. DOOM—must have been akin to pinning down mercury. . . . Fernando goes a long way in presenting the man behind the mask (who died in 2020) without revealing all of his spaced-out secrets that made him special." —A. D. Amorosi, *Variety*

"This is an ambitious, wide-screen, hugely colorful undertaking. Putting to bed some long-held rumors and mistruths, the book also zones in on what makes DOOM such an entrancing figure—in placing a spotlight on his life and work, the author often locates further deposits of genius. A tome worthy of the iconoclastic rapper." —Robin Murray, *Clash*

"There's a lot more going on in *The Chronicles of DOOM* than gushing over a fallen hero. . . . [Fernando] tells a larger story about reinvention, a process familiar to anyone who has had to rebuild a life, and an identity, when things fall apart." —Chris Vognar, *San Francisco Chronicle*

"Fernando has offered a definitive road map to a great artist whose output can still be daunting to the newcomer." —Michaelangelo Matos, *Carbon Sound*

"Skiz's chronicle of the famously secretive rapper offers something unexpected." —Jacob Rosenberg, *Mother Jones*

"Fernando provides a comprehensive look at DOOM's life and career, meticulously researched through interviews with the rapper's many collaborators and those closest to the man behind the mask. His track-by-track breakdowns of DOOM's albums will have sample spotters diving into their record

collections. A perfect pairing with Dan Charnas's *Dilla Time* (2022), this is an essential exploration into the world of 'your favorite rapper's favorite rapper.'"
—Carlos Orellana, *Booklist* (starred review)

"*The Chronicles of DOOM* is superbly written, and incredibly well-researched, but also full of heart and the pure love and appreciation of any true DOOM fan. Here you get everything you would want to know about the man, the myth, the mask. It is written as compellingly as the origin stories of the greatest superheroes and supervillains. If you love DOOM, I could not more highly recommend this book."
—Tommy Orange, *New York Times*–bestselling author of *Wandering Stars* and Pulitzer Prize finalist for *There There*

"This authoritative guide to one of hip-hop's most enigmatic figures peeks behind the mask to reveal Daniel Dumile's rebellious spirit and creative genius."   —Rob Kenner, author of *The Marathon Don't Stop: The Life and Times of Nipsey Hussle*

"*The Chronicles of DOOM* is a thoroughly researched and at times poetically written tome about the life and work of MF DOOM. . . . [It] has something for the old-school hip-hop heads, the comic-reading and cartoon-watching nerds, the DIY indie kids, the esoteric stoners, and everyone in between just like DOOM's music."   —Logan Dalton

THE CHRONICLES OF
DOOM

ALSO BY S.H. FERNANDO JR.

The New Beats: Exploring the Music, Culture and Attitudes of Hip-Hop (1994)

From the Streets of Shaolin: The Wu-Tang Saga (2021)

THE CHRONICLES OF
DOOM

UNRAVELING RAP'S MASKED ICONOCLAST

S.H. Fernando Jr.

ASTRA HOUSE
NEW YORK

Copyright © 2024 by S.H. Fernando Jr.

All rights reserved. Copying or digitizing this book for storage, display, or distribution in any other medium is strictly prohibited.

For information about permission to reproduce selections from this book, please contact permissions@astrahouse.com.

Astra House
A Division of Astra Publishing House
astrahouse.com
Printed in the United States of America

Library of Congress Cataloging-in-Publication Data

Names: Fernando, S. H., Jr., author.
Title: The chronicles of DOOM : unraveling rap's masked iconoclast / S.H. Fernando Jr.
Description: First edition. | [New York] : Astra House, 2024. | Includes bibliographical references and discography. | Summary: "The definitive biography of MF DOOM, charting the reclusive and revered hip-hop artist's life, career, and eventual immortality"—Provided by publisher.
Identifiers: LCCN 2024020778 (print) | LCCN 2024020779 (ebook) | ISBN 9781662602177 (hardcover) | ISBN 9781662602184 (epub)
Subjects: LCSH: MF Doom. | Rap musicians—England—Biography. | LCGFT: Biographies.
Classification: LCC ML420.M4246 F4 2024 (print) | LCC ML420.M4246 (ebook) | DDC 782.421649092 [B]—dc23/eng/20240509
LC record available at https://lccn.loc.gov/2024020778
LC ebook record available at https://lccn.loc.gov/2024020779

ISBN: 9781662603242 (pb)

First paperback edition, 2025
10 9 8 7 6 5 4 3 2 1

Design by Alissa Theodor
The text is set in WarnockPro-Light.
The titles are set in AmasisMTStd.

For Sid

SONNET 55

Not marble nor the gilded monuments
Of princes shall outlive this powerful rhyme,
But you shall shine more bright in these contents
Than unswept stone besmeared with sluttish time.
When wasteful war shall statues overturn,
And broils root out the work of masonry,
Nor Mars his sword nor war's quick fire shall burn
The living record of your memory.
'Gainst death and all-oblivious enmity
Shall you pace forth; your praise shall still find room
Even in the eyes of all posterity
That wear this world out to the ending DOOM.
So, till the Judgement that yourself arise,
You live in this, and dwell in lovers' eyes.

—WILLIAM SHAKESPEARE

CONTENTS

SONNET 55   vii
INTRODUCTION   3

I. THE MAN
1. BACK IN THE DAYS   13
2. THE GAS FACE   24
3. PEACHFUZZ   34
4. BLACK BASTARDS   44
5. THE TIME WE FACED DOOM   54

II. THE MYTH
6. HERO VS. VILLAIN   71
7. MONSTER ZERO   81
8. TAKE ME TO YOUR LEADER   90

III. THE MASK
9. SUSPENDED ANIMATION   103
10. DEEP FRIED FRENZ   110
11. WHO YOU THINK I AM?   121
12. THE MIC   128

IV. THE MUSIC
13. MF DOOM/*OPERATION: DOOMSDAY*   139
14. METAL FINGERS/*SPECIAL HERBS*   155
15. KING GEEDORAH/*TAKE ME TO YOUR LEADER*   168

16. VIKTOR VAUGHN/*VAUDEVILLE VILLAIN*	183
17. MADVILLAIN/*MADVILLAINY*	199
18. MF DOOM/*MM . . FOOD*	219
19. DANGER DOOM/*THE MOUSE AND THE MASK*	234
20. DOOM/*BORN LIKE THIS*	249
21. JJ DOOM/*KEY TO THE KUFFS*	266

V. THE LEGEND

22. NEVER DEAD	289
EPILOGUE	299

VI. THE CATALOG: A DOOMOGRAPHY

Bibliography	316
Notes	323
Acknowledgments	335
About the Author	337

THE CHRONICLES OF
DOOM

INTRODUCTION

The year 2020 will always be remembered as the "Year of the Mask"—our humble response to the outbreak of a global pandemic and its attendant lockdowns, restrictions, and overall uncertainty that sent the world into a tailspin. But for serious rap fans, that designation hides a double meaning, recalling the year's heartbreaking conclusion. On December 31, we discovered that one of the most creative, original, and beautiful minds that hip-hop had ever produced—in the person of Daniel Dumile, aka MF DOOM, or simply DOOM—had passed away at the age of forty-nine. The announcement came via a poignant Instagram post by his wife, who wrote:

Begin all things by giving thanks to THE ALL!

To Dumile:

The greatest husband, father, teacher, student, business partner, lover and friend I could ever ask for. Thank you for all the things you have shown, taught and given to me, our children and our family. Thank you for teaching me how to forgive beings and give another chance, not to be so quick to judge and write off. Thank you for showing how not to be afraid to love and be the best person I could ever be. My world will never be the same without you. Words will never express what you and Malachi mean to me, I love both and adore you always. May THE ALL continue to bless you, our family, and the planet.

All my Love
Jasmine.[1]

Readers of this unforeseen obituary were further confounded by the revelation that DOOM had passed away two months earlier, on October 31. For grieving fans, it seemed weirdly apropos since everyone had an excuse to wear a mask on Halloween, and DOOM never appeared in public without one. Honoring the privacy he so fiercely protected in life, his wife offered no further details of his death.

Reaction to the MC's untimely passing came swiftly on social media—especially among his contemporaries. A roll call of rappers, from Denzel Curry to Playboi Carti, tweeted their respects to the artist popularly regarded as "your favorite rapper's favorite rapper," a term coined by Q-Tip from A Tribe Called Quest. Former collaborators, like Radiohead's Thom Yorke, also chimed in, crediting him as a "massive inspiration." From the *New York Times* to everyone's favorite podcasts and blogs, the tragic news was tempered with massive tributes. DOOM was even lionized in places one wouldn't normally expect. The entertainment industry bible, *Variety*, for example, called him, "One of the most celebrated, unpredictable and enigmatic figures in independent hip-hop."[2]

But a real measure of his influence and impact came from the legions of fans worldwide, who bombed social media with DOOM-inspired artwork and graffiti homages to the man, who himself wielded a wicked can of Krylon. Some, like Ryan O'Connor, were even moved to pen poignant tributes online, writing, "He may have been rap's comic book villain but he was the most beloved character rap ever birthed."[3] Adam Davidson, meanwhile, managed to distill the feelings of countless others who enjoyed a deep and personal relationship with the artist through his music, concluding, "Here's to one of the best friends I never met."[4] The overwhelming sense of shock and sorrow among DOOM's boosters and supporters was accompanied by the realization that a unique and irreplaceable talent had been forever lost.

Though regarded as a hero to most, DOOM was more comfortable claiming the title of "Supervillain," a persona he inhabited with verve and gusto. But while examples of his villainous behavior abound—including sending imposters to perform in his stead—this pose was largely obfuscation on his part. In reality, he exemplified the antithesis of the fame-obsessed, money-hungry, attention-seeking, and self-absorbed artist. He fancied himself a man of the people and came across as both humble and down-to-earth in interviews, revealing a unique worldview. "I always tend to root for the villain. That's just me," he told BBC Radio 1 in 2012. "You know he's probably going to lose in the end or whatever, but he always comes back. The villain tends to be the more hard worker, yunno? He speaks for the working-class man."[5] In another interview, he said, "I look at DOOM as representing the average Joe. The outlaw can sympathize with DOOM, or the cat who doesn't have too many friends, or the cat who doesn't have the best sneakers on. If you're not as cool as Jay-Z, you don't have enough money to buy his records or buy a gold chain—I don't wear no chain—I'm your man, yo! I'm the one you can relate to. I got a pot belly. Come holler at me!"[6] Leaving no mystery about where his allegiances lay, his idiosyncratic nature set him apart from the crowded and competitive field of braggers and boasters who battled for mic supremacy.

A true workhorse, DOOM proved himself incredibly prolific and dedicated to his craft as both an MC and a producer during a career spanning more than three decades. From his first incarnation as Zev Love X, who alongside his brother Subroc (Dingilizwe Dumile) formed the core of the group KMD, he promptly distinguished himself with a star-making guest spot on the gold single "The Gas Face" from 3rd Bass's *The Cactus Album* (Def Jam/Columbia, 1989). After KMD parlayed that opportunity into a record deal of their own, their promising debut *Mr. Hood* (Elektra, 1991) spawned the memorable hit "Peachfuzz." On the back of that modest success, they returned to the studio to make a follow-up, *Black Bastards*, an album that was unfortunately shelved due to music industry politics and what was then considered controversial cover art.

After suffering the twin tragedies of his brother's untimely death and the termination of his record deal, DOOM spent several years in the existential wilderness, on the brink of homelessness, as he often admitted in interviews. But out of the darkness, inspiration struck like a lightning bolt as he reinvented himself as his comic-book alter ego, based on the Marvel villain Doctor Doom. Reemerging on the rap scene via the fight club of open-mic nights, he cobbled together tracks produced at various friends' home studios and released *Operation: Doomsday* (Fondle 'Em, 1999), the first full-length under his new persona. Arriving at an opportune moment, it provided the precious antidote for rebel rap kids disenchanted by the "jiggy" era personified by the likes of Puff Daddy and Jay-Z. While these platinum-selling artists repackaged the art form for commercial consumption, staging million-dollar video shoots aboard borrowed yachts, DOOM, like an experimental submersible, took us into uncharted depths.

Indeed, his glorious second act came at a time when rap cleaved into rival factions, creating two distinct camps. Indie rap, like its much-hyped cousin, "alternative rock," may have been a convenient marketing term, but, in hindsight, it also proved the existence of a healthy market for non-major-label music that pushed boundaries both lyrically and sonically. A grizzled veteran of hip-hop's golden era, DOOM found himself at the nexus of this independent movement, enjoying his most prolific phase between 2001 and 2005, while working on several albums simultaneously. After *Operation: Doomsday* was rebooted in 2001, with wider distribution and a national press campaign, he followed up with the first in a series of instrumental albums known as *Special Herbs*, of which he eventually released ten volumes under the moniker of the Metal Fingered Villain.

In 2003, not content with one alter ego, DOOM expanded his brand with several other alternative personas. King Geedorah, based on the three-headed flying dragon from the Godzilla movie franchise—popularly known as Ghidorah—released *Take Me to Your Leader* on British indie label Big Dada in June. Only a few months later, in September, the *Vaudeville Villain* LP, credited to Viktor Vaughn, appeared on the start-up Sound-Ink Records, out of New York. Slowly building up steam, DOOM's *pièce de résistance* came as a collaborative effort with LA producer Madlib, his partner in the duo called Madvillain. Released by Stones Throw Records in March 2004, the resulting *Madvillainy* was widely hailed as the *White Album* of indie rap. DOOM had finally arrived as a real contender in his own right, surpassing even the relic of his former self, Zev Love X. Continuing his assault, he returned with Viktor Vaughn's *VV:2 (Insomniac)* in September and a follow-up DOOM album, *Mm..Food?* (Rhymesayers), in November. The following year his collaboration with producer Danger Mouse, *The Mouse and the Mask* (Epitaph, 2005), sold a staggering 350,000 copies, vaulting him onto the *Billboard* charts. Releasing eight albums on eight different labels in a six-year span marked an unprecedented achievement in rap, establishing the consistency and high standards on which DOOM earned his reputation.

But the early aughts proved only a warm-up for the inventive rapper who told journalist David Ma, "Hip-hop is so saturated with the same old same old that people always expect the guy to actually be the guy. They want you to be real and straight from the streets and all that. I make hip-hop but use DOOM as a character to convey stories that a normal dude can't."[7] By eschewing the usual street verité of rap, along with its accompanying tropes and clichés, he, instead, distinguished himself as a writer of fiction.

"You have writers that write about crazy characters but that doesn't mean the writer himself is crazy," he explained. "DOOM is evil—let's not forget that—but that doesn't mean I'm evil."[8] Never before in the "keep it real" realms of rap had an MC sought refuge in fiction, writing and rapping from the third person perspective. For Daniel Dumile, DOOM represented a character comparable to the outrageous right-wing pundit persona styled by Stephen Colbert on Comedy Central. Using a similar approach, the rapper created his own unique niche, distinguishing himself from all other MCs in the process.

DOOM's rhyme style, too, elevated lyricism to a whole 'nother level. Not only did he perfect the use of internal rhyming and alliteration, in which consecutive words within a single line all rhymed, but he regularly employed techniques like onomatopoeia, double entendre, puns, and punchlines to staggering effect. While the smartest rappers may have consulted a thesaurus, DOOM's secret weapons were *Merriam-Webster's Dictionary of Allusions*, *The Dictionary of Clichés*, and *Depraved and Insulting English*. Employing a vocabulary worthy of a wordsmith like Shakespeare, he displayed a command of language rarely seen in rap. His stream-of-consciousness writing style that obsessives could really sink their teeth into—allowing for multiple interpretations of his work—defied an era of mumble rap, where not really saying anything dominated the mainstream.

But if there was one unifying spirit or theme to his work, it was laugh-out-loud humor. "When I'm doing a DOOM record, I'm arranging it, I'm finding voices," he told writer Ta-Nehisi Coates. "All I have to do is listen to it and think, oh shit, that will be funny. I write down whatever would be funny and get as many 'whatever would' funnies in a row and find a way to make them all fit. There's a certain science to it. In a relatively small period of time, you want it to be, that's funny, that's funny, that's funny, that's funny. I liken it to comedy standup."[9]

On the production tip, DOOM, who considered himself a producer first and foremost, was no slouch either. "I try to find beats that'll have you buggin'," he once said. "You know, like questioning what you could possibly say on that beat, but stuff that's still funky, you know what I'm sayin'? Beats that push the envelope."[10] To this end, he went to great lengths to find singular source material, often turning to cartoons and other children's programming or obscure YouTube videos. Other times he flaunted conventions, sampling quiet storm R&B hits, or even earlier rap songs. Whether rapping over other producers' beats or his own, he always sought to engage and challenge the listener with something different.

Amid the colorful cast of characters and personas who have distinguished themselves in rap—from Rammellzee to Kool Keith, Ol' Dirty Bastard to Busta Rhymes—DOOM shines as another true original. When asked about the best advice he had ever received, he replied, "A wise man once said, 'Do you.' I know what he meant, but I didn't really grasp what he said until maybe a year later. And that was like the wisest statement I heard out of any book or anything I ever read: 'Do You.' Be yourself and that's the best thing you could be. Anytime you try to copy someone you're not being genuine to yourself."[11] In the same interview he added, "I'm constantly striving for perfection, so what I'm doin' is constantly elevatin' and educatin' myself in a way that, all right, I'm better than I was the previous day. Yunno, so, that could go on forever, there's really not ever going to be a top, you know? I don't think I'll do it in this lifetime."[12]

True to his words, DOOM may not have ascended to the top of the charts or become a Fortune 500 rapper like Jay-Z. But in carving out his own space within hip-hop, he became an icon nonetheless, ultimately transcending the art form. At the same time, he was regarded as a maverick and an iconoclast, who rigorously challenged rap's status quo during its most overtly pop phase. Though his creative output may have been cut short, he remains revered to this day, and still very much shrouded in mystery. Yet the crater-sized impression he left begs greater examination and analysis.

The Chronicles of DOOM: Unraveling Rap's Masked Iconoclast delivers a long-awaited and unprecedented look at a most enigmatic and reluctant public figure. As a complex character who cherished his privacy, DOOM's very nature precludes any efforts to get behind the mask and into his head. Instead, his story unravels like a ball of yarn as told through the people who worked with him and knew him best. While laying out his tangled but compelling narrative, this book offers unparalleled insights into the making of a true hip-hop legend. It also demonstrates that we all have something to learn from this self-professed Black nerd, who went against the grain and broke from convention, turned tribulation into triumph, and, ultimately, like Sinatra, did it his way.

DOOM, like most of us, led a messy and complicated life that doesn't conveniently adhere to a conventional narrative arc, so the book, necessarily, takes a nonlinear approach. While maintaining a basic chronology, it skips backward and forward in time to explore DOOM's work on several projects simultaneously. The book also takes pause to drill down and offer deeper insights into the influences that shaped him—comic books, monster movies, and the esoteric ideas that contributed to his unique worldview. Such a detour is essential to even begin understanding his prodigious catalog, which we delve into in detail. In summation, we discuss his important legacy and the savvy approach he took to maintaining it, the cherished place he now inhabits in the hearts of those touched by his work, and his exalted perch in the pantheon of hip-hop.

THE MAN

All things are possible. Who you are is limited by who you think you are.

—THE EGYPTIAN BOOK OF THE DEAD

1

BACK IN THE DAYS

You have to decide who you are and force the world to deal with you, not with its idea of you.

—JAMES BALDWIN

Preachers and presidents are typically the ones to get streets named after them, not rappers. That's why it was no small deal when the Long Island city of Long Beach—population circa thirty-four thousand—voted overwhelmingly to christen East Hudson Street, between Long Beach and Riverside Boulevards, "KMD - MF DOOM Way," in homage to some of her most famous sons. Daniel Dumile Jr., aka MF DOOM, and his younger brother, Dingilizwe, aka Subroc, who spent their formative years growing up at 114 East Hudson, joined the ranks of rap's fallen soldiers—in the fine company of Jam Master Jay, Scott La Rock, MCA of the Beastie Boys, Phife Dawg, The Notorious B.I.G., and Big Pun—to be officially enshrined in the public consciousness for their contributions to the art form and culture. On a sunny Saturday in July 2021, neighbors, fans, friends, and family (including the surviving Dumile siblings, Dimbaza and Thenjiwe, up from Georgia), gathered at an unveiling ceremony to celebrate their lives and reminisce about the brothers, who were closer than two peas in a pod.

Spearheading the drive to gather a petition of over ten thousand signatures, longtime resident Dr. Patrick Graham kicked off the festivities, proclaiming of DOOM, "His hip-hop lyricism represents some of the best linguistic metaphors, garnering intergenerational and interracial admiration."[1] Though his undeniable raw talent had made him widely popular, he still managed to evade mainstream success. But as DOOM embodied such concepts as freedom and redemption, Graham observed, "His life and art symbolize the resilience we need in our present context."[2]

For DOOM, writing rhymes and making music did not revolve around money, fame, fashion, or hype, but the act of creativity itself, to which he dedicated his whole being. He knew full well that art, though a product of individual self-expression, embodied transcendent powers—to heal, transform, transmit ideas, and even bring people together. It was a means of seeing and engaging with the world. An artist in the truest sense of the word, DOOM owed his entire existence to the creative act.

Ashlyn Thompson first met Daniel Joshua Dumile Sr. at a weekly art show in Long Beach in 1970. A native of Marabella, Trinidad, the lithe eighteen-year-old had emigrated to the US the previous year to join her family. Her mother, Henrietta, had been the first to arrive stateside in the mid-sixties, working as a domestic. Now well on her way to making her American dream a reality, Mrs. Thompson had started a nursing agency to provide home care for the aging Jewish population in the area, squirreling away enough funds to purchase the four-bedroom house at 114 East Hudson Street with her husband, Joseph. After establishing employment and permanent residency, the Thompsons, like many typical immigrants, started bringing over their eleven children. Education being a priority, Ashlyn, an honor student, arrived in time to complete her senior year at Long Beach High before enrolling in courses at nearby Molloy College. She was still finding her footing in her new surroundings when a chance encounter introduced her to her future husband, who was selling his paintings in the town center at Kennedy Plaza.

Dumile (pronounced "Doo-me-lay"), also an immigrant, hailed from Zimbabwe in southern Africa. Besides being an accomplished artist, a hobby he pursued in his spare time, he was proficient enough in math and science to win a full scholarship to attend university in the US in the mid-sixties, a rare achievement for a foreign student. Initially, he ended up studying in upstate New York, but a taste of his first harsh winter was enough to make him transfer. Consulting a state map, he spotted the name "Long Beach," which enticed him with visions of the sunnier climes he had left behind. Without so much as a visit, he decided to relocate there, enrolling in nearby Hofstra University in Hempstead. At least the "City by the Sea," as his new home was nicknamed, offered a magnificent view of the Atlantic from its sprawling wooden boardwalk.

Upon graduating, he briefly taught math and science at Long Beach High before helping to establish the Harriet Eisman Community School, an alternative night school catering to troubled students left behind by the public school system. Having lived under apartheid, Dumile was a natural-born activist who espoused solidarity with the civil rights struggle in America. His main goal became helping to empower Black people. Smart, multitalented, and committed to his ideals, he made enough of an impression on Ashlyn that, in spite of her strict upbringing, she was soon sneaking out of the house to meet him. Not long into their surreptitious and whirlwind courtship, she found herself expecting her first child, and they married.

That summer, Ashlyn made a trip to London, England, to visit her older sister Marlene, who was attending nursing college there. Also a recent newlywed, Marlene had just welcomed a baby girl named Michelle into the family. While staying with her sister in the borough of Hounslow, Ashlyn unexpectedly went into labor, giving birth to a healthy baby boy, Daniel Jr., on July 13, 1971. As soon as mother and child were able, they returned to the US a couple of months later, the baby traveling on a British passport since he was officially a British citizen. By this time, Daniel Sr. was renting a small house in Freeport, Long Island, where they lived. Over the next few years, the Dumile family grew to include Dingilizwe, born in August 1973; Dimbaza, born in October 1975; and finally a girl, Thenjiwe, born in May 1977. Not content to remain a housewife while raising her brood, Ashlyn found time to enroll in the nursing program at the Nassau County Vocational Education and Extension Board. By the time her daughter was born, she had graduated, becoming a licensed practical nurse.

Meanwhile, Daniel Sr. continued with his teaching and activism. In addition to his role in establishing the Eisman school, he helped found the Martin Luther King Community Center for neighborhood youth. He also played an instrumental role in getting the first Black officer hired by the Long Beach Police Department. Considering the deep influence of Louis Farrakhan and the Nation of Islam on certain segments of the Black community in the seventies, it came as no surprise when Daniel Sr. and his wife joined the organization and started regularly attending a mosque in neighboring Roosevelt. Never very religious, he found inspiration in the Nation's emphatic message of Black empowerment.

Though raised as a Christian, Ashlyn dutifully adopted the hijab and started reading the Quran. Always intellectually curious and an avid reader, she passed on her appreciation for language and the written word to her children. Despite her training as a nurse, she displayed a progressive bent, embracing naturopathic medicine and practicing yoga, meditation, and vegetarianism long before they were in vogue. While her husband channeled his creativity into painting and woodcarving—taking over their basement as his studio, where he stored stacks of finished canvases and art supplies—Ashlyn enjoyed designing and sewing clothes for herself and her family.

Early life for the Dumile children, who grew up in a stable, two-parent, middle-class household, could only be described as normal. Despite the Nation's preoccupation with discipline, they were allowed to be themselves, gravitating toward their own interests like skateboarding and riding BMX bikes. Their father did, however, exercise strict control over the media consumed under his roof, favoring the educational programming of NPR and PBS. But the kids were still permitted to indulge in the weekly ritual of Saturday morning cartoons and other children's programs.

Daniel Jr. did not demonstrate a particular aptitude for school, though his teacher praised his ability to draw. In one of his very first report cards, dating back to first grade, she described him as "a quiet boy who gets along well with his peers."[3] She further assessed, "Dumile can decode words and understand what he reads. He has good ability but very poor work habits, . . . poor listening skills, and does not follow directions."[4] Apparently, "DOOM," his mother's pet name for him (and one that stuck, which we will use herein in his preferred form of all caps), was already moving to the beat of a different drummer. Despite receiving mostly Cs, he did manage to get an A for attitude, but only a D for effort.

As a member of Gen X, DOOM belonged to the first generation that grew up immersed in rap. Though far too young to attend those early parties in the Bronx, he turned eight in the summer of 1979, when the novelty of reciting rhyming words over a beat finally reached national prominence with "Rapper's Delight," the breakout sensation by the Sugarhill Gang. In addition to establishing rap in the public consciousness, that song set off schoolyard ciphers everywhere as kids raised on Mother Goose attempted to imitate its seductive flow. Fads have always been the currency of youth, but DOOM took rapping more seriously than most. "Ever since third grade, I had a notebook and was putting words together just for fun," he recalled. "I like different etymologies, different slang that came out in different eras, different languages, different dialects. I liked being able to speak to somebody and throw it back and forth, and they can't predict what you're going to say next. But once you say it, they're always like, 'Oh, shit.'"[5]

But even before rapping became the talk of the town, all eyes were on the deejay. When DOOM was around eight or nine, he and his siblings would spend several days a week down the block at their babysitter Dolores's house. She lived with her two grown sons, Charlie and Doug, aged seventeen and twenty, respectively, who sported Afros and were heavily into music. In the basement of their Freeport home, they set up a pair of turntables and a mixer to practice deejaying, spinning the popular jams of the day—like "Bounce, Rock, Skate, Roll" by Vaughan Mason and Crew, Chic's "Good Times," and "Genius of Love" by Tom Tom Club.

"We used to look up to them," DOOM recalled of Dolores's sons, "like go peekin' down in the basement at what they were doin', you know?"[6] From spying from atop the basement stairs, he was eventually invited down to take part in the action. "So that's my first experience with what we would call hip-hop," said DOOM, "You know, see how the record feel when you spin it back. How the fader feel when you hit it, you know what I mean?"[7] The tactile sensation of manipulating records with their hands offered instant gratification for this young novice and his brothers, who were soon addicted. Though still far removed from having their own setup, they practiced whenever they could at the homes of friends and relatives, wrecking many needles and vinyl albums along the way.

But those carefree days of childhood—of endless summers, no responsibilities, and the comfort of being together—were soon shattered when divorce fractured the family. While Ashlyn retained custody of the children, moving back in with her mother at 114 East Hudson Street, she had no problem allowing her ex-husband visitation rights. Though the split was amicable, and the children appeared remarkably resilient, there was no way to really gauge the consequences of going from one happy family to a single-parent home. Without a place of her own, Ashlyn felt like a child herself. Living with her mother and a couple of younger siblings created a dynamic that made it impossible for her to stay in Long Beach for too long.

Fiercely independent and determined to do her best for her kids and keep them together, she spent the next two years trying to get back on her feet. Despite working constantly, she moved around the metropolitan area several times chasing rents she could afford. For a time, the family lived on Lispenard Street in lower Manhattan as well as north of the Bronx in more suburban Yonkers and Mount Vernon. But regardless of the challenges they faced, the kids remained inured to their situation, finding refuge in fantasy. "That's when we was really really collectin' comics," DOOM recalled. "The whole Marvel universe was our shit. Straight up. Iron Man to X-Men to Fantastic Four to even like Alpha Flight. All the dope shit. All the spin-offs and everything. The whole Marvel universe—the way they designed it—everything played a part in everything."[8] In addition to sparking the imagination, comics provided an all-encompassing world—actually a universe—that they could get lost in.

Despite a revolving procession of schools, friends, and neighborhoods, hip-hop provided another anchor that kept them grounded and engaged. They first heard Harlem rapper Kurtis Blow performing his smash hits "Christmas Rappin'" (1979) and "The Breaks" (1980) on superstar DJ Frankie Crocker's show on WBLS, New York's premier urban station. But the real, raw hip-hop could only be found on underground stations broadcasting on the far ends of the dial. When their mom was at the hospital working a graveyard shift, the brothers would stay up late, tuning the crappy clock-radio dial to 105.9 WHBI-FM in Newark, New Jersey, for the *Zulu Beats* show, on Wednesdays from one to three in the morning. The hosts, DJ Afrika Islam and Donald D, counted themselves among Afrika Bambaataa's mighty Zulu Nation, who had overseen the Bronx's transition from violent gang turf to a cauldron of creativity, leveraging the disparate elements of rapping, deejaying, breakdancing, and graffiti writing into a celebration of peace, love, unity, and having fun.

"They used to just spin breaks, but they'll have voice-over pieces on top of it," DOOM recalled. "You have like 'Funky Drummer,' or you have 'Apache' rockin', you know, and you'll have like something from like an old comedy joint like a Monty Python piece will be playing," adding, "I always found that real bugged out, you know what I'm saying? 'Cause I ain't know where it was coming from. So, you had another layer of digging, you know? So not only did you have to find what the break was from, you gotta figure out, wait, wait, what is that voice, you know? So, it was always interesting to me."[9] The Awesome Two (Special K and Teddy Ted) and The World-Famous Supreme Team (Cee Divine the Mastermind and Just Allah the Superstar) also hosted shows on WHBI that the brothers would tape. Lacking any formal musical training, DOOM, like many others of his generation, was drawn to hip-hop for its accessibility, originality, and the novelty of using old records to create something new.

Around 1983, after two years of roaming, the family returned to 114 East Hudson in Long Beach, thanks in part to lobbying efforts by DOOM and his siblings. Though back under their grandmother's roof, they could, at least, count on the built-in support network of family and friends instead of trying to make it on their own. Within striking distance of Queens, Long Beach had stuck out as a unique enclave in the New York metropolitan area since its incorporation in 1922. Occupying the westernmost barrier island off Long Island's South Shore—a strip roughly three and a half miles long and less than a mile wide—it was originally dubbed the "Riviera of the East" for its wealthy population and prominent boardwalk. Quiet residential blocks of single-family homes with manicured front lawns characterized the town, which remained predominantly white (about 84 percent) in the eighties, with a smattering of Blacks, Latinos, and Asians.

Long Beach stood at the crossroads of suburbia and the big city, a hybrid environment where skateboarding and BMX bikes could coexist with graffiti and breakdancing. In middle school, DOOM and Dingilizwe, both avid skaters, built a wooden half-pipe in their driveway out of salvaged scraps. They were also skilled enough to strip a used BMX bike down to its frame, rebuilding and repainting it to look brand new. When graffiti was enjoying a renaissance in the early eighties, the brothers made their mark as writers. Too young to be running around train yards after hours, DOOM tagged walls with thick markers, simply writing "Art," his first official pseudonym, in the bubble lettering popular at the time. Dingilizwe, who mostly went by his Muslim name, Raheem (or Heem for short), chose the moniker Subroc, the name for a submarine-launched nuclear warhead developed by the US Navy in the sixties. After breakdancing became the next urban craze to go mainstream, thanks to movies like *Flashdance* (1983), *Breakin'* (1984), and *Beat Street* (1984), they jumped on that bandwagon, too. As neighborhood youth started carrying pieces of cardboard around so they could throw their bodies on the concrete, spinning around without losing any skin, the brothers Dumile eagerly followed their peers, also mastering the robotic movements of "popping" and "locking."

With the decline of New York's notorious gang scene in the seventies due to violence and drug abuse, hip-hop helped fill the void in the eighties, encouraging the formation of crews, which were defined by any group of youth who hung out together and shared common interests. "And everybody in the crew might add one thing to it, or, you know, bring a different angle to it," said DOOM. "So, graffiti was like something that we just did, doodling, you know, art in general. It turned more to graffiti at first and then the breakdancing came into it. And it turned out the hip-hop part, music-wise, sound-wise, got more popular and started to be something that we practiced more, making tapes, and we took it from there."[10] One of the highlights of having a crew was choosing a cool name. The brothers settled on KMD because they liked how the letters sounded together. Taking a page from the outlaw spirit of graf, considered by some to be vandalism, KMD evolved into a backronym for "Kausing Much Damage."

The return to Long Beach solidified the brothers' connection to hip-hop, to which they committed themselves fully and with the all-out zeal of youth. Still too poor to afford their own turntables, they could at least watch their neighbor, Fred Harris, who was around eighteen at the time, practicing on the pair of Technics 1200s that he kept in his garage. Fred happened to be a protégé of DJ Reggie Reg, a popular local DJ who spun at parties. They also met Ahmed Brandon and Otis McKenzie, a couple of older teens who were accomplished breakdancers. Ahmed lived around the corner, and his mother worked for DOOM's grandmother's nursing agency. Both he and Otis were members of GYP or "Get Yours Posse," a larger crew of neighborhood youth bonded together by various aspects of hip-hop culture. Though rap was fast establishing itself as the face of the movement, each of the other elements were considered equally important to true B-boys, who dabbled in them all. Before money entered the picture, creativity was the currency, and earning respect from one's skills. KMD easily blended into the larger GYP, whose membership ran to over forty members deep at their peak.

Perhaps because their mother tolerated the neighborhood youth, 114 Hudson became a home base for GYP. "We're just kind of hanging out, drinking, eating, snapping, having fun. And that would be all day long. All day long," recalls Uncle E, a GYP member who spent a significant amount of time there. Funny enough, the place had the vibe of a neighborhood barbershop, as a fourteen-year-old Subroc, barely in high school, started cutting people's hair as a side hustle. As word spread quickly through the town, friends waited their turn to get a "tape-up" or "fade" on Friday and Saturday nights. Instead of charging cash, Sub took his payment in vinyl LPs that his customers usually lifted from their parents' record collections. He and his brother were now actively "crate-diggin" or looking for samples to make music, so they needed the raw materials of their trade.

By this time, they had saved enough to buy a single turntable and begged their mother to get them the new Casio SK-5 for Christmas. Though it looked like a toy, this consumer-model keyboard had the ability to sample sounds. As one of their first pieces of equipment, it set them on a path toward music production and encouraged their crate-digging. In a first-floor room just off the porch known as "DOOM's room," the neighborhood youth would hang out and listen to music, or just shoot the shit while waiting for their turn in the barber's chair that Sub set up in the foyer. DOOM usually played the background: reading a book, writing rhymes, watching a documentary on PBS, or sometimes just staring off into space absorbed in his own thoughts on the couch.

As the brothers started making their own music, they also learned some hard lessons about the burgeoning cottage industry surrounding rap—namely, that it was not all fun and games. Of the top MCs of the day that DOOM respected—names like Rakim, Slick Rick, and Just-Ice—one of his favorites was KRS-ONE of the group Boogie Down Productions. In fact, he said, "The whole BDP crew—he and Scott La Rock—influenced me the most being there was two of them like me and my brother. My brother was the DJ and I'm the MC, so we always looked up to them and followed their career."[11] Lawrence Krisna Parker (aka KRS-ONE) had been a homeless teen from a troubled background when he met and befriended Scott "La Rock" Sterling, an employee at the shelter where he was staying. Bonding over their mutual love of hip-hop, the duo eventually started working together, releasing a slew of independent singles. In the process, they got embroiled in one of rap's first major rivalries, or "beefs," taking on Marley Marl, deejay on the popular WBLS mix show *Mr. Magic's Rap Attack*, and his partner MC Shan over a supposed diss.

In the bigger picture, the so-called "Bridge Wars" were ostensibly fought over turf and which borough got bragging rights for giving birth to the beats. Shan struck first on the street sensation "The Bridge" (Bridge Records, 1986), implying that Queensbridge, the sprawling housing project complex in Queens that he and Marley called home, was where hip-hop got its start. But Boogie Down Productions, whose very name proudly touted their affiliation with the borough that started it all, set the record straight with "South Bronx" (B-Boy Records, 1986), which name-checked all the originators from Kool Herc to Grandmaster Flash. Shan responded with a song called "Kill That Noise" (1987), but it was no match for BDP's reggae-inspired rejoinder, "The Bridge is Over" (1987), a ferocious diss record that settled the score once and for all. Both BDP songs appeared on their classic debut *Criminal Minded* (1987), a highly influential and popular record of its era, released through the independent B-Boy Records. After signing to the RCA-distributed Jive Records for their next album, BDP were poised for even greater glory. Then tragedy struck.

A younger member of the crew, Derrick "D-Nice" Jones, got involved in a petty argument on the streets over a girl. After catching a beatdown at the hands of a jealous boyfriend, he called his mentor Scott La Rock to set things straight. La Rock responded by making a trip up to the Highbridge Homes on University Avenue in the Bronx, where the attack took place. Accompanied by three other members of the BDP crew, he went looking for the perpetrator—not out for revenge, but rather to squash the beef. With a promising career in music on the horizon, he knew they didn't need to deal with any unnecessary bullshit. Unfortunately, the streets operated according to their own rules.

At Highbridge, Robocop, a member of BDP, shook down some random guys in an attempt to find the person they were looking for. With no luck, the four men got back into the jeep and were about to drive away, when La Rock suddenly slumped over in his seat. He had taken a single slug to the back of the head from an unknown assailant, probably positioned on a nearby roof. Though they rushed him to the hospital, on the following day, August 27, 1987, he was pronounced dead.

La Rock's murder was one of the first high-profile deaths in hip-hop, occurring just as BDP's star was on the rise and while working on their major-label debut, *By All Means Necessary* (Jive/RCA, 1988). "When that happened, and we both peeped it, automatically we thought of ourselves in those shoes. If the same thing was to happen to one of us, you know what I'm sayin', what would we do," DOOM recalled. "So, we saw how Kris handled that situation. He could have quit. We didn't know what he was going to do. Was he going to come out with another album? Then he came with that shit—*By All Means Necessary*. So that showed us what to do in that situation. You persevere, you keep going, you strive, and you do it. So, it made us ready for something to happen in life."[12]

2

THE GAS FACE

A grin shows a trick up a sleeve
What a tangled web they weave
Deceivers, stupefied through fable
Say "Let's make a deal" at the dinner table
Put you on tour, put your record on wax
Sign your life on the X.

—PETE NICE,
"THE GAS FACE"

On the other side of the Nassau County line, Michael Berrin was steadfastly pursuing his love for hip-hop, too. White and Jewish, he may as well have been a yeti in the heavily Orthodox Jewish neighborhood of Far Rockaway, Queens, where he grew up. No yeshiva for him. Instead, he attended public high school at Music and Art, then located at West 135th Street in Harlem. To secure a coveted spot at the school made famous by *Fame*, he sang for his audition. Trained in opera, he hoped to someday become a cantor in a synagogue.

But all that changed after hearing a bootleg tape of the park jams happening in the Bronx. He was equally amazed to discover that some of his own schoolmates—namely the Kangol Crew, featuring "Slick Rick" Walters and "Dana Dane" McCleese—were already ghetto celebrities, well-known for rocking crowds with their lyrical prowess. Not only were these guys the flyest cats in high school—coming to class decked out in stylish mock neck shirts and creased slacks with Bally loafers or Clarks Wallabees on their feet, and, of course, the signature fuzzy Kangol hats to top it off—but both were talented enough to secure record deals after graduating, with Def Jam and Profile, respectively. Maybe, Berrin thought, there was a path for him, too.

Though rap was relatively new, it wasn't unheard of for white guys to rhyme. In fact, another classmate, Blake Lethem, was already rocking the mic as Kid Benetton or Vanilla B, before settling on the moniker Lord Scotch. But he gravitated more toward graffiti, writing the tag *KEO*. So, Berrin made an assiduous leap of faith, from opera to MCing, choosing Serch as his nom de rap because he felt like he was constantly searching for a place to fit in and belong. Hanging out at hip-hop hotspots like the Latin Quarter in Times Square, he would often be an anomaly—the token, wannabe-down white guy. But far from feeling intimidated or out of place he held his own, basking in the exclusivity.

Following high school, Serch abandoned cantorial aspirations entirely, linking up with Brooklyn producer Grand Wiz Tony D. (aka Anthony Dick) to release the independent single "Melissa" (Warlock Records, 1986), which managed to crack the airwaves on KISS-FM. It was the kind of breakthrough that made him grind even harder. One day while hanging out on the boardwalk in nearby Long Beach, trying to pick up girls and capitalize on his status as a rapper with a record on the radio, he ran into Ahmed Brandon and Otis McKenzie, who were showing off their breakdancing moves. "We started talking about music and then, you know, we started talking about dancing and Ahmed and Otis were nice on their feet and I was nice on my feet," Serch recalls. They ended up back at Ahmed's basement on Park Avenue going toe to toe and trying to one-up each other. "So, you know, that's how we just kind of became friends," he says.

Creeping on a come up and looking to boost his nascent rap career by any means necessary, Serch pounced on every opportunity to get onstage and rock a mic. One day, he performed at an open-mic talent show at Long Beach's Martin Luther King Community Center that his future protégé happened to be attending. "We heard him first before we seen him, you know what I'm sayin'?" DOOM recalled. "Somebody was rhyming, so, anytime somebody's rhyming it's interesting. So, then we peeped this dude, and he did his thing by himself, solo."[1] Later that day, he and Serch met for the first time through their mutual friend Ahmed.

Since Long Beach was only a ten-minute drive from Far Rockaway, Serch quickly became somewhat of a fixture in the neighborhood. It certainly didn't hurt that Ahmed's mom had cable TV and liked to cook. Whenever he came over to catch Mets and Knicks games or watch HBO, she often whipped up some oxtails or fried fish. Serch and his new friends would also check out the 18–21 nights at Club Z in nearby Island Park and dance to hip-hop. Sometimes, they would hang at DOOM's, where Subroc sealed their friendship, sculpting Serch's "Jewfro" into a high-top fade for the first time. Serch witnessed firsthand how the brothers were constantly crate-digging for samples, spinning records, and writing their own rhymes. Though, respectively, four and six years older than DOOM and Sub, creatively, he felt like he was in the company of equals. "If I wasn't going to the Latin Quarter or if I wasn't making a move into like Brooklyn or whatever, just trying to get my name out, or if I wasn't doing promo shows, I was with them," says Serch.

On Friday nights, their friend Shamon, aka Mr. Hood, used to borrow his dad's 1979 Cadillac Sedan deVille so he and other members of GYP could cruise around to parties. Sometimes they trooped as far as the Bronx or Riverhead in Suffolk County, Long Island. If there was nothing else happening, they would pile into the car seven deep and head to the upscale Roosevelt Field mall to try their luck picking up girls. But first, everyone had to chip in a few dollars for gas.

Inevitably, the outcome of these missions yielded more strikeouts than a perfect game. "These girls would scrunch up their face and give us this look of total disgust," says Serch, "like how dare you, you peon. How dare you even look in my direction let alone ask for my number. And Subroc said, 'Man, we spent all that money on gas to get a face like that.' And we all started laughing."[2] Someone else dubbed the pained expression the "gas face," according to Serch, who says, "It was the funniest shit I ever heard, and we started running that shit to death."[3]

Crews routinely created their own slang—coded language evoking shared experiences that defined a group identity. "Vocabulary was a priority," says Mr. Hood, "'cause vocabulary creates our uniqueness." Serch, who usually rolled solo and had been craving the camaraderie of a crew, really embraced GYP and saw Ahmed, Otis, DOOM, and Sub as the brothers he had been seeking. He told them that when he "got on" with respect to his music career, he would bring them along—no small promise, but not an idle one either.

It turns out that Serch was by no means the only Caucasian enamored of hip-hop. In 1983, a punk band formerly known as the Young Aborigines released their first "crossover" single, "Cooky Puss" (Rat Cage Records). What started off as a joke—a prank call to a Carvel ice cream franchise—morphed into a popular underground hit in New York. The newly christened Beastie Boys—composed of Michael Diamond, Adam Horovitz, and Adam Yauch—had just embarked on their wild ride like the Merry Pranksters. These upper-middle-class Jewish boys could claim no real connection to hip-hop culture besides having a savvy ear to the street, but with loads of chutzpah, attitude, and ambition to match, they traded in their instruments for microphones, making a bold musical swerve.

Their secret weapon was Rick Rubin, incidentally, a Long Beach High graduate, who functioned as their first deejay, DJ Double R. At the time, he was just a student at NYU, dabbling in rap production and putting out records on his newly formed independent label, Def Jam, which he ran out of his dorm room. Following the success of Run-DMC, who had incorporated the sound of electric guitars into their eponymous 1984 debut, the Beasties released their second single, "Rock Hard," that same year on Def Jam. By the time their third single, "She's on It" (1985), dropped, Rubin had convinced downtown impresario Russell Simmons to come aboard to co-helm the label, greatly expanding its profile with a distribution deal from Columbia Records and a movie deal with Warner Bros. As a result, that song appeared on the soundtrack to the movie *Krush Groove* (Warner Bros., 1985), a fictional portrayal of the Def Jam story, blowing the doors wide open for the Beasties and all the other acts on the label.

Managed by Simmons, the trio hustled their way onto the opening slot of Madonna's *Like a Virgin* US tour in 1985, making headlines for their raucous, frat-boyish behavior. You could take the punks out of rock, but they stubbornly maintained their rebellious attitude. The following year they piggybacked on Run-DMC's *Raising Hell* tour along with Def Jam stalwarts LL Cool J and Whodini. Their meteoric rise culminated in November 1986 with the release of their gargantuan debut, *Licensed to Ill* (Def Jam/Columbia), the first rap album to reach the top of the *Billboard* Top 200 chart, where it lingered for five weeks. Despite an irreverent approach that made it seem like they were making fun of rap—while not taking themselves too seriously either—the Beastie Boys were living proof that a white rap act could sell records and achieve great success without being corny. And they were still only nubiles on their multi-decade musical odyssey. Serch filed this information away for later as he released his second independent single, "Hey Boy!," featuring K. Love and Tony D. (Idlers, 1987). He also squarely set his sights on Def Jam for his next release.

Since the entire white rap community was so minuscule at the time, any Caucasian with MC aspirations probably knew Mark Pearson, who attended the exclusive Saint Ann's School in Brooklyn with Mike Diamond from the Beasties. After graduating, he met Pete Nash, aka Pete Nice, who hailed from the vicinity of Belmont Park in Queens, because they were both recruited to play basketball at Columbia. He also counted Serch's classmate Blake Lethem among his tribe. They knew each other from summer camp and later the graffiti scene, where Pearson wrote as SAKE. Inspired by the Beasties' success, he wanted to start another white rap group, but, unfortunately, couldn't rap. So, he did the next best thing and linked up his two friends who did.

As committed as Pete was to basketball, he was just as serious about rhyming. In high school, he had been in a group called Sin Qua Non, who went as far as performing at Brooklyn's Empire Ballroom on a bill including Dana Dane, Sparky D, Ultimate 3 MCs, and Stetsasonic. Though the group dissolved when its members went away to different colleges, Lumumba Carson, son of activist Sonny Carson (and a future member of Afrocentric rappers X-Clan), managed them during their brief career, sticking with Pete when he went solo. But progress was not coming fast enough for the aspiring MC, who was now caught up in college hoops. So, Pete proactively made some rough demos on his own, playing them for friends in Queens, who knew Kid 'n Play's managers, Rich Ahee and Len Brown—known collectively as RichLen Productions. Since they also managed producer Hurby "The Love Bug" Azor, he figured they had the connections to land him a deal.

Meanwhile, Lethem, formerly Vanilla B, had been collecting his props on the mic as Lord Scotch. Chain-smoking Marlboros didn't do wonders for his stamina or breath control as an MC, but at least he walked the walk and talked the talk, boasting legitimate street connections to boot. For his first meeting with Pete, he showed up wearing an acid-washed jean jacket and Brooklyn Dodgers cap, flipping a razor blade around his mouth like an OG. He cut the figure of the prototypical "wigger" before the term even existed. But Pete liked his style and thought he was an ill character. When they decided on working on a demo together, Lethem moved into his dorm room in Columbia's Johnson Hall for two months.

As a group name, they came up with Servin' Generalz, a play on surgeon general. Lethem relished his role as streets ambassador, taking Pete to spots like Brooklyn's Albee Square Mall, the headquarters for gaudy "truck" jewelry where rappers got gold "fronts" fitted on their teeth. He also introduced him to people like Dante Ross, a white skate rat, who was then working at Rush Management; Clark Kent (Rodolfo Franklin), who was Dana Dane's DJ; and his boy Shameek, who became the group's beatboxer. One night at Latin Quarters, Lethem introduced Pete to Serch for the first time, though they already knew of each other from afar.

At the end of his sophomore season in 1987, Pete suffered a knee injury, and took to walking with a cane (which would become his trademark prop later on). Instead of being redshirted and having to pay another year's tuition, he decided to quit the basketball team and focus on rap. That summer he lobbied Columbia University's radio station, WKCR, to start its first rap show and was granted an hour-long slot on Tuesday nights that he called the *We Could Do This Show*. The plan was to involve his whole crew, including Clark Kent cutting up records on the turntables, Shameek beatboxing, and him and Lethem trading rhymes during a live segment.

Unfortunately, the first show proved to be a disaster, as Kent ended up getting stuck on the subway, and Lethem was missing in action, leaving only Pete and Shameek to hold it down. Lethem, in fact, never reappeared, having been arrested on drug charges and sent to Rikers Island. Shameek shared a similar fate after a conviction for armed robbery. Only Kent proved reliable, sending his cousin DJ Richie Rich as a substitute whenever he had scheduling conflicts. But one night, he messed up, too. After bringing some of his crew to do the show with him when Pete couldn't make it, the station ended up being trashed and records went missing. The program director had no choice but to cancel the show after only four months.

The only upside for Pete was that it gave him more time to focus on his music. He and Richie Rich started working on a demo at Brooklyn's Funky Slice Studios that Kool DJ Red Alert played on his popular mix show on 98.7 KISS-FM. With his name getting around, Pete finally felt like he was making some headway. After recording another demo to the instrumental of Sweet T and Jazzy Joyce's "It's My Beat," he gave it to Dante Ross, who, in turn, passed it on to his bosses, Russell Simmons and Lyor Cohen. Impressed, they wanted to sign Prime Minister Pete Nice as a solo artist on Rush Management.

In the meantime, Serch had also been busy. Unbeknownst to Pete, he had also caught the ear of Lyor Cohen, the Israeli American who started out as Run-DMC's tour manager before becoming Simmons's partner in Rush. Only a month earlier, in June 1988, Cohen had signed MC Serch as a solo artist as well. Both he and Pete were given studio time at Chung King Studios in Chinatown, where they worked independently on their demos with producer Sam Sever (Sam Citrin), another friend of Ross. A friendship grew organically between the two MCs as they clocked hours in the studio with Sever and started hanging out after hours at clubs with Ross. Since Simmons wasn't quite sold on their solo progress, Pete and Serch decided to join forces as a group with Sever as their DJ-producer. They had even settled on the name Three the Hard Way. Unfortunately, Sever couldn't commit to the arrangement since he was getting a lot of outside production work at the time. But his shoes were eventually filled by DJ Richie Rich. When Simmons balked at the group's name, they changed it to 3rd Bass. After half a year of shopping the group to different labels, he finally brought them home, making them the sixth act signed to Def Jam in February 1989.

After inking the deal, things started moving into high gear. Serch had already introduced Pete to his crew out in Long Beach, whom he did not forget about. He made good on an agreement with Ahmed that in exchange for finishing high school, he and Otis could join 3rd Bass as backup dancers.

Meanwhile, DOOM, who was still in school—when he felt like attending—remained focused on writing rhymes. He, too, was in the process of refashioning KMD into a rap crew, adding another MC from the neighborhood, Jade One (aka Rodan), as the third member.

By this time, DOOM had joined the Ansaaru Allah Community (Helpers of Allah) based in Bushwick, Brooklyn. While donning white robes and the trappings of Islam, this group largely studied the Bible. They offered DOOM a spiritual foundation as well as the kind of education that made him more conscious of himself and his place in society. Influenced as well by the progressive raps of Public Enemy and KRS-ONE, DOOM went as far as changing the meaning of KMD. Instead of "Kausing Much Damage" it now stood for "a positive Kause in a Much-Damaged society." As his nom de rap, he chose "Zev Love X," which spelled "X evolvez" backward, a reference to himself as the next evolution of Malcolm X. Before even beginning work on their own album, Pete and Serch established a production company, Rhyming Is Fundamental (RIF), as many rap groups did to develop new talent. They chose KMD to be the first act on their roster.

In May 1989, Pete graduated magna cum laude from Columbia with a degree in English. Meanwhile, 3rd Bass's first single, "Steppin' to the A.M.," was already in heavy rotation on radio, introducing MC Serch and the sinister Minister to the rap world. The video for the song featured Ahmed and Otis making highly choreographed moves flanking Serch, in addition to cameos from a very young DOOM and Subroc. The opening black-and-white shot showed a hooded figure making his way through a phalanx of GYP members, slapping hands as he walks by. When he gets to the end of the line, Video Music Box's Ralph McDaniels pushes back his hoodie to reveal Serch with the signature "3rd Bass" shaved into his fade, courtesy of Subroc. The brothers Dumile had made their long-awaited splashdown.

While Sam Sever had overseen production on most of the 3rd Bass album, and the Bomb Squad contributed a couple of songs (including "Steppin' to the A.M."), Pete also asked Prince Paul (Paul Huston), fresh off his work on De La Soul's platinum-selling *3 Feet High and Rising* (Tommy Boy, 1989), for beats, and the producer provided two. The first, containing a sample of the Emotions' "Best of My Love," was earmarked for "Brooklyn-Queens," an older song that Pete had already written on his own. The other track, based off a piano loop from Aretha Franklin's "Think," was up for grabs, and Serch suggested doing a song called "The Gas Face" featuring DOOM. "So, immediately, from the beginning, we told DOOM we would put him on," says Pete, "and that was the best way to put him on—put him on one of our records to get him a deal."

The only problem was that neither of them had ever heard DOOM rap. "I mean here was the thing about DOOM," says Serch, "like DOOM would write rhymes all the time, but he wouldn't let me hear 'em. He would just be writing for himself. That was his process. He was very private—with us even." When Serch would challenge him to a rhyme battle, DOOM always demurred. "'Gas Face' probably never would've happened. Because that was just a GYP thing. And that was a KMD thing," Serch says, "and if he didn't wanna rhyme on it, more than likely, we probably would've came up with another idea for another song or another concept or something, but we wouldn't have done 'Gas Face.'" Sensing a once-in-a-lifetime opportunity, however, DOOM rose to the occasion.

As one of the last tracks they recorded for the album, the song came together pretty quickly. With the beat already done, the three MCs wrote their rhymes on the Long Island Rail Road while en route to record vocals with Prince Paul. Arriving at Island Media Studios in Babylon, Long Island, Serch and Pete both laid down their verses in one take. As Paul's friend Don Newkirk, the voice behind some of the zany skits from the De La album, was around, they asked him to act as master of ceremonies and introduce each rapper's verse. When it came time for DOOM to enter the vocal booth for the first time ever, on the surface he appeared as his usual calm self. But Serch remembers him asking everyone to leave the room.

"My first impression was just that he was flawless, and I just remember never hearing a style like that," says Paul, who had remained behind with the engineer. "Like I couldn't say, okay, he sounds like this person or that person. It's his own thing. He was also professional. He came in and just knocked it out." While everyone in attendance was happy with how the song turned out, Pete saw a potential single. "I just thought it was dope that he was just spitting," says Serch, like a proud papa, "like, ah, cool, yo. My dude got lyrics. That's dope." They were also probably a little relieved that their faith in DOOM had not been misplaced.

After that session, Paul ended up keeping in touch with the young rapper, eventually becoming a trusted friend and mentor. "He gave me his number and wrote it on a piece of paper. I still have the paper from the day inside the studio when he gave it to me," says Paul, "and so we kept in contact after that session because he was just so inquisitive about things. He was like, 'How'd you do this? How'd you do that? Da, da, da,' you know—just production stuff. And since he was so cool, I didn't mind."

3

PEACHFUZZ

As you start to walk on the way, the way appears.

—RUMI

On November 14, 1989, "The Gas Face" followed "Steppin' to the A.M." as the second single off *The Cactus Album* (Def Jam/Columbia, 1989), becoming something of a phenomenon, and helping push the album toward gold sales. Its zany, tongue-in-cheek video was notable for three reasons: 1) it sparked a major beef by throwing shade at MC Hammer, who had the top rap song in the country at the time with "U Can't Touch This," a full-scale rip-off of Rick James's "Superfreak"; 2) it featured a slew of high-profile cameos from the likes of comedian Gilbert Gottfried, label boss Russell Simmons, and rappers Flavor Flav, EPMD, and Run-DMC—not to mention an appearance by then Def Jam employee Bobbito Garcia, who would play a pivotal role in DOOM's future; and 3) no longer relegated to the background, Zev Love X finally hit prime time, closing out the song with a featured verse.

Cracking a Mona Lisa smile, the rail-thin rapper—sporting his trademark John Lennon wire frames with a gold hoop piercing his right nostril—almost stole the show with his effortless delivery and the laid-back demeanor, firmly embedding him in the minds of the MTV generation. Subroc popped in briefly, too, during the line, "Subroc cut at you with a clipper," mugging next to the 3rd Bass insignia he had carved in Serch's fade. At the video's conclusion, Zev, wearing a service-station attendant's overalls, jokingly gave the "gas face" to his friend Dante Ross, whom he had met through Pete and Serch. The former Rush employee was now working as an artists and repertoire (A&R) rep for Tommy Boy Records.

In heavy rotation on *Yo! MTV Raps*, the breakout success of "The Gas Face" made it the obvious choice to perform on television when 3rd Bass was invited to appear on *The Arsenio Hall Show* in 1990. The late-night talk show had only premiered the previous year, but already made for must-see TV among the young, urban demographic at whom it was aimed—the show's rise coinciding with rap's steady march toward the mainstream. Consequently, the charismatic host with the teeth-baring grin earned a rep for giving many rappers their first leg up on network TV, where an appearance as his musical guest meant instant exposure nationwide. Crouching inconspicuously on the DJ platform as he waited to drop his verse, Zev was clearly not accustomed to such attention, but performing live helped pull the quiet kid from Long Beach out of his shell.

In addition to *Arsenio*, he accompanied 3rd Bass to Harlem's legendary Apollo Theater as well as numerous promotional gigs, including their album release party at LA's Palace Theatre in January 1990. That's where a photographer captured a shot of him posing with Pete Nice and N.W.A's Dr. Dre and Eazy-E. In April, when the group kicked off a big arena tour, sharing the bill with Big Daddy Kane and Digital Underground, who brought along a young dancer named Tupac Shakur, Zev was right there in the mix, rhyming in front of packed audiences. "Those shows were fuckin' crazy, man," he recalled. "Coliseums in North Carolina type shit—10,000 people. At that time, I was just doing my verse from 'Gas Face' for 3rd Bass so I'm only onstage for 16 bars—one minute. Nervous as hell, though. Every time. But as soon as I get offstage it goes away, and the crowd is spinning like, 'Ohhhhh!' So those times kinda set it off. In my mind, those were the best times."[1] His journey into the spotlight had been swift and unexpected, thrusting him into the center of a scene of which he was formerly only a fan. "Back then, Kane would come over and we'd kick it with him sometimes," he added. "I used to talk to Pac a lot. We used to be like the two extra guys going onstage, so we'd be talking backstage and at the hotel about working on our own shit."[2]

After "Gas Face," it was on, according to Serch, who says, "It was like a hundred miles an hour. Like all of a sudden, we were rhyming on the tour bus. We were rhyming with Pac and Shock G in hotels. Everywhere we went, we would rhyme, like everywhere. It was like a broken faucet that once you turned it on, you couldn't turn it off." Despite the long hours on the road coupled with the sudden and drastic change of lifestyle, Serch says, "He was still very much a practicing, devout Muslim on the road. He didn't change. One thing about DOOM, DOOM didn't change just because of where he went. Now, he might have become more worldly, you know? As we all did, right. We all kind of discovered different shit. And so, it was very much this amazing time." But behind the novelty and allure of the experience, their youth and naivete helped obscure the fact that they were really nothing more than glorified record-company employees. As much fun as they may have been having, they were hamsters running on the fast-paced wheel of the music industry and, therefore, subject to its dictates.

Rap, like Zev, was growing up, and the former rebel sound of the streets found itself in an awkward adolescence. One indication was that the big boys (i.e., major labels) started paying it serious attention. *The Source*, formerly a stapled newsletter run out of the dorm room of two Harvard rap fanatics, transformed almost overnight into a thick, glossy monthly with a salaried staff and offices on lower Broadway, thanks to a corporate advertising windfall. The magazine had declared the eighties the "Rap Decade," charting the art form's rise from obscurity onto the national stage. But 1990 proved to be a pivotal year, the beginning of what could be considered the battle for the soul of rap. Two distinct camps—mainstream and underground—emerged, continually at odds over the course of the new decade. On one hand, acts like MC Hammer and Vanilla Ice dominated the charts with multiplatinum major-label debuts that pulled rap firmly in the direction of pop. But that same year also saw hardcore releases by Ice Cube (*AmeriKKKa's Most Wanted*), Public Enemy (*Fear of a Black Planet*), EPMD (*Business as Usual*), Boogie Down Productions (*Edutainment*), and Eric B. & Rakim (*Let the Rhythm Hit 'Em*)—all uncompromising voices who repped the culture to the fullest without selling out.

In between these two poles, artists both new and old were vying for a share of the expanding audience. Some, like Run-DMC and LL Cool J, attempted comeback bids to mixed success. On the West Coast, the seeds of gangsta rap planted by N.W.A continued to flourish through the efforts of Compton's Most Wanted, Above the Law, and King Tee. Meanwhile, back east, a more cerebral, conscious rap found expression in the works of newcomers like Brand Nubian, Poor Righteous Teachers, X-Clan, and A Tribe Called Quest. Tribe, of course, represented the latest incarnation of the Native Tongues posse, a loose affiliation of like-minded artists who melded streetwise slang and Afrocentric concepts with jazzy, abstract beats. Their initiation into the industry came after appearances on albums by their predecessors, De La Soul and Jungle Brothers. Due to a lack of experienced A&R people familiar with rap, established groups often fulfilled the role of discovering and developing new talent, as 3rd Bass had done with KMD.

Pete and Serch had always intended to put their brothers on, but as it turned out they didn't have to try too hard. Their old friend Dante Ross, formerly of Rush and Tommy Boy, had recently made the move to Elektra Records, then part of the expansive Warner family along with Atlantic, known collectively as WEA. With the power of the purse behind him, he was actively assembling a top-notch rap roster that included New Rochelle's Brand Nubian and Leaders of the New School from Uniondale, Long Island. "Even when Dante was at Tommy Boy, I had told him about DOOM and KMD. And then finally, when he went to Elektra and actually had more power, you know, he was always talking about like, 'Yo, let's get DOOM. Let's see what they can do on a demo,'" Pete recalls, "So it was already like that. Dante already had the inside track."

One would imagine that Def Jam had an interest in the group since they first appeared on the label, but according to Pete, "Def Jam would've only given like the regular deal of $125,000 and Dante was talking like a much bigger number." Serch adds, "The only time it became a negotiation is at the very last minute, Tommy Boy offered us more money. We went back to Bob Krasnow and Dante and we're like, look, just match this deal. We don't want more money, but we can't take less money. So just match this deal. And Dante had some feelings about that. Like he thought we were sticking him up, but we weren't sticking him up." Elektra wound up playing ball, signing KMD for $250,000 in 1990.

From the perspective of teenagers still in high school, the deal may have seemed like hitting the lotto. But in the music industry, well-known for exploiting artists, things were never as they appeared. After lawyers and management each deducted their 10 to 15 percent fee, the lion's share of remaining funds went to covering studio costs, paid out in installments. That didn't leave much left for the artists themselves. But Ross, who described the Dumile brothers as practically twins, who were "really endearing and charming,"[3] took them under his wing. In order to save money, he gave them access to a preproduction studio that he and his partners John Gamble and Geeby Dajani—known collectively as Stimulated Dummies (or SD50)—leased in the basement of the Westbeth artists building in Manhattan's West Village. Working dutifully most nights, they demoed the whole album there over the course of four or five months, before mixing it at Calliope Studios on Thirty-Seventh Street.

Just prior to their signing, Zev added a new third member to the group to relieve him of some of the lyrical duties, as Sub was still mainly focused on production. Unfortunately, their homeboy, Jade One (aka Rodan), had recently been kicked out of high school in Long Beach, so he had to transfer upstate to finish his education. Taking his place was Onyx the Birthstone Kid (Alonzo Hodge), a fellow Muslim youth from the neighborhood, who was not even writing rhymes at the time. Onyx had first bonded with the Dumile brothers following an incident in which he had been chased down the street by a vicious neighborhood mutt. While trying to take refuge at their house to escape getting bit, he accidentally put his hand through a window and badly cut himself. After Sub accompanied him to the hospital to get stitches, Onyx ended up with a friend for life.

Describing the workflow on that first album, *Mr. Hood*, Zev explained, "Me and Sub would do whatever we could do. It wasn't necessarily sectioned off. It was really just for fun in a lot of ways. I would dig in the crates, find loops, and come up with a concept. Then, I'd usually get close to finishing it, but I'd be too lazy. I never liked messing with computers or programming drum machines or samplers. I left a lot of beats half done and Sub would come in and finish a lot of them. Onyx was only vocals. He didn't fuck with the music at all. He added a lot of humor to what we were doing. His angle was ill."[4]

While backing up Zev on album cuts like "Mr. Hood at Piocalles Jewelry/ Crackpot," "Who Me?," "Figure of Speech," "Bananapeel Blues," "Trial 'N Error," "808 Man," and "Boy Who Cried Wolf," Onyx appeared on only one solo jam, "Boogie Man!" Sub, who had just started coming into his own on the mic, contributed verses to "Humrush," the posse cut with Brand Nubian; "Nitty Gritty"; and "Soulflexin'," while taking a solo turn on "Subroc's Mission." The bulk of the production was credited to KMD, except for "Hard Wit No Hoe," credited to Sub alone, and "Humrush" and "Boogie Man!," for which SD50 supplied the beats.

On the surface *Mr. Hood* reveled in tongue-in-cheek humor and inside jokes, but its content actually proved to be much more subversive. "We based the album on the *Sesame Street* concept, incorporating loads of puppets and learning, which will get kids into it," Zev explained. "So, we incorporated that humor with education, with confrontation, with touchy subjects that people don't want to hear about."[5] Case in point, "Who Me?," in which they go right after racism, is a song that contains samples from a *Sesame Street* audiobook, *Shapes & Colors: Ernie's Favorites!* (Golden Books, 1986). In it, Zev takes exception to the black-faced caricature known as Little Black Sambo, rapping, "Pigment, is this a defect in birth? / Or more an example of the richness on Earth? / Lips and eyes dominant traits of our race / Does not take up 95 percent of one's face / But still I see, in the back two or three / Ignorant punks pointing at me." In an ironic twist, however, the group adopted the controversial image of Sambo as their unofficial mascot, who makes a cameo in the song's video as well as on the album cover. It proved to be a means of redeeming such a racist symbol in the same way that Black people made the N-word into a term of endearment when used among themselves.

More emblematic of the album, however, would be the ubiquitous Mr. Hood, a character whose stiff accent and dialogue, sampled from a Spanish-language instructional record, served as the conceptual glue to tell a larger story. "So, the whole record was based around us schooling him from being this drug dealer type, just dropping little jewels on him, schooling him, bringing him into the crew kinda thing," Zev explained. "But by the end of the record, he gets it into his skull, he starts being more aware, more conscious of what's going on."⁶

Unlike Sambo, however, Mr. Hood wasn't just a fictional character, but paid homage to a member of GYP, who had been a friend of the Dumiles since middle school. He earned his nickname by being a neighborhood fixture—that guy who was always in the middle of the action and got along with everybody. "If the 'hood was human," says GYP's Uncle E, "he was just the embodiment of that, you know. [He] liked to hang out, liked to be at the house parties and, you know, just having a good time snapping, you know what I mean? He was, like, all the fun things that all the kids liked to do in the hood." DOOM and Sub thought enough about their friend that they wanted to include his image on the album cover alongside theirs. "I didn't know I was actually gonna be on the album cover," says Mr. Hood, "Although they did tell me they was gonna name the album after me. But it kind of went through one ear and out the other, you know?"

Then, one random school day when he happened to be eating lunch, Sub popped his head into the cafeteria. "He was like, 'Yo, we gotta go.' I forgot exactly where he said, but he said, 'Yo, we gotta go to the city.' And I didn't think nothing of it, you know, we were always getting into something," says Mr. Hood. "I was just so happy to see them." After joining DOOM and Sub in a rented limo, they stopped to pick up some other friends. Next, they made a pit stop at Burger King before proceeding to a photo studio on Twenty-Second Street in Manhattan. Upon arrival, Mr. Hood was dispatched to the makeup room against his will. He wound up arguing with the makeup lady for twenty minutes before finally relenting. "They gave me a hood, 'Yo just, put this on and take this picture, whatever.' And I actually didn't like that hoodie they had on me, I was like, 'Yeah, I could've brought my own,'" he says. "The next thing you know they show me the album cover, like a week after. I just was like, wow, I couldn't believe it. It still didn't like sink in."

The cover of the *Mr. Hood* album featured a vintage, black-and-white photo of kids playing hopscotch on a Harlem street in the fifties, taken by renowned street photographer Arthur Leipzig. He was still alive when contacted for permission for its use, and enthusiastic about his work being reimagined for a new audience. In the era before Photoshop, art director Carol Bobolts had to manually doctor the original to include color photos of the three group members posing in the background with Mr. Hood's face in the foreground—a study in contrasts. She used a special Scitex printer, found only at HBO Studios, to achieve such a distinctive look. A cartoon graphic of Zev's hand-drawn Little Black Sambo with a red line through his face adorned the top right-hand corner, while the letters "KMD" were superimposed to look like colored chalk on the hopscotch board. Though he couldn't claim credit for finding the photo, Zev was probably drawn to it for the same reasons that Leipzig clicked the shutter—it captured the innocence of youth, a magical time to which there was no going back.

While working on the album's lead single, "Peachfuzz," DOOM and Sub got an assist from their younger brother Dimbaza, who was only fourteen at the time. Like the Three Musketeers, they had come up together as B-boys, with Dim always in the orbit of his elder brothers, whether engaged in deejaying, writing graffiti, breakdancing, or rhyming. They developed an informal system of passing on skills, according to Dim, whereby, "Sub will always be the learner and then make DOOM the one who's a student when he comes home and then they'll bring me into it and make sure I'm just a backup who also knows. And it always worked that way." Despite not being an official member of the group, Dim contributed in any way he could while they were working on the album. "My brothers practically gave me the assignment to just stay open to hearing shit, stay open to whatever sounds dope," he says.

At the time, he was involved in a group of his own with his best friend Lou, a Puerto Rican kid from the neighborhood. While messing around one day, Dim recalls, "We sampling, we checking loops at Lou's house for our shit. And as soon as we heard the 'Peachfuzz [sample] we looked at each other and was like, 'Yo, that was dope!' We knew that it was too dope for our little garage band project that doesn't have any traction, no labels interested. We were like, all right, we gotta bring this over to my brothers." The sample in question, which featured a smooth bossa nova beat punctuated by a melodic piano, was lifted from the opening bars of "On a Clear Day You Can See Forever" (Columbia

Records, 1967) by O.C. Smith, a singer probably best known for recording "Little Green Apples," one of the breakout hits of 1968.

"We was like, 'Yo, check this out. Y'all gotta hear this. This is dope. What do you think?'" says Dim. "And they played it and they was, like, 'Yo! yeah.' That's when we learned that they were trying to find a beat for the song. They just had the concept, the idea, and knew that that was gonna be the first single." Pairing the piano sample with another drum loop from O. C. Smith's "Sounds of Goodbye" (CBS, 1969), KMD came up with the most memorable track on the album. A metaphor for the transition between childhood and adulthood, "Peachfuzz" signaled that they were growing up, and that life was no longer simply fun and games as responsibilities beckoned.

The video for "Peachfuzz," which debuted on December 5, 1990, on MTV and BET's *Rap City*, portrayed a daily slice of life for the members of KMD. As adherents of the Ansaaru Allah Community, they were dressed in all-white robes and turbans, selling incense and educational pamphlets on the streets. Despite their supervisor's reminder to "Be humble," they couldn't repress their teen spirit, comparing themselves to rap stars in magazines and trying to impress girls. Incidentally, one of these girls was Zev's real-life girlfriend at the time and eventually the mother of his first child. Of course, 3rd Bass made an obligatory cameo—this time with Serch sporting a "KMD" carved into the back of his fade—as did Grand Puba Maxwell, of Elektra labelmates Brand Nubian, playing the xylophone. "Peachfuzz" represented a kinder, gentler, more playful style of rap, not designed for dancing, making a statement, or trying to call attention to itself, but compelling and exciting just the same.

The only other single to merit a video was "Who Me?," released on April 24, 1991. Featuring more of the same shots of Ansaars selling incense and KMD clowning with friends and riding BMX bikes, it also introduced their Sambo character, played by someone dressed in a costume resembling a sports team's mascot. Once again, KMD proactively employed humor to deflect any hint of controversy. In a bizarrely prophetic twist, the video also showed the group rapping under a street sign that read "KMD Street," which would not become a reality until 2021, after the passing of both DOOM and Sub.

Mr. Hood came into the world on May 14, 1991, the same day as albums by De La Soul (*De La Soul Is Dead*) and Ice-T (*O.G. Original Gangster*). Only two weeks later, N.W.A's much-anticipated *Niggaz4Life* debuted at number two on the *Billboard* Top 200 before claiming the top spot the following week. Compared to such high-profile competition, *Mr. Hood* barely registered a reaction, reaching number sixty-seven on *Billboard*'s Top R&B/Hip-Hop albums chart, though "Peachfuzz," the album's most successful single, peaked at number eleven on the Hot Rap songs chart. Regardless of mainstream perceptions, *The Source*, then the sole arbiter of taste in hip-hop circles, gave it a 4 (out of 5) mic review—equivalent to a very affirmative thumbs up. In a longer feature about the group, they called it, "One of the most innovative and original albums since [A Tribe Called Quest's] *People's Instinctive Travels*."[7] By the hairs of their chinny chin chin, KMD had arrived.

4

BLACK BASTARDS

See, I became underground since the life in the street
The love of the beat, large is the fleet
That will remain underground for all my boys whose souls sleep
Six feet deeper than the soles of my feet.
—ZEV LOVE X, "BLACK BASTARDS!"

As far as industry standards were concerned, *Mr. Hood*, which sold about 150,000 copies, would not be considered a triumphant debut. But it hardly tanked either. It managed to slip in at an opportune moment when the majors were still throwing money at their new cash cow, while trying to figure out what worked and what didn't. Who would have thought, for example, that a soulful, sing-songy rap about "Tennessee" by a Southern group called Arrested Development could win a Grammy in an era when gangsta rap ruled the airwaves? Relationships mattered, too, and KMD were lucky to have a true believer in their corner in A&R man Ross. "We didn't recoup on the first record, so when it came time to talk about another one, the label wasn't sure," he says, "I convinced them that they should, but they set the budget at $200,000, which was a lot less than *Mr. Hood*."[1] Though their major-label debut may have been but a momentary blip on rap's radar, it proved to be a learning experience for the brothers that helped broaden their horizons.

When they hit the road to promote that first record, touring with labelmates Brand Nubian and Leaders of the New School, they had to forge their own identity independent of 3rd Bass. Image Crafting 101 was not a class offered in high school, yet it was essential in the cutthroat field of entertainment into which they had been catapulted. Initially, KMD appeared onstage, as in their music videos, wearing the Ansaar uniform of white robes and kufis. While obviously trying to set themselves apart, they came across as a little too different—not to mention awkward—since appearing like religious zealots didn't quite jive with the playful vibe of their music. After a few shows, however, they switched up to regular street clothes, helping them better connect with their audience.

Despite being practicing Muslims, the Dumile brothers also succumbed to peer pressure this time around, and started experimenting with alcohol and weed. After all, the Five Percenters in their touring party—namely Brand Nubian and Busta Rhymes—bound by no such restrictions, were having too much fun. Zev's initial concession to loosening up involved drinking red wine, but he chose Manischewitz, the kosher brand, as opposed to the forty-ounce bottles of malt liquor favored by his peers. On the West Coast leg of the tour, headlined by De La Soul, he also indulged in marijuana for the first time. Years later he recalled, "On those long stretches, I think 15 days out there, days would get longer and longer. So, it just made us relax I guess."[2] While the first album captured a snapshot of young adolescents, these new experiences marked a coming of age, providing fodder for their next album, *Black Bastards*, which they worked on over the course of the next two years.

The contrast between the two records could not have been more stark. On a track like "Sweet Premium Wine," Sub declared his newfound taste for alcohol, rapping, "You know I'm complex-cated like a Rubik's Cube puzzle / Who said I drink? I don't drink, I guzzle." Meanwhile, numerous references to weed cropped up in tracks like "Smokin' That S*@%!," "Suspended Animation," and "Contact Blitt." The latter, in fact, related a true story in which the whole crew smoked so much on the tour bus that even the bus driver caught a contact high. He was so stoned, in fact, that he attempted to extort them for money in order to continue driving. Zev set the scene, "My rap label mates, they all smoke blunts / Went on this tour once, the bus was loco / From Albuquerque to like Acapulco / See it was Lord J, Sadat, Alamo / Busta and myself in the back with the whole O.Z."

Another obvious departure from those innocent times of yore was "Get-U-Now," on which a revved-up Zev boasted, "I've got a brand new .380 in the box, made like Glocks / A shoebox of bullets, two clips, no safety lock." Rapping about guns and drugs hardly covered new territory, and for a group so often compared to the conscious collective of the Native Tongues, it seemed like a complete 180-degree reversal. "So, all those new things we were learning, a lot of the weirdness that came out of being in the business, went into that record," Zev explained, "that's where you get a lot of the edge on it, almost bitterness I would say. It's like a talk shit kind of record almost. A bit like, 'Well, fuck y'all,' we're still going to do our thing."[3] Transitioning into young adults, they were obviously heavily influenced by the swirling currents around them, as well as the many new heads coming into their cipher.

"I first met DOOM in 1989 on the set of 'The Gas Face' video,"[4] says Bobbito Garcia, a Wesleyan University grad whose first job in the music industry was working in the mailroom of Def Jam. After getting bumped up to promotions, he made sure his friend Jorge Alvarez took over his former position. Bob and Jorge knew each other as neighbors at 160 West Ninety-Seventh Street, located in the rapidly gentrifying but still crime-prone area known as Manhattan Valley on the Upper West Side. Robert Hill, who ran the independent Zakia label that released Eric B. & Rakim's first singles and album, also lived in that building, as did a young graf writer named Kadi Agueros, who left his tag, "EROTIC," on any flat surface he could bless with a fat cap. Right around the corner, at Ninety-Eighth and Amsterdam, was the unassuming playground of PS 163, the Alfred E. Smith School, better known as "Rock Steady Park." In the eighties it served as the headquarters of legendary breakdancers, the Rock Steady Crew, many of whose members lived in the neighborhood and perfected their acrobatic moves on that same asphalt.

Growing up in an area steeped in hip-hop, Kadi, a fan of BDP's first album, formed a graffiti crew known as CM, which stood for "Criminal Minded." Fellow writers Kae-Nit (Hill's son), Nice-O, Dev, and Style formed the core of this crew, but other friends from the area who dedicated themselves to different elements of the culture were down as well. Percy Carey, a former child star on *Sesame Street* and currently the rapper known as MF Grimm, gravitated toward the CM Fam, as did his DJ, Roc Raida (Anthony Williams), a Harlem native who would clinch the DMC World DJ Championship in 1995. "There were so many people involved—neighborhoods, people on the street corner, people older than us. Even if they were the neighborhood wino, they were down with CM,"[5] says Grimm.

Apartment 6G, where Jorge Alvarez lived, served as the crew's unofficial clubhouse, where dudes would hang out and listen to the latest jams while drinking 40s, puffing on blunts and Newports, playing video games like Super Mario, or scarfing down $2.50 fish sandwiches from the Chinese deli downstairs. "It's just my people, that's how we grew up," says Jorge, who also met Zev at the same time as Bobbito. "Me and DOOM got cool quick. He would come around my way and before you knew it, he was family."[6] On his frequent forays uptown, Zev spent many a night at 6G, soaking up the vibes and making new connections that would last a lifetime.

Though he never really aspired to be an MC, Jorge loved to snap and make jokes. While stuffing envelopes in the Def Jam conference room, he would channel this humor into freestyle raps over the Honey Drippers' old-school break "Impeach the President." Egged on by other rappers he knew like King Sun and MF Grimm, he eventually wrote a rhyme and performed it for Bobbito, who gave him further encouragement. Bobbito went as far as setting his friend up with a European producer called the Duke of Denmark to make his first demo, "My Intro." But Jorge soon found other opportunities to rhyme, linking up with Prince Powerrule, a Puerto Rican MC with a deal on the independent Revenge Records. They went into the studio to record more demos, including "9mm Rhymes" and "Rhythmic Insanity." Jorge also appeared on the track "Young Stars from Nowhere" off Power Rule's album debut, *Volume 1* (Interscope, 1991).

One day, while Jorge was dubbing copies of his demo in the office of Faith Newman, Def Jam's head of A&R, she overheard it and was instantly impressed. After passing on the tape to her boss, Russell Simmons, Jorge received a promotion. Simmons also expressed an interest in signing him and making a record, but, apparently, the young rapper had already made a verbal agreement with Pete Nice, who was making moves of his own.

The second and final album from 3rd Bass, *Derelicts of Dialect* (Def Jam/Columbia, 1991), had dropped only a month after KMD's debut. Despite spawning the hit "Pop Goes the Weasel," a diss of Vanilla Ice that helped the album go gold, success could not compete with a litany of personal issues stacking up between Pete and Serch. Six months after the album's release, while on tour to promote it, they announced their intention of going their separate ways. Serch relinquished his stake in their company, RIF productions, and, therefore, no longer had anything to do with KMD as he pivoted toward a solo career. Meanwhile, Pete, after forming a duo with DJ Richie Rich, scored a label deal at Columbia to start developing his own artists. He brought Bobbito on to run day-to-day operations and act as A&R. Jorge, whom Bob had nicknamed "Kurious," after the popular children's book character Curious George, became the first act signed to the newly established Hoppoh imprint distributed by Columbia.

Bobbito was also diversifying his portfolio during this period. The former Def Jam employee partnered on a rap radio show at Pete's alma mater, Columbia, with freshman Adrian Bartos, who called himself DJ Stretch Armstrong. Between Stretch, who already had a reputation from spinning at New York clubs, and Bob, who had one foot in the music industry and another in the underground through his CM connections, their show on 89.9 WKCR became a much-followed alternative to commercial rap radio—as well as highly influential. It served as a one-of-a-kind vehicle for introducing new talent, airing exclusive material, and highlighting live freestyle and scratching sessions. Not coincidentally, Jorge, now going as Kurious, appeared as one of the show's first guests. KMD also dropped by for the first time on February 17, 1991, to promote *Mr. Hood*.

Meanwhile, Dante Ross, who was busy building his rap roster at Elektra, had signed his first West Coast artist, Del the Funky Homosapien (Teren Delvon Jones), a bohemian rapper from the Bay Area. Not only was he Ice Cube's cousin, but Del also helmed his own crew of abstract wordsmiths out of Oakland known as Hieroglyphics. Following Del and the Hiero crew's first appearance on *The Stretch Armstrong and Bobbito Show*, freestyling with

Kurious, they all became fast friends and started hanging out at Kurious's apartment whenever they were in New York. That's where they met KMD for the first time, too.

"They was over there on a record player, fooling around with an Ultramagnetic record of some sort. They was just buggin' out like, 'Yo, Ultramagnetic!' just going crazy," recalls Del. "I'm just thinking like 'Yeah, that's my shit, too! As much as they was goin' off over that record, I was the exact same way. So, I knew from that, like, 'Ok, I'ma fool with these fools,' you know what I'm sayin'? Like they kindred."[7] As labelmates, they were already familiar with each other musically, but hanging out together as part of the CM Fam allowed Del to start getting to know the brothers Dumile on a personal level.

With a reduced budget for *Black Bastards*, KMD could not afford to squander time or money at expensive studios. The group had also been downsized after the departure of Onyx, who apparently left over creative differences, so they needed to consolidate their energies and step up their game. Capitalizing on their Ansaar connection, they decided to record the album upstate at the community's compound in Monticello, New York, where Dr. Malachi Z. York, the Ansaar leader and a former musician himself, maintained a studio. In addition to establishing himself as the charismatic and controversial leader of multiple religious movements even prior to the Ansaars, York had moonlighted as a singer-songwriter in the early eighties, specializing in R&B and gospel. His musical career went as far as starting his own label, Passion Records, which later became York's Records, and building a studio that he used and rented out to other artists. KMD initially blocked out two hundred hours at the upstate facility, but when the Ansaars suddenly uprooted and made a mass exodus to Georgia in the summer of 1992, the group had to move their effort closer to home.

While working on *Dust to Dust* (Def Jam/Columbia, 1993), his post–3rd Bass album with DJ Richie Rich, Pete had met Rich Keller, a freelance engineer at Chung King. Keller also operated his own studio in his house in Leonia, New

Jersey, but unlike most home setups, he invested in a good microphone with pre-amps and a two-inch tape machine, the industry standard at the time. The additional gear allowed him to track and record vocals from home and then take the two-inch reels to mix at any professional studio. Through the latter part of 1992 and continuing into the spring of 1993, KMD became his main clients.

They would work in spurts of a week or two, with a week or two off. Arriving at Keller's in the late afternoon, they usually toiled well into the night. "I feel like they moved in," the engineer recalls, "like they brought crates of records." Unlike their first album, where Subroc was focused more on production, but played the background lyrically, the dynamic was shifting. He was slowly coming into his own—not only as an MC but as a man. At eighteen, he and his girlfriend had just brought a new life into the world—a little girl—and with her came a total change of perspective.

According to Keller, "He was more animated and outspoken. He acted more like the rapper in the group during our sessions. I know DOOM was the main MC, but Subroc acted like he was. He had the machismo and had more attitude. DOOM was more about the music and the 'mission' when I was with them. He lived the music; every song was a proclamation that he had to get out. I was inspired by his dedication to the music."[8] Before the record's completion, DOOM, too, would experience the birth of his first son. The vagaries of life helped transform the brothers into different people as they worked on the new album. No longer as loose and carefree, they could feel the pull of responsibilities as they became the main providers in their family.

As far as the division of labor on this album, Sub was credited with producing seven songs compared to Zev's sole contribution, "Contact Blitt." They produced the remaining six tracks together, though their younger brother Dimbaza, credited as Q4, got another assist on "Constipated Monkey," for which he found the drum loop. While Zev still handled most of the vocal duties, Sub rapped on five tracks, including "It Sounded Like a Roc," a solo effort. This album also included several cameos. "Smokin' that S*#%" was a posse cut featuring members of their uptown crew—Kurious, Earthquake, and Lord Sear—while "F*#@ Wit' Ya Head" showcased their boys from Long

Island: H2O (Hard 2 Obtain) and CMOB. The "What a Niggy Know? (Remix)" featuring MF Grimm was a late addition to the album.

KMD had already established their affinity for skits on *Mr. Hood*, and this album, too, opened with a two-minute sonic collage laid over an acoustic bassline and breakbeat called "Garbage Day #3." "That track was Subroc's idea, he put the whole thing together," according to Zev, "It was movie pieces from the 60s and shit like that."[9] Before the advent of Pro Tools, assembling this track involved a lengthy and painstaking process where Sub stayed up all night watching cable TV with a portable DAT player handy. After recording pieces of dialogue, he cut those clips together the next night using the MPC60 that the brothers had bought from Dante Ross.

Gone, however, were the *Sesame Street* snippets, as they borrowed instead from deeper, darker material like Melvin Van Peebles's blaxploitation classic, *Sweet Sweetback's Baadasssss Song*. In fact, the film's graphic opening scene depicting a prostitute taking a young boy's virginity stands as a fitting metaphor for the entire album and the group's loss of innocence. A favorite sample source they returned to again and again was the free jazz and spoken word album *The Blue Guerilla* (Juggernaut, 1970) by Gylan Kain, a founding member of the Last Poets. John Gamble of SD50 had introduced the brothers to the album, and it obviously struck a serious chord. They also happened to know Kain's son Khalil, who starred in the movie *Juice* (1992), and, perhaps, felt they could sample it liberally without fear of a lawsuit.

Aside from using numerous snippets of spoken word and instrumental pieces, they borrowed the whole title of "Constipated Monkey." In the original version, Kain, with typical gravitas, said, "So you sit up at the counter like a constipated monkey / Starin' into an empty bottle, lookin' for God." When taken out of context, however, "constipated monkey'" sounded hilarious, and, no doubt, resonated with the CM Fam, who became associated with the term after Kurious adopted it as the title of his own debut album.

If KMD seemed like a whole new group, it was not lost on the people close to them. After securing a deal for Kurious, Pete wanted to sign a white rapper by the name of Cage (Christian Palko), who was featured on "Rich Bring 'Em

Back" from *Dust to Dust*. Through his appearances on Stretch and Bobbito's show, Cage entered the orbit of CM, becoming good buddies with Subroc. "So that whole crew was running together at that time," says Pete, "and, you know, unfortunately, they were all dropping acid and doing tabs and doing all types of crazy shit. Now, at this point, you look at DOOM who's a devout Muslim, bringing his prayer rug and doing daily prayers on the tour bus, you know. You go from that to DOOM and Sub just smoking blunts, drinking forties, dropping tabs. So, it was like a total 180-degree pivot that they made. And then you see like with *Black Bastards* how different it was." Ross adds, "There was an immense change with the guys in-between records, both as people and artists. They were hanging out in the city a lot, often with Constipated Monkeys, and they were experimenting with a lot of mind-altering drugs. Like a lot of them. Even so, I still felt good about what might become of the record."[10]

Despite the inevitable growing pains, KMD still showed plenty of promise and potential, as well as having the unflinching support of their peers. But even as their careers progressed, not all was well on the home front. According to Dimbaza, "My brothers got a record deal, but that shit did not take my mother off of food stamps." For a certain period, when an injury forced her to stop working and collect disability, bills would pile up, and sometimes the electricity was cut off. Such a precarious situation was enough to upend the fallacy that rappers got rich off record deals. At a time when studio costs were prohibitive, even if a record sold well, royalties could be recouped against the advance, along with any additional marketing and promotional costs. The business model of the music industry had always been to nickel-and-dime the artist as much as possible, charging them back for any expenses to keep them in debt to the label. Being young people with no prior experience managing money further complicated matters.

Rich Keller, who saw a lot of the brothers during this time, remembers, "There was a point where I felt like, you know, we got personal. Like they had some issues. Pete was pretty tight with the money. I gotta say, the money was not flowing. I know they had family issues back at home that they talked about, just based on not having enough money, you know, for rent, bills. Things were kind of tough at home. So, I contributed to help them out." In addition to buying them lunch during studio sessions, at one point, Keller remembers giving the brothers extra pillows and blankets to take home to their siblings in Long Beach. With everything riding on getting the album out, the group was, no doubt, feeling the pressure.

5

THE TIME WE FACED DOOM

For every prohibition you create, you also create an underground.

—JELLO BIAFRA

Ever since N.W.A had the cojones to record "Fuck tha Police," off their groundbreaking debut *Straight Outta Compton* (Ruthless/Priority, 1988), rap has been well acquainted with controversy, repeatedly butting heads with the powers that be over issues of free speech. But the hubbub over that song elicited only a comparative slap on the hand—in the form of a letter of disapproval from the FBI to their record label. Meanwhile, Ruthless founder Eric "Eazy-E" Wright was invited to attend a Washington luncheon for what was billed as the Republicans Inner Circle after making a generous donation of $1,250.

Not long afterward, Miami's 2 Live Crew tested the limits of the First Amendment when US district court judge Jose Gonzalez declared their third studio album, *As Nasty as They Wanna Be* (Skyywalker Records, 1989), legally obscene due to hit songs like "Me So Horny." This decision was eventually overturned, however, and the album went on to become the group's best-selling release, moving over two million units thanks to the added attention.

That's not to say that censorship didn't have its victories. Tipper Gore and a group of "Washington wives," whose clout derived from being married to prominent politicians, established the Parents Music Resource Center (PMRC) in 1985. Parlaying their proximity to power into well-publicized congressional hearings, they successfully pressured the RIAA (Recording Industry Association of America) into policing itself, allowing for "Parental Advisory" stickers on any content deemed violent, sexual, or drug related. But apparently, this move did not go far enough.

On May 14, 1991, Ice-T released his fourth studio album *O.G. Original Gangster* (Sire/ Warner Bros.), which, incidentally, landed on the same day as KMD's *Mr. Hood*. The new record introduced his side project, the metal band Body Count, featured on a song by the same name. When Ice-T headlined the inaugural Lollapalooza concert later that year, he performed a split set featuring his solo rap material as well as him fronting the band, a savvy move that greatly expanded his crossover (read: white) audience. One of their hypest songs was a revenge fantasy called "Cop Killer," which invoked the names of LA police chief Daryl Gates and black motorist Rodney King, whose March 1991 beating at the hands of four LAPD officers was captured on video tape. Long before the advent of smartphones put a video camera in everyone's hands, it was the first time the general public could bear witness to the police brutality that was commonplace—especially in the black community. No one with a beating heart, who had seen the video, was unaffected. Body Count eventually released their eponymous debut, which included "Cop Killer," at the end of March 1992, also on the Warner-distributed Sire Records.

Barely a month later, on Wednesday, April 29, all hell broke loose in Los Angeles when a mostly white jury acquitted the four officers charged with beating King. The verdict set off almost a month of rioting, unrest, and massive destruction of property in one of the nation's major metropolises, totally changing people's perspectives on songs like "Fuck tha Police" and "Cop Killer." If there was any silver lining to the LA riots, it was the temporary truce between Crip and Blood street gangs, who finally realized who their common enemy was. For rappers like N.W.A and Ice-T, this mass rebellion swelling up from the streets was nothing short of vindication for issues they had been speaking about for years. But it also pushed rap into the crosshairs of the culture wars.

By June, the Dallas Police Association along with the Combined Law Enforcement Association of Texas (CLEAT) started protesting "Cop Killer" and demanding that Body Count's record be pulled from store shelves, threatening a boycott of parent company Time Warner, which owned Warner Bros. Records. At the company's annual shareholder meeting in July, actor turned conservative activist Charlton Heston read aloud the lyrics to both "Cop Killer" and another song from the album, "KKK Bitch," which name-checked Tipper Gore. Even the current administration at the time weighed in, with President George H. W. Bush calling the record "sick," while Vice President Dan Quayle described it as "obscene."

In the face of such powerful and widespread opposition, the co-CEO of Time Warner, Jerry Levin, went on the offensive in an op-ed for the *Wall Street Journal* that same month. "It doesn't incite or glorify violence," he wrote of the record, "It's his [Ice-T's] fictionalized attempt to get inside a character's head."[1] Regardless, Warner Bros. record execs received death threats, and some stockholders threatened to pull out of the parent company. While the controversy proved great for sales, pushing the album toward a gold certification, in August— the same month that Ice-T appeared on the cover of *Rolling Stone* wearing a police uniform and clutching a nightstick in his hands—the rapper, of his own volition, finally asked his label to pull the song from the album. After months of protest and pushback, Ice-T, whose last album had been titled *Freedom of Speech... Just Watch What You Say!* (Sire, 1989), had learned a hard lesson.

"When I started out, I was signed to Warner Brothers and they never censored us. Everything we did we have full control over," said Ice-T. "But what happened was, when the cops moved on Body Count they issued pressure on the corporate division of Warner Brothers and that made the music division— they couldn't out fight 'em in the battle—so even when you're in business with somebody whom might not want to censor you, economically people can put restraints on 'em and cause 'em to be afraid. I learned that lesson that you're never really safe as long as you're connected to any big corporation's money."[2] He eventually made an amicable split with Sire/Warner Bros. over a dispute about the artwork to his next album, *Home Invasion* (1993), which was eventually picked up by the independent distributor-label Priority. But it was hardly Warner's last brush with the issue of censorship and rap.

Of course, Ice-T already had a proven track record as a bankable entertainer when the shit hit the fan. In addition to a solid rap pedigree and this latest foray into heavy metal, he had also made the pivot to acting—ironically, playing a cop in the 1991 blockbuster *New Jack City*. But when a lesser-known rapper from the West Coast, Paris, courted similar controversy with his sophomore album *Sleeping with the Enemy*, slated for release through the Warner-distributed Tommy Boy, his deal was terminated. Paris attempted to push the envelope even further with a protest song called "Bush Killa," another revenge fantasy detailing the assassination of a sitting president, whom he felt had no concern for Black people and had led the country into a meaningless war with Iraq (the first Gulf War). The rapper didn't leave empty-handed, however, using the low six-figure settlement he received from the label to put out the record independently through his own Scarface imprint in November 1992.

Around the same time, the Jungle Brothers had turned in their third LP to Warners, only to have it rejected over censorship of another kind—this time on the grounds of being too experimental. In the three years since the release of their masterpiece *Done by the Forces of Nature* (Warner Bros., 1989), the group had been hanging out with the likes of avant-garde producer Bill Laswell and working out of his Greenpoint Studios in Brooklyn, where they had been introduced to an impressive lineup of progressive artists such as John Zorn and free-jazz pioneer Ornette Coleman. After immersing themselves in loads of new information, cutting-edge sounds, and psychedelic drugs, and running through a recording budget of almost $500,000, they delivered a piece of real art that took hip-hop into the outer limits.

For their bold artistic vision, risk-taking, and disregard for convention, however, they were reeled in by their corporate handlers, who insisted that the whole album be retooled and remixed for popular consumption. The result was *J. Beez wit the Remedy*, a pale imitation of the original record, which eventually saw light in June 1993. The experimental version circulated through underground channels before being independently released in much-truncated form as the *Crazy Wisdom Masters* EP (WordSound/Black Hoodz, 1999). But the whole episode further illustrated the extent to which the corporate powers could and would exercise their influence over artists—especially rappers.

Rap had already been singled out in a landmark ruling against unauthorized sampling in December 1991, in which Judge Kevin Duffy invoked the Ten Commandments, warning, "Thou shalt not steal." The case came as a response to rapper Biz Markie using portions of Gilbert O'Sullivan's "Alone Again

(Naturally)" without permission for his song "Alone Again." As a result, Biz's third album, *I Need a Haircut* (Cold Chillin'/Warner, 1991), which contained the song in question, was pulled from store shelves—a blow to his career from which he never quite recovered. In the bigger picture, the ruling had a major impact on sampling in general, paving the way for huge clearance fees and implying that rap's reliance on other recorded music made it somehow less creative. The incident provided further incentive for labels to pay more attention to policing their own product, a lesson that the "Cop Killer" controversy hammered home.

As New York emerged from the winter of 1993, KMD was solely focused on the completion of their new album—not any of these other distractions. With only a couple of songs left, the finish line was in sight, and they were already contemplating the possibility of doing solo projects next. Though still as close as ever, both lived with their girlfriends and had children to support, so they weren't spending as much time together outside studio sessions. Zev had been hanging out uptown with Kurious Jorge and MF Grimm, while Subroc had grown close with the white rapper Cage, who was the same age. "Cage was a legit MC," says Dimbaza Dumile, "Sub recognized that and was like, 'Yo, I'll help you.' So, he was one of the first people who was like, 'You can get on with me. I will help you get on as a rapper.' He believed in him—that was Sub's pet project."

On the night of April 22, the two friends met for dinner downtown in the Village. Then they went back to Cage's place on Great Jones Street near the now defunct Time Café and smoked a few blunts. After playing several games of chess, the weed got the best of them, and they eventually passed out. By the time Cage woke up the next morning, Sub had already left. He called the house in Long Beach and spoke to Mrs. Dumile and Sub's sister, Thenjiwe, to see if his friend had made it back yet, but he hadn't. A couple hours later they called him back, somewhat concerned that Sub had still not arrived.

That evening Cage received a conference call from Pete Nice and Bobbito informing him of the unimaginable. Sub had been found unconscious on an exit ramp of the Long Island Expressway near Rockaway Boulevard, and currently lay in critical condition at Mercy Hospital in Rockville Centre, where he might not make it through the night. Sure enough, he passed away later the following day, April 23, 1993, apparently due to blunt force trauma to the head. He was only nineteen years old.

"It shocked me," Cage recalled, "I know he died because of injuries because he was hit by cars, and I remember hearing he had contusions of the brain which were caused by the accident. Some people said they saw him running into traffic, others say he was chased into traffic. And [the cops] never investigated it. They just closed the case."[3] He added, "That was a fucked-up time. And for a long time, people speculated that I had something to do with it. For a good year."[4]

Because news of Sub's death came so unexpectedly and out of the blue, those close to him seriously entertained the possibility of foul play. Did he have beef with anybody? Was he abducted and beaten up before being dumped on the exit ramp? Since Cage was the last person within his circle to see him alive, he naturally fell under suspicion, as did the influence of drugs. According to Dimbaza, "Aside from me feeling like, 'Hmm, something sketchy happened,' Sub was on some serious Jimi Hendrix acid use where he couldn't make music if he wasn't tripping, okay. So, his behavior didn't help matters when it came down to us feeling like, wait a second, what could have possibly happened?" He says that Sub did have a bad trip only weeks before he died.

Of Cage, Dimbaza adds, "That was totally his trip buddy. I think Cage introduced him to that rule where you gotta trip with somebody. It's truly true, you do gotta trip with somebody and they both were using acid so heavily. They were perfect for each other." At the same time, he absolves Cage of any blame or responsibility in the matter, saying, "I don't like the way people trying to bring up that he might have something to do with it." But to this day, rumors and speculation regarding the details of Subroc's untimely passing abound, making the truth as elusive as ever.

While Sub was fighting for his life in a hospital bed, Zev was none the wiser. After having been picked up for an open-container violation, he had spent several hours in police custody. Mayor Rudy Giuliani's campaign to improve the "quality of life" in the city included fining or even arresting people for carrying an open beer on the street or dancing in bars that didn't have a cabaret license.

When finally released in the wee hours, Zev phoned home to check in, and his mother delivered the crushing news.

Five days later on April 28, Sub's wake was held at the John N. Moore Funeral Home in Roosevelt, Long Island, before his body was interred at Rockville Cemetery in Lynbrook. In homage to his brother, Zev set up a boom box beside the casket and played finished tracks from the album. On the closing verses of Sub's solo track, "It Sounded Like a Roc," he raps, "Attitude nonchalant / I do what I want / If I be ghost / Expect me back to haunt." Pete Nice described the entire experience of hearing the album at the wake as "surreal." The funeral program included a poem written by the deceased called "The Value of Life." In it, he says, "The less you value it, the more it is worth / Less disappointments so there's no loss." He ends by saying, "Life is not valuable, happiness is." There was also an obituary penned by Kinetta Powell-Dumile, the mother of Zev's first son, that ran in the July 1993 issue of *The Source*. In part, it read:

> *Subroc was academically, musically, mechanically, and artistically inclined. He was very skilled, talented, thoughtful, and able to master everything he put his mind to. He thought what others couldn't perceive to think. He knew what others couldn't begin to know. He understood what others couldn't begin to understand. He did what others wouldn't try to do. He was what no one else could be. And now he still stays one step ahead of us.*[5]

Everyone from the Dumiles' extended family of aunts, uncles, and cousins to members of GYP and CM crews to well-known rappers filled the funeral parlor that day. "Everybody was heartbroken and devastated," says Mr. Hood, "It affected the whole crew. Everything changed. Everything changed 'cause Sub, you know, was the master link—the master link to everything. So, when you have a chain, you have the master link and that link is not there, you know? It just changes everything."

With emotions running high, a bit of a commotion ensued as well. According to Pete, "Serch showed up at the funeral home and he wasn't just asked to leave. He was, you know, basically escorted out. And I think he still hung out outside, but he was not welcome at the memorial service." The split that had ruptured 3rd Bass was obviously felt by Zev and Sub, who had chosen sides when they went with Pete. Though the actual reasons for the animosity between them and Serch went much deeper, Pete will only say, "DOOM had personal and artistic and philosophical differences. So, they were not fuckin' with Serch."

Psychologists have identified seven stages of grief that usually follow in ordered progression—from disbelief and shock to denial; guilt and pain; bargaining; anger; depression; and finally, acceptance. But depending on which of his friends you ask, Zev seemed to be bouncing back and forth between these stages erratically like a pinball. Probably the closest person to him at the time besides his family, Kurious, said, "Each man feels his feelings on the inside, the way he does, but all I can say—just from being around DOOM—I'm sure that's something very strong to go through, but he handled it like a man, like really cool. He just seemed very strong about it."[6] Even though, he adds, "You saw a couple more bottles of Henny now, a couple more forties, he'll talk about it and he'll put a positive spin on it like from a metaphysical standpoint and he'll kind of stay there. But you know he's feelin' the human aspects of the pain and missin' his bro, you know what I mean?"[7]

Dante Ross, on the other hand, said, "I think some part of DOOM was gone when Sub died. Sub's death, understandably, made DOOM a very angry person."[8] The rapper Del saw it that way, too, saying, "DOOM really took that super duper hard. Like I was with him one night and he was just buggin' out, you know what I'm sayin'? Like we was trying to get a cab and I think the cab was like not trying to pick us up, so DOOM started like beating on the window of the cab like trying to break the window damn near. I'm like, 'Chill, chill,' you know what I'm sayin', but he was just amped off the whole situation, like it was still fresh. He was goin' through it, you know?"[9]

At other times, he seemed to retreat further inside himself. "DOOM's always been like a very laid-back, quiet person and it just took him down another notch," says Mr. Hood. "Subdued" is also how Michelle Mitchell, an elder cousin by only a few months, described him. She says, "I don't even think he had the chance to grieve—privately maybe—but not like how everybody was grieving. He didn't grieve. And I think that everybody needs to grieve. If you don't have a chance to really grieve, it will start to affect you in different ways." Even his engineer, Rich Keller, noticed the change in DOOM, remarking, "He was even more resolved and quiet, you know, he seemed just even more serious, like the tragedy just turned him more inside to himself. He was just more focused on his work."

Another CM member, Big Ben Grimm, aka Benn Klingon (Alfred Morgan II), started spending more time with DOOM after his brother passed. He describes the rapper as being someone who was already laid-back and a bit of a recluse, adding, "So, I wouldn't say it was much different when and after Subroc died than it's been for the rest of the years since we've been family."[10] DOOM started spending more time uptown, where he could count on the unconditional support network of the CM Fam. But he had neither the time nor luxury to wallow in grief because he had an album to deliver.

Recalling the pledge that he and his brother had made to each other following the death of Scott La Rock—when KRS-ONE had carried the torch solo and released a new BDP album—DOOM did the only thing he could do. "I still went and finished the record despite there only was a little more to do," he said, "So, you know, one of us is going to finish it anyway. If it would have happened to me, he [Sub] would have finished it."[11] Even so, he took his time, finally completing the album about eight months after Sub's death.

When it came time to mix, instead of returning to Chung King or Calliope, DOOM wanted to work a little closer to home. Keller arranged to lock out a week at his friend's studio, Cove City Sound in Glen Cove, Long Island, which featured a vintage Neve mixing console. They also tracked vocals for "Smoking That S*@%," featuring Earthquake, Kurious, and Lord Sear, there. As a late addition, DOOM decided to feature his friend MF Grimm on a remix of "What a Niggy Know?," the first single. In January 1994, they finally put the album to rest following a mastering session at Masterdisk in Manhattan.

Had DOOM grown up in the place of his birth, he would, no doubt, have been familiar with the "Golliwog," a children's book character that inspired a rag doll popular in the UK and Australia up through the seventies. The friendly-looking figure, whose pitch-black skin contrasted with its eye-popping expression, prominent lips, and fuzzy hair, even served as the mascot for a popular brand of jam, appearing not only on its label but in print and TV advertising as well. The "Golly," as he came to be called, traced its origins to author and cartoonist Florence Kate Upton's children's book, *The Adventures of Two Dutch Dolls and a "Golliwogg,"* published in 1895.

Only a few years later, however, in 1899, Scottish author Helen Bannerman wrote and illustrated *The Story of Little Black Sambo*, another children's book that enjoyed a much wider degree of popularity. Though Sambo was not even of African descent—rather a Tamil boy from southern India—the rudimentary drawings of him that appeared in the book became conflated with the Golliwog, so, his name and likeness came to be associated with Black people. Though not inherently racist in the context of the children's stories in which they appeared, both the Golliwog and Sambo took inspiration from the blackface minstrel shows popular in America in the early half of the nineteenth century. During the post-Civil War and Jim Crow eras, these names came to denote derogatory terms representing racist tropes.

For a subversive, mischievous guy like DOOM, who liked to stir things up, the image of Little Black Sambo proved irresistible. "We had used the Sambo character before on *Mr. Hood* graphics. It was kind of like our logo, our mascot," he explained, "We were about deading the whole stereotype thing. It was a mockery of a mockery. And we took it to the next level on *Black Bastards* by hanging the dude."[12]

Indeed, for the cover art of the new album, he drew his own black-and-white rendition of Sambo hanging from a noose with the album title spelled below—minus the letter *A*'s, which tied it to the popular children's game Hangman. It was an ingenious metaphor for getting his point across in the most fun, tongue-in-cheek way possible. "By me putting it out there, I'm really trying to provoke thought," he added, "It's not the hanging of a person, it's an idea being executed—the whole concept and stereotype of our people being displayed as minstrels or servants or fools."[13] Unfortunately, not everyone saw it that way.

"The album got mastered and turned in, and the artwork had gone through the Elektra system, and no one ever questioned it," according to Dante Ross. "Then, all of a sudden, the artwork got leaked to Terri Rossi and *Billboard*. At the time, a lot of older, bougie black people weren't feeling hip-hop. I'd put her in the same bag with C. Delores Tucker and Dionne Warwick. She just didn't get it."[14] Chalk it up to the generational divide, but in her "R&B Rhythms" column in *Billboard's* weekly industry tip sheet called *Airplay Monitor*, Rossi wrote, "I know the officers at Elektra and Time Warner are just kidding us. To promote lynching is just plain evil.... Maybe [KMD] needs a refresher course on the entire Civil Rights movement. Martin Luther King is spinning in his grave."[15] It was clearly the visceral and reactionary response of an individual who had no idea where the group was coming from and probably didn't even bother listening to the lyrics.

A lone voice of disapproval may have rung hollow and proved inconsequential had it not been supported by a similar take by freelance journalist Havelock Nelson, who penned *Billboard's* more visible biweekly rap column. "Regardless of what the group was attempting to achieve with this imagery and the term," he wrote in April 1994, "Many in the black community will find them offensive. It's inexcusable that the executives at Elektra allowed these images to slip through."[16] Ironically, his comments appeared right next to a photo of the kings of gangsta rap, Dr. Dre and his protégé Snoop Doggy Dogg. Signed to Interscope, formerly part of Warner, they were moving millions of units with violent content and liberal use of the N-word. But regardless of the mounting controversy, the major-label machinery had already sprung into motion. The first single, "What a Niggy Know?" (changed last minute from "What A Nigga Know?"), was just cracking the airwaves along with its accompanying video; a release date of May 3 had been announced for the album; and advanced cassettes were mailed out to the press.

On Thursday, April 7, 1994, DOOM was summoned to a meeting at Elektra the next morning, where he was completely blindsided by the powers that be. Dante Ross already knew that the label was unhappy about the artwork for *Black*

Bastards, but he also expected to be able to defend their position, which he had clarified to his boss Bob Krasnow, chairman of Elektra Entertainment. He and DOOM arrived at the Time Warner building on Columbus Circle just before nine in the morning on Friday.

"We got there, and they had the [cover] artwork proofs out on the table," DOOM recalled. "There were a couple of people in the room, including one old dude I had never seen before. He was speaking on behalf of Elektra. It seemed like they had everything planned out already, like they knew how everything was going to end before we said anything. And they said they weren't going to put the album out. They didn't even want us to change the cover."[17] DOOM, who apparently showed little reaction at the time, was presented with a check for $20,000 as a conciliatory gesture, and the original artwork was returned.

Krasnow wasted no time issuing a statement saying, "The groundswell of reaction produced by the cover imagery of KMD's new album has exacerbated concern within Elektra, and the decision has been made that it was best that the record be taken in its intended form elsewhere."[18] All of this went down only a week before Time Warner's annual shareholder meeting. With the controversy ignited by "Cop Killer" still fresh in their minds, it was obviously a preemptive response by the label.

Due to the lag in publishing, Nelson's short piece ran in *Billboard* the following week on April 14. "Definitely looking back at it, I would've investigated more. I would've, you know, talked about what the meaning of the cover was, what the references were. I didn't at the time 'cause it was maybe a deadline day. I cannot recall what the conditions were," he offers in hindsight. "But reflecting on it, I definitely would not have been so harsh to come out saying it's so debasing and so negative," he adds, saying, "I didn't get it at the time I wrote about it, and I should have, honestly, you know, waited to like, call the label or get with the group and kind of see where they were coming from." Rossi, who was contacted by *The Source* in the days following Elektra's decision, expressed a similar regret.

In a scathing editorial entitled "Corporate Hysteria," in the June 1994 issue of *The Source*, editor in chief Jon Shecter, who had met with DOOM on the same day that the rapper was dropped, observed:

> Rap music and corporate America share a peculiar relationship. Rappers like Snoop and Onyx [the group] achieve mind-blowing, massive acclaim sending their pure, uncut material through the vast channels of multinational corporations. But as we've seen over the years, it doesn't take much for the bottom-line bigwigs of big business to flip on hip-hop. It seems inevitable that the raw honesty of many rap records would offend enough of mainstream America to put the product at odds with the company selling it.... The message this incident sends is clear. There is no more tolerance for "controversy" in the boardrooms of a media giant, rap is quite simply expendable. But what did you expect from corporate America?[19]

Ross was quoted in the same editorial saying that the label was basically "scared" to put it out. "I think Elektra knew that the album wasn't going to be a huge hit, and they didn't want black people mad at them, in the community and at the company. So, they figured they should just cut their losses,"[20] he said.

According to Pete, who was managing DOOM at the time, "He was just distraught. You just lost your brother; you just lost your deal. I have a sheet of paper of every single person I called up to try to place the *Black Bastards* album and not one of 'em bid on it. I mean, you have a totally finished, classic album, and because of that whole bullshit at Warner, everybody was just scared off. It was just shameful. I mean, it's like, you know, Russell [Simmons], Def Jam, Profile, like everyone, I called up everybody and no one wanted to fuck with it. And you know, at that point, DOOM was just, like, so disenchanted."

A couple months later in June 1994, a feature on KMD that was supposed to coincide with the album's release ran in *The Source*. Writer Ronin Ro had conducted the interview earlier in March, before the album was shelved, and it already painted a grim portrait of Zev Love X, who was still coping with the loss of his brother. Dressed in all-black fatigues and puffing on a blunt, "his face is a mask of torment," said Ro, who cannily observed, "Death has cast a shadow on Zev, yet he pretends it hasn't. It has made him take a more realistic look at his life, the people in it and what he has to do with it. He realizes you only live once and you have no time to please other people by being anyone other than yourself. This whole record shit he knows is temporary. At any minute, label executives can cut him off and send him back to relative obscurity (as they have done to so many others who have proved unprofitable)."[21] As they listened to tracks from the album together, Zev remarked, "It seems like I'm listening to two different people, to tell you the truth. I'm not even that motherfucker from before. I don't know. Different times. What I'm doing now, creatively, is totally different. It's like him and me combined as one type shit."[22] The metamorphosis of Zev Love X was already in progress.

THE MYTH

I do not come to you as a reality, I come to you as the myth because that is what Black people are: myths.

—SUN RA

6

HERO VS. VILLAIN

> *Comics are a gateway drug to literacy.*
> —ART SPIEGELMAN

Far from flights of fantasy or pure fiction, myths are the stories we tell ourselves that lend meaning and legitimacy to our lives in our quest for ultimate truth. Establishing a context for the present, they also connect us to a rich past and, often, at their core, provide the seeds of our belief systems. Folklore, too, fulfilled a similar role among cultures and communities favoring an oral tradition—including Indigenous populations like the Native Americans or captive Africans brought to the New World. Of course, the unique challenges presented by slavery necessitated alternative forms of expression, information dissemination, and commentary that ultimately contributed to the survival of those suffering under its yoke. In the process of dealing with desperate circumstances, new myths were also born.

Take the African archetype of the trickster, which became embedded in the imagination of the African American for generations to come. Known by various names—including *Esu-Elegbara*, *Exu*, *Echu Elegua*, or *Papa Legba*—this character from West African Yoruba mythology, personified in Anansi the Spider, found expression in such distinctly African American folk heroes as Br'er Rabbit and the Signifying Monkey. In tales passed on via word of mouth, these unlikely saviors were revered for their ability to outsmart more powerful opponents (i.e., "Massa") using creativity, guile, and wit, thereby transmuting vice into virtue. A "slippery tongue," for example, facilitated one's removal from a sticky situation. That same "gift of gab" offered the ability to cajole, manipulate, lie, and generally talk circles around those trying to assert their dominance or authority. Such a rhetorical strategy, known as "signifying"—or more colloquially, "jivin'" or "talking shit"—became a legitimate superpower for coping with an unjust world.

Though slavery eventually ended, life did not appreciably change for the newly emancipated, who still had to contend with restrictive Jim Crow laws that laid the foundation for the institutional racism that plagues us to this day. In this post-slavery landscape, the archetype of the trickster became more fluid, morphing into the authority-flouting "Badman" to create a uniquely African American anti-hero. While traditional heroes, possessed of the best intentions, were always striving for a just outcome or goal, the Badman, who often exhibited pathological tendencies, proved to be a little more complicated.

Due to severe limitations placed on all aspects of Black life—from housing to education to employment—the Badman operated on the fringes of established society and, therefore, outside the status quo. Malcolm X once remarked, "Only a fool fights by the ground rules that his enemy has laid down for him," but the Badman had already internalized such logic. In fact, becoming a key figure in the underground or counterculture might explain how he earned his reputation in the first place. The Badman's involvement in everything from gambling and prostitution to illegal drugs and alcohol, which had no place in polite society, provided the only available means to make a decent living. In treading this path, he also placed himself in opposition to the police, who replaced the former enforcer, the slave master. But to his community, the Badman struck a righteous figure like Robin Hood, flouting what was permissible under inequitable laws.

One of the earliest and best examples of the Badman as anti-hero was "Stagolee" or Stagger Lee, whose name, in its various renderings, has been lionized in myriad songs, ballads, toasts, and stories. Ironically, he wasn't a defender of the race, railing against a corrupt system, but rather took the life of another black man who dared touch his Stetson hat. Their deadly dispute boiled down to an issue of respect and preserving one's honor, which was always worth defending. Lee, according to author Cecil Brown, "came to personify the collective feeling of blacks at the bottom of society, and it was in this sense that Stagolee became a symbol of the Black community."[1]

Had he merely been a myth or contrived, his story might not have resonated among so many musicians and performers, from Cab Calloway to Bob Dylan. But not simply a figment of the folkloric imagination, Stagger Lee Shelton was a known St. Louis pimp in the 1890s, whose reputation for toughness could only be matched by his way with words. In this regard, he could be seen as a worthy predecessor of today's rappers, who have subsumed the persona of the Badman while perfecting the practice of signifying, taking it to the pinnacle of pop culture.

A century after Stagger Lee saw the emergence of characters like Nas Escobar and The Notorious B.I.G., originally Biggie Smalls. Nas, of course, was comparing himself to the infamous Colombian drug lord, who revolutionized the cocaine trade, while copyright issues forced Biggie to change his name from that of the gang leader of the 1975 film *Let's Do It Again*. While adding the adjective that introduced his all-caps persona, he alternatively called himself the Black Frank White, after the drug kingpin played by Christopher Walken in *King of New York* (1990). As products of the crack era, these counterculture bards of the nineties wholly embraced the archetype of the Badman as part of their cultural inheritance. But for DOOM, assuming the persona of one of the most iconic comic book villains of all time involved more than simply adopting a pseudonym.

"Back in the day, the first thing that hit me and gave me ideas in terms of characters and creative writing were comic books,"[2] he said. Having already established a connection to Doctor Doom through his own nickname, he took the time to delve further into the character's backstory, adding, "In the case of Doctor Doom, he was supposed to be a bad guy, trying to take over the Earth and whatnot, but where he's from [Latveria] he's revered as a king, he's loved. So, it's a matter of perception, it depends on whatever angle you're looking from."[3]

DOOM went on to observe that "the way comics are written shows you the duality of things—how the bad guy ain't really a bad guy if you look at it from his perspective. Through that style of writing, I was kinda like, if I flip that into hip-hop, that's something niggas ain't done yet. I was looking for an angle that would be brand new. That's when I came up with the character and worked out the kinks—that's the Villain."[4] Clearly on a mission to murder stereotypes and one-up all the other MCs out there, he staked his claim to be the baddest of them all, declaring, "From the point of view [of America] we're the villains. But I'm the SuperVillain."[5]

Joseph Campbell, known for his comparative study of worldwide folklore and mythology, concluded that "the artist is the one who communicates myth for today."[6] His statement applies as much to DOOM as to the genre that heavily influenced him—superhero comic books—which only came into being comparatively recently, with the introduction of Superman in 1939. According to author Bradford Wright, "Comic books had the power to indulge fantasies and create myths for a young audience hungry for empathy and easy explanations. Here was an entertainment industry catering exclusively to the tastes of the young and impressionable, controlled by urban young men with worldviews far removed from Victorian middle-class ideals and guided, above all, by the pursuit of quick profits. It was a combination that heralded a cultural and market revolution."[7]

The urban men to whom he was referring were largely lower-middle-class, second-generation Jewish immigrants like Jerry Siegel and Joe Shuster, who created Superman for DC Comics while still in high school. Another collaborative team, who had a huge impact on the comic book industry—especially after hitting their stride in the sixties—was Stanley Lieber (aka Stan Lee) and Jacob Kurtzberg (aka Jack Kirby), who formed the creative core of DC's main competitor, Marvel Comics. At a time when the industry was struggling, they single-handedly revived interest in superheroes with the introduction of the Fantastic Four, an unlikely pairing of idiosyncratic individuals, who acquired remarkable powers following their exposure to cosmic rays during a spaceflight. The Fantastic Four quickly rose in popularity to become the flagship book for Marvel, who followed their success with equally compelling but conflicted characters such as Spider-Man, the Hulk, and Thor. The Fantastic Four were also among the first comic book characters to get their own animated TV series, beginning in the late sixties. While diverse in their skill set, all shared a similar profile—awesome abilities coupled with human frailties that brought them down to Earth and made them relatable. Such traits became the defining characteristics of Marvel heroes.

As Wright noted, "Marvel presented its cautionary tales not through moral platitudes but in the form of alienated antiheroes. On the surface these characters were not sympathetic, they were hopelessly selfish individuals who planted the seeds of their own destruction. Yet in these pathetic characters, readers recognized familiar human feelings and glimpsed their own anxieties."[8] In this regard, DOOM's flawed supervillain persona perfectly conformed to the template.

In addition to the angst-ridden hero archetype, which, for a time, was copied by the entire industry, Marvel's innovations extended to an entire intricate universe, in which such characters interacted, often crossing over into each other's story lines. As unbelievable as some of the plots and concepts may have appeared, they always offered commentary on real issues of the day that placed them a cut above mindless entertainment. Look no further than Hollywood's enduring fixation with big-budget superhero movies to understand how influential and impactful these humble comic books would eventually turn out to be.

What is considered the Marvel Age of comics officially kicked off with the introduction of the Fantastic Four, who debuted in November 1961. Reed Richards, aka Mr. Fantastic, who could contort his body in impossible ways, helmed a motley crew of superheroes, including his girlfriend Susan Storm, who had the power of invisibility; her brother Johnny, known as the Human Torch for his ability to spontaneously combust; and Richard's best friend, Ben Grimm, a former football player whose acquisition of superhuman strength was accompanied by the breakout of his stony complexion that gave him the name The Thing. In need of a worthy nemesis, their creators obliged, giving them Doctor Doom, whose hubris and awesome abilities made him as compelling a character as the heroes themselves. A "mad scientist" in the greatest sense of the term, Doom had the ability to shoot electricity from his hands, time travel, and even play God, wresting his mother's soul from the hands of the devil himself. Following the character's first appearance in *Fantastic Four* #5 in July 1962, Doctor Doom eventually took on a life of his own.

Author and comic book enthusiast Douglas Wolk, who has read the entire Marvel oeuvre of some twenty-seven thousand issues, writes, "Doom is genuinely monstrous. He never removes the armor with which he has covered his flesh, or the metal mask he built so that nobody could ever see his scarred face. He's prideful, supercilious, and allistic, devoid of compassion, prone to bursts of contemptuous rage. He maintains his power through violence, and it's of paramount importance to him to appear to be in absolute control at all times."[9] At the same time, however, he concedes, "In the stories Kirby drew, we most often see Doom in the business of consolidating his power, or plotting his revenge on Reed Richards, as he does here, rather than something more broadly nefarious. We are to understand he is a villain because he fights the Fantastic Four, and that the Fantastic Four are heroes because they fight him; his understanding is just the reverse."[10]

Embedded in the background, Doctor Doom did not even receive an origin story until a couple of years later in *Fantastic Four Annual* #2. By 1965, he was not only fighting his usual foes, but also making appearances battling Spider-Man, the Avengers, and Daredevil. For someone who didn't even get his own book(s) until much later in 2006, when Ed Brubaker compiled and expanded his whole backstory into the six-volume *Books of Doom*, he seems to have exerted an oversized influence on the Marvel Universe. He even figured prominently in the Fantastic Four's animated TV series, produced by Hanna-Barbera, that first aired in 1967.

"Doom is a compelling villain because he is unabashedly the hero of his own story," says Wolk. "Like as far as he is concerned, he is out to make the world a better place and the world would be a better place if he were running it. And he might be right about that. He has, in fact, been the person who has saved everything more than once." Rationalizing the character's more pathological behavior, he adds, "He has a weirdly tormented past. He has not necessarily good, but kind of defensible reasons for hating the people he hates and being obsessed with what he's obsessed with." Like the flawed heroes for whom comic book audiences rooted, Doom cut the figure of a villain, who, perhaps, wasn't all that bad ("a killer who loves children," as his namesake admitted in rhyme). After taking over the world in the late eighties, for example, he abolished apartheid in South Africa, which begs the question: How evil could he be?

Even bad guys were children once, and young Victor Von Doom's story begins in the fictional Balkan nation of Latveria, where he is born into a nomadic tribe of Gypsies known as the Zefiro, a persecuted minority. His father, Werner, is a man of science and medicine, while his mother, Cynthia, who practices magic, is considered a witch. Science and mysticism, then, represent the twin pillars of influence in Victor's life that are crucial to his character's self-realization and development. Premised on logic and reason, science utilizes reproducible methods of experimentation to derive consistent and observable results. Magic represents exactly the opposite, existing in the abstract, intuitive realm where faith, belief, and miracles comingle. The eventual loss of both parents in a violent and unexpected manner provides the impetus that sets Victor on his path to becoming the infamous Doctor Doom, as he devotes himself to the study of these two divergent approaches to explaining the unknown.

He lives like a hermit, shunning most people, only sharing his true self with his girlfriend, Valeria. But when the Baron of Latveria's forces come after him, he must leave her, escaping by inventing a lifelike mechanical double—the prototype Doombot. (DOOM would brilliantly exploit this important detail in the story later on in real life.) Victor's invention attracts the attention of the US government, who offer him a full scholarship to college in exchange for access to his research.

In college, the budding scientist meets Reed Richards, the future Mr. Fantastic, who asks him to be his roommate. After Victor spurns this overture, however, Richards ends up rooming with Ben Grimm. It turns out that the scholarship is simply a means to an end for Doom, who is provided a lab to help the US government develop an army of robotic soldiers. He uses the facilities to further his practice of the dark arts, working on a time machine that would allow him to enter the demon Mephisto's realm and free his mother's soul.

Victor successfully propels himself to the other side, but only briefly, as the unstable energy he generates unleashes a fiery explosion. After regaining consciousness in the hospital, he finds his face has been scarred. The degree of his disfigurement has always been debatable, however, as different writers contributed to the character's story after Kirby left Marvel. Following the accident, Victor decides to terminate his agreement with the US government, allowing his robotic soldiers to destroy his research and self-destruct before he himself flees the country.

Returning to Eastern Europe, he lives in relative anonymity thanks to the bandages that cover his face. After reconnecting with his childhood love, Valeria, he seems to have finally found the peace and stability he needs. But living "happily ever after" is not in the cards for Victor. When KGB agents discover his true identity, they attempt to persuade him to work for them, using Valeria as a bargaining chip, but almost end up killing her. Victor's neighbor, Otto, comes to the rescue. Masquerading as a harmless drunk, he turns out to be a member of a secret order of monks from Tibet. In Victor he sees the fulfillment of an ancient prophecy, which says that a man who hides his face would lead them, and urges him to go and study with the order.

In the years that Victor is away, immersed in training and honing his abilities in both science and the mystic arts, he learns that the Baron, who persecuted his tribe and family, has ascended to the throne of Latveria. Meanwhile, his former rival Reed Richards has become a renowned scientist. The news is enough to spark a fit of jealousy and rage, making Victor realize that he has unfinished business to attend to (the same feelings DOOM probably experienced when he saw all these corny MCs coming up). Enlisting the aid of the other monks, Victor devises a high-tech suit of armor that he dons like a medieval knight, along with a green cape and hood. The final piece of the outfit is a forged metallic mask that he hastily puts on before it's had a chance to fully cool. The unfortunate result is that he sears the flesh off his entire face, becoming permanently disfigured and making the final transformation into Doctor Doom.

The accident only serves to toughen his resolve while deadening his empathy and emotions. Despite Valeria's best efforts to dissuade him, Doom is more determined than ever to return to Latveria and start exacting his revenge. His first move is to marshal his tribe of Zefiros to help rebuild his robot army and reclaim the country. By this point he is so formidable an opponent that no one dares challenge him. He carries out a mostly bloodless coup, killing only the king. Having "liberated" his own country, Doom now sets his sights on the world. It's not your ordinary megalomaniac power grab either because, as far as he is concerned, people have demonstrated such an inordinate capacity for violence, hate, and destruction that he feels like he's rescuing humanity from itself. Doom, eventually, fulfills this ambition as well, though his greatest personal achievement is battling Mephisto to finally free his mother's soul from eternal damnation.

Even in abbreviated form, this backstory provides plenty of parallels between the comic book character and the MC. The most obvious similarity they share are lives irrevocably altered by tragic loss. In the fictional Doom's case, the death of both parents determines the path he pursues in life. For DOOM, the unexpected loss of his brother coupled with the termination of his record deal delivers the one-two punch that took the floor out from under him, setting the stage for serious transformation. In both cases, revenge provides the impetus for change, whether a score to settle with humanity or with the music industry.

While plenty of rappers have assumed comic book alter egos—from David Banner to Jean Grae (based on Jean Grey from the X-Men) to Tony Starks (Ironman, aka Ghostface Killah)—only DOOM fully inhabited his character. His most obvious homage to his namesake was the trademark metal face mask that made his transformation complete. Employed primarily for theatrical effect, the mask helped him subvert the whole paradigm of fame, allowing him a modicum of privacy in his personal life. He also used it to deflect attention from himself so that people would focus more on the content of his words. But one might also argue that the mask eventually morphed into his entire image, especially when he created his own DOOMbots, letting them loose to perform in his stead. Such villainous behavior earned him a significant backlash from his dedicated fans, who, expecting to see the real DOOM, were hardly fooled.

Other parallels were not so obvious. Like his namesake, DOOM was a recluse who valued his privacy and enjoyed spending time alone. Completely dedicated to his art, he exhibited the same relentless work ethic as the good doctor. In fact, if not for his prolific output, we might not be talking about him today. But once back on his feet, he imposed himself on the rap scene as the alternative to the status quo. Like his character's quest for world domination, he was on a self-declared mission to destroy commercial rap. In a way, DOOM also possessed a time machine like his comic-book alias, taking rap back to the fundamentals of dope beats and clever wordplay.

Hip-hop, like comics, boasted no shortage of larger-than-life personalities with egos and mouths to match, but DOOM managed to dominate them all. When it came to puns, punchlines, metaphors, and straight bragging, he beat rappers at their own game. When asked about his inspiration for the character of Doctor Doom, creator Jack Kirby referenced the Grim Reaper, the personification of death. One also saw echoes of Doom in one of the big screen's ultimate badmen, Darth Vader. In modeling such villainous behavior, DOOM had big shoes to fill, but he approached it with tongue planted firmly in cheek. As one reviewer commented, "If there is anything truly villainous about DOOM, it's that he subverts hip-hop's foundation of taking oneself way too seriously by acknowledging that it's all just tall tales."[11]

The strongest point of intersection between the man and the myth—missed by most casual observers—was their dedication to both science and mysticism, two opposite approaches to explaining the world. Like his namesake, DOOM's father was a scientist and mathematician, while his mother, though a nurse, leaned toward alternative therapies and spirituality. Both contributed to their son's erudite approach to everything from mastering the technology of various electronic beat machines to his love for hidden knowledge and the occult. DOOM remained a student of the universe for life, always thirsty for knowledge, wisdom, and understanding. The fruits of his research resurface in rhymes, rich with obscure references that people will be decoding for years to come like some latter-day Shakespeare. In his later years a diminished musical output coincided with a deeper devotion to the esoteric—everything from harnessing the power of crystals to constructing geodesic domes and orgone pyramids. Certainly, if the roles were reversed, and in some parallel universe the fictional Doctor Doom had to choose a real-life analog, he could have done no better than the person of Daniel Dumile.

7

MONSTER ZERO

> *Monsters are tragic beings. They are not evil by choice. They're born too tall, too strong, too heavy: That is their tragedy. They do not attack humanity intentionally, but because of their size, they cause damage and suffering. Therefore, man defends himself against them. After several stories of this type, the public finds sympathy for the monsters. In reality, they favor the monsters.*
> —ISHIRŌ HONDA, DIRECTOR OF *GODZILLA* (1954)

On March 1, 1954, a blast brighter than the sun electrified the skies above Bikini Atoll in the Marshall Islands, whipping up smoke, debris, and vaporized water into that dramatic harbinger of devastation, a mushroom cloud. US military testing of the hydrogen bomb, the most advanced weapon of mass destruction ever unleashed on the planet until then, exceeded all expectations, impacting a much wider area than was previously estimated and raining radioactive fallout on residents of two nearby atolls, who were not evacuated until three days later. The crew of the ironically named Japanese tuna trawler *Daigo Fukuryū Maru* (*Lucky Dragon No. 5*), who had the misfortune of casting their nets in the vicinity, suffered severe radiation poisoning from the flurries of toxic grey ash that floated down from the sky, settling on their skin. In the wake of the calamitous bombings of Hiroshima and Nagasaki that ended WWII nine years earlier, this tragic incident only served to exacerbate existing emotional wounds and galvanize the anti-nuclear movement in Japan.

That same year saw Toho Studios' release of the original *Godzilla* (*Gojira* in Japanese) movie, in which a prehistoric sea monster "awakened" by nuclear testing wreaks havoc on the populace. Though fantastic in nature, the film seemed like a veiled attempt to come to terms with the bomb's devastation by the only nation to experience its awesome power firsthand. Indeed, it proved to be cathartic, as author David Kalat writes, "Nuclear horror rains down on Tokyo, but without America playing any role in the proceedings or even being mentioned once. Godzilla, a symbol of the Bomb, gave audiences a mechanism by which to rage against the damage done to their country, to decry the arms race, to see their nation as both victim and savior, without transgressing the many taboos that postwar life had imposed on such discussions."[1]

Inspired by the 1952 re-release of the original giant monster movie, *King Kong* (made in 1933), and modeled after 1953's *The Beast from 20,000 Fathoms*, *Godzilla* instantly rose to become a popular hit, without aspiring to the same art-house pretentions that characterized other foreign films of the era. On the contrary, its production values and special effects—considered cutting-edge at the time—involved a man in a latex-rubber suit stomping around painstakingly produced miniature sets. Americans saw a significantly different film with the release of *Godzilla, King of the Monsters!* (1956), two years later, featuring new footage of actor Raymond Burr intercut with the original as well as dubbing in English. Though the film was still regarded as somewhat campy and schlocky, these additions powered its success stateside, where it grossed $2 million at the box office—ten times that of the previously highest-earning Japanese film, *Rashomon* (1950).

That classic period piece, directed by world-renowned auteur Akira Kurosawa, shared much in common with its lowbrow counterpart, including the same cast, crew, and studio. *Godzilla* director Ishirō Honda even called himself a close personal friend and creative consultant to the Japanese master. While Kurosawa's oeuvre came to earn the highest respect of cinephiles worldwide, *Godzilla* went on to become a global pop-culture phenomenon, qualifying as the longest-running film franchise ever made, and spawning a whole genre of Japanese films known as *kaiju eiga* ("strange beast movies") that featured an assortment of giant monsters. To date, the franchise has been responsible for some thirty-eight films—thirty-three produced by Toho, one by TriStar, and four by Legendary Pictures (the latter two being US film studios).

Over the course of that prolific run, the fearsome beast, originally conceived as a metaphor for the destruction wrought by nuclear weapons, morphed into a likable creature and savior of humanity, who defended Japan against some of his equally bizarre counterparts, such as Rodan, the giant flying Pteranodon, and King Ghidorah, the three-headed, two-tailed, winged serpent from outer space. "Godzilla's transformation into a heroic defender of the Earth was more than just the softening of a once terrifying movie monster into a family friendly icon. The change represented something about Japan as a nation. Like Japan, Godzilla was sometimes right, sometimes wrong, but always acting on the same underlying principle: the defense of its territory," Kalat writes. "Perhaps, in some way, the fictional construct of Godzilla helped provide a metaphor . . . to show that great forces can have both good and bad effects in the world, without being all of one or the other."[2]

If there remained some ambiguity about Godzilla's motives and intentions, Ghidorah offered an appropriate foil—the unapologetic bad guy you loved to hate. Appearing in multiple movies, beginning with *Ghidorah, the Three-Headed Monster* (1964), the monster quickly rose to become the archnemesis of Godzilla and probably the second most popular of all the *kaiju eiga*. Conceptually, its name derived from the Japanese pronunciation of Hydra, the mythological Greek sea monster with nine heads, though local legends also spoke of an eight-headed, eight-tailed dragon called *Yamata no Orochi*. Sometimes referred to as Monster Zero, Ghidorah moved more gracefully than Godzilla and could shoot destructive "gravity beams" from its heads while whipping up gale-force winds with its wings.

Always portrayed as an existential threat originating from off-planet, the golden-scaled creature further distinguished itself from the pantheon of earthly monsters by claiming the title of "king," suggesting its superiority. But only those with more than just a cursory knowledge of the franchise could appreciate such nuances. Not surprisingly, the biggest fans of Godzilla and his minions were younger audiences exposed to such B-movie fare via TV reruns. Imagine a young DOOM, already a sponge for comic books and cartoons, considering the merits of such a monster.

"Out of that whole Godzilla stuff, Ghidorah was always the villain," he says. "So, I thought, OK, he's the oddball. Let's show a little bit more of his personality—a side of him that people don't see."[3] Like Doctor Doom, he recognized there was more to the character than just being a bad guy. But since Ghidorah didn't speak, aside from some high-pitched shrieking, DOOM, the writer, attempted to get inside his head. He ended up settling on an alternative narrative, using the character to hold a mirror up to humanity. "His whole mission is the evolution of humans, to show humans from his extraterrestrial point of view, what we look like,"[4] he explained. DOOM's motive for assuming another villainous persona, then, remained consistent with his recurring theme of redemption. Just like his "killer who loves children" persona, Ghidorah was meant to challenge our allegiances. "I design my characters from the point of view of someone who's looking at them and thinking of them as bad guys," he says. "They're not necessarily bad guys. Hopefully, once you get to know them, you build your own opinions of who they are."[5]

Back in the late eighties, when Public Enemy's Chuck D called rap the "Black CNN," he unwittingly set the stage for the "keep it real" movement of the nineties. He wanted to speak truth to power as he compared rappers to street journalists telling the stories of an invisible underclass whose voices had been marginalized in the mainstream media. MCs following in his wake felt further compelled to offer their own truths as they saw or experienced it. "Keeping it real," then, evolved into a mantra representing rappers' preoccupation with authenticity—not necessarily a bad thing until it became circumscribed with certain unwritten rules. You couldn't say it if you hadn't done it, for example, was a warning to the glut of fake gangstas out there who talked the talk but couldn't walk the walk. As the line between reporter and first-person participant became increasingly blurred, stereotypes started piling up on top of clichés. In the wake of the crack epidemic's scourge on urban

America, selling drugs—or rapping about it—found justification, even glorification, as an acceptable alternative to a minimum-wage job at McDonalds. The term "real," itself, became twisted, painting a monochrome portrait of ghetto life as representing the entire Black experience.

Perhaps this trend or movement was simply a reaction to rap's increasing commercialization courtesy of the Hammers and Vanilla Ices, who upended the art form from its humble roots in a quest to cash in. In contrast, the "keep it real" nineties centered rap back on the streets where it was born. Rugged workwear like Carhartt, Dickies, and Timberland boots reflected the era's non-fashion aesthetic as music videos were often shot against a backdrop of crumbling urban decay. Rampant materialism and conspicuous consumption had yet to poison the art form, and rappers remained focused on serious issues affecting their communities. Leading the pack were conscious, committed artists, who reflected the struggle as they saw it—without compromise or apology. As a result, the decade produced no shortage of classic music. Unfortunately, all the promise and grassroots energy of those times eventually unraveled with the deaths of two of the biggest stars of the day, Tupac and The Notorious B.I.G., only six months apart in 1996.

Ironically, Biggie's label, Bad Boy, helmed by the flamboyant Puff Daddy (Sean "P. Diddy" Combs), was well-positioned to pick up the pieces. They transitioned seamlessly into the "Jiggy" Era—coined after pop-rapper Will Smith's 1998 Grammy Award–winning hit, "Gettin' Jiggy Wit It"—known for its slick, glossy sound, coupled with an appetite for luxurious living and conspicuous consumption. With its finger on the pulse of late-stage capitalism, rap may have been moving more units than ever before, minting an exclusive club of black millionaires and moguls in the process. But for those who had followed the music since its inception, the inevitable big sellout had begun. After all, wasn't that the American way—to start from scratch, make something out of nothing, and then cash out to the highest bidder? Far from being simply a commodity, however, hip-hop remained a cultural expression with deep roots that could not easily be compromised. In the late nineties, when rap was undergoing a huge transformation—from gritty to glitzy, and no longer dominated by the coastal powers of New York and LA—an out-of-work DOOM observed from the sidelines, analyzing the situation. Looking for a way to fit back into the narrative, he decided the only course of action was to keep it way unreal.

"In hip-hop, we get kinda confused. I think we limit ourselves with the whole, 'I'm the guy' kinda thing," he observed. "So, I'm like if hip-hop is all about bragging and boasting, then I'm going to make the illest character who can brag about all kinds of shit. Like why not? It's all your imagination—go as far as you want."[6] Choosing to model his new persona on a comic-book villain with whom he already shared a nickname was not much of a stretch. "This is the fun part of the approach of the DOOM stuff. I'm not that dude at all. I'm writing about a character. It's a little based on my personality but it's definitely exaggerated,"[7] he explained. To underscore the point, he became the first and only MC to rap in the third person, referring to his alter ego as "he." But if his first stab at fiction wasn't bold enough, he truly took it to the next level with "King Ghidra" (later spelled Geedorah in an effort to absolve himself of any copyright infringement), putting himself in a class of his own.

"Well, it's really because I consider myself a writer. When I write, I write from different characters, I write through different scenes, different times," DOOM explained. "I look at it like I'm a fiction writer or someone who writes novels, you've got a wide range of characters—even someone who writes scripts for movies, a playwright. It always makes things more eventful. It would be corny if I was just writing from me. [That's why] I've got a whole slew of characters."[8] By stepping outside the accepted parameters of the art form, he had stumbled upon a brilliant conceit that no one else in rap had even considered.

"So, I figured out a way where, all right, this time I'm doing it, but it's going to be done like how they do it in the movies. They'll have a character in it, but the character is spawned from the imagination," he said. "As wild as it may be, if you're a writer, you can go there and make it real. I like to stick to the writing aspect of it and write these scripts, write these screenplays. The character can do anything. Regular MCs can't really do that."[9] For inspiration, DOOM credited late-night talk show host and comic, Stephen Colbert, who for a good chunk of his early career, parodied a conservative political pundit in the mold of Bill

O'Reilly. Under the aegis of such a character, he had license to make humor out of the most outrageous and provocative statements. DOOM applied the same formula to Mcing, saying, "For people who are attracted to hip-hop music, it's our job to spark their thoughts, to make them say, 'What the fuck is he saying that for? Why's he doing that?' Then, when they find out it's just a character, it's a mind-opening thing. Plus, it's like, damn, the temptation to just fuck with people's head like that, I just can't resist."[10] Chalk up the reign of rap's King Geedorah to creativity and vision combined with a healthy dose of playful humor and mischief, all qualities overflowing in the mind of DOOM.

His adoption of this nonhuman character did not occur in a vacuum either. DOOM's fertile imagination had already met its match in his buddy MF Grimm, a true collaborator who acted as a sounding board to bounce ideas off. It was Grimm's idea to append the "MF" prefix to their rap names as another way to set themselves apart from other MCs. Sure, everyone was already familiar with the role of a master of ceremony, but "MF" offered a riddle without a definitive answer. According to Grimm, its meaning was fluid and might stand for "Mother Fucker," "Mad Flows," or "Multiple Frequencies." In DOOM's reading, the acronym translated to "Monkey Feet," "Manhattan's Finest," or, most popularly, "Metal Face," as befitted the character of Doctor Doom.

At the time, the only rappers challenging the orthodoxy of the "keep it real" era, while still being firmly ensconced within it, were a group from Staten Island who called themselves Wu-Tang Clan. As their name suggested, these nine MCs, all members of the Nation of Gods and Earths (Five Percenters), had adopted the imagery and mythology of kung-fu films popular in the seventies and eighties. They even renamed their home borough of Staten Island, "Shaolin," after the legendary Chinese martial arts academy. Among the many ways they changed the game, both creatively and business-wise, Wu-Tang's influence loomed large over nineties hip-hop. With provocative and outlandish pseudonyms like Ol' Dirty Bastard and Ghostface Killah and multiple identities, they gave license to rappers to indulge in a bit of fantasy and role-playing, inspiring no shortage of copycats along the way. Both DOOM and Grimm, like pretty much everyone else in rap, were enamored by the group, who were running things between 1994 and 1995.

Using the Clan as a template, Grimm conceived of his own rap crew, based not on martial arts, but on the monster movies of Japan popular in his youth. Assuming the role of Godzilla, the trademarked star of the genre, would have been a little too obvious and perhaps begging for a lawsuit. Instead, Grimm chose to call himself Jet Jaguar after the giant, self-aware robot who helped Godzilla defeat his foe in the film *Godzilla vs. Megalon* (1973). DOOM, in keeping with his villainous nature, latched onto Godzilla's archnemesis. Between 1995 and 1998, DOOM and Grimm would assemble a cast of largely unknown, underground MCs and call themselves Monsta Island Czars (M.I.C).

Though the fictional Monster Island represented Manhattan, they recruited MCs from all over the city, asking them to adopt the names of different monsters from the Japanese *kaiju eiga*. From Long Beach, DOOM enlisted Tommy Gunn (Thomas Rollins), who assumed the alias Megalon; Rodan (aka Jade One), an original member of KMD, who had moved back to the area after completing high school upstate; and Kongcrete, who shortened his name to Kong (as in King Kong) for this project. Spiega (Traver Brown), who took his name from the giant spider who first appeared in *Son of Godzilla* (1974), hailed from neighboring Freeport. A Queens rapper known as Kwite Def (KD), of the group Dirt Nation, chose Kamackeris as his new moniker, based on the giant mantis Kamacuras, who also appeared in *Son of Godzilla*. A Puerto Rican MC from Virginia, whom DOOM brought into the fold, assumed the alias Gigan, after another one of Godzilla's giant reptilian opponents. Rounding out the roster and recruited to help produce the album was DOOM's old friend Web D in his monster persona of King Cesar, the lion/reptilian hybrid who first appeared in *Godzilla vs. Mechagodzilla* (1974). Like the Clan, their plan was to strike first as a collective before branching out with solo projects. But the lack of a recording budget, along with the logistics of coordinating so many MCs, made for slow progress. So, M.I.C evolved into a long-term marquee project on which DOOM and Grimm pinned their hopes for a come up.

For now, DOOM had all the time in the world, and he used it to tweak Geedorah's character, bringing the monster in line with his own mythology, which was a work in progress. "So Geedorah, he's really into hip-hop. He does it, thinks it, feels it, all that," he explained. "But the only way he can really express it in 3D here is by telepathically communicating with DOOM and having DOOM write down and relay the messages that he's sending. So how Geedorah comes vocally on records, there's almost a spiritual connection between him and DOOM. Geedorah's style is different and the way you can tell the difference is Geedorah's more like, how can I say, more royal in his presentation. He's on a grander scale. That's how you can tell the difference between the two."[11] While this explanation bordered on the absurd, once the listener accepted the conceit of a rapping dragon from outer space, pretty much anything else was possible.

DOOM could skillfully flip all the silliness into something substantial and profound—for example, when he stayed in character as Geedorah during an interview with CMJ. "They call Godzilla the beast?" he asked. "The equivalent of the beast on Earth would be institutionalism, the big systems, the jails, the police, the fucking government, anything that's oppressing you. So, of course, I got beef with the beast. That niggas fuckin' shit up constantly, and when I come and stop the nigga, he gotta get like eight other motherfuckers to try to stop me."[12] Geedorah might be beaten back or even suffer defeat. But like any villain worth his salt, he would always return another day to raise hell.

8

TAKE ME TO YOUR LEADER

I eat no pork / So why can't I be as smooth as my man Dr. York.

—ZEV LOVE X, "PEACHFUZZ"

For channeling the persona of a giant flying reptile from outer space, DOOM gets the trophy for boldly daring to go where no other rapper had ventured before. Such a display of eccentric bravado, however, found precedent in another musical iconoclast—jazz avant-gardist Sun Ra, who always claimed to be from off-planet (specifically Saturn) and whose whole life embodied the concept of Afrofuturism. But, as a youth growing up, DOOM fell directly under the sway of someone closer to home—Dr. Malachi Z. York, a self-proclaimed spiritual leader, who in Brooklyn in the early seventies founded the Ansaaru Allah ("Helpers of Allah") Community, to which the rapper belonged.

And why not? York cut a colorful character who assumed as many identities as his organization underwent complete makeovers during their thirty-year-plus history—claiming, once, to be *Yaanuwn*, a green-skinned reptilian from the planet Rizq. His syncretic teachings, drawn from the world's three major religions, included such widely eclectic sources as Buddhism, Egyptology, Freemasonry, Rosicrucianism, Moorish Science, Kabbalah, the New Age movement, yoga, Black nationalism, apocalyptic prophecy, conspiracy theories, occult magick, and ancient alien theory. He is, therefore, responsible for introducing DOOM to an entire underground of esoteric knowledge and fringe philosophy that became an ongoing focus of interest and study throughout his life.

After his family joined the Nation of Islam, DOOM and his younger brother, Dingilizwe, gravitated to the Ansaars sometime during the eighties following their parent's divorce. At the time, the community, based on Bushwick Avenue between Willoughby and Dekalb Avenues, promulgated a more orthodox version of Sunni Islam. As York presented himself as a gifted, knowledgeable speaker and charismatic personality, it did not take long for the brothers to become regular attendees at his Sunday lectures at the Bushwick masjid. They also served as street peddlers, selling incense, oils, and their leader's self-published treatises in support of the cause.

At the height of their run in the late eighties, the Ansaars were an impressive sight to behold in their signature white robes and kufis (with full veils for women), providing a living example of Black unity, cooperation, and discipline. Not only did they establish a firm foothold in Brooklyn, offering an oasis of calm and tranquility in a neighborhood plagued by crime and drugs, but they exported their model of independence and self-sufficiency, opening satellites in Baltimore, Cleveland, Atlanta, Newport, Virginia, Philadelphia, and Washington, DC, as well as international chapters in Canada (Montreal and Toronto), the UK (London), Trinidad (Port of Spain), and Jamaica.

The proliferation of the Ansaars began with the opening of a chain of bookstores known as the Tents of Kedar. They used these sites to conduct classes in their esoteric philosophy, as well as Q&A meetings to recruit new converts. Unlike the Nation of Islam, the largest Black Muslim organization at the time, and its prominent offshoot, the Nation of Gods and Earths (also known as the Five Percenters), whose beliefs originated from the same source—a set of questions and answers known as the Supreme Wisdom Lessons—York debunked the notion of Black people as "Asiatic" peoples. Instead, his whole cosmology centered on Africa, but with a definite aim toward empowering African Americans. In the limited literature on him that exists, author and academic Susan J. Palmer writes:

> York argues that his people originated from the Sudan region of Africa. His disciples today define themselves as "Nuwaubians" (as opposed to "Nubians"); a term that refers to the masses of African Americans still sleeping under the "Spell of Kingu" (a figure from Mesopotamian mythology, sometimes associated by York with the biblical Leviathan), not yet

> *awakened to "Right Knowledge." Starting with the ancient kingdom of Nubia in Sudan, York traces the lineage of his people back to the Sumerian and Egyptian civilisations, and even beyond that, to the stars. He finally expounds the "ancient astronaut" theory proposed by Zecharia Sitchin of the Anunnaki, angelic extraterrestrial astronauts who arrived from the planet Rizq, colonized our planet, and built the first great civilisations of Sumeria and Egypt.*[1]

As fantastic as some of these claims may seem, the fluid nature of York's beliefs and the way he constantly reinvented and sometimes contradicted himself make it virtually impossible to nail down a cohesive point of view, only adding to the air of mystery that surrounds him. As one observer noted, "One simplifies the Nuwaubian phenomenon only at the cost of accuracy."[2] But to Palmer's point, pop culture and even the Pentagon may have finally caught up to York: the latter finally admitting the existence of UAPs (unidentified aerial phenomena), while the popular History Channel series *Ancient Aliens* introduces some of his controversial ideas to the mainstream. DOOM, however, saw more practical applications to his teachings, saying, "A lot of the things he speaks about is finding a better way—a way to improve us spiritually, mentally, physically. So, it's almost like reaching that vacation place, where we're all at total peace."[3]

Though not much is known about his early life, York, whose given name was Dwight, was apparently born in Boston on June 26, 1945, and grew up in New Jersey. At age nineteen, according to a 1993 FBI report, he was incarcerated for the statutory rape of a thirteen-year-old, possession of a dangerous weapon, and resisting arrest, and ended up serving two years before being paroled. Upon his release, he started frequenting the State Street Mosque in Brooklyn, founded in 1928, which served all manner of Muslims, from Arab, African, and South Asian immigrants to African Americans whose introduction to the faith had come through Noble Drew Ali's Moorish Science Temple or the Nation of Islam. It was in this heterogeneous setting that York first came across Sudanese immigrants from the Dongola region, who were to change the course of his life, introducing him to an indigenous African Islam with roots in mystical Sufism. "The Ansar," according to the exiled Sudanese leader at the time, Sadiq al-Mahdi, "draw from all schools of thought and we are not bound by any school of law. We recognize the original texts and seek new formulation, conscious of changes in time and place."[4] Classical Islam, in contrast, centered the Sunnis and especially Saudia Arabia as the ultimate authority on Muslim thought.

Tensions between local and foreign-born Muslims provoked a rift at the State Street Mosque that York exploited to his advantage, striking off on his own in 1967 with an organization known as Ansaar Pure Sufi. A bookstore by the same name on Rockaway Boulevard in Brownsville served as its headquarters. In the years that followed, this organization would grow from a handful of followers to hundreds, undergoing several different transformations, beginning with the Nubian Islamic Hebrew Mission (1968), not to be confused with the Black Israelites. Following that incarnation came the Ansaaru Allah Community (1973–1992), Holy Tabernacle Ministries (1992), United Nuwaubian Nation of Moors (1993), and, finally, Yamassee Native American Moors of the Creek Nation (1994).

A major turning point for York came in the early seventies, when he visited Sudan, linking up with the powerful clan of Sudanese Al-Madhi, Muhammed Ahmad. The Al-Mahdi was recognized as a kind of millenarian leader who would restore Islam to glory before the end of the world—similar in concept to the second coming of Christ. When York returned to the US, he appropriated the title, appending it to his own name and claiming to be a direct descendant of Ahmad. Behind the name change, he dropped all previous Hebrew vestiges—except his logo of an upturned Islamic crescent below a six-pointed Star of David—and started building his Ansaar community in Brooklyn.

Over the course of the decade, it came to include a distribution center at 717 Bushwick Avenue, where the incense and oils his peddlers sold were made and packaged; a bookstore at 716 Bushwick, offering his many treatises; a "Children's House," where the younger members of the community were sequestered together, away from their parents, and schooled in Hebrew and Arabic; a masjid, or gathering place for prayer and question and answer sessions; and an office at 415 Hart Street, where an all-female (and unpaid) staff consisting mostly of his wives and concubines put together York's numerous publications. Add to this a Nubian laundromat, two grocery stores, a recording studio, and a pizza shop selling a delicious wheat-crust pie made with a touch of honey, and York's vision of an independent, disciplined, and righteous Black community bonded together by his teachings seemed a reality. It's no wonder he gained hundreds of followers during this period, while exporting his model to other cities and countries.

Adding to his successes as a community organizer and spiritual leader, he also managed to maintain a career as an R&B recording artist, collaborating in several groups in the early eighties before going solo as "Dr. York" in 1985. To this end, he ran an independent production company and record label, releasing such quiet-storm material as "It's Only a Dream" or "What Is He to You?," which managed to receive some radio play. Perhaps his recording career might have taken off had he had access to the proper channels of distribution and promotion. Ironically, the "smooth" musical side of Dr. York was no secret to DOOM and other Ansaars, and actually enhanced his appeal as a spiritual leader. "We all rationalized the 'Dr. York' persona by assuming he was trying to reach all people by switching roles like he did, so no one considered his actions to be inappropriate. We considered it necessary,"[5] according to Ruby Garnett, another AAC member, who eventually became one of York's wives at age nineteen.

It was in this latter role of recording artist, producer, and independent studio/label owner that York crossed paths with several prominent rap artists of the era. Though not explicitly Ansaar, hip-hop pioneer Afrika Bambaataa, founder of the Universal Zulu Nation, considered himself a follower of Dr. York's teachings, as did Doug E. Fresh and Posdnuos of De La Soul. Certainly, the Native Tongues crew, who enjoyed their height of popularity concurrently around the late eighties and early nineties, would have found the Ansaar's Afrocentric ideology right up their alley. Meanwhile, Rakim and groups like Onyx, Force MDs, and Stetsasonic, who all had affiliations with the Five Percenters, rented time at York's studio.

Before KMD immortalized the Ansaars in their video for "Peachfuzz," which depicted the brothers Dumile in the trademark white robes and kufis, selling oils, incense, and literature on the streets, Jay-Z's mentor, The Jaz (Jonathan Burks), was the first to include scenes of the Bushwick community in his video for "The Originators" (1990). It featured plenty of shots of brothers wearing white robes or red, black, and green leather jackets emblazoned with the logo of the Nubian Islamic Hebrews, and even a shot of a young Jigga rapping in an uncharacteristically fast style. Meanwhile, The Jaz holds a portrait of Imam Isa Al-Mahdi (York) himself, looking every bit the Sufi mystic with his prominent white turban and ancient stare. Though the Five Percenters exerted a formidable influence on hip-hop—even adding certain slang like "peace" and "word is bond" to the rap lexicon—the impact of the Ansaars could be seen as a little more understated.

From his foothold in Brooklyn, York continued to expand. In 1983, he purchased a lodge on an eighty-acre tract of land outside the village of Liberty in the Catskills—ostensibly as the community's summer retreat. But Camp Jazzir Abba came to serve a much more important function beginning around 1992, when the entire Brooklyn community started pulling up stakes and boarding up buildings to relocate upstate. The unexpected move was accompanied by yet another name change—to Holy Tabernacle Ministries—as York seemingly made a dramatic swerve in ideology, suddenly denouncing Islam altogether. According to Palmer, "The HTM was characterized by a rampant eclecticism and syncretism, embracing Hebrew motifs blended with ancient Egyptian, Babylonian symbols, ufology and Masonic lore."[6] While such actions may have confounded outsiders, York had good reasons for doing so.

It may have had something to do with the fact that his provocative preaching and ideology were earning him enemies not only among Five Percenters and the Nation of Islam, but other traditional mosques as well. Chief among his critics was Bilal Philips, a Jamaican-born Sunni Muslim, who published *The Ansar Cult in America* (1988), a book that totally derided York as a charlatan, heretic, and huckster, who had built a cult of personality that bore no resemblance to true Islam. Following a close brush with El Sayyid Nosair—the assassin of Meir Kahane, founder of the Jewish Defense League—who paid the Bushwick masjid a visit, York had good reason to believe that people within the Muslim community wanted him dead.

But to his followers, he presented a different story. According to Garnett, "He'd called a meeting and asked us all to come up with ideas on what kind of clothing we wanted to start wearing because he said we'd eventually end up being targeted if we didn't start to appear more western. He told us that the world would eventually start to target Muslims and it would be imperative for us not to be associated with anything related to Islam."[7] On this last count, York was either extremely prophetic or lucky because the explosion that rocked the World Trade Center in Manhattan on February 26, 1993, unleashed the specter of "Islamic terrorism" on the world for the foreseeable future.

After initially garnering Mayor Ed Koch's praise in the eighties for ridding their Bushwick neighborhood of drugs and crime, the Ansaars eventually found themselves the subject of an FBI investigation as a possible front for a criminal organization. By 1993, a Bureau report produced in association with the NYPD, Department of Welfare, IRS, INS, and orthodox Muslim mosques implicated the organization in welfare fraud, tax evasion, arson, vigilantism, and intimidation. The first murmurs of sexual abuse also started to leak out from former members of the community.

York's retreat upstate, then, had everything to do with self-preservation as he circled the wagons, making the community even more insular. But if he thought a simple change of address could rid him of his problems, he could not have been more wrong, as the allegations followed him. In the rural, often racist environs of Sullivan County, the community faced constant harassment for improper permitting of the buildings they erected. They were also viewed suspiciously by neighbors for maintaining an active shooting range and arsenal of weapons. As a result, they didn't last too long there either.

York's response was to purchase 475 acres of farmland in the heart of Georgia's dairy country, near Eatonton, where he moved the group, once again, after changing their name to the United Nuwaubian Nation of Moors. The UNNM, according to Palmer, "had become a self-contained 'spiritual supermarket' offering access to an eclectic range of doctrines, myths, theories, and rituals that had been appropriated from other groups."[8] They set about building a sovereign nation called Tama-Re, an Egypt of the west, complete with two pyramids and other Egyptian-inspired statutes. Perhaps, to blend in with their rural surroundings, they initially wore cowboy boots and hats. But coinciding with yet another name change—this time to the Yamassee Native American

Moors of the Creek Nation—they also adopted the attire of Plains Indians and York started calling himself Chief Black Eagle.

After a brief honeymoon, during which their Putnam County neighbors viewed them as somewhat of a harmless curiosity, troubles resumed over the issue of building permits. At first, county commissioners were turned away from the property by armed guards. After the local sheriff intervened, they were allowed to perform their inspection. But when York disregarded orders to bring several new constructions up to code—including a huge warehouse that doubled as a nightclub—authorities padlocked the buildings in question. So began a full-scale war between the county and its new transplants, who went aggressively on the attack, even playing the race card. They circulated fliers calling county officials racist while referring to Black council members who opposed them as "house niggers." They attempted to infiltrate the local chapter of the NAACP and even hosted a visit by the activist Rev. Al Sharpton in 1999, while pushing the narrative that Putnam County wanted them out. The conflict moved into higher gear, however, when they issued threats of violence against Sheriff Howard Sills and other officials.

With the disastrous 1993 government siege of the Branch Davidian compound in Waco, Texas, still fresh on everybody's mind, both sides became increasingly paranoid. Sills started getting tips from former Nuwaubians about alleged sexual abuse that was going on in "The Land," as they called it, which he referred to the FBI. By the spring of 2002, they received even more conclusive evidence of such crimes after having interviewed more than thirty-five of York's victims and determining that he may have fathered as many as three hundred children. They also learned of a weapons stockpile at the compound. In an effort to stave off another Waco, Sills and the FBI concocted a plot to raid Tama-Re when York was off-site, so he'd be unable to issue the order to retaliate.

On May 8, 2002, York and his main wife were picked up after leaving the compound in a black SUV. Then a combined task force of some three hundred federal and state law enforcement officers descended upon Tama-Re, securing it in under five minutes after receiving no resistance from the one hundred or so Nuwaubians present. After securing weapons, cash, and other evidence, the authorities encountered about two hundred more members as they left later that evening, but by that time the game was up. Bloodshed had been successfully averted.

Subsequently, following a 2004 conviction, the man once known as Al Imam Isa Al Haadi Al Mahdi, Rabboni Y'Shua Bar El Haady, the Lamb, Ammunnubi Raakhptaah, Chief Black Eagle, Dr. Malachi Z. York, Dr. York, or just plain Doc, assumed his current alias—inmate #17911-054. He is currently serving 135 years at the US Penitentiary supermax prison in Florence, Colorado, for more than one hundred counts of child molestation and multiple RICO violations. The organization he started remains mired in controversy and largely in tatters. Its few remaining apologists can only claim racist intervention by the US government bent on extinguishing any semblance of Black power.

Following the passing of his brother and the organization's move down south, DOOM had not been active with the Nuwaubians since the early nineties. While living in Atlanta, however, he attended the Saviours' Day festivities in the summer of 1999 and even managed to catch Dr. York's last lecture prior to his arrest (which he attended with friend and collaborator, Stahhr the Femcee). In 2000, when asked about his opinions of the group, he replied, "What I think, that's just a projected guess. I try to look at the facts about it. The vibe is good—unlike I've ever felt anywhere else. It's one of the first places I ever seen where there's more than 100 people and nobody smoking a cigarette. As far as how it's been going, and what he's [York's] been saying, and raising the children, keeping people together on some real property? Well, I'm looking at it like it's working."[9] DOOM was not alone in his praise. Jesse Jackson, who visited Tama-Re in 2002, prior to the raid, applauded it as an example of "The American Dream."

Even as the criminal case against his spiritual mentor was proceeding in the courts in 2003, DOOM thought enough about the man to name his second son, Sean Malachi, after him, perhaps as a sign of solidarity or act of defiance. After all, as York had provided such a positive role model, it would have been a bitter pill to swallow to learn that someone who commanded so much respect and gave so much to his followers hid a secret life as a pedophile. But as Garnett, a former wife of York's, wrote in her memoir, "Imam Isa the teacher is different from Imam Isa the man."[10] It was a revelation to which only certain female members of the community would have been privy, as well as the cause for much cognitive dissonance among the "true believers." DOOM, however, appeared nonplussed. While he never publicly mentioned his mentor again, he still followed the "right knowledge" that York spoke about, and his interest in esoteric subjects never waned, but, in fact, grew even stronger.

THE MASK

I was ashamed when I realized life was a costume party and I attended with my real face.

—FRANZ KAFKA

9

SUSPENDED ANIMATION

Be alone, that is the secret of invention; be alone, that is when ideas are born.

—NIKOLA TESLA

Today a young man on acid realized that all matter is merely energy condensed to a slow vibration, that we are all one consciousness experiencing itself subjectively, there is no such thing as death, life is only a dream, and we are the imagination of ourselves. Here's Tom with the weather.

—BILL HICKS

In some Native American cultures, male members of the community, upon reaching the cusp of manhood, would take part in an important tradition known as a vision quest. This rite of passage involved venturing out alone into the wilderness, often to a sacred site, and fasting for several days to induce dreams or visions that would help that individual discover his life's purpose or determine his role within the community. By stripping away everything he was familiar with; withholding food and sleep, vital for normal functioning; and convening with nature, the idea was that the initiate would turn deep inside himself, and in this way acquire the kind of inner wisdom potentially accessible to all but drowned out by the distracting din of daily life. Prophets of antiquity such as Moses, Jesus, and Mohammed followed a similar shamanic path on their way to receiving the mystic revelations on which the world's major religions were founded. Undergoing suffering, isolation, and deprivation of a different kind, DOOM was involuntarily thrust into something like a vision quest that lasted not days, but years.

The period between 1994 and '98, when he retreated from the public eye and practically fell off the map, is often considered his "missing years," which found him broke, near homeless, and traumatized by grief. But this time on his own, below the radar, also provided a crucial opportunity to begin the healing process, while establishing the foundation for his return. Lost and vulnerable as he may have been during his "dark night of the soul," it was all a necessary part of the process of finding himself. While self-medicating with alcohol and drugs to deal with his emotional pain, DOOM never abandoned what he felt deeply to be his true calling—writing lyrics and making beats—doubling down on the only activities that gave him a sense of purpose. It was this dedication to his craft that eventually served not only to sharpen his skills, but to revive his confidence after experiencing so great a fall.

At twenty-three, the conscious rhymer, who had never held a real job in his life, was suddenly forced to support himself. He ended up turning to what anyone in his situation might have done—selling drugs—not with Scarface ambitions, but rather, simply to sustain a basic level of survival. Though New York had always been the center of his universe, DOOM kept it moving during these interim years, bouncing around the East Coast from Boston to DC and Virginia and, finally, all the way down to Georgia, where he would eventually settle in the new millennium. Effectively starting from scratch, he battled serious odds, as the music industry was not known for offering second chances. But thanks to his prodigious work ethic and strength of will that he developed during his years-long vision quest, DOOM was able to pull off one of the greatest comebacks in history—not only in rap but in the annals of music.

Using the severance allotted by Elektra, he was able to get an apartment in Manhattan after losing his record deal. Unfortunately, Sub had been in sole possession of the key (and whereabouts) of a storage unit that contained most of their equipment, crates of vinyl, and a gold-record plaque for "The Gas Face," so all of that was effectively lost. But DOOM managed to hold onto his MPC60, and he borrowed a Casio FZ-10 rack-mount sampler from engineer Rich Keller that allowed him to continue making beats.

His initial place in Midtown, off Eighth Avenue, he shared with another rapper, Shelly B, whom he was producing and dating. Ray Davis (aka Web D), a deejay and producer from Long Beach, who knew DOOM years before he was signed, worked in Manhattan at the time and often visited. "He was in a bad place," Davis recalls of the post-Elektra era, "so, I would see him and me and him was like drinking buddies. We would sit around and get high and drink forties of OE [Olde English 800 malt liquor] all the time. And I told him, I was like, 'Yo, you ain't got [all] your equipment, man. If you need to use my shit, you can use my shit, my records, do whatever the fuck you need to do, da, da da. I'll help you.' You know?" DOOM would eventually take him up on the offer, but for the time being he improvised, making the most of what he had.

Kevin Hutchinson (aka Chicken Lover), a member of the CM Fam and Jungle Brothers' Bush Camp clique, recalls visiting DOOM in midtown as well. "I see what he did now—he was making an arsenal of beats," he says, laughing. "He didn't want people to say, 'Oh, well, that's KMD.' He wanted to be known for a different style that he had. I mean he had catalog. I went there with Kae-Nit [another member of CM], and he was letting us hear tons of stuff." DOOM was obviously keeping himself well occupied. Hutchinson adds, "As I remember him, I could always say that dude is dangerous. 'Cause I seen him, I heard it. We were sitting there for hours, like 'shroomed out for like ten hours—sometimes all night—just listening to music he had made."

While DOOM also spent a lot of time at Kurious's place on Ninety-Seventh Street, working on music or writing lyrics, he leaned on his youngest brother for support as well. "He didn't really function without me at that time," says Dimbaza Dumile, who was only nineteen when he joined DOOM further uptown at an apartment at 157th and Amsterdam. "We started taking acid more after Sub passed going to '94, '95, listening to [the] Raekwon album [*Only Built 4 Cuban Linx*] and just listening to shit," he says. "We were tripping every day at that Manhattan apartment. I mean I used to go pick up 250 mescaline tabs in Central Park." At the time, a certain section within the park was known as the spot to procure LSD or mescaline. "I would go pick it up 'cause I was innocent enough looking," says Dimbaza. "DOOM would try to hustle 'em to make money, but we were eating most of them. We would sell just enough to re-up and the rest we were just taking for the head. We were trippin' like fuck. Sub would have been impressed."

Prior to his brother's death, DOOM hadn't messed with anything stronger than alcohol and weed, both depressants. But psychedelics offered the opposite of a sedative effect—not to mention a real escape. Certainly, such powerful psychoactive substances as LSD and mescaline, the active ingredient of the peyote cactus, which some Native American tribes considered a sacrament, were nothing to be taken lightly. Depending on a multitude of factors—including setting, dosage, and the current mood or disposition of the user—such substances affected one's brain chemistry, tearing the mask off our perceived reality to deliver a heavenly, transcendent experience, or, just as easily, hell. Often misunderstood, and miscategorized as Schedule I drugs, along with the infinitely more lethal and addictive heroin and cocaine, the efficacy of psychedelics in treating such disorders as PTSD has been acknowledged by mainstream medicine today. Though such substances were not physically addictive, whatever DOOM was experiencing under the influence kept him coming back for more. Perhaps they served as a form of therapy as the psychedelic state lifted the veil into other dimensions, where he might have felt closer to his departed brother.

When they weren't navigating this realm beyond the senses, DOOM and Dimbaza sometimes visited Grimm, who had spent many months in rehab following the New Year's Day 1994 shooting that left him paralyzed from the waist down. Now confined to a wheelchair, he was just regaining the breath control indispensable to any MC and longed to get back into rap. Over games of chess, Grimm and DOOM dreamed and schemed together about a comeback, plotting future collaborations, and generally leaning on each other in their combined hour of need. When the Dumile brothers needed a break from the city, they went to hang out with homeboys in the Roxbury neighborhood of Boston. But eventually, when the money ran out, DOOM had no choice but to go back to where he started.

"So, 1995, I guess we're in Freeport again," says Dimbaza, "My father bought a crappy house—a piece of work—but it was a house, and we can always be there, right? So, he's basically living back at his dad's house." The younger Dumile refers to this period as his brother's "John Coltrane phase," as he was spending a lot of time around the house, doing little else besides reading and a lot of thinking, accompanied by daytime drinking to the tune of Trane, Pharoah Sanders, and Ornette Coleman courtesy of an AM jazz station. "We drinking liquor that we stole from my uncle," says Dimbaza. "We seen those bottles of liquor sitting there at my uncle's fuckin' bar since we little as hell, and you know he ain't drinking that shit." So, the brothers helped themselves, switching up from psychedelics to scotch.

While it may have seemed like DOOM was tuned out, he was always, at least subconsciously, affected by his environment—especially whatever information or stimuli he was receiving. Later on, he would observe, "People like Ornette Coleman or John Coltrane chose to go in a direction that people couldn't accept. But now, their stuff's seen as classic. That helped to show me that even if people don't get what I'm doin' now, they'll get it eventually."[1]

Despite having his basic studio setup intact, he was still not inspired to create. "DOOM was in a low right now musically," according to Dimbaza. "He wasn't making music." Knowing his brother only too well, he felt an obligation to remedy the situation. One day while messing around on the turntables looking for samples, Dimbaza cued up a copy of the Spinners' *Mighty Love* album (Atlantic, 1974). Dropping the needle on the second song on side one, "Ain't No Price on Happiness," made his ears instantly perk up since its opening bars sounded like a dope loop. When he tried to get DOOM's attention, however, his brother initially brushed him off.

"I was like talking to DOOM, and he sounded down and during this down conversation—'cause it was a very bluesy time, you know, for both of us—he is trying to talk like he ain't, you know, he don't got no music," says Dimbaza, who pressed him to listen to what he had found. "I got him out of that bluesy conversation to come over to the record player and listen to the sample," he says. "And thank fuckin' God he heard what I heard and immediately started working on it. He didn't let his Debbie Downer attitude be like, 'It's dope, but I'm gonna work on it in the morning.' He started working on it and he made 'Go with the Flow.'"

DOOM paired the Spinners loop with the staccato drum track of Kool G Rap & DJ Polo's "Truly Yours" from the album *Road to the Riches* (Cold Chillin', 1989). In the song's opening ad-lib, G Rap says, "Go with the flow," which DOOM also samples, thus explaining the track title as well. Though songs like "Dead Bent" and "Gas Drawls" were subsequently credited as being the first official MF DOOM recordings, both were originally made in 1994 during the *Black Bastards* sessions, according to Dimbaza. "'Go with the Flow,'" he says, "kind of came after that and that's when he started accumulating songs." It marked a definite breakthrough for his brother, and the first time in a while that he approached music with renewed zeal and energy.

But if there was an even more important eureka moment for DOOM during that summer of 1995 back in Freeport, he revealed it to journalist and label owner Peter Agoston many years later. "Summertime, it was a beautiful day out, and I'm trying to think of shit," he said. "It just hit me one day. If I was to come back, it would have to be as DOOM. It just popped in my head, like if I ever get a chance to really do it again, that's how I would do it—on the surface level, on the public level."[2]

He further elaborated, "You know in a lot of ways it prevents a lot of bullshit from happening. Like a lot of bullshit associated with this particular genre of music, you know what I mean—paparazzi, the haters, whatever fuckin' bullshit. In any other writing job, you don't get this shit, but this rap shit, it's almost like people expect you to be the dude you writin'. Like, I'm a writer, yo, I write for different characters, know what I'm sayin'?"[3] As if a switch had flipped in his mind, he acknowledged the important distinction between himself, the person known as Daniel Dumile, and the character he was portraying.

DOOM had arrived at this conclusion by really digging deep to analyze the essence of rap's appeal. "So, I'm like, I take a look back at that shit and I say,

'OK, what is it that people like about what we do?' It's rhyming, the way we fuck with the words on the beat. None of that other shit in between matters at all,"[4] he said, citing trivialities like where you're from or what you're wearing. "So, I'm like, if people want to hear raw rhymes—and the iller the rhymes [the better]—you could come with anything and get the light, catch the wreck. So, I'ma test that theory. Let me change my name, all that, come out as a totally different motherfucker, totally new style, not ride the coattails of KMD—I mean there was good stuff that we did, but I wanted to just go in another direction. So, all right, boom, you do the DOOM and see how the public takes it."[5] This realization proved to be transformative. Of course, he was still broke and without the means to put out his music, but, at least, he had found a way forward. "I'm totally designing the character from scratch, but to me, I was having fun,"[6] he said. He probably hadn't admitted as much in years.

10

DEEP FRIED FRENZ

No man is an island
Entire of itself;
Every man is a piece of a continent
A part of the main.

—JOHN DONNE

Friends, how many of us have them? Friends, ones we can depend on.

—WHODINI

Battered by the vicissitudes of life, like a ship tossed around in a storm, DOOM's disappearance during the so-called "lost years" proved essential to his rebirth. Another casualty of the music industry, he could just as easily have called it quits, opting instead for the steady paycheck of hourly wage labor. But he kept largely to himself and, taking the time to process his grief, did nothing. Only while adrift in the calm waters of solitude did he even begin to heal and regain a sense of purpose and direction in life. But once resolved on a path forward, and committed to a course of action, the universe conspired to help. Executing his master plan required the cooperation and support of practically everyone he had known up to that point, as well as new allies and enablers, and, in most instances, the stars aligned to make that possible. Though DOOM eventually wrote a song railing on fake friends, he obviously knew the ones he could count on, too.

Alfred Morgan II (aka Big Benn Klingon) didn't rap, write graffiti, breakdance, or deejay, but by virtue of growing up at Ninety-Seventh and Columbus, he inevitably hung out at nearby Rock Steady Park, and became a junior affiliate of the CM Fam. "The vibe of the park was snapping," he recalls. "We was always the funniest cats—playing ball, telling jokes, getting drunk and talking shit."[1] In the immediate aftermath of Sub's death, DOOM gravitated to that environment, where he could count on the unconditional support of his CM brothers, and his friendship with Morgan started blossoming. In August 1993, however, Morgan had to leave for DC, where he was recruited to play football at Howard University. Though it took some time and convincing, the burly athlete, who majored in education and early childhood development, eventually persuaded his grieving friend to come down and spend some time with him.

Initially, DOOM crashed in Morgan's dorm room as he familiarized himself with the DC scene. Despite its starched, white-collar reputation as the seat of government, the nation's capital also happened to be a lively college town humming with the energy of youth, boasting hip bars and clubs, and plenty of music. Morgan liked to show off his friend's skills, so DOOM vanquished many wannabe MCs on campus. He also met Deanna, a redhead who was already friends with Morgan, Kurious, Kadi, and other members of CM. When they started seeing each other, he often stayed at her place. DOOM's excursions below the Mason-Dixon Line became more frequent when he realized that this town was far more than simply a pleasant distraction. There was money to be made here.

In addition to forging new friendships, DOOM unexpectedly ran into some former acquaintances. Jason Fragala (aka Optical), a local MC/producer, and his deejay, Dialtone, were shocked when they stumbled into him and Deanna outside a club in DC. The two men along with partner, Zechariah Wise (aka Mister Wise), were part of a group called Team Demolition, which they had started back in high school. One night, after attending a solo Pete Nice show in the area, they had connected with his dancers, Ahmed and Otis, also formerly of 3rd Bass, and gave them their demo tape. The two Long Beach residents, who were down with GYP (DOOM's Long Beach crew), saw some potential and expressed an interest in managing the group. They invited Team Demolition up to New York for a visit, which was their first occasion hanging out with DOOM—then Zev Love X—who they knew through KMD.

In the aftermath of Sub's death, however, they found a damaged and devastated person, not quite whom they expected. They were huge fans of the conscious lyricist of the *Mr. Hood* album, but this former teetotaler was now drinking heavily and chain-smoking. He also appeared subdued, often staring off in the distance, lost in his own thoughts. After hearing a sneak preview of *Black Bastards*, which hadn't even been completed yet, the Team Demolition crew were even more surprised by KMD's drastic change in direction—from happy-go-lucky to angst-ridden. Although they hung out in New York a few more times, when the proposed business arrangement with Ahmed and Otis didn't pan out—since Pete lost his label deal with Columbia—both parties eventually fell out of contact.

In the meantime, Team Demolition had evolved into a production company as Mr. Wise opened Depth Charge Studios in the basement of his home in Burke, Virginia. Following their fortuitous reunion, Fragala invited DOOM to check out the space, picking him up a few days later from Deanna's place, where he was accompanied by Kurious. Never wasting an opportunity in the studio, DOOM brought a bagful of DATs (Digital Audio Tapes) and wanted to know if they could dub them onto cassette for him to listen to. "And the first beat that came on was the beat that's the interlude that runs throughout the first DOOM album. And this is '96 you know," Wise recalls. "So, he's playing us all the beats off of the first DOOM album. Like there was very little cutting room floor with DOOM. Everything that he did got used."

As they caught up on old times, Wise and Fragala were thrilled to have the former KMD rapper in their presence. Slightly balding, the twenty-five-year-old appeared much older than his years, as his scrawny frame had filled out, but that wasn't the only change they noticed in him. "We wanted to push him to come to the studio more, but he was really on some drug shit at first, which kind of took us aback 'cause this was Zev Love X," says Fragala. "He wanted to give me a rack of drugs to sell, but it worked out because we started doing both, and once we got 'em to the studio they didn't want to leave, you know what I'm sayin'? They loved it down there."

At the time, Wise was working with a fairly basic setup consisting of a Mackie 24×4 mixing board, an eight-track ADAT, an ASR-10 keyboard workstation, and turntables. But compared to what DOOM was using at home, it may as well have been the Hit Factory. As a result of their prior history and mutual connections, Wise wouldn't dream of charging for studio time, thereby giving his old acquaintance further incentive to come down more often. But DOOM's movements, like his behavior, were erratic. "He tried to live the personas he was developing—he was an enigma on purpose," says Wise. "Like, he'd just disappear. You wouldn't see him for a couple months. 'I was in Atlanta. I was back in New York. I was over here. I was doing this.' And again, a lot of it was centered around dope, you know, hustling. But some of it was music related."

The longest stretch that DOOM spent in Virginia occurred during the summer of 1996, soon after they first reconnected, as he split time between Wise and Fragala's basements. "I was selling a lot of drugs in the street at the time. I was young and dumb," Fragala admits. "So it was a good connection, you know? We started making a lot of money real quick." Beginning with an inventory of acid, ecstasy, and magic mushrooms, all drugs which appealed to the college crowd, the pair soon expanded to cocaine.

According to Wise, "I would get a knock on my door, and it's a package from DHL addressed to Depth Charge Studios, care of my boy. And I'd open it up and it'd be like an ADAT tape and Jason, my boy, would be like, 'Okay, look inside' and you'd crack open the ADAT tape and it'd be stuffed with cocaine. And he's [DOOM] not telling me this." Identical to a VHS tape, an ADAT could fit about a half ounce of the drug. The return address might say from "Viktor Vaughn" or "Monster Island," according to Wise, who notes, "He had all that nomenclature developed already. Like he was developing all the King Ghidorah and all the Monster Island/Godzilla shit already, you know, in his mind. But it was weird for us."

Once DOOM even sent them a peanut butter sandwich via overnight courier. "I opened it up and inside was a sandwich bag full of ecstasy pills," Wise recalls. "It was wild man. Like, this dude is sending me a peanut butter and jelly sandwich stuffed with like thirty ecstasy pills. And like, again, that was not my thing back then. I'd hand it to my boy, like, 'Clearly this is something for you,' and he's like, 'Yeah.'" After Fragala sold the product, he would send DOOM the money via Western Union and wait for the next re-up via mail. Eventually,

DOOM taught him the Five Percenters' Supreme Mathematics to use as code when speaking on the phone. The number five, which stood for "power," meant cocaine.

DOOM's studio sessions at Depth Charge proved to be equally insane. "When we'd be working on stuff together, he'd get really fucked up," says Wise. But a typical session always started with dinner. DOOM would order the Dragon and Phoenix (lobster with chicken) from the Chinese restaurant in the strip mall across the street. He'd wash that down with a gallon jug of Riunite wine from the local Giant supermarket that would be killed over the course of the night. Plenty of blunts were smoked, too, but DOOM's high of choice was mescaline, which would keep him up all night, sometimes speaking to unseen entities. One night, while particularly out of his skull, he appeared to address the air, blurting out "devils" to his hosts, but he just as soon snapped out of it. Then he turned to Wise, telling him how much he reminded him of his brother since they were both so technically adept with the equipment. "And like, we didn't know what to say, 'cause this was still like us kind of getting to know him, you know," says Fragala. Regardless, there was a method to his madness.

"So, like he would come in, and basically I would sit there at the ASR-10 and he'd be like, let's loop this up," says Wise. The first track they worked on, "Dead Bent," featured a prominent string sample from Isaac Hayes's "Walk on By" (Stax, 1969), married to the programmed beat and part of the hook of BDP's "Super Hoe" (B-Boy Records, 1987). "He was like, 'I wanna loop up the Isaac Hayes shit. Let's do this. And you have the "Super Hoe" drum track?' I was like, 'Yeah, I got the "Super Hoe" drum track.' Like he had all the ideas and then I would just facilitate it," says Wise. Using recognizable samples didn't really cut it in that era of obscure crate-digging, due to high clearance fees and simply out of creative concerns. But according to Wise, "He was kind of going against the grain of what was happening in the current hip-hop that was being made at those times. He didn't care about any of that. He was breaking rules."

Though he kept his productions relatively simple and stripped down, not spending much time on them, DOOM was a perfectionist when it came to recording vocals. He often made multiple passes on the same track before redoing them all. "It was almost like he was figuring out how he wanted MF DOOM to sound, you know what I mean?" says Wise. "Like the vocals on the ones that he did with me, he's fuckin' out of his mind. He's inebriated, he's wild. It's a totally different voice, like way more flamboyant." But on the final version of "Dead Bent" that eventually saw release, DOOM rapped in monotone with a laid-back delivery that would become his signature style.

As they continued working with him, Team Demolition witnessed the metamorphosis of Zev Love X into MF DOOM. In addition, they got a sneak preview of what was to come, although they didn't always know what to make of it. DOOM would constantly toss out different ideas, such as doing a whole album whose concept revolved around food. "He seemed to know, like, exactly what he wanted to do. Like he had everything laid out," says Wise. "And he had all the backstory of all the characters laid out as well, like very early on." Without going into specifics, he even let them in on what was to be the defining feature of his main persona. "He would talk about the mask and say, 'When I come out with this shit, no one's ever gonna see my face,'" says Wise. "Like he preconceived all of that. He knew what he was gonna do. He didn't even like being photographed. I have maybe three or four photographs with him."

According to Fragala, "Everybody was kind of biting off Wu[-Tang] a little bit, but all DOOM would talk about was Wu at this time. I mean that was his inspiration in a lot of ways to do his music. He always talked about the RZA and how they got kung fu shit with their music, and he wanted [to use] Godzilla, for the same shit, pretty much." As Wu-Tang based their whole concept around martial arts movies, DOOM told them he wanted to use the Godzilla franchise in a similar manner with his Monsta Island collaboration with MF Grimm.

Of all the Clan members, he particularly liked how Ghostface Killah wore a stocking cap to conceal his face during the early days of Wu-Tang. But, at the same time, he didn't want to bite his style. Once Ghost started showing his face in videos and public appearances, however, the mask became fair game. Dimbaza offers confirmation, saying, "He respected that Ghostface wearing a mask first thing so much and he definitely did need confirmation that Ghost wasn't gonna keep rocking with it before he could say, 'Aiight, yo, I'm gonna do that then.' He was honoring that. That's a true story."

Only three months older than DOOM, Michelle Mitchell enjoyed a close relationship with her cousin growing up. Both a friend and confidant, she could be counted on for many things—not least of which was introducing him to girls. "It was just like every girl he'd meet was somehow through me in some kind of unofficial way," she says. "Like, he just would tell everybody, 'Yeah. I date all her friends.' It's not something that was intentional in any kind of way or form, but it just ended up that way."

Michelle had played matchmaker when Kinetta Powell, who was two years her junior and attended the same high school, expressed an interest in meeting her cousin. She remembers introducing them at the Macy's at Roosevelt Field mall, where Powell was working, and says that in no time the two became a couple. In 1993, they became parents of a baby boy, Daniel Joshua Dumile III, known as DJ. In the turbulent period that saw Sub's death and the termination of their record deal, Michelle says, "I think maybe the blessing to him was his child. It helped him hold on." Unfortunately, a casualty of those times was DOOM's relationship with his baby's mother. When she became a flight attendant, often traveling out of town for long stretches, he assumed full responsibility for his son as a single parent. "And I always gave him props for that," says Michelle.

Later, in the late nineties, she introduced DOOM to the woman who would not only become his business partner, but partner in life. She had known Jasmine Thomas since they both attended Nassau Community College and worked at the same bank branch. But they didn't really become close until the Jones Beach Greek Fest when Jasmine got separated from her friends and Michelle ended up helping her find them. Afterward, Jasmine, a resident of nearby Freeport, became a frequent visitor to the Mitchell home in Long Beach, where she inevitably ran into DOOM. Starting out as friends, their relationship would grow organically. Since Jasmine owned her own car, DOOM would sometimes hit her up for a ride when he had an errand to run or someplace to be.

"So many years later I was living in Georgia and my mother was living here [in Long Beach] and I think my father was out of town at the time," says Michelle. "And I said to DOOM, and I also said to her, 'Hey, can you guys, every now and then, stop and check on my moms for me because I'm far away.' So, it happens that one day they both stopped in at the same time. It's like you know somebody, you grew up around them, be around them for a long, long time and you never saw them in that way, and then, all of a sudden, you see them in that way. So that's basically what kind of happened with them, and they developed an actual strong relationship."

At one point, Michelle enticed her friend to come down south for a visit. "I was like, 'Girl, you know, people can get these mansions out here for like, what we paying in rent.' It's crazy," she says. "And I think I told her, 'Why don't they come check it out.'" Jasmine and DOOM took her up on the offer and drove down to look after her house while Michelle returned to New York to see her ailing father. "And I remember her saying, 'Oh yeah, I really like it. It's dope,'" she says.

Michelle eventually moved back to New York and was living in Queens the next time she ran into them. The couple dropped by unexpectedly, spending the entire day with her, and it was only then that she found out that they had tied the knot. "They did like a Vegas number," according to Michelle, who knows no other details about the nuptials. "They were super, super private," she concedes. About a year later, on a trip to Georgia, Michelle discovered that Jasmine had made the big move to the Atlanta area and was living in the suburb of Kennesaw. DOOM would often visit from New York before permanently relocating there in mid-2000.

DOOM was hardly the only disgruntled artist in the music industry. When his album, *A Constipated Monkey*, dropped in January 1994, the debut release on Pete Nice's Columbia-distributed Hoppoh imprint, Kurious was so unhappy and disillusioned by its lack of promotion and the resulting poor sales that he contemplated a break from rap. But that decision was eventually made for him. Not only was he dropped, but Hoppoh lost their label deal after 1995's *Pre-Life*

Crisis by Count Bass D tanked, making Pete and partner Bobbito Garcia redundant as well.

Swearing off the music industry entirely, Pete retreated upstate to focus on his other passion—baseball memorabilia. The enterprising young Garcia, an amateur baller and sneaker enthusiast, looked toward a fresh start as well. On a lark, he opened up Bobbito's Footwork, a boutique located in the tiny basement of 323 East Ninth Street in the East Village, which specialized in sneakers and hip-hop vinyl. He also continued his popular underground rap radio show with Stretch Armstrong on WKCR, though that was strictly a labor of love.

Meanwhile, Kurious, who started binging on psychedelics to cope, gravitated toward the street life to make ends meet. In DOOM he found the perfect partner in crime, and they started bouncing out of town on money-getting missions to DC and Virginia. When not on the road, they were still spending a lot of time at Ninety-Seventh Street, one of the few spots where DOOM felt comfortable working on his music. One day, after having just copped a "loosey" at the corner store, they were outside on the street when DOOM started kicking a rhyme style that Kurious had never heard before. He described it as, "That delivery that's more, you know, conversational. It's like a little deeper; it's not as animated, know what I'm sayin'? It's kinda more inside like a host, like a comic book host."[2]

Like his predecessors Rakim and G.U.R.U. Keithy E from Gangstarr, DOOM had discovered the power of the monotone. Nine out of ten rappers favored an animated, expressive delivery, electing to shout to project their voice. But by not modulating his pitch and taking the time to enunciate his words, DOOM stumbled upon a style that lent both gravity and a matter-of-factness to his delivery simultaneously. It also made it much easier to understand and appreciate what he was saying. Kurious admits, "Yo, it took me back for a second, but I was like, 'Yo, that's kinda ill, 'cause its DOOM. You gotta always know that there's something to it—there's always substance. So, I remember hearing that and getting the first taste of that, only to see that shit go crazy later."[3] Privy to the music DOOM was making at the time, Kurious suggested that he hit off Garcia with a demo to play on the radio.

In the meantime, fed up with the politics of the major-label system, the part-time radio host had launched his own independent imprint, Fondle 'Em—partly out of frustration, partly as a joke. Since he was receiving a steady stream of demos through the radio show, his friend Rich King from Big Daddy Distribution had suggested releasing some of them. King subsequently went on to partner with Joseph Abajian, a deejay and owner of the record store Fat Beats, to start a distribution company under the same name dedicated to independent hip-hop. He offered Garcia a manufacturing and distribution deal, financing his first release by the Cenubites, a side project by Ultramagnetic's Kool Keith and Godfather Don. Released in December 1995, the center label of the Cenubites' EP read, "Fondle 'Em Records, A Division of Tickle 'Em which is a subsidiary of Squeeze 'Em Ent." Along the bottom edge it proudly declared its no-frills credo, "No Video, No Sticker, No Promotion, No Marketing." Even though CDs dominated the marketplace, the record was issued on vinyl only without artwork—essentially a "white label" geared toward deejays and true hip-hop heads.

Since the days of "Rapper's Delight" and "King Tim III (Personality Jock)," rap had been primarily the purview of independent labels. Even in the eighties, labels like Def Jam, Cold Chillin', and Tommy Boy essentially functioned as independents though distributed by majors. In keeping with hip-hop's DIY tradition, Fondle 'Em was among a vanguard of independent labels that created another seismic shift in the rap landscape in the mid-nineties, providing an alternative to the mainstream that was becoming increasingly slick, glossy, and commercial.

"We have no interest in getting picked up by a major. This is straight indie," says Garcia. "Like this is all we are, and DOOM fit into that ethos so well, because similar to the vision of the label, he was like, 'Yo, I already went through the major-label thing. Like, I don't wanna go through that again.'"[4] After DOOM played him his only completed song, "Dead Bent," Garcia suggested doing a white-label twelve-inch and throwing it out there to see what would happen. He offered DOOM his standard agreement: a fifty-fifty profit split once expenses were recouped, with the artist owning his masters and publishing. He asked for two more songs to justify a proper release, and they sealed the deal with a handshake.

In order to make the record happen, DOOM turned to another friend, Stretch Armstrong, who had a decent home studio and an expansive record collection at his apartment at 407 East Ninety-First Street. His setup consisted of both the SP-1200 and MPC60 drum machines, an Akai S-950 sampler, two ADATs, an eight-track reel-to-reel, and a Mackie sixteen-input mixer as well as some basic outboard processing units. "I don't know how DOOM ended up in my apartment to do this," Stretch concedes. "I don't remember the conversation. I think what happened, however, was he got to my place. Once he understood the library of records and also got a feel for my place, there was something about DOOM where it just felt right to let him have access to that in any form that he wanted."[5]

Toward the end of 1996, Stretch ended up giving DOOM the keys to his apartment for a period of two to three weeks so he could use the studio. The scrappy MC took full advantage of this opportunity. "DOOM barely slept. He'd sit on my couch and fall asleep for a little while when he got tired, then he'd get up and go back to work," Stretch recalls. "I was super busy at the time—barely at home. So, when I'd come home, he'd be there. He was in the zone so I wouldn't talk to him too much."

Besides sampling a 1972 Scooby-Doo soundtrack that Stretch owned, DOOM's choice of records bordered on the bizarre, favoring the eighties R&B of the SOS Band, Sade, and Atlantic Starr. He also used a snippet of Scott La Rock scratching from the BDP song "Poetry." According to Stretch, "Back then, if you were like a hip-hop beat nerd and you sampled another rap record for the drums or for the scratches, you know, you'd be laughed out the room."[6] He adds, "DOOM is at my crib like breaking every rule and doing things that at the time, I gotta be honest, like it made no sense to me. And thank God he did because now when I hear those records, I'm like, wow, this is genius. If, you know, he was told to do something one way, he'd be like, 'Nah, I'm doing it my way.'"[7]

11

WHO YOU THINK I AM?

Invent yourself and then reinvent yourself.
—CHARLES BUKOWSKI

The year 1997 marked a pivotal moment for hip-hop as it transitioned from insurgent outlier to darling of the mainstream, though not without significant growing pains. Fulfilling their promise of industry domination, Wu-Tang Clan literally blasted out of the gates with "Triumph," the first single off their heavily anticipated *Wu-Tang Forever* (Loud/RCA), the follow-up to *Enter the Wu-Tang (36 Chambers)*. It was accompanied by a slick, CGI-heavy video by soon-to-be Hollywood mainstay, Brett Ratner, which cost a cool $800,000 to make. Barely a month later, the rap world was mourning the tragic loss of one of its biggest stars, The Notorious B.I.G., victim of a drive-by shooting in LA on March 9. His death followed in the wake of that of another icon's—Tupac Shakur—only six months earlier, and in an identical manner. What all three acts had in common were much-hyped double albums (B.I.G.'s delivered posthumously) that moved millions of units, dominating the charts. Amid all the hubbub, DOOM's first Fondle 'Em twelve-inch—an anonymous white label, catalog number FE008—quietly slipped out into the world, illustrating the deep divide between major labels and independents.

As rap joined the upper echelons of big business, DOOM was just happy to have a record out for the first time in six years. His under-the-radar single included "Dead Bent"; "Gas Drawls," recorded and mixed at his buddy Web D's studio in Long Beach; and "Hey!," recorded and mixed at Stretch Armstrong's apartment, along with the instrumentals on the B-side. That's as much information as the center label provided besides "produced, mixed, written, arranged

& flipped by MF DOOM." The only artwork appeared on the B-side—a black-and-white scanned image of his comic-book namesake's mask, cropped so only the eyes and nose were visible, beneath the logo for Roaring Spring Compositions, a brand of marbleized notebooks popular among elementary school kids and MCs.

But cryptic illustrations aside, the only thing that really mattered to DOOM was how these songs, mastered from four-track cassette, sounded. "DOOM's style at times was very basement demo-esque and that was deliberate," observes Fondle 'Em chief Bobbito Garcia. "And it was brilliant because if you think about the context of '96 to '98, that's the Bad Boy era where things are like super mega polished and very like radio playable, and DOOM, you know, was like the complete opposite of that—still quirky and still nice with his rhymes, and still a wordsmith, you know, [with] vocabulary and cadence, but the quality of the recordings wasn't great. But that's what endeared the audience to it."[1] Whenever he played these demos on the radio, Garcia says the telephone lines always lit up.

The printed credits also told only part of the story. Earlier versions of these songs had been recorded at Rich Keller's New Jersey studio, Depth Charge Studios in Virginia, and a mystery spot in Atlanta run by DOOM's friend and sometime-collaborator Mr. Fantastik, an equally shadowy figure who would come to inhabit the Villain's freaky multiverse. About Mr. Fantastik, whose true identity has become the subject of much internet speculation, DOOM only offered, "He's from New York, but he moved out to Atlanta before I did, and he been out here for a while. And he always tryin' to get me to get a crib down here, and, you know, I'm always comin' back and forth, chillin' with him. He's straight baller status, so every time I come down, it's like, whatever, everything is on him—strip clubs and all that shit. He's straight ballin', but, you know, he's the one who introduced me to down here."[2] Since Fantastik only ever appeared on two tracks with DOOM, and nowhere else, it's fair to assume that he didn't depend on rap to earn a living. Furthermore, his maintaining a low profile might be attributed to the fact that, like his friend, he valued his privacy and didn't want to put his business out there.

Sold through Bobbito's Footwork, Fat Beats, and early e-commerce websites such as Sandbox Automatic and HipHopSite.com, the first pressing—all one thousand copies—was quickly scooped up by a growing audience disheartened by rap's mainstream trajectory. Even DOOM was pleasantly surprised, saying, "Damn! We do that every month, it'll be on!"[3] And he wasn't wrong. Considering that zero money was put into the record's promotion, and it sold strictly by word of mouth, the release proved an unqualified success, paving the way for two more singles.

Later in 1997, Fondle 'Em dropped "Greenbacks," credited to "King Ghidora featuring Megalon," with "Go with the Flow" on the B-side, credited to MF DOOM and Sci Fly (who were one and the same). Following in 1998 came "The M.I.C." with "Red & Gold"—both produced by Metal Fingers, DOOM's production alias. Aside from Megalon, a member of the Monsta Island collective, every other credit on those releases belonged to DOOM, who was apparently already enjoying confusing people with his numerous alter egos. His confidence buoyed with each sold-out pressing, he eventually decided that the time was ripe for an album. Garcia, in fact, was so psyched about releasing only the second LP in his catalog (after the Juggaknots self-titled debut) that he suggested doing full-color artwork this time around.

It was at this crucial juncture that the universe serendipitously reinserted Blake Lethem into the mix. Lethem had gone AWOL years earlier after forming a group with Pete Nice. Landing in jail for dealing drugs, he had spent the past ten years in and out of the system for parole violations. Finally returning to the city in 1996, he started hustling for artwork jobs to support himself. After hearing the buzz on the streets about Fondle 'Em, he decided to pay Garcia a visit at Footworks.

As Lethem recalls, "DOOM walks in and he's asking Bob, 'Yo, you know any good artists who can put this together?' And I happened to be in the corner, and Bob points to me. And we just clicked. And it turned out we had this long history. Even though I didn't know DOOM from the KMD days, I'm pretty much behind-the-scenes responsible for all of that."[4] Certainly, Lethem's sudden disappearance had left the door open for Pete Nice and Serch, whom he had introduced, to join forces as 3rd Bass. And without the efforts of 3rd Bass, KMD might never have had the opportunity to appear on a hit record or be signed to a major label. Sharing a common lineage in the game, these two OGs had rediscovered each other when they each had something to prove and needed each other the most. Their synergy would leave an indelible impression on an art form entering its pop phase at the turn of the millennium.

DOOM had already arrived at a title for his full-length—*Operation: Doomsday*—from the best-selling Sidney Sheldon thriller *The Doomsday Conspiracy* (William Morrow, 1991). Loosely based on the Roswell incident of 1947, the story follows passengers on a bus in Switzerland who witness the crash of a UFO, that authorities claim as a weather balloon. The protagonist of the story, a member of US naval intelligence, stumbles on a plot called Operation Doomsday to keep the witnesses silent and cover up the fact that aliens have been in communication with governments on Earth for a long time. For DOOM, the title played perfectly into the concept for his new persona as he declared his mission to destroy rap.

Despite already being an accomplished visual artist in his own right, he may have felt he needed help with the artwork, as this was the first time he was putting together an entire album by himself. Perhaps the whole *Black Bastards* cover imbroglio remained fresh in his mind as well, prompting him to remove himself from the process. Regardless, Lethem provided an excellent collaborator to bounce around ideas while also being able to execute concepts that were in DOOM's head.

The cover image, featuring an illustration of Doctor Doom wearing his trademark metal face mask and green cape, came from an actual frame from a Marvel edition of *The Fantastic Four*. Lethem modified the cape to look more like a hoodie by substituting drawstrings for the clasp, but the mic in DOOM's clenched metal fist was part of the original illustration. Using graffiti-style lettering, he signed it "MF DOOM?"

By far, Lethem's biggest contribution to the DOOM mythos, however, was designing the infamous mask, which the rapper never failed to be seen without in public. "DOOM was very interested in maintaining his anonymity and I immediately saw the benefit of that 'cause we used to sit in the club at the bar and drink and nobody would even look twice at him. Nobody bothered us," he says. "Then he could throw on the mask and jump onstage and the whole crowd is, like, in awe and rhyming along with every lyric. A lot of artists don't enjoy that kind of freedom, so the mask was important to him."[5]

Though DOOM respected the way Ghostface Killah kept his identity concealed beneath a stocking cap, he was also looking for something a little more substantial and permanent. "He wanted something unique and something that spoke to the metal face persona," says Lethem, "so the first thing we copped was, you know, these Halloween masks with the rubber band in the back, and it's plastic with a little mouth hole cut out—what you wore as a kid."[6] Initially, they bought a facsimile of the mask worn by the pro wrestler Kane at a ninety-nine-cent store. Lethem used a razor blade to cut and shape it into a slightly different form, squaring out the eyes like Doctor Doom. Then he spray-painted the entire mask with metallic silver Rust-Oleum. Though it bore some resemblance to the comic-book character's visage, it didn't cover the whole face, cutting off at the top lip with two extensions on either side of the mouth. Since this early prototype of the mask wasn't very sturdy, it didn't survive DOOM's first video shoots, when a crew member accidentally sat on it between takes.

Lethem next proposed trying to procure a helmet from a real medieval suit of armor. He stumbled upon the next best thing at Forbidden Planet, a store on Broadway in the East Village that specialized in toys, graphic novels, comics, science fiction, manga, anime, T-shirts, statues, art books, posters, games, and movie memorabilia. The movie *Gladiator* (2000), starring Russell Crowe, had just been released, and in the store's window display, Lethem spotted a replica of the mask that Crowe wore in the film. Rendered in heavy-gauge metal, it weighed about twenty-five pounds. He brought it to his neighbor on Second Avenue, a German sculptor who owned welding equipment, to make some modifications, removing the faceplate from the helmet, and sanding down any rough edges. Then, he had to figure out how to keep the mask mounted on DOOM's face. Lethem found the solution by using the webbing inside a construction worker's helmet. "I took the webbing out and I put two screws through the temples of the mask and put a hinge and a screw into the webbing of the construction helmet," he says. "So, now you had, like, a fitted cap in the back of this metal [face] plate."[7]

DOOM did his best to take care of it, even procuring a small metal case as its home, but signs of wear inevitably started showing. When he guzzled Jack Daniel's, for example, the mask developed a patina of rust around the mouth. This prompted several modifications, including taking it to an auto body shop to get the whole thing chromed. A gem enthusiast, DOOM also had a ruby, his birthstone, embedded into the forehead as symbolic of the third eye. Over the years, he added even more customization on the interior, to which, obviously, not everyone was privy, including padding around the cheeks, crushed pieces of amethyst, and a copper spiral at the forehead. The mask naturally evolved into a huge part of his identity and aesthetic. Previously, only superheroes and, perhaps, pro wrestlers wore masks. Rappers were still too preoccupied with authenticity, but DOOM one-upped them all.

"I'm not that dude at all," replied DOOM, when asked about the mask. "I am writing about a character. It's a little bit based on my personality, but it's definitely exaggerated, you know. If you gonna have a character, make him into a character.... [Then] you can have the character be able to do or be able to say anything."[8] After all, DOOM always claimed that his own life was way too boring to write about—imagination was where it was at. He further clarified, "Zev didn't rock a mask and I have other characters that don't wear masks, too—and they all have their own thing that makes them stand out. My albums are all characters and together they're part of this lineage of stories and albums written by me."[9] But where performance was concerned, he was as much of an actor as a writer, ascribing the mask as a means to further develop the character.

Another equally important reason for donning a mask was to allow himself some measure of privacy by creating distance between his personal life and what he did for a living. "I like to separate my situation—my home life and my family life," he said. "The people I know in the neighborhood don't even know what I do. I'm just a dude who lives right there, or the dude down the street that comes into the store. I need my life. I'm not trying to change my life for this rap shit, for real.

Definitely not. Come on, not when you can do both. I enjoy music—making music. I make money with this music, live off music, share music, but you still need to have your life."[10] Simply by virtue of being a low-key individual, who had already experienced the pitfalls of fame at an early age, he was over the concept of celebrity and actively sought to subvert it. Therefore, the mask offered anonymity.

DOOM disavowed a lot of the trappings associated with rap—the jewels, the cars, the fashion. "It don't matter what you look like—your race, your style, if you're cute or fuckin' ugly," he said. "None of that shit matters when it comes down to the music. In jazz, that's what it used to be like. But with hip-hop, it's such a new form of music that it got exploited to the point where what you look like and what you're wearing and how big your chain is matters first. Then people check out the album and see how whack it is. So, DOOM is just your average Joe, understand? It's all about the skills, so it don't matter what he look like. He could be you. He could be me."[11] Like Miles Davis, well-known for playing trumpet with his back to the audience, DOOM was making a bold statement: Don't look at me but listen to the content of my lyrics and my music.

While acknowledging rap as a live performance medium, he said, "I wanted to get onstage and orate, without people thinking about the normal things people think about. Like girls being like, 'Oh, he's sexy,' or 'I don't want him, he's ugly,' and then other dudes sizing you up. A visual always brings a first impression. But if there's going to be a first impression I might as well use it to control the story. So why not do something like throw a mask on?"[12]

Pushing thirty, with a spare tire slowly spreading around his midsection and his hair thinning on top, DOOM also realized that he was no Adonis, but would have to compete against a younger generation of rappers coming up. Covering his face allowed him the advantage of being someone else, so he could let it all hang out. Whether a genius gimmick or marketing tool, the mask was obviously something he had put a lot of thought into, and it seemed to be the answer to many of his concerns. "Plus, it's like, damn, the temptation to just fuck with people's heads like that, I just can't resist," he admitted. "The funny thing is, many people, from fans to press, et cetera, seem to have bought the story to the point where they forget you're not actually a supervillain."[13]

12

THE MIC

People will laugh at you for having to start over. Meanwhile, they haven't even started.

—MIKE TYSON

*Competition is none, I remain on the top like the sun,
And I burn whoever come in the chambers of torture, I caught ya
You should'a brought ya, whole neighborhood to support ya.*

—RAKIM, "NO COMPETITION"

Long before the advent of rap records, the art form cut its teeth as a live performance medium, with MCs engaging in verbal warfare to make a name for themselves while eliciting audience participation with call-and-response chants. Indeed, since the days of the park jams, rap's gladiatorial aspect has proven a vital part of its DNA. Battling became a way for MCs to test their skills against each other, allowing the crowd to be the real-time arbiter of victory. Competition, in fact, spawned the braggadocio and hyperbole associated with freestyling, a random, stream-of-consciousness flow that didn't adhere to any specific style, subject matter, or cadence. Contrary to popular belief, freestyle raps could be either pre-written or entirely improvised. The bottom line was that a rapper was assessed on the strength and quality of his or her performance—specifically the ability to move the crowd—leaving absolutely no quarter for Milli Vanilli MCs.

Amid a music industry takeover in the nineties, however, as records rose to prominence, rap's performance aspect suffered a severe blow. DATs replaced live deejays at shows and battling took a backseat to record sales, a much more reliable metric of popularity. Of course, battles on wax persisted—for example, the clash of the Roxannes and the legendary "Bridge Wars" between KRS-ONE and MC Shan—but even the novelty of such clashes could not replace the energy and excitement of those original hip-hop jams or parties, which thrived on a sense of unpredictability and improvisation.

Though Boston transplant Rocky Montagne had never attended any of those early jams, he helped usher in a revival of the live, DIY-style, grassroots hip-hop party when he arrived on the scene in 1993. Such an incubator allowed unknown and up-and-coming talent a chance to shine, giving birth to a whole new generation of stars. While working the door at the legendary Village Gate jazz club, Montagne had seen a performance of Cult Jam, Lisa Lisa's backing band, fronted by the rapper D-Nice of Boogie Down Productions. "I'm looking at that, and that gave me the idea to do an event basically with live musicians and rappers," he says. He decided to add spoken word to the mix when his friend Calvin Gaines, a bassist, producer, and brother of the poet Reg E. Gaines, tipped him off about a nascent poetry revival taking place.

Together with another promoter, Montagne started a short-lived night called Bebop, on the first Monday of every month, featuring MCs and poets performing before a house jazz band. Capturing the zeitgeist of the early nineties, Bebop created a buzz almost instantly, and by the second installment, they were filling their two-hundred-capacity room. Unfortunately, success proved to be too little and too late, as the Village Gate, teetering on the brink of insolvency, lost their lease and closed for good in February 1994. This temporary setback forced Montagne to move Bebop across the street to a club called Kenny's Castaways. Then he heard about the poetry slams going on at the Nuyorican Poets Café in the East Village.

Originally started in 1973, out of the late Puerto Rican–born poet Miguel Algarín's apartment, the Nuyorican had already established a radical-chic reputation for underground poetry recitals. It maintained that bohemian vibe when the café was restructured as a nonprofit in 1981, raising funds to secure a permanent space on East Third Street between Avenues B and C. Dealing with the ravages of heroin, crack, and AIDS, which severely impacted the neighborhood, it took several years to renovate the rundown tenement that housed the café. But, by the time of its grand reopening in 1989, the Nuyorican managed to live up to its promise, playing host to the next generation of poets—names like Paul Beatty and Maggie Estep—whose work displayed the unmistakable influence of hip-hop.

Montagne's contribution involved bringing MCs into the mix, thereby establishing the venue's connection with the burgeoning independent rap scene. He approached the Nuyorican with an ambitious proposal: Give me a Monday night and I will fill the room. Mondays were typically tough for nightlife establishments, but after seeing video footage from Bebop that he had taken, the club went even better, offering him a Wednesday-night slot instead. In the meantime, through his former partner, Montagne approached Bobbito Garcia to serve as master of ceremonies for the new night that would be called All That. Since the radio host already had a strong following through his show on WKCR, Montagne knew he would be a vital asset in helping to promote the night.

All That debuted at the Nuyorican in 1994 as an open-mic event featuring poets and MCs performing before a live jazz trio. Anyone who paid the five-dollar admission was eligible to participate by adding their name to a hat from which performers were picked at random. Popular from jump, that party led to the spin-off of another more hip-hop-centric night called Words in 1995, held on the first Saturday of every month. Instead of a house band, they featured a DJ, as well as a live drummer, to accompany the poets. As both nights surged in popularity and attendance, Montagne eventually partnered with Garcia, who started booking up-and-coming rap artists for Words.

"That whole nineties [era], the Nuyorican was really, really popular. I mean, the room legally sits 120. We were doing like 400 people [a night]," according to Montagne. The poet Saul Williams was one of the first artists to be discovered and score a record deal after performing there. In 1998, an unknown white MC from Detroit called Eminem also created quite a sensation there. After appearing at the more industry-oriented Lyricist Lounge showcase a month later, he was quickly signed by Dr. Dre. The chanteuse Erykah Badu, along with rappers Mos Def and Talib Kweli, built their reputations at the Nuyorican, which became an important part of New York's indie rap ecosystem, along with labels like Fondle 'Em and stores like Fat Beats. It was only a matter of time before DOOM would reintroduce himself to the world there as well.

Wu-Tang Clan cast a huge shadow over nineties hip-hop, and their influence on DOOM, in particular, cannot be understated. Like him, the Clan's elder statesmen RZA and GZA had been previously burned by the music industry, providing the impetus for their reinvention and ultimate resurgence. Instead of following the usual path to a deal by shopping a demo, they showed that a rap group could press up and sell their own records and have major labels court them. Leveraging that independent clout into dictating the terms of their deal, they effectively changed the power dynamics in an industry known for exploiting artists. Then, after infiltrating the industry as a group, the Clan spun off solo deals with multiple major labels—another unprecedented move at the time. For a moment, they had competing corporations tripping over themselves to elevate the Wu-Tang brand. Upstart independent outfits from the South like No Limit and Cash Money took heed. Other veteran artists like Kool Keith and Prince Paul were quick to catch on as well, resurrecting careers that had somewhat stalled. After buzzworthy independent releases—*Dr. Octagon* (Bulk Recordings, 1996) and *Psychoanalysis: What is it?* (WordSound, 1996), respectively—they were eventually wooed back into the major-label system.

By the latter half of the nineties, however, the independent scene was coming into its own. As the stylistic and aesthetic gap between indie and major transformed into a chasm, a major-label deal no longer held the cachet it once did. Many artists favored creative control as well as having a greater input over their career that working with an indie label offered. Signing to a major was no longer an end in and of itself since it was possible to make an impact and move units on independents as diverse as the New York–based Rawkus, Stones Throw on the West Coast, and Rhymesayers in Minneapolis.

In this respect, DOOM's timing and approach was impeccable, primed as he was to take advantage of this new wave of opportunities. Dedicated to his craft, he had amassed an archive of material and concepts—more than even he could use alone. Alongside his main collaborator MF Grimm, he plotted several projects, the most ambitious of which was the multi-person crew styled after Wu-Tang called Monsta Island Czars (M.I.C). While they were putting that project together, they pounced on any opportunities that came their way.

Boston deejay Papa D (Adam DeFalco) had formed the independent Brick Records and Backpack Music Studios (BPM) out of his home in Malden, Massachusetts, in 1996. When friend and fellow deejay Ninja B mentioned that he had made tracks with Grimm years ago, the pair contacted him about releasing some of that material. According to Papa D, "To be honest, I don't know if it was my idea or his idea or what, but somehow it was like, can we get DOOM to do a couple of songs and we'll do like a split MF record."

Working at the Boston-based, independent hip-hop distribution company Landspeed, he was already a fan of DOOM's Fondle 'Em singles. He and Grimm agreed on a price that now escapes him, but as Papa D recalls, "It was a buyout. At the time, yunno, it was a pretty good cash advance." To underscore the point, he adds, chuckling, "It was to the point where I had to borrow money from my brother to make it happen." With the advance committed, it took a good year before the MF EP came to fruition. But it provided a blueprint for the type of collaborative projects for which DOOM would be known throughout the rest of his career.

Caught up in the daily operation of survival, life was still hard for the rapper, who was splitting time between making music—whenever and wherever he could—and hustling. In mid-May of 1998, DOOM boarded a Greyhound bus at Port Authority for the four-hour trip down to DC, as he had done on so many previous occasions. Only this time, when they stopped in Baltimore to let passengers off, two police officers with dogs got on the bus and proceeded down the aisle for a random search. After catching the scent of a bag that had been stowed in the overhead rack, the animals started barking. The cops asked passengers who owned the bag, and after receiving no response, proceeded to look inside. Staring back at them was roughly a kilo of crack cocaine bagged up for street sales. Since no one claimed ownership, the officers decided to pull DOOM and another suspect off the bus, whisking them away to central booking.

Despite no direct evidence linking him to the drugs, the rapper was quickly embroiled in a case. Charged with importing a controlled substance into the state, he had his fingerprints and mugshot taken, before being remanded into custody. He used his free telephone call to contact Deanna, the girl he was seeing in DC, who in turn notified Kadi from the CM crew in New York to see if Garcia could possibly post bail. Word of what had happened soon filtered through DOOM's network. "My brother's locked up for crack, and I'm like, 'Fuck!'" Dimbaza recalls. But DOOM brushed off the charges and maintained his innocence. "He ended up getting a lawyer that was able to prove that that wasn't his bag. This was all mistaken identity bullshit, blah, blah," says Dimbaza, adding, "And he actually got out shortly thereafter after waiting patiently. He didn't even mind the bid. He didn't mind being there while he was waiting for that to happen."

Initially charged on May 14, DOOM wasn't arraigned until almost a month later on June 12, when he beat the charge. Apparently, Deanna's father was able to secure good representation for him that made all the difference. According to Dimbaza, "He got out based on the level of lawyer he had and the stupid ass circumstances. It got thrown out. So, I believed him—what he said. He never told me the story like, 'Yo, I got out, but it was really my crack.' No, he fuckin' like, they pinned that shit on him. It wasn't his, and I believe him 'cause the level of work that he's supposedly caught with." DOOM didn't deal in kilos, but ounces or half ounces, usually sent through overnight couriers. "So that package that they found, it was kind of at a level that he wasn't at, and we don't hide our shit like that," says Dimbaza. "We smart enough niggas to know like, no, my shit ain't gonna be where they rip open the bag and just see a bunch of crack bags. My brother is a petty crack mover. I just knew it wasn't his."

Regardless, DOOM was incredibly lucky to have dodged a bullet that could have easily derailed his whole comeback effort. But the fact that he was able to take everything that life threw at him in stride, without being crushed or deviating from his path, spoke volumes about his inner strength. He made it through that short bid, according to his brother, by staying close to the Muslim inmates and keeping himself occupied with his rhymes. In fact, on "Doomsday," the title track from his forthcoming album, he rapped, "I wrote this one in B.C. D.C.

O-section / If you don't believe me, go get bagged and check then / Cell number 17, up under the top bunk." Not only did he give the Baltimore City Department of Corrections a shout-out, but DOOM broke character revealing a rare piece of personal information, which he seldomly shared in his rhymes. With his freedom secured, he might have shrugged off the incident as if nothing had ever happened and gone back to business as usual. But he didn't.

DOOM's close brush with the law and the possibility of doing serious time was, no doubt, cause for a serious reality check. Since first reconnecting with the guys at Depth Charge, and going into business with Fragala, he had been steadily moving all kinds of product through the area—not just cocaine. The situation had even reached a point where they had to shift the drug business to a random house in Arlington, Virginia, where Fragala employed several young "flunkies," as he described them, who were also aspiring rappers, to help him move product. DOOM even stayed in that house sometimes.

Not long after the Baltimore incident, however, the rapper disappeared. Fragala says, "He just never came back to town, kind of dis-attached himself from everybody for a minute, even me for a good minute. You know what I'm saying?" He also claims that DOOM owed money to some people, who were actively looking for him, and it was more convenient to simply disappear. "He never did nobody in my crew dirty, he was stand up with us," Fragala maintains. "I know he did some cats dirty in DC, but he always had a home with us. Like it wasn't like he left on bad terms at all with us. It was almost like we had a good thing going—what happened?—type shit. And you know, he did a lot of that shit." But in the final estimation, he adds, "He did all that shit for his family. And he was a real friend, you know what I'm saying? Like he was a genuine dude. If he said he was gonna do something, he was gonna do it."

Following the release of his third Fondle 'Em twelve-inch in 1998, and appearances on the *Stretch Armstrong and Bobbito* radio show, the buzz on DOOM started moving into higher gear. Most people, however, remained ignorant of the fact that he was the reincarnation of Zev Love X, since no one had yet seen his face. Around this time, he forged a relationship with Nice and Nasty Vaz, an up-and-coming DJ, who was also managing Bobbito's Footwork. Vaz had just started a new hip-hop show on WKCR called *Nightrain*, along with DJ Eli Escobar; Apex, from the live hip-hop band Dujeous; and Kinetic from the group Arsonists. "He asked me to be the connection between him and the underground hip-hop scene in NYC," says Vaz. "He asked me to filter out any bullshit and co-sign any upcoming potential live performances and promoters."[1]

The young DJ was obviously psyched, not only because he was a huge DOOM fan, but also since he was starting a new night at the Nuyorican to promote his radio show. The premier *Nightrain* showcase, scheduled for September 19, 1998, already featured a bill packed with underground stalwarts Mazzi, J-Treds, Pumpkin Head, Wiseguy & Gaston, the High & the Mighty, 7L & Esoteric, Mr. Lif, Yeshua da Poed, and DJ Mr. Len. Though Vaz invited DOOM to perform, the rapper was initially reluctant about stepping on stage, since he hadn't done a live show in quite some time. So, it took some convincing. "Hey, let's not put you on the bill. Let's make this a surprise performance," suggested Vaz. "And he was crazy open to that; he thought it'd be a dope idea to just get onstage and blow everybody's mind. And we're talking about a really tight-knit group of hip-hop heads."[2]

DOOM wore a Kool-Aid smile on his unshaven mug as he strode up to the Nuyorican that sultry Saturday evening. With the line already stretching around the block, he knew the place would be packed for his live baptism by beats. He had come ready for battle in the no-frills attire of jeans and a wife-beater, a red Phillies cap angled on his head. In those pre-mask days, he attempted to conceal his identity by wearing a sheer stocking pulled down over his eyes and nose. Still, hardly anyone recognized him or made the connection to Zev Love X. When Vaz announced that MF DOOM would be performing, however, a surprised rumble went through the crowd. No one had expected to be seeing the rapper responsible for underground hits like "Hey!" and "Dead Bent."

DOOM took the stage with longtime associate Megalon. According to Vaz, "He does 'Greenbacks' for the first time and even though the record hadn't been out that long, 90 percent of the crowd knew every word to every fucking song he did."[3] DOOM followed that up with the unreleased "Doomsday," rapped in a much faster cadence than he did on record. From there, he went into "Dead

Bent" and, finally, "Hey!," to raucous applause and hoots of approval. He was obviously having a great time as he interacted with members of the audience.

"The Nuyorican shit was real intimate, real lyrical," he later recalled, "like the stage must have been shorter than a table so you see the reactions of the people, kinda joke around with them."[4] In a previous life, DOOM had rocked huge arenas and Arsenio Hall, but he felt very much in his element at the tiny venue that helped relaunch his career. After not performing live for the better part of the decade, this show was indispensable in helping to rebuild his confidence—not to mention sparking the hype behind his new persona. Before long, he was rocking stages everywhere.

THE MUSIC

We are what we repeatedly do. Excellence, then, is not an act, but a habit.

—ARISTOTLE

13

MF DOOM/*OPERATION: DOOMSDAY*

> *It is the fool who always rushes to take sides. Do not commit to any side or cause but yourself. By maintaining your independence, you become the master of others—playing people against one another and making them pursue you.*
> —ROBERT GREENE, *THE 48 LAWS OF POWER*

Through no small effort, DOOM's uncompromising vision finally came to realization on October 19, 1999, with the release of *Operation: Doomsday*, an album of many firsts. Coming a decade after his introduction to the music industry, it marked his inaugural solo effort, as well as the first time that DOOM exercised complete creative control over his music and how it was presented. The first long-player in the Fondle 'Em catalog to feature full-color artwork, this album could also compete with all the other LPs filling record store racks, as it aspired to more than merely a naked white label aimed at a select audience of deejays. In fact, the record felt right at home among other rap releases that dropped the same day—including Handsome Boy Modeling School's *So... How's Your Girl?* (Tommy Boy/Warners), Pharoahe Monch's *Internal Affairs* (Rawkus/Priority), and U-God's *Golden Arms Redemption* (Wu-Tang/Priority).

With his foot in the door, DOOM was, once again, primed to make an impression on a whole new era of rap that saw major-label dominance challenged, not only by a healthy independent scene, but also the technological innovations of digital downloading and streaming. Earlier, in June of that year, Napster had emerged as a file-sharing application that allowed individuals to swap whole music collections online, and the novelty of it all was changing the way people consumed music. Despite the revenue lost from sales of physical product, artists inherited a new form of promotion in the ability to go "viral" online, and all these emerging trends worked in DOOM's favor. He no longer needed to rely on the established infrastructure of the music industry to promote and sell his music. He also acknowledged the virtues of being small and independent. By remaining uncompromising in creativity and quality, and consistent in output, the audience would seek him out, allowing him to grow his career without the support of multinational companies, which is exactly what he did.

Operation: Doomsday marked the first in a succession of independent releases that saw DOOM dominating rap in the early aughts, despite not having a major-label deal and barely registering on the charts. Like the alter ego he created for himself, he practically inhabited his own parallel universe. It's as if he had taken a page—or pages—out of Robert Greene's *New York Times* bestseller *The 48 Laws of Power*, published the month before his album dropped. Law 25, for example, stated, "Do not accept the roles that society foists on you. Recreate yourself by forging a new identity, one that commands attention and never bores the audience. Be the master of your own image, rather than letting others define it for you. Incorporate dramatic devices into your public gestures and actions. Your power will be enhanced, and your character will seem larger than life."[1]

It seems as if DOOM took such advice to heart during his prolific run—preserving, as well, his free-agent status by refusing to commit to one label. His motivations for doing so, however, appear born out of necessity more than anything else because he was still in survival mode. As he told an audience at the Red Bull Music Academy in Madrid in 2011, "So one of the things that we did was made sure we had control over the entities, control over the business, you know, not to where you sign a deal where you could only make records for one company. Threw that out, know what I'm saying?"[2] Compared to his prior experience at Elektra, the simple and straightforward dealings with Garcia had converted him into a true believer in the independent route. "So, what it freed up was, it made it possible to solicit work to other people," he added. "So as much work as you could do, now I had the freedom to put it out. With the success of the Fondle 'Em stuff, other cats wanted me to do maybe a verse here or do a record for them, so as many people as was coming to me, it's like, 'All right, yo, I'll do it, I'll do it.' I had to get back up and get this bread, you know what I'm saying? But I guess on the outside, it looked like I was doin' a lot of records, which is cool, though."[3]

While money may have been a major motivation, DOOM also demonstrated a keen understanding of his audience as well as the lane he was creating for himself in rap. "I feel like it's not really like an overextended thing, it's more of a niche thing," he said, "Certain people like certain things. It might be thrift store clothes; you know what I'm saying? So, they'll go to the thrift store instead of going to Macy's to get whatever's supposed to be the high-end shit. It's a certain quality that people look for, and we provide that same quality."[4]

Considered a classic today, *Operation: Doomsday*, the lynchpin of DOOM's subterranean dynasty, still had to fight an uphill battle for recognition, released, as it was, without any traditional promotion. Sonically, too, it remained somewhat of an anomaly, relying heavily on syrupy quiet-storm hits of the eighties and other rap records as sample sources, which violated the unspoken standards of crate-digging.

"Yo, that shit came from the fuckin' deejay parties in the park and bein' on some like, the girls want to hear one thing and the niggas want to hear one thing," said DOOM, stubbornly defending his creative decisions. "See I always looked for that blend to keep the party movin' when I was deejayin'. So, I took that style and incorporated it into makin' beats, you know what I'm sayin', to achieve the same effect except with lyrics on it."[5] In hindsight, it was a genius move that made his music more accessible. In addition, it wasn't too far removed from how a hit-maker like Puff Daddy built his Bad Boy empire, co-opting eighties classics like the Police's "Every Breath You Take," and serving up a kind of rap karaoke version—albeit infinitely more polished and cleaner than anything DOOM ever did.

But the fact that DOOM's production style was purposely sloppy also helped endear him to an audience of hip-hop heads. While taking the better part of five years to make, the record still sounded somewhat half-baked. Back in the days, Subroc had been the finisher, polishing up and putting together ideas his brother had painted with broad strokes. Now that DOOM was operating on his own, he lacked that important editing function. Esteemed *Village Voice* music critic Robert Christgau observed, "As concept, this could get tedious fast. . . . the album never comes into full focus. But it does flow, as music and as signifying."[6] While not dismissing the record entirely, he did acknowledge something special about DOOM, adding, "Message: this smart guy had some horrible setbacks and came out the other side, a role model, you might say."[7]

Of the album's nineteen tracks, seven had already been released on twelve-inch singles. But, to his credit, DOOM took the time to remix them, sometimes even redoing the vocals. Out of the twelve new tracks, five comprised extended skits that incorporated snippets from various Fantastic Four cartoons and the early hip-hop film *Wild Style* to outline DOOM's back story. "Hero vs. Villain," a spoken-word track featuring DOOM's friend E. Mason, who had helped him assemble all the material for the skits at his DC studio, was the only track on which DOOM does not appear. So that left six new vocal tracks, four featuring members of Monsta Island Czars.

Grimm got the nod on "Tick, Tick . . . ," which famously sampled the cascading strings at the end of "Glass Onion" from *The Beatles* (Apple, 1968). Longtime collaborator, Tommy Gunn, who first served as DOOM's lyrical foil on "Operation: Greenbacks," returned on "The Finest," named after the SOS Band song it sampled. He also resurfaced as Megalon on "Who You Think I Am?" a "Protect Ya Neck"–style posse cut also featuring King Cesar, Rodan, Kamackeris, and Kong (along with DOOM as King Ghidra)—clearly a setup for the Monsta Island project that was in progress.

In addition to giving his crew some shine, DOOM employed the guest vocals of an unknown singer he had met randomly named Pebbles the Invisible Girl. She popped up on the title track, "Doomsday," singing the hook from Sade's "Kiss of Life" (Epic, 1992), on which the song was based, and returned on "The Finest." Though the two never worked together again, DOOM established a precedent—to always include some female representation on his albums, whether an MC or singer. Incidentally, he wasn't shy about breaking out into song himself as he did on the intro to "Dead Bent," singing, "Ooh, you're like the sun / Chasing all the rain away," an interpolation of the lyrics to Atlantic Starr's "Always" (Warner, 1987).

Of course, he couldn't forget about his homeboy Kurious, who made a guest appearance on one of the album's most personal tracks, "?." Over a sped-up loop of Isaac Hayes's "Vykkii," (HBS, 1975), which set the sentimental mood for the track, DOOM stepped out of character, once again, to reminisce about his deceased brother, whom he addressed directly:

> *Like my twin brother, we did everything together*
> *From hundred raka'at salats to copping butter leathers*
> *Remember when you went and got the dark blue Ballys*
> *I had all the different color Cazals and Gazelles*
> *The "SUBROC" three-finger ring with the ruby in the "O", ock*
> *Truly the illest dynamic duo on the whole block*
> *I keep a flick of you with the machete sword in your hand*
> *Everything is going according to plan man.*

It's a poignant moment that stuck out from a general tone of humor and zaniness, and those perceptive and familiar enough would have finally made the connection to KMD. DOOM delved into his personal space only one other time, for the hook of the album's title track, on which he rapped, "On Doomsday, ever since the womb / 'Til I'm back where my brother went, that's what my tomb will say / Right above my government; Dumile / Either unmarked or engraved, hey, who's to say?" Sub's legacy obviously hovered over the entire proceedings. As testament to their bond, the back cover of the LP included a black-and-white photo of the two brothers at Dr. York's upstate New York compound, dressed head to toe in the white robes of the Ansaars (with a black bar over DOOM's eyes to conceal his identity).

Operation: Doomsday, which saw DOOM raising a new flag and planting the seeds for plenty of more projects to come, represented his organic evolution as an artist. Not content to simply pick up where he left off, he went out of his way to develop a new style and break new ground while staying committed to his ideals. Against the backdrop of slick, commercial product being churned out by the music industry, the album may have appeared somewhat of a hot mess, but, in hindsight, it provided the perfect antidote to the so-called "shiny suit" era, attracting a large following in the underground.

Thanks to the buzz built by the singles and his occasional appearances, live and on the radio, the album sold steadily via word of mouth. "The total records pressed were 4,500—everything sold by Fat Beats," says Garcia. "There was no demand for reorders. So, me and DOOM just kind of like shook hands, you know, I paid him for everything that was due. It was super clean."[8] With a vinyl LP wholesaling for between $5.99 and $7.99 at the time, DOOM's cut may have only amounted to a modest profit. But the satisfaction of making money off music again, after the better part of a decade, must have felt incredibly redeeming. This small victory inspired many larger ones to come.

Bigg Jus (Justin Ingleton) first met DOOM at the video shoot for "The Gas Face" in 1989. At the time, the Company Flow MC was just a young graf writer, tagging along with his man Shake, a dancer for Run-DMC, who knew about the shoot. He had a chance to kick it with a young Zev Love X, himself a newcomer to the industry, but that was the extent of their interaction. "The next time I seen him again was around the time he got dropped from his label, and I was literally driving by," says Jus. "I think he was in the Village. I drove past him. He had like a full-size canvas of the *Black Bastards* album that he was holding. He had his head down, and I was going to stop, but he looked sad as hell. I knew about his brother and everything and I just let that one be."

In the meantime, Jus joined El-P (Jaime Meline) and DJ Mr. Len (Leonard Smythe) to form one of the biggest groups to emerge from the New York underground. Though Company Flow only released one album, *Funcrusher Plus* (Rawkus, 1997), they exerted an inordinate influence on the scene—their rallying cry, "independent as fuck," reverberating long after their breakup before the turn of the millennium. Jus left the group to pursue a solo career, but like former partner-in-rhyme El-P, who founded Definitive Jux as a home to release his music, he ended up starting an independent label of his own with a couple of partners. But years earlier in 1997, Jus ran into DOOM for a third time while shooting Company Flow's first official video for Rawkus.

Shot at the Transit Museum on Court Street in downtown Brooklyn, "End to End Burners" was about graffiti pieces that covered a whole car. "It's like the way the museum is set up, it's a train station and you have different train cars from different eras," says Jus. "So, at some point in time when the video shoot was winding down or they were shooting different scenes, I started going through the cars and when I went into one car, I looked and it was DOOM sleeping on the train like a homeless person, basically. Like I guess he wasn't, you know, on top of his shit then either at that point in time. He was still kind of maybe messed up in the game." He had apparently accompanied Bobbito Garcia to the video shoot. After waking him up, Jus spoke to him briefly, reminding him of the last time they had met. The significance of such strange synchronicities—bumping into each other in the least likely of places—would eventually come into focus for both of them.

Fiona Bloom, a British transplant who attended college in Georgia, had worked in the music industry since 1994, when she conducted the marketing campaign for Gang Starr's fourth album, *Hard to Earn* (Chrysalis/EMI, 1994). Though hip-hop was her passion, as a white woman, she was finding it difficult to be taken seriously. She ended up as director of media relations at an indie rock label called Zero Hour Records. After paying her dues there, she caught a break in 1998, helping to broker a multimillion-dollar deal between Zero Hour and her former employer, EMI. As thanks, her boss gave her her own hip-hop imprint, which she called 3-2-1 Records.

Her debut release through the new label was a compilation of hip-hop and dub called *Connected* (1998). Featuring an eclectic assortment of artists—including Kool Keith, Cokni O'Dire, The Angel, and Blackalicious—the album received a decent amount of press thanks to her efforts. The Oakland-based Blackalicious, who were signed to Mo' Wax in the UK but practically unknown in the US, were so impressed that they asked to be signed, and she was only too happy to indulge. The following year, she also signed Rubberoom out of

Chicago and Bigg Jus, fresh from his split with Company Flow. He also convinced her to sign Brooklyn's Skeme Team and Scienz of Life from New Jersey, before eventually becoming an A&R rep for the new label.

Everything seemed to be going well, until the mother company, Zero Hour, went bust in June 1999. Bloom found herself in a catastrophic situation, suddenly owing money to multiple artists, as well as unpaid bills for mastering and manufacturing. It was a stressful time for her, illustrating how unpredictable and merciless the music industry could be. Thankfully, her friend Alan Ket, editor of *Stress* magazine, referred her to a possible investor, who might be able to save the day.

Peter Lupoff of Lehman Brothers, a former musician himself, was looking to leave Wall Street and get into the music business. In 1998, he had already formed a company with producer Nile Rodgers and another partner called RRL Entertainment to invest in entertainment industry properties and projects. Ket arranged a meeting, according to Bloom, "And I ended up bringing Bigg Jus as my partner, because I didn't wanna be a white chick with another white guy starting a hip-hop label. I wanted to do this right."

Lupoff, apparently, had the same intentions. Already attracted to independent hip-hop through the work Rawkus was doing, he felt he could do it better. "Maybe we can tease out some new models with the internet coming on and Napster, like let's just embrace that and find some clever way," he said. "Let's find a new model to give artists ownership in their masters and maybe ownership in the label so that they are partners for real." Following a week of further talks between the three principles, Sub Verse Music was founded.

"Like he [Jus] and I conceived of the idea of the name Sub Verse together— 'sub' [meaning] below, 'verse' [meaning] spoken word as a way of talking about underground. And we got launched," says Lupoff. "If Jus is our partner on creative, Fiona's sort of outward facing, and I'll just deal with, you know, the operational business finance. I didn't really intend to be that involved. I had to get really involved because the music industry went into the shitter, but that wasn't the intention."

But even before the industry apocalypse, Lupoff was fully committed to the success of this new enterprise. His personal investment paid off the former 3-2-1 artists monies they were owed in exchange for delivery of an album master. Then, with seven masters under his belt, he was able to approach the EMI subsidiary Caroline for a manufacturing and distribution deal, netting an advance of $250,000. Using those funds, he was able to secure office space at a converted office furniture warehouse in lower Manhattan on Washington and Vestry Streets, subletting the bulk of it for additional income. By late 1999, Sub Verse Music was on the map and ready to unleash a trove of releases from Blackalicious, Bigg Jus, Rubberoom, Micranots (from Minneapolis), and Scienz of Life.

Though the independent hip-hop scene of the late nineties was gradually expanding, it still represented a niche market. From Plainfield, New Jersey, the crew Scienz of Life, composed of John Robinson (aka Lil' Sci); his brother Michael (aka ID 4 Windz), the group's producer; and Inspector Willabee (Rashan Coleman), already called themselves friends and neighbors of Bigg Jus. They also knew Bobbito Garcia from the radio show and his live nights at the Nuyorican. In fact, at one of those nights, Robinson passed him a cassette demo to play on the air and was pleasantly surprised a couple weeks later when he found a message from Garcia on his answering machine. The host/label owner was interested in releasing a twelve-inch of their song "Powers of Nine Ether," which led to a handshake deal on Fondle 'Em. The group would often meet Garcia at Footworks to handle business, and once when they came in, he informed them that they had just missed DOOM. They were so hyped, Robison recalls, "We run out, catch up to DOOM up the block, and we're literally able to just meet him quickly as he's getting into a cab and just let him know who we are and, you know, let him know we're not crazy. We work with the same label, with Bob, da, da da."

Their next encounter with DOOM occurred a couple years later in 1999, when they drove down to Atlanta with Bigg Jus to perform their first show there. "We get to the sound check at the venue MJQ and DOOM is outside, you know, maskless, no mask, none of that. Like, yo, what up?" says Robinson. Since he and Jus already knew each other, they kicked it for a bit, but DOOM didn't even stay for the show. But the group's inaugural trip down south made a serious impression on them. "It was really our first time in Atlanta to get introduced to the underground scene in ATL," says Robinson, "It was, like, really powerful. We realized, oh wow, this is like a melting pot of artists from all over the country here, just doing different styles and things, but all in the name of hip hop." They realized then that New York, or even LA, could no longer claim to be the center of the hip-hop universe.

Back in New Jersey, Jus was feeling restless. "Something was telling me to get the fuck up out the city," he says. "And I didn't know what it was, but because of my upbringing and stuff like that, I got like strong intuition about things." According to Robinson, "Bigg Jus who I consider a very quiet, super innovator to this day—when Bigg Jus speaks about things that sounds crazy that means listen, cuz that shit's definitely gonna happen in some capacity."

With Sub Verse on the verge of starting up, he talked to them about opening a satellite office in Atlanta, where they would work for the label making calls and deliveries to retail in exchange for their living expenses. "So, when you're calling to talk about your record, you're asking about Micranots and Rubberoom and the other artists. When you're moving about on tour, doing retail runs, going into the record stores, or doing an in-store, you're asking about the other records in the retail scapes and blah, blah, blah, really learning the game hands on," says Robinson. "But also, like having rent paid, having a gas card and a van and, you know, just all these things to kind of keep the machine going." As working artists, committed to growing their careers, such considerations made a lot of sense to them—especially since a new wave of gentrification was making the New York area a prohibitively expensive place to live.

Throwing in their lot together in 2000, Scienz of Life and Bigg Jus piled their lives into a moving van and drove down from the apartment complex where they both lived in Harbortown, New Jersey, to a converted cotton mill/loft complex in Newnan, Georgia, about forty miles southwest of Atlanta. DOOM had already relocated earlier that year, renting a townhouse with his wife Jasmine in Woodstock, which was about thirty-six miles northwest of the city. "He was one of the few people I knew down there," says Jus, who had attended military school in Georgia. "He was kind of like my barbecue buddy, basically, in Atlanta." Though they lived an hour apart, the two would occasionally hang out. "So, he would come to my spot and do recording and stuff and I'd go to his spot and hang out," Jus recalls. In speaking, DOOM strongly believed that *Operation: Doomsday* had more mileage, and Jus says, "I remember trying to organize a deal in Atlanta, you know, talking with him at one of these barbecues."

At the same time, Scienz of Life, who had practically set up a hip-hop bootcamp in the 3,500-square-foot loft where their five-man crew lived, worked, rehearsed, and exercised together, were just getting to know the Villain. "DOOM would come check us at the loft space there, bring the MPC, sometimes work on beats there," says Robinson. "And then we really just started connecting more on, I would say spirituality, really, like, you know, just talking about different books, whether it was Dr. York's books or whether it was, you know, some other spiritual leader. We connected on that tip a lot. I felt like that was the glue, you know, that was the brotherhood. The music was there too, but I felt like at the time the building sessions were about just the world and what was going on and how to prepare yourself, how to be in tune, how to stay in tune and plugged in to the right information." He adds, "That was a big part, I feel, of DOOM's m.o. to not be so public and, you know, open and always accessible."

"So, it's probably late 1999, early two thousands. I'm having regular conversations with Bobbito about any number of things we might do," says Lupoff. "And at one point he says to me, 'You know, *Operation: Doomsday*, you should think about taking this up because I've done everything I can do with it. I put it out on vinyl on Fondle 'Em and I don't know that there's more to get done, but, you know, DOOM is sort of back on track. He's anxious to kind of get going again and you're the right aesthetic and you all could work this out.'

"And while that was happening," Lupoff adds, "I think simultaneously the artists in the Atlanta area were also working with him and getting to know him better—Jus and the Scienz of Life. And, so, I think DOOM was getting comfortable that there was like a simpatico here and that he would be safe working with us because he's hearing it from Bobbito, he's hearing it from people in Atlanta." After meeting with DOOM personally at the Sub Verse offices in 2000, Lupoff began to discuss the details of a deal.

"And we got to a place where we agreed to an advance and where, you know, the master reverted back to him at the end of a short period of time, I think it was like five years or four years, which was kind of our way, you know. It just sort of felt, like, equitable," he says. "And then almost as an afterthought, he's like, 'Well, if you're gonna take *Operation: Doomsday*, you want *Black Bastards* too?' It's like, absolutely, we'll put that out. And, so, I forget what the economics was. I forget what the dollar amount was. It might have been 15 or 20 grand for *Doomsday*. And I think he said, 'Well, how about the same for *Black Bastards*?' I said, fine."

The universe was slowly opening doors for DOOM. In November 2000, only weeks after signing with Sub Verse, he had the opportunity to shoot his first music videos for the songs "?" and "Dead Bent." Though essentially no-budget videos made by then NYU film student Adam Bhala Lough (aka Piston Honda), he still had to buy the rapper a new pair of Timberland boots and a bottle of Jack Daniel's to ensure his participation (for which the label eventually reimbursed him). But these simple, unpolished productions, which find DOOM wearing the first, plastic version of mask, perfectly complemented the rawness of the music, further contributing to the burgeoning cult of DOOM.

A hip-hop fan from Virginia, Lough had ostensibly come to New York for film school, but spent much of his time frequenting Fat Beats and venues like the Nuyorican, where he could experience the music he loved. He had discovered DOOM through the Fondle 'Em release of *Operation: Doomsday*, an album that he describes as "unpolished" but "weirdly addictive," adding, "I'd never heard anything like it." When the opportunity arose to see DOOM performing live at the Knitting Factory, on a bill featuring Minneapolis duo Atmosphere and Chuck D's rock band, Concentration Camp, he made sure to attend. He watched from the balcony, along with a wheelchair-bound MF Grimm, as the audience of fifty or so flocked to the front of the stage to see DOOM. Though the rapper disappeared immediately after his performance, as he was prone to do, Lough was able to meet a guy named DJ Fisher, who called himself DOOM's manager, and pitch him on making a free video. After exchanging numbers, Fisher told the young film student he would speak to DOOM and get back to him.

Though Lough had never shot a music video, DOOM requested some samples of his work, so he sent him a VHS of experimental shorts that he had made for a class. Afterward, they spoke by phone and finally met in person at the Sub Verse offices a couple weeks later. Lough had initially pitched doing videos for "Red and Gold" and "Hey!," but DOOM wanted to do "?" so they scheduled the shoot for the weekend of November 18th when he would be back in town.

It was an unseasonably warm day in Brooklyn's Sunset Park when they reconvened. Although the call time was set for seven in the morning, DOOM didn't arrive until midday, insisting that they stop at the Foot Locker on Fourteenth Street for a new pair of Tims, which pushed their starting time back even further. When they finally arrived in Brooklyn, Kurious and one of his buddies were already waiting. Before shooting commenced, DOOM passed around the bottle of Jack that Lough had purchased the night before. With only a few hours of light left, a skeleton crew that included Lough, his friend Ethan Higbee, and cinematographer Ben Rekhi managed to capture most of the footage they needed for the simple and straightforward video.

Shot on film with an ARRI-S 16mm camera, DOOM rhymed—with and without the mask (though his face was obscured)—on a brownstone stoop and park bench. They also shot Kurious walking down the street while reciting his verse, and the two of them playing chess in the park. DOOM happened to bring Sub's machete, which figures prominently as a prop as does the bottle of Jack. It's not hard to notice the World Trade Center towering in the background as well. After finishing up for the day, they planned to continue shooting the next day at Lough's apartment in the East Village at 205 First Avenue.

As the director went out to pick up more film the following morning, he was listening to *Operation: Doomsday* on his headphones for the umpteenth time. Suddenly, he was seized by an inspiration to do another video for "Dead Bent," a stream-of-consciousness song with no hooks. Lough envisioned DOOM rhyming while getting up and going to the corner bodega, where he steals a bunch of produce. He would shoot it in one continuous take, but twice, with DOOM re-creating all his actions in reverse. Then they would present both takes side by side in a split screen. Arriving a few hours late, once again, DOOM seemed partial to the idea. So, after completing the shots they needed for the "?" video, they ran through several takes of "Dead Bent." Everything proceeded without incident until the cameraman, Rehki, accidentally sat on the mask, which had been left on the couch, squashing it. Understandably, DOOM was not amused, and he abruptly ended the shoot.

With footage for two videos in the can, however, Lough had his work cut out for him, and spent the next few months in the editing room. After cutting in photos of Subroc and clips from an episode of the Fantastic Four cartoon, he sent copies to DOOM and Garcia, getting good feedback from them. A self-conscious DOOM wanted to cut out a shot that revealed his bald spot, but Lough kept it in, anyway. He turned over the finished copies to Sub Verse, who were able to get the videos aired on MTV Europe.

The whole experience left an indelible impression on Lough, who later wrote about it, saying, "Throughout the four or five months working with him, DOOM came across to me as a genius, undoubtedly brilliant, slightly nerdy, but also dodgy, capricious, and an unapologetic hustler. He smiled a lot, laughed a lot, drank a lot, and was warm and open in social situations. He'd trust you with certain details from his life, yet not trust you by a damn sight with other things."[9] That was the last he saw of the complex and enigmatic rapper until the following summer when DOOM was performing a show at S.O.B.'s.

Fiona Bloom describes DOOM's August 15, 2001, appearance at the well-known downtown venue as "the most infamous S.O.B.'s show ever." According to her, "If you talk to the owner of S.O.B.'s, Larry Gold, he says, still to this day, people ask him about that show." Months after his Sub Verse release, with his star on the rise, DOOM sold out the 450-capacity club on a Wednesday night. When showtime arrived, he trooped onstage backed up by some of the Monsta Island Czars with Bigg Jus as his deejay. The excitement in the crowd was palpable.

Bloom says, "He had a good, or I should say, a warped sense of humor, you know. He was a funny, crazy guy, a disturbed guy, sweet guy, sweetheart, teddy bear at the end of the day, not a scary guy at all, you know, a lovely guy, but he liked to get things wild up, and yeah, so he staged this fight." Though she witnessed it all, buried in the crowd, like most people who were there, she still was not sure exactly how and what actually transpired.

"From what I remember DOOM was doing his set and then he was bringing Megalon," says Jus, who had a better vantage point, being onstage himself. "S.O.B.'s is not really a big stage or whatever, but he was walking back and forth, and he walked toward Megalon and pushed him, I think, playfully. But Megalon kind of got embarrassed and just jumped on DOOM and pummeled him real quick." DOOM's gold fronts went flying into the crowd. Somewhat taken aback, he jumped off stage to escape, and one of his Timberlands slipped off. He ended up fleeing the club wearing one boot with Megalon giving chase. Meanwhile, according to Jus, "The whole crowd is stunned and don't know what's happening."

Chaos ensued. "There was like blood everywhere, and people thought that somebody was killed, or hurt," says Bloom, "And next thing you know, everybody's bum rushing to the door and lights are on and the show had stopped, and people were freaking out and screaming and everything was a blur." People were running out of the club to see what happened.

Jus ran out to see about DOOM and found the rapper pacing back and forth down the block, looking frazzled. "DOOM was like, hella embarrassed. Like he was like, 'What just happened?' And I just told him like, 'Yo, just say the shit was staged,'" he says. "And then he kind of gathered himself, came back in and acted like the shit was staged. But no, it was not staged from the start." Upon returning to the club, somebody gave him back his gold fronts, and he was able to retrieve his Timberland as well. Says Jus, "That's how the show ended. It was kind of brilliant." According to Bloom, "All I can remember was it was like one of the most historic, crazy experiences I'd ever encountered. And everyone said the same thing."

If Fondle 'Em put DOOM back on the map, Sub Verse spread his name far and wide, greatly expanding his cachet as an artist. Despite their modest investment in licensing the two records, the label was determined to get the most bang for their buck, releasing a remastered *Operation: Doomsday* (with a bonus track, "I Hear Voices") in May 2001 and *Black Bastards*, with its original, controversial cover art, only a month later. Bloom, who handled marketing and promotion, capitalized on the story of DOOM's redemption after losing his brother and his major label deal, which hip-hop centric publications like *Ego Trip*, *Stress*, and *Mass Appeal* found irresistible. But her Rolodex was deep, and she was also able to get him coverage in such national outlets as the *New York Times*, *Entertainment Weekly*, *High Times*, *Rolling Stone*, and *Spin*. Thanks to the press bonanza, a flurry of ads taken out by the label, and their wide distribution channels that stretched around the globe, they were able to register some decent sales. According to Lupoff, "In the time that we were tracking it, we probably moved 75,000–80,0000 of *Doomsday* and maybe 65 to 70 [thousand] of KMD. They were pretty close for a couple of years." But beyond the impressive numbers, their marketing and promotion campaign firmly placed DOOM back in the public eye.

Far from dealing with a faceless corporation, DOOM was treated like family by Sub Verse and took full advantage of it. "So absolutely DOOM would ask for a lot of stuff and we gave him everything—pretty much everything he asked for—whether it was wardrobe, recording equipment, microphones, you know metal face mask, weed. We got it for him," says Bloom. When DOOM's plastic mask was wrecked during the "Dead Bent" video shoot, Lupoff paid Lethem the $300 it took to purchase and refit the steel mask from *Gladiator* that became DOOM's defining feature. DOOM might even have done another record for Sub Verse if not for one simple reason. According to Bloom, "We were having major success and DOOM was very happy. Everybody was very happy. But then, just remember where we are, Washington Street in Tribeca, right? 2001, right? 9/11 happened."

14

METAL FINGERS/*SPECIAL HERBS*

Enough about me, it's about the beats.
—MF DOOM, "BEEF RAP"

The carnage and destruction wrought by the September 11 attacks on New York's World Trade Center, broadcast around the world on infinite loop, were enough to leave anyone watching with PTSD. But for New Yorkers, this calamity fundamentally affected their daily lives, irrevocably changing the place they called home. For months afterward, a sense of dread, paralysis, and defeat pervaded the city, accompanied by the acrid smell of burnt buildings permeating the air. The smoldering gap in the Manhattan skyline, where an iconic landmark once stood, marked a hole in the soul of the once mighty Big Apple.

"We could not get into our office for months," Bloom recalls. "Peter had a huge flat on Greenwich Street, four blocks from World Trade. He lost his flat. He was in a hotel for about eight months. I was living in Brooklyn at the time in Fort Greene. Jus thought it was Nostradamus, wigged the fuck out, and disappeared. And me also wigging out, and not really knowing if I even want to go back—not just to the office—but if I even wanna do what I'm doing anymore, because 9/11 changed everything. It changed the way I felt about life." She was hardly alone in this sentiment, and eventually wrote a heartfelt letter to her partner Lupoff before walking away from the label in which she had invested so much of herself to help create.

Even prior to her departure, however, the writing on the wall did not bode well. The label's breakout success with DOOM was underwriting losses on other releases, a situation that could only last for so long. "We're putting out music we're really proud of. We love the sound of it, we believe in the artists, but there's not a basis for us to distribute this music in a way in which we can make more than what it costs to put out," says Lupoff. After losing his primary partners, he was left running the company solo with only one other full-time employee, OP Miller, who was appointed label manager. Though it would have been a no-brainer to offer DOOM, their biggest seller, another deal to possibly help jump start the label again, Lupoff, too, was in a different place following 9/11. After having already sunk a large personal investment into the company, his priorities had shifted. He was also about to get married.

"I even remember saying to him [DOOM], too, it's like, I don't think we're a great partner for a next project," he says. "You're really entitled to a new advance. You're really entitled to new money to get that going. We don't have that. I think that, organizationally, for this to work, I needed the whole team to kind of be there to do it, too, and we just didn't have the wherewithal." Though the label was able to maintain itself for another year, he says, "We did wind down Sub Verse in 2003 and we let all the masters revert [back to the artists]."

The advent of file-sharing that accompanied a dip in the wholesale price of CDs made it a challenging time for the music industry in general. But independents, especially, bore the brunt of the pain—whether a Sub Verse, with its high overhead, or a nimbler outfit like Fondle 'Em, which folded in 2001. But as 9/11 provided the death blow to many flagging or bloated operations, it also cleared the way for more smaller labels to rise from the ashes. DOOM may have been out of a record deal, but it wouldn't be for long.

After years in the wilderness, spent grieving, drinking, tripping, scheming, and dreaming, DOOM was finally on the path to reclaiming his mojo, immersing himself in multiple projects, some not even his own. In 2000, he helped his friend MF Grimm put together an entire album during a small window of time before the latter had to serve time for drug and conspiracy convictions. DOOM not only produced several tracks for what was to become *The Downfall of Ibliys: A Ghetto Opera* (Day by Day Entertainment, 2002), but also oversaw its creation. He elicited additional production from Count Bass D, Dr. Butcher, DJ Eli, Cas, Protest, and dminor, and mixed the whole thing himself, serving in the same capacity as Large Professor did for Nas's *Illmatic* or the RZA on Ghostface's *Supreme Clientele*. Testament to the close bond he and Grimm shared, the project was especially important to his partner since it allowed him to maintain some semblance of a career while incarcerated.

Just before Grimm, who was out on a $100,000 bond, was to turn himself in, he reached out to DJ Rob Swift (Robert Aguilar) of the turntablist crew the X-Ecutioners (formerly the X-Men), to whom his DJ, Roc Raida, also belonged. "He's like, 'Yo, Rob, man, I'm about to go in, like, I'm about to do a bid, and I'm sitting on songs that are like halfway done,'" says Swift. "So, he was like, 'Yo, can I please go to your house and record all of these songs?' And I was like, of course, come through."

Swift remembers the first time he met Grimm in the early nineties. "It was like at a battle," he recalls. "And I just remember his intensity. He was in there as if he was in a boxing match. It wasn't like a rap battle to him. Like he was in there, ready to take off heads, figuratively and literally, yeah. Like that was Grimm, very intense." They eventually became very close and spent hours messing around in the studio together making demos, or, sometimes, even just hanging out and playing Nintendo at Grimm's place.

Now that his friend was confined to a wheelchair, Swift figured he might be bringing someone to assist him. But several days later, when he buzzed him into his apartment building in Jackson Heights, Queens, he didn't expect to see DOOM, sans mask, pushing him out of the elevator. As they approached, he recalls, "Grimm said, 'Rob, thank you, man, for letting me come through. By the way, yo, this is DOOM.'" Swift was shocked because the Villain was a known name on the underground now. But formalities aside and with time of the essence, the three of them plunged immediately into the task at hand.

Swift's basic home setup consisted of a sixteen-track Mackie mixing board, several drum machines—an SP-1200, MPC60, and MPC2000—and an E-MU E6400 sampler. He had also just purchased a Roland VS-1680 digital audio workstation, which was an all-in-one desktop studio, but didn't know how to use it yet. He was about to get the manual when DOOM told him, *Don't worry about it, Rob. I know this machine like the back of my hand.* After Scienz of Life and Bigg Jus had introduced him to the 1680, DOOM liked it so much that he used some of his advance money from Sub Verse to get one himself. Quick and easy to use, the machine soon became his main production tool.

"Actually—and this was so cool—he was like, 'Yo, just sit by me as I work it so that you can kind of learn as we go,'" says Swift. "And that's what I did. I just stood by him. And what I thought was gonna be maybe like a two, three-hour session, I think we were in my studio for at least five, six hours minimum, just working on song after song. I'm not exactly sure how much, but it was a lot of songs that we recorded."

His guests had come prepared with discs of samples and songs that had been laid out and arranged. Since Grimm had already written rhymes for these tracks, they just recorded vocals before mixing everything down. Having arrived in the early afternoon, it was getting dark outside by the time they left. According to Swift, "It was so organic and real and there was nothing fake about that moment, dude. There was just friends helping each other out, whether it was like me helping Percy record these songs before he went to jail or this new friend I met, who knew this toy better than I did. And he was gonna teach me how to play with it. So, I learned that Roland 1680 watching DOOM."

The new millennium saw the release of Brick Records' split *MF EP* (BRK012), featuring DOOM and Grimm, each of whom contributed three tracks along with their instrumentals. DOOM's side featured "Doomsday (remix)," "No Snakes Alive," and "Impostas." Grimm's side included "The Original" and its remix, "Break Em Off," and "Dedicated." Label head Papa D had suggested doing the "Doomsday" remix since the original track was already out.

"So, what happened was, when we decided we were gonna do the remake, he [DOOM] had sent me an acapella," he says. He enlisted his friend Mr. Jason (Jason Katsohis) of Boston's Porn Theatre Ushers, to produce the remix beat. "Once we agreed on what beat and everything, I brought Jason over, recorded the beat, and then we like flew in the vocals," he adds. "And the first time I did it, I sent it back to DOOM for approval and he was like, 'No, this is off.' He's like, 'Send me all the stuff.' And then he sent it back and we mixed it." Of the other two unreleased tracks, DOOM eventually recycled "No Snakes Alive," featuring King Ghidra, Jet Jaguar, and Rodan, for his King Geedorah project.

Papa D didn't meet either of the artists in person until he and a photographer went down to New York for the cover shoot during the summer of 1999. Though DOOM didn't wear the mask at the time, "He was kind of like, don't really get my face, you know," recalls Papa D. "But I think me and the photographer took it as he was just on some b-boy shit, you know, hat low, whatever—not like, really don't show my face, you know what I mean?" When it came time to approve the artwork, however, DOOM was adamant. Papa D says, "He was like, 'Nah, you can't use any of those with my face in it. Like, when my face is clear, you gotta scrap those.' And I was like, Oh, word really? Like it was news to me, you know? Luckily, we had enough where it's not like a straight on view of his face that we could still do something dope for the art."

The final package, a fancy, full-color double gatefold, featured images of DOOM and Grimm chilling uptown outside the apartment building where the former was staying with his now seven-year-old son. DOOM wore a red polo shirt, Red Sox baseball cap, and denim shorts, while a bespectacled Grimm was dressed in a wifebeater and jeans. One shot placed Grimm in the foreground with DOOM standing high up on a balcony in the background. They also captured the reverse angle with a close-up of DOOM, cradling a bottle of Beck's beer with Grimm, below, in the background. Afterward, they took a trip downtown, to a park near Fat Beats on Sixth Avenue, where they took more pictures of the artists playing chess. "DOOM and Grimm apparently did that a lot," says Papa D, adding, "Everybody had a couple of beers, and we just chilled." DOOM's son even tagged along for the shoot as he was often prone to do since his dad was his sole guardian.

At a time when college radio and record pools were not only still relevant, but essential for promoting independent releases, Brick put in the necessary groundwork of servicing deejays with the EP and making follow-up calls. When all was said and done, they ended up moving about five thousand copies through Landspeed Distribution, with whom they shared office space—decent numbers for an independent record with little promotion. Not long after its release, however, Grimm went to prison, and Papa D lost touch with them both. Brick went on to become a respected indie label in the Boston area, releasing the work of such artists as Mr. Lif, 7L & Esoteric, and Big Shug.

Meanwhile, on the West Coast, Peter Agoston was just getting his foot in the door of the music industry. Tucked away in the sleepy pothead town of Arcata, California, he was working on a journalism degree at Humboldt State University. His byline had already appeared in music magazines like the cutting-edge *URB*, based in LA, and he deejayed as well. To that end, he maintained a relationship with several independent record labels and artists, including the Bay area collective Anticon, who happened to run their own distribution company, 6months.

Following high school and before heading west, Agoston had worked at Sandbox Automatic, an early online retailer specializing in hip-hop, where he had first come across *Operation: Doomsday*. "I remember when the CD version came out and I was like, man, I can't believe they put a CD out," he says. "They sold out, you know, CDs are whack." A vinyl purist, he dreamed of helming his own label, but with a twist. "It's gonna be instrumental-only releases," he says. "That was like the original intent." Anticon's Sole (aka Tim Holland), who worked at 6months, encouraged him to take the plunge, offering to manufacture and distribute his releases.

Agoston's plans were set in motion in mid-2000 when he received a call from the Orlando-based DJ Fisher, who was running Day by Day Entertainment on behalf of MF Grimm during his incarceration. "I think at the time people were liking DOOM as a rapper, but you could not deny his prowess as a producer, especially, like, at that point," says Agoston. "[He] was just like, so distinctly old school, like blend tape style production, which is a very simple art form, but a very effective one." Familiar with the relationship between DOOM and Grimm, he told Fisher, "I would love to see if DOOM would be down to do an instrumental version of *Operation: Doomsday*. To my recollection, DJ Fisher was like, 'I'll bring it up to him.'" By this time, DOOM was living with Jasmine in the suburbs of Atlanta, and before long, Fisher put them in touch directly.

"So, we just started talking and he and I would talk on the phone like pretty often," says Agoston, who eventually conducted one of the most intimate interviews with DOOM for the Atlanta-based *Elemental Magazine* in 2003. "He was very open and down and interested and we had good chemistry and stuff. I think he liked me. He got a kick outta me, and I was just like this guy in California, you know, that had a little record label."

DOOM asked him for a thousand-dollar advance as the price of doing business. While a paltry sum in music business terms, it was a large enough number for a guy who was still a student, so Agoston approached 6months, who agreed to cover the sum. But instead of simply doing an instrumental version of *Operation: Doomsday*, DOOM had more ambitious plans. *Why don't we do a whole series of instrumental albums?* he suggested. *We'll do ten of them and it'll be dope.* It also gave the rapper a chance to flex his production alias, "The Metal Fingered Villain," which was eventually shortened to Metal Fingers, another variation on the MF title. Agoston says, "So, I think he saw where I was headed with the idea and perhaps in his own mind could see that like, 'Yeah, I'm sitting on [a lot of] those types of beats.'"

They quickly came to terms without any kind of formal, written agreement. "We're like, okay, let's do this record. It's gonna be vinyl only. We're only gonna make a thousand copies, and it'll be volume one of what will be a ten-volume set called *Special Herbs*. And originally it was *Special Herbs & Spices*," says Agoston. "So, we started that up and that was the very first record I ever put out." The novel concept of the series—literally a vinyl beats tape—anticipated an interest in purely instrumental hip-hop that eventually became a thing later on. But not many people were doing it at the time.

It didn't take much effort to put together on DOOM's part, as he already had a ton of material in the vaults. Even so, of the album's nine tracks, he still included four instrumentals from *Operation: Doomsday*, renamed accordingly—"Saffron" ("Doomsday"), "Shallots" ("The Hands of Doom" skit), "Charnsuka" ("?"), and "Monosodium Glutamate" ("Rhymes Like Dimes"). Other titles came to be used on future projects. "Arrow Root," for example, provided the instrumental for "Next Levels," which showed up on the King Geedorah album. "Fenugreek" and "Sumac Berries" were both beats that DOOM ended up giving Ghostface for the tracks "9 Milli Bros." and "Jellyfish," respectively, off his 2006 comeback album, *Fishscale* (Def Jam).

Released on December 18, 2001, the inaugural release on Agoston's newly formed Female Fun label, the cover of *Special Herbs, Volume 1* (FF001) featured a frame from a Fantastic Four comic that helped illustrate DOOM's whole concept. "Only I have the power to remove my mask... by manipulating the many-faceted ring on my finger. And now the final precaution," says Doctor Doom, displaying his ringed metal hands. Someone out of the frame replies, "We shall cover your ring with special herbs, camouflaging it so completely that none will see it."[1] The back cover contained DOOM's own artwork—a picture of himself wearing the mask and a Panama hat in homage to the logo of Optimo cigars. The record, which also bore the mask logo of DOOM's own Metal Face Records, a pending joint venture with Jasmine, sold out in a couple months with virtually no promotion. That prompted them to re-press another thousand. "I think we sold, like the lion's share in California, you know, just 'cause it was made in California, and that was when we had Amoeba and Rasputins," says Agoston, referring to two legendary West Coast record stores. "We probably sold half of the copies in between the Bay Area and LA.

"And then other interests from other record labels started coming in and places that had a little more infrastructure than me," he adds. "I mean, I was working out of my bedroom, you know, with other people's money, but that's what made it amazing, too—I mean that he didn't really care about that." Agoston credits DOOM's laid-back personality, and what an affable guy he was, saying, "It was just like, 'All right, you're cool. Like I dig where you're coming from.' But who was I? He didn't know me. But he was like, artistically, a very trusting dude, which is pretty cool, you know? 'Cause in hip-hop a lot of people are kind of like, standoffish, especially back in the day." The two hadn't even met in person, maintaining a close working relationship via phone, and they wouldn't cross paths until early 2002.

Back east, Devin Horwitz was making moves as well. A budding journalist and photographer from suburban Maryland, he attended Boston University, where he counted rapper Aesop Rock (Ian Matthias Bavitz) and producer Blockhead (Tony Simon) among his friends. Upon graduating, he moved to New York and started writing for *The Source*, *Vibe*, *XXL*, and *Rap Sheet*. He also interned at the well-respected jazz label CTI (Creed Taylor Inc.), home to such luminaries as George Benson, Ron Carter, and Bob James. He eventually scored a choice paying gig as a production assistant at *High Times*. His tenure at the esteemed counterculture magazine serendipitously coincided with their expansion into music. When Mike Esterson formed High Times Records in 2002, he tapped Horwitz's expertise as the resident hip-hop head to help put together the label's first release, *T.H.C., Vol. 1*, an abbreviation, and obvious double entendre, that stood for the hip-hop collection. It was Horwitz's first experience as an A&R and executive producer.

Ever since the early nineties influence of Cypress Hill, Redman, Dr. Dre's *The Chronic* (Death Row/Interscope, 1992), and the Phillies Blunt craze, everyone knew that weed and hip-hop went together like peanut butter and jelly. And who better than *High Times* to capitalize on that relationship? Armed with a decent budget and the magazine's stoner credentials, Horwitz was able to entice such artists as the RZA, B-Real, the Beatnuts, the Pharcyde, and Black Moon to contribute weed-related tracks. Just starting to dabble in beat-making himself, he was also able to slip in one of his very first tracks, made under his production alias, The Prof. He asked none other than DOOM to drop lyrics over this track.

In high school, Horwitz had published his own hip-hop zine called *Down Low*. In 1993, while interviewing Del the Funky Homosapien at the Elektra offices in Manhattan, he had unexpectedly run into the then Zev Love X, who was gracious enough to sign an autograph for him. As a huge fan of KMD and now *Operation: Doomsday*, he was psyched to have the chance to work with DOOM—this time as collaborators, and in a real studio.

They recorded vocals for "My Favorite Ladies" and "All Outta Ale" at D&D Studios on Thirty-Seventh Street in Manhattan, DJ Premier's home base. The former track, slated for the compilation, was straight-up boom bap with a warped string sample that sounded like something the RZA might conjure up. It provided the appropriate backdrop for DOOM to wax poetic about his favorite stimulants, thinly disguised as various girls' names. Mary, who had a "fragrance like a flower," for example, was obviously marijuana. Ally, short for alcohol, "always kept me happy." Evie, who "make me feel all fuzzy inside," was none other than ecstasy, while Lucy, "so fly, she should be in the sky with diamonds," was a Beatles reference to LSD. DOOM ingeniously weaved them all together into a clever narrative, not forgetting Cookie, a white girl from Colombia, who "helped me get money," an obvious allusion to cocaine.

Due to a slight tempo change in the track, however, Horwitz had to ask DOOM to re-record his vocals, for which the rapper demanded additional funds. As an alternative fix, he ended up resampling the entire acapella into his MPC and punching it in, verse by verse, over the track with DOOM's supervision. It was February 2002. Coincidentally, Agoston stopped by the studio to meet DOOM in person for the first time that very same day.

When the fourteen-track *T.H.C., Vol. 1* was released at the end of April 2002, the label sponsored an eleven-city tour of the East Coast and Canada to help promote it, featuring several of the artists who had contributed. DOOM, however, couldn't make it. Though the album was well received, sales of physical records, in general, were starting to take a hit due to the encroachment of illegal digital downloading. After dropping several other releases, including compilations of stoner rock and reggae, High Times Records was finding it hard to hang in a business so rapidly changing. They eventually folded in 2004, but not before putting out *Volume 2* of DOOM's *Special Herbs* series (released with the first volume as a bonus), thanks to Horwitz's efforts.

The experience of acting as A&R and assembling a whole record from start to finish had proved an ideal fit for Horwitz, influencing his decision to start his own label, Nature Sounds. He announced the new venture with a 2003 compilation called *Nature Sounds Presents The Prof. in... Convexed*, featuring him laying down beats for the likes of Aesop Rock, Sean Price, and Masta Killa. "All Outta Ale" appeared on that debut release, as well as another track featuring DOOM called "Bells of DOOM." For the price of a new pair of New Balance sneakers, Horwitz was even able to convince DOOM to appear in a suitably no-budget video for "My Favorite Ladies," made by a start-up production company called Greenpoint Pictures, who leased office space in the same building as Nature Sounds in rapidly gentrifying Williamsburg, Brooklyn.

"Ultimately Devin ended up putting out most of the *Special Herbs* stuff," says Agoston. "So, at first, you know, that kind of upset me 'cause I thought it was like our project," referring to him and DOOM. "But then, we all became like a friend group, and I got over myself and realized that this is just like kind of a lesson in working with DOOM," he says, chuckling. "And it was like an important lesson to learn. I was just grateful that we did not only the first one, but I ended up doing another volume, too, volume three."

Released in pairs (i.e., 1&2, 3&4, etc.) between 2001 and 2005, the *Special Herbs* series proved to be a consistent seller that appeared in many incarnations. After the High Times release of *Volume 2*, Nature Sounds took over the series from *Volume 3* (releasing the vinyl version, while Agoston did the CD) through *Volume 6*. Then DOOM gave his friend John Robinson of Scienz of Life the opportunity to release *Volumes 7–10* on his independent Shaman Work imprint. Following these initial runs, Nature Sounds returned to reissue the entire series with different cover art. Originally, *Volumes 1–6* pilfered the frames of Fantastic Four comics for covers—for example, Doctor Doom's metal hands on a keyboard (*Volumes 5&6*)—prompting Marvel to issue a cease-and-desist order.

For DOOM, the series began as an outlet to release beats that he didn't use in any other context, but morphed into a library from which he could draw material for projects as needed. Both *Special Blends 1 + 2*, a kind of mixtape featuring DOOM beats matched with acapellas from such artists as MOP, Ghostface, Jeru the Damaja, and Mobb Deep, and *Special Herbs & Spices*, the same concept except with Grimm handling all lyrical duties, were spun off from this series. Plenty of double dipping occured as well. Individual tracks like "Orris Root Powder (sometimes appearing as "Orris Foot Powder") from *Special Herbs 9&0*, for example, based on borrowed orchestral strings from Arthur Verocai's "Na Boca Do Sol" (Continental, 1972), was used in no less than four other songs—including "Black Gold" by John Robinson, "Monsters" by DOOM and Trunks, Masta Ace's "In Da Spot," and "Rhythm N Poetry" by Hell Razah. This recycling of beats became somewhat problematic when DOOM started submitting the same work to different labels, but he didn't care in the least, just as he exhibited zero concerns over sampling.

Though some of his source material tended to be very well-known or recognizable, he released it regardless without clearances—obviously an issue that the small labels with whom he partnered didn't bother about either. "Black Snake Root" from *Special Herbs, Volumes 5&6*, for example, sampled the funky riff from Boz Scagg's "Lowdown" (Columbia, 1976), a Top 40 pop hit. "Mandrake," from *Special Herbs, Volumes 7&8*, was based on the well-known piano riff from the Doobie Brothers' hit "What a Fool Believes" (Warner Bros., 1978). DOOM probably assumed that he was too far below the radar for anyone to take notice, but as his reputation grew in stature, it's amazing in retrospect that no one came after him for copyright infringement.

Taken in its entirety, the ten-disc set, with a running time of over six hours, offered a great overview of DOOM's unique production style, which, like the majority of good hip-hop, hardly reinvented the wheel. His beats were simple and straight ahead—usually no more than a two- or four-bar loop supplemented by some programmed drums. What stood out was his choice of samples, and the subtle ways in which he manipulated them. DOOM, for example, cornered the market on sampling children's TV shows, where he found hidden gems. Take the suspenseful interlude from season six, episode 130, of the seventies series *The Electric Company*, used for "Fo Ti" (*Special Herbs, Volumes 7&8*). To supplement such samples, he often played the drum machine live, never using the quantize function, which would have put everything he played directly on the beat. His drums, therefore, always have a looser feel.

Sometimes he dispensed with additional programming entirely and just sampled various parts of the same song into his MPC that he played live on the pads. In "Lavender Buds," from *Special Herbs, Volumes 5&6*, he took vocal and piano parts from the Blackbyrds' "April Showers" (Fantasy, 1974) and essentially made his own remix of the song. On other occasions, such as on "Valerian Root," from the same disc, he finger-played a kick and snare from the MPC over the entire song, a loop of New Birth's "Do It Again" (RCA/Victor, 1974), adding variation and a live feel to a sampled production. But double-dipping was always an issue, as he used the same beat for "Emblica Officinalis" from *Volume 7&8*.

Though *Special Herbs* couldn't claim to be the first dedicated example of instrumental hip-hop—DJ Shadow's *Endtroducing.....* (Mo' Wax, 1996) and Prince Paul's *Psychoanalysis: What is it?* (WordSound, 1996) paved the way—it seemed to anticipate an explosion of interest in lo-fi beats in the early aughts. Other bedroom producers were obviously influenced by DOOM's very basic approach to beat-making and felt empowered to have a go as well. Considering DOOM went against the grain, sampling what others wouldn't—predominantly cheesy eighties and nineties R&B, smooth jazz, children's TV shows, movie soundtracks, infomercials, and canned Muzak—the *Special Herbs* series could also be seen as anticipating the development of vaporwave, a microgenre of electronic music popular in the 2010s that used these same sample sources that DOOM helped popularize, but manipulated to bizarre effect. Apparently, DOOM's metal fingers were planted firmly on the pulse of what was happening.

15

KING GEEDORAH/*TAKE ME TO YOUR LEADER*

Out of suffering have emerged the strongest souls; the most massive characters are seared with scars.

—KHALIL GIBRAN

"He definitely had some demons that he was fighting, but it seemed that they were beginning to tame over the time that I knew him and was seeing him in New York during that era of 2000–2003," says Peter Lupoff of Sub Verse. "I think he was in a good relationship and was with somebody very supportive, and I think that gave him a really good foundation. And eventually I think that helped with DOOM's persistence and continued successes after Sub Verse, and he matured into recognizing that."

Lupoff is, of course, referring to DOOM's wife Jasmine Thomas, a truly silent partner and even fiercer advocate of his privacy, who helped him get his life and business in order. She was the reason he went to Georgia in the first place, trading the nonstop hustle of New York for the small-town comfort of Kennesaw (population 33,036), where the pace of life flowed slower than molasses. As a guy living on the edge and trying to raise a young son, he was lucky to have found her. In early 2002, Jasmine was responsible for setting up Metal Face Records LLC, as an outlet to release or reissue his music. After years of friends or random fans filling the role, she eventually became his manager, establishing Dogfoot Management LLC in 2006 and DOOM's official Gas Drawls website later in 2011. More recently, of course, she maintained his social media presence on Twitter and Instagram, from which DOOM's passing was subsequently announced.

But beyond handling his business concerns, she offered a stabilizing influence, making a comfortable home for DOOM and his son, where he could focus on his creativity without all the other distractions that came with basic survival. He had certainly earned as much. Here, he could lay down the mask and just be himself—balding, bespectacled, and now boasting a prominent beer belly. The last place you'd expect to find the Villain was chilling in a two-bedroom suburban townhouse under sunny Georgia skies. In the large, unfinished basement, beneath harsh fluorescent lights, DOOM set up his lab on an OfficeMax desk.

Cocooned from the concerns and demands of the outside world, he remained fully engaged in his craft, staying busy on a variety of projects. Hustle and good fortune had put a lot on his plate, including Grimm's *The Downfall of Ibliys* album, the Monsta Island Czars project, and *Special Herbs*. Additionally, he was doing one-offs and guest spots—for fellow Atlanta rapper Count Bass D (Dwight Farrell), the High Times compilation, and making an appearance on Prefuse 73's debut for the well-respected UK label Warp. Prefuse 73's "Black List," featuring DOOM and Aesop Rock, appeared on *Vocal Studies and Uprock Narratives* (2001), an album that veered more toward electronic music than hip-hop, but helped introduce DOOM to a whole new audience overseas. Capitalizing on any opportunity that came his way, he expanded his influence organically.

While producing Grimm's album, he most often worked at Bigg Jus's studio, which he found preferable to his own. Jus, at the time, was using an Ensoniq Paris pro system, a digital audio workstation on par with his former Roland VS-1880. It combined software and hardware into an all-inclusive unit that allowed recording, editing, and mixing. "Since I worked with him more in the capacity of an engineer when he recorded on my system, that's the part I probably honor the most," says Jus. "He was very straightforward in what he wanted to do. He was very B-boy about what he wanted, and he was just on point—wasn't nothing odd or out the ordinary. And that's the thing that I honor the most, we was just regular, straight up B-boys working on shit together, not having to get too bent or anything like that." At the same time, he adds, "Now I have seen him, doing shows together, drink a half a bottle of Jack Daniel's, straight to the head at six in the morning." Those closest to DOOM, who were privy to his drinking, tended not to make an issue about it. But when pressed, many have classified him as a functional alcoholic based on his dependence—despite the fact he remained productive. Drinking was a problem lurking in plain sight that would eventually catch up to him.

DOOM's shortcomings in other areas became plainly apparent as well. "He didn't have a grasp on his business affairs, and he let a lot of fuckin' fans do a lot of the legwork for him," says Jus. "He always had people working to push projects, someone who was like an unofficial manager, like a super fan who was doing work for him. I'll just leave it at that. It's the brilliance of his villainy." Pressed to elaborate, he only says, "If you think about it, he literally was thinking like a villain, like a comic-book villain. The way sometimes he had people do things and the way he organized what he needed to be done, it was kind of like a comic-book villain. And I want to acknowledge the brilliance of that." Certainly, lingering behind the affable image he projected, DOOM's powers of manipulation were persuasive as he sometimes resembled a puppet master, pulling the strings.

For Jus, however, "He was more like my badass brother." He says he bonded with DOOM over the fact that they were both former graf writers, whom he describes as being "advanced motherfuckers" because they took risks while always staying ahead of the curve. "There's a lot of shit I can't really say," Jus admits. "He was just an advanced dude, but he was into shit that I couldn't get into. I was busy trying to run a label and shit like that. I couldn't, you know, deal with most of the stuff that the artists were doing 'cause I had to kind of keep a straight focus. Other than that, he was a completely genuine, nice, down to earth, humble dude, who, you know, was much wilder in his earlier years than he was kind of later." Jus's evasiveness when it comes to sharing certain information about his friend reveals as much about the loyalty DOOM inspired—especially among his inner circle, who were uber-protective of his cherished privacy. But it's not difficult to read between the lines. "Did he do regular other shit that entertainers do when they get famous?" Jus poses rhetorically, "Yes, he did all of that. I don't consider that villainous either. I don't know what you call that."

Another artist, who had a chance to get up close and personal with DOOM in Atlanta, was John Robinson (aka Lil' Sci) of Scienz of Life. After leaving the Newnan loft and looking for new digs, he was invited to stay at DOOM's place, where he remained for almost two months. "It was epic because, you know, I got to really see a lot of the creative process that normally I wouldn't," he recalls. "For real, there's a method to the madness." Something that struck Robinson, for example, were the shingles of sticky notes covering DOOM's studio walls, containing couplets like "Chinese slippers / Guyanese strippers," or sometimes longer parts. He wasn't sure of their purpose until they collaborated on the song "Yikes" from Scienz's second album for Sub Verse, *Project Overground: The Scienz Experiment* (2002).

"We almost didn't do it," says Robinson of the collaboration. "We were headed to New York touring, and he was like, 'Yo, I'll just do it when y'all get back.' And we was like, 'No, we can't. We're going to master the album while we're in New York.' And he's like, 'All right.' And then I just decided, you know what, let's take a ride." While the group took a trip to the store, DOOM vibed out with the track. Robinson says, "By the time we got back, he had some new part of a verse written. He started taking things off the wall of sticky notes and, boom, the verse was ready to go. And [he] spit it. Maybe one or two takes. And we were like, 'Yep, this is it.' Let's go." Having recorded DOOM's verse directly into their Roland VS-1880, they headed off to New York, and "Yikes" became one of the standout cuts on the album.

"DOOM jokingly said to me one time, you know, when *Special Herbs* was moving and just all this music was coming out and everyone's like, ah, man DOOM is crazy prolific," Robinson recalls, "He said to me like, 'Yo Sci, I'm lazy as hell with this shit. I just had a lot of music stacked. Not for nothing, I do this all the time, you know?' And he's just laughing, but I loved his work ethic because it was intentional, you know? His process was literally like, yo, make a little bit of the beat and just let that play and walk away from it."

DOOM told him: *I might go play a video game. I might go cook some food. I might sweep or mop the floor. You know, I might read while that shit is playing, or I might turn it off and go do something else and then come back to it and add to it.*

"It was this nice, consistent, slow bake where it was like, oh shit, I see the build. And I like the fact that there's no rush. I'm not rushing. I'm letting the vibe carry the creation, you know?" says Robinson. "He said, 'This is kind of how I do it. Like for real, you know,' And that was dope to see. And it made sense to me."

Once, while he quickly needle-skipped through an album looking for possible samples, DOOM started laughing at him. *Bro, you sampling 20 seconds into the record, like play the record. How you know it ain't something dope in the middle. How you know it ain't a bridge at the end that you could flip. Yo, just play the song, light something up, and just chill and listen to that shit. It's the least you could do.* Once again, Robinson took such advice to heart.

DOOM also offered him some tips on rhyming: *No ad-libs. I'm rhyming to the whole world in a room sitting in the chair right across from one person at a time, basically. So, when the people are hearing it, they're hearing me. People don't speak with ad-libs. You don't have two voices and all these crazy effects. That's cool for live performance and club shit. But it's like, yo, when people are listening and taking in this experience, I like to keep it conversational—no ad-libs.*

The man of many aliases eventually convinced Robinson to do a project under his government name called *Who Is This Man?* (High Water Music, 2008). "Just to create another lane," he says. *Yo, you're doing business already under that name. People know the Scienz of Life and Sci. It just creates a different mystique. You know, it won't take away. It'll only grow.*

During Robinson's stay with the Villain, they made the song "Next Levels," featuring himself; his brother, ID 4 Windz; and Atlanta-based Stahhr the

Femcee. DOOM used to watch and tape all kinds of late-night cable, including a BET show that aired in the 90s called *Jazz Impressions*. The show's smooth-jazz title theme—a mellow horn-piano-and-upright-bass riff—was just the kind of sonic source he loved. Besides its slight cheese factor, the theme's origins were opaque and its composers unknown—criteria that made it hard to trace by the sample police. Many years later, however, a fan from the Netherlands successfully tracked down its source, which DOOM also used as the basis for "Arrow Root" on *Special Herbs, Volumes 1&2*.

"One of DOOM's favorite quotes was, 'It's all about the rec,'" says Robinson. "And what that means is like, 'Yo, it don't matter what I look like or what I got on, if I got a big chain on or not. Is that shit [the music] dope, period? It's all about the rec[ognition].' And you know, that was one of the things that was the standard." He also adds, "And another thing, how he moved, period, was on a need-to-know basis." Obsessively private, DOOM avoided signaling his moves in advance or even letting anyone know what he was up to at any given time. As the advent of social media coaxed everyone—including celebrities—to constantly share the minutiae of their lives, DOOM went in the opposite direction, thereby enhancing his mystique.

"Paid in Full" (4th & B'way/Island, 1987), the fifth single off Eric B. & Rakim's game-changing debut of the same name, became one of the first rap singles to cross over to the clubs, laying the blueprint for a fusion that has grown even stronger today. The runaway success of that song started in Europe thanks to the "Seven Minutes of Madness" remix by a young, up and coming British duo known as Coldcut. Matt Black, an ex-computer programmer and Oxford-educated biochemist, and his partner, Jonathan More, a former art teacher and silversmith, had met while deejaying on pirate radio. They were quickly thrust into the ranks of hot producers thanks to their audio collage/cut-up technique that blended vocal snippets from TV and film along with scratching and additional samples, like the sublime hook by Israeli singer Ofra Haza.

Taking full advantage of the newfound attention to produce pop artists like Yazz and Lisa Stansfield, the duo really fancied themselves as funk renegades, who didn't have much respect for the mainstream music industry. To show their commitment to more underground and left field sounds that they and their friends were producing, they started their own independent label, Ninja Tune, in 1990. No doubt, their early beat experiments—for example, the five volumes of DJ Food's *Jazz Brakes* series that included some of the first instrumental hip-hop—made them mavericks in the trip-hop scene that emerged in the UK in the early part of the decade. Their ambitious creative vision and consistency have also made the label one of the most successful and longest-enduring independents.

About a year after Ninja Tune was up and running in London, recent Oxford grad Will Ashon was finding his legs while on the dole (the UK's version of unemployment) in Brighton. Into music and books, he began reviewing the latter for a local publication. But his editor let him in on a little secret that has launched many a journalism career: If you ring up record labels, they'll give you free records to review. A jazz aficionado by default of his father's collection, Ashon also gravitated toward the hip-hop of the day—groups like Public Enemy, Wu-Tang Clan, De La Soul, Tribe Called Quest, and Freestyle Fellowship. He listened to UK rap, too, which he viewed as underground rap with an English accent. Serendipitously, one of the first labels he hit up for free records was Ninja Tune. With his work appearing in such UK magazines as *Hip-Hop Connection*, *Muzik*, and *True* (later *Trace*, where he served as music editor), Ashon started building a reputation as a writer.

"So, what I tended to do was I'd get an interview for *Muzik* where someone would fly me to New York and then I'd hang out and stay in New York for a bit longer and try and write something else for *Trace*," he says. "And I was really obsessed with underground hip-hop as it was called. I used to come to New York, and I'd go to Bobbito's store at the time and admire all the T-shirts and buy the twelve-inches." On one such trip he was introduced to the music of DOOM, who he was surprised to discover was Zev Love X from KMD, with whom he was already familiar.

At one point, Ashon realized that some of the music he would pick up on his travels and write about was not available in the UK. He came across plenty of homegrown artists bubbling beneath the surface who deserved exposure as well. "So, that was why I went to Ninja Tune and asked them if they'd be interested in doing something," he says. Peter Quicke, who still runs the label, agreed to start off by releasing a few singles. Between 1997 and 1998, the first twelve-inch releases by English rappers Alpha Prhyme (aka Juice Aleem) and Gemini Twins, followed by American artists Abstract Rude and Saul Williams, dropped on the newly formed Big Dada Recordings, a subsidiary of Ninja Tune.

"To be honest, I wasn't expecting to make any money on it," says Ashon. "I was doing it because I wanted to put out records. I wanted to be involved. There was all this exciting music. So, I'm not even sure we had a proper deal at first, but I think once we moved to albums, the deal was, we'll give you a split of the profits because all Ninja's deals with their artists were profit split deals."

By the time Ashon released Big Dada's first album—the rap ragga dub classic *Brand New Second Hand* (1999) by Roots Manuva—he was still a freelance writer, doing the label thing on the side. Then two things happened to change his status: he lost his main gig as music editor when *Trace* relocated to New York, and his first daughter was born. Meanwhile, the Roots Manuva album kept selling until it reached an astonishing sixty thousand copies in the UK alone, garnering stellar reviews along the way. Its success propelled Big Dada into becoming a recognized name in the indie rap game. Banking on his good ear and instincts, Ashon finally asked Ninja Tune to put him on the payroll.

Around the end of 2000 or beginning of 2001, he received a random call from the states from someone he didn't know—most likely Big Benn Klingon. "He said he was managing DOOM, and would I be interested in doing a record? I said, 'Fuck, yeah, I'd love to do a record. Absolutely,'" he recalls. "'This is how much money we've got.'" Ashon offered an advance of $20,000, the going rate for projects released on the label. "They came back and said, 'Look, DOOM says he can't do it for that. It's not enough money, but he could do a King Geedorah record for that amount of money,'" he says. "Throughout the whole time I ran Big Dada, it was a problem that American artists obviously came from a bigger market and a market where hip hop was more established, and they wanted more money." Though he really had no idea who this King Geedorah geezer was, Ashon agreed to sign him.

"Geedorah is an interesting character, you know. I mean the whole direction of Geedorah is like, OK, he's not even from Earth, he's from outer space. And he channels the information to DOOM in order for DOOM to produce or what not," DOOM told an audience at the Red Bull Music Academy in Barcelona in 2011. "He just straight reptilian. Like he would be like a three-hundred-foot, three-headed dragon, like golden. He's actually from the Godzilla films, so, again, it's like the villain theme—the bad guy. Geedorah's like the classic bad guy."[1]

While rappers like Kool Keith popularized the use of multiple aliases, DOOM took it to a whole new level of surrealism. If a Black Elvis wasn't high concept enough, how about a giant reptilian creature from outer space? It all seemed like a bit much—even though everyone did fall for the mask. But at least DOOM did his research, not only assuming the name, but fully inhabiting the character by creating a revisionist narrative of the celluloid version. Though he doesn't take it at all seriously, he lays the bait for us to—another measure of his villainy—as we scramble to fathom what Geedorah is all about.

For DOOM, it's all purely metaphorical. "If you really look at it," he observed, "Geedorah is really stronger than all of them, but he's still that oddball, you know what I'm sayin'?"[2] It's a telling quote in that the qualities that attracted him to the character in the first place—strength and weirdness—could apply to DOOM himself. Monsta Island connection aside, his whole purpose in developing a new character was to offer a fresh perspective, which he probably did as much for his own entertainment as for everybody else's.

"Coming from one particular character all the time makes the story, to me, boring," DOOM explained. "I get that mainly from novels and that style of writing, or movies, you know, where there's multiple characters to carry the storyline. This way I could come from one point of view, [then] another point of view, and they might even disagree on certain things."[3] This schizophrenic approach put him in a class of his own among MCs since not even Kool Keith rapped in the third person. Now DOOM had the gall to channel a fictional monster. Though a huge departure, to say the least, it was probably only something he could pull off.

DOOM, of course, did nothing for the hell of it, so there were practical considerations behind his decision. Releasing this project under a different alias freed him up from the expectation of carrying most of the lyrical duties, so he could focus more on production. Indeed, of the album's thirteen tracks, he only raps on five of them—two as MF DOOM—much to fans' dismay. Following, as it did, on the heels of the Monsta Island release, he showcased group members Jet Jaguar, Gigan, Biolante (Kurious), and Rodan, but also featured several newcomers—including Trunks, who makes a cameo on "Lockjaw," and Hassan Chop, another New York transplant living in Atlanta, who made his debut on the poignant "I Wonder." While juggling other projects such as Viktor Vaughn and *Mm.. Food*, the follow-up to *Operation: Doomsday*, DOOM proceeded at his own unharried pace. If there was a deadline to turn in the album, someone forgot to give him the memo.

"So, I found a string of emails of me going, 'Hey man, how's it going? How are you getting on?' And then I'd get a one-line email back saying 'I'm on the road, man, you know? Yeah, I'll get back to you when I'm back in New York. It's all coming along great.' And that was the process—this long gap of me chasing [him]," according to Ashon. "But basically, what then happened was that I would occasionally get a CD-R through the post, just with King Geedorah written on it, in, like, Sharpie, spelled differently every time. Nothing else in the envelope." The CD-Rs were the cheap kind that cracked easily, and each contained only two or three tracks. Ashon recalls receiving at least three or four of these over the course of about a year and a half.

"I mean it was a short album anyway because I think he kind of ran out of steam on it," says Ashon, who believes DOOM put the minimum effort into making this album happen. "But the beauty of the Geedorah record was that we put everything that we had on there 'cause that was everything that he gave us." The final running time clocked in at a spare forty-two minutes, which also meant it fit onto a single vinyl. "To me that felt like the perfect length for an album. That's the length at which you leave it, and you leave it wanting more," says Ashon. But it came at a time when most of the artists he dealt with liked to max out their releases, using the full seventy-four minutes that fit onto a CD. DOOM, of course, had to be different.

"I think he just sent me the tracks. I got it mastered. I put it in an order that I thought worked. I sent it over to him and he said, 'Yeah, sure,'" according to Ashon. "I don't know what he's been like on other projects, but it never felt like he was completely engaged. And I always felt that was because I was always slightly paranoid that we hadn't paid him much money and it was just some silly label in England that he wasn't that invested in it. But maybe he was like this with all the records he made." The fact that both parties had an ocean physically separating them probably made it feel that way.

Says Ashon, "It was probably one of the most long-distance releases I've ever done in terms of the amount of contact I had with DOOM, because he was hard to get a hold of, but that kind of added to the romance for me because it played into the whole kind of mystery of MF DOOM, you know, the mask and everything." At the same time, he concedes, "I was always worried throughout the whole time that he was never gonna deliver the record because I always felt like I didn't really know him. I'd never met him. I don't think at that point he had a manager, or the manager had changed." But DOOM wasn't the type to leave money on the table.

"My favorite story is there's the line where he says—it's the end of one of the tracks—but he said something like 'no homo,' and I remember being really worried about this, really uncomfortable," says Ashon. He's referring to an audio collage at the end of "The Fine Print," where a voice says, "Are you a homo . . . we help thousands of homos every month." DOOM snagged it from a late-night infomercial that actually says "homeowner," but the last part drops out. "So, I rang DOOM up and said, I'm a bit worried about this," says Ashon. "And he said, 'But, Will, it's a giant three-headed lizard. He's talking about Homo sapiens. (Cue the laugh track.)'

"And I was like, 'Oh shit, yeah.' And that was the moment where I thought, okay, DOOM's really got into character as a three-headed giant lizard. And when he says this, he means no Homo sapiens. And even if it wasn't true, just to say this off the bat just seemed so clever and so brilliant to me. I was just like, oh, okay. Yeah, I can live with that."

"Long story short, the King Geedorah album is from television," says John Robinson, who was around during its making and saw it all come together. "All the samples are from TV. And creating it was a slow bake." Sure enough, eight of the album's thirteen tracks were built on loops from obscure TV themes or movie soundtracks. The cheesy strings from the opener, "Fazers," for example, came from a porn movie. "An old ass porno with some skinny dude in cowboy boots, like '79," according to DOOM, who added, "But right there is that loop with the violins. I'm like, 'Ooh, that shit is sweet.'"[4] It was just the kind of syrup that he liked to douse his tracks with. DOOM was gracious enough to give his friend E. Mason the only co-production credit on the album for finding that sample and helping him program the drums beneath it. But lyrically, he owned the track, breaking in his new persona like a pair of sneakers fresh out the box.

> *King Geedorah, Take me to your leader,*
> *Quick to claim that he not no snake, like "me neither,"*
> *They need to take a breather,*
> *He been rhyming longer than Sigmund the sea creature*
> *Been on Saturday feature,*
> *Pleased to meet ya.*

Channeling Geedorah with an arcane reference to a children's series from the seventies, DOOM's internal rhyming and alliteration game was just getting started. With deadpan wit and tongue planted firmly in cheek, he offers his revisionist take on Godzilla's arch nemesis as, "His own biggest fan / And got a fan base as big as Japan." Despite the big conceit we're all supposed to swallow, DOOM sometimes blurs the line between personalities, declaring, "Half up front, half upon mastering / Would you like that in cash? / Last thing you should ask the King," a mantra that he lived by. Regardless, Geedorah bangs harder than some skinny dude with cowboy boots could.

Unfortunately, after such a promising start, the reptilian star of the show returns only twice more—on "No Snakes Alive" and "The Fine Print." The former track, featuring Jet Jaguar and Rodan, originally appeared on the *MF EP* (Brick Records, 2000). But DOOM, no doubt, felt that the song's warped groove that sped up halfway through—lifted directly from a scene from *Godzilla vs. Megalon* (English dub, 1973)—justified a revisit. All three MCs slay the track with distinctly different styles and flow, but DOOM's effortless humor always wins the day. He says, "Sort of mellow type fellow / Who sometimes spaz on wife like Othello / Hell no, he won't use words like Illuminati / Or Gotti or shotty, he might use karate," slipping out of character again to demonstrate the contradictions in his own personality with a Shakespeare allusion, before declaring that he would never use the clichés that most rappers do.

If Geedorah's appearances on the album were few and far between, the rapper made only two cameos as DOOM. The lead single, "Anti-Matter," was the first of two collaborations that he did over his career with the enigmatic Mr. Fantastik. As fiercely private and guarded a person as DOOM, everything we know about this part-time MC comes directly from his rhymes. "I get the cash, take niggas out like trash / Known to stack a mean stash, they used to call me Pure Math / Back in the days, all I did was stay paid," Fantastik raps over a guitar and bass-driven groove from the Whatnauts' "Message from a Black Man" (Stang, 1970). Based on his own description—along with other lines like "Feds try to creep me, somehow always miss me"—he comes off like a drug dealer who's trying to keep his identity a secret, while rapping for the fun of it. Whatever the case, he is obviously the same Pure Mathematics—a righteous Five Percenter name, incidentally—whom DOOM shouted out at the end of "Go with the Flow" and said he had met at an arms deal on "Deep Fried Frenz." DOOM's only other cameo is on "The Final Hour," a forty-nine-second track that samples the soundtrack to *Dark Shadows*, a popular sixties show that dealt with the supernatural.

Not letting the eerie music go to waste, however, DOOM reprises it on "Take Me to Your Leader," one of three skits featuring DOOM's trademark aural collages, constructed of snippets from vintage Merrie Melodies cartoons and *Fist of the North Star*, a Japanese manga. On "Monster Zero," he attempts to explain the origin story of King Geedorah via sampled dialogue from the films *Godzilla vs. King Ghidorah* (1991), *Invasion of Astro-Monster* (1965), and *Ghidorah, the Three-Headed Monster* (1964) as well assorted bits from *The Twilight Zone, Star Trek*, and CNN. The final collage, "One Smart Nigger," which reprises the *Stone Killer* theme (Cinephile, 1973) used on "Lockjaw," is a darkly comic critique of racism that sounds like it could have been an outtake from KMD's *Black Bastards* album.

"It was just ill, you know, where he's painting these pictures with different vocal samples," says Robinson. "If you really listen, it's so meticulous and intentional down to every little word. Like it's not just, 'Oh, I just put this on 'cause it's DOOM talking, and it sounds cool.' It's like, no, listen to what he's saying. 'Cause he's explaining the mission, you know." This technique worked well on *Operation: Doomsday* to define the character of DOOM. In this case, however, those not previously acquainted with the Godzilla franchise might be scratching their heads as to what was going on conceptually with this album.

"It's like an ongoing process," said DOOM, discussing his audio collages. "Sometimes it's months of gathering pieces, you know? Sometimes I leave it alone for a few months and I'll come back to it and find that one last piece that it needed. I mean when it's done, I'll just know it's done by—it'll be full. But I could really work on it forever."[5]

The label had to push back the release date a couple times because the album just wasn't ready. When it was finally mastered by Big Dada, DOOM did not approve—twice—finally remastering it himself, which contributed to further delays. King Geedorah / *Take Me to Your Leader* finally arrived on June 17, 2003, almost two and a half years after its inception.

Though it may have seemed like forever for DOOM to deliver the album, for Ashon the wait was worth it. "It was just brilliant. If you were gonna go gritty, if you were gonna go underground, this was it. This was the real deal," he says, grateful for the experience of working with DOOM. "It turned out to have been probably one of the most consistently selling records we ever put out. It just went and went. It's another one of those things that without a huge amount of fanfare we put out and it just rolled and rolled and rolled, you know, which is kind of like the holy grail for any small label—a record that just keeps selling."

The record did so well that Big Dada wanted to exercise their right, per contract, to option DOOM's next release as King Geedorah. By that time, however, he had blown up, and wanted much more money, according to Ashon, so a follow-up was shelved. Perhaps that's another reason why DOOM never again revisited the giant reptile from outer space, who was technically signed to Big Dada. It's indicative of his mercenary nature to never be too firmly attached to the characters he created. But, at the same time, DOOM's imagination seemed like a bottomless well at this point, with no shortage of other projects and personas to keep him busy.

16

VIKTOR VAUGHN / *VAUDEVILLE VILLAIN*

One power alone makes a poet: Imagination. The Divine Vision.

—WILLIAM BLAKE

It's April 30, 2001—Monday night at Fluid, where a voracious crowd of two hundred packs the small South Fourth Street hot spot to see MF DOOM's first throwdown in the gritty city that birthed another celebrated underdog, Rocky. Metal face gleaming under the lights, he's ripping it up beside the small DJ booth where Rich Medina and Cosmo Baker, the night's promoters, hold court. Big Benn Klingon, DOOM's unofficial manager/hype man, hangs out as well. As DOOM delivers a hype performance, the crowd responds in kind, parroting his rhymes like karaoke. But the show's flow is marred by a gaggle of hecklers at the back, who start taunting him after the second song. *Yo! That shit sucks! Fuck you!* Probably just some rabble rousers from neighboring Camden, New Jersey, DOOM ignores them and skates through his set. But the jeering persists. Finally, after about the seventh or eighth song, the Villain has had enough.

"Yo! Stop the music!" he commands in a booming voice of thunder. Turning to Klingon, he points at the hecklers, yelling, "Get 'em!" The former gridiron giant bounds off stage with a quickness that belies his size, beelining toward the offending party as the crowd parts like the Red Sea. An arm the girth of a Burmese python wraps around one of the hecklers' necks as Klingon wrangles him out of the club. Stunned, the guy's friends follow, as does OP Miller, Sub

Verse's label manager, who has accompanied DOOM on this road trip. Even DOOM jumps offstage and makes his way outside, but not before stashing the mask in its metal attaché case.

"It's a mess," observes Miller. "I get outside. Ben has this dude still yoked up in a headlock, and the dude looks like he's about to die—like he was basically kinda gasping for air. His boys are starting to come after Ben to try to get him off, and as they come out, DOOM comes outside, and he has the metal attaché case in his hand." One of the guys instantly runs up on the Villain. "And as he comes," Miller continues, "DOOM swings up, hits the guy; comes back down, hits him again; and hits him a third time and knocks him out. All the dudes are now just like shook 'cause the one guy's in the headlock; one guy's knocked out. They're all kind of like, 'What do we do?' And then finally security kind of comes and starts breaking stuff up." DOOM and Klingon, meanwhile, hop into the Enterprise rental vehicle and disappear into the night.

"The way creativity works for me, it comes to you like it's an energy stream or it comes in waves kinda," DOOM once explained. "So, you just gotta be ready for the wave when it come. And when it subsides and go back, that's when you step back for a second."[1] Between 2001 and 2005, he was pretty much riding a tsunami of creativity, juggling no less than four albums simultaneously. "I'm constantly working," he said during that period. "It's a never-ending battle goin' on and on and on, unfolding."[2] Yet his well of creativity ran deep, and the fruits of his hustle produced such memorable characters as King Geedorah and, of course, Viktor Vaughn, who were not your average MCs.

"Viktor's a young cat, maybe he's 19 or 20 years old," DOOM explained of his new alias, a sort of prequel to DOOM. "He's full of spunk type thing and real witty with his. Music is his thing, too. Hip-hop, of course. That's the one thing all the characters have in common is their love for hip-hop music. So, Viktor he's more of an MC guy—no real political agenda. In a lot of ways, he's coming from the same direction as the average cat on the street who rhyme."[3] The character he was describing could have easily been a younger version of himself, with a twist. "How he differs from the average MC, or the average soloist is in the fact that he's from another dimension totally—like an alternative universe," DOOM explained quite seriously. "It's more like, you know, Superman he's on Earth, but then Bizarro is like Superman's equivalent in another twisted universe type thing. So, Vik is like from that other twisted universe which is similar to Earth but not quite."[4]

Playing off his Marvel alter ego's origin story, Viktor Vaughn was nothing more than a corruption of Victor Von Doom, who transformed into Doctor Doom when his scientific experiments went awry, scarring his face and forcing him to don the metal suit and mask. In the comic books, the good doctor also invented a time machine, which DOOM incorporated into Viktor's story, saying he was temporarily Earth-bound due to the machine's malfunction. To pass the time, he hooked up with some Earthlings and ended up releasing an album—because, what else would a stranded time traveler who was into hip-hop do? Other than such nuances of character, DOOM described Viktor as being a normal fellow, "Into the girls, he's into just b-boying around. His album is in that field. He drop [lyrics] about high school or, you know, just hanging out."[5] In this regard, he sounded suspiciously like the hedonistic, trouble-prone Bobby Digital alter ego that RZA created in 1998 to channel his younger self's preoccupation with partying and bullshit.

But coming on the heels of King Geedorah, Viktor Vaughn represented the extended rollout of DOOM's own multiverse. Inspired by the Marvel model where various characters across different stories sometimes interacted with each other, he hatched an ambitious plan to do the same. He signaled as much, as early as the second Fondle 'Em twelve-inch, on which King Ghidra featured on the A-side, "Operation Greenbacks," while the B-side's "Go with the Flow" was credited to MF DOOM. He even admitted, "To me, everything just flows better when I got multiple characters portraying the story."[6] Aside from introducing a new persona, the *Vaudeville Villain* album represented a real departure for DOOM, as the first project that he did not produce. "It was a breath of fresh air to just really be the MC and not the producer this particular time," he said. "I could concentrate strictly on the rhymes and concepts."[7] As the first fully collaborative project that DOOM ever worked on, it also provided a template for his future output.

The cultural mecca of New York has long been a magnet for art school graduates, but for Max Lawrence and his friends from the Rhode Island School of Design, Philadelphia seemed like the better option. With gentrification gobbling up affordable housing in the late nineties, where else could you rent five thousand square feet for only $1,000 a month? Lawrence and crew established their very own slacker's paradise on the second and third floors of an old industrial building in Philly's Chinatown, which they dubbed Space 1026. "We built a gallery and a halfpipe and all kind of lived there. There was just a bunch of us, like straight nerds, you know, and all of our records. And we did monthly shows of people's artwork and music events and stuff like that," he fondly recalls. Embodying a staunchly anti-corporate, punk-rock, DIY aesthetic, he credits a similar organization in Providence called Fort Thunder, several of whose members went on to prominence in the art world, for providing the inspiration.

"So, in our DJ crew, we just, like, were super record nerds, like typical DJs, you know, just geeking out on record hunting and that kind of thing," Lawrence elaborates. It wasn't long before a friend introduced him to DOOM's music through the Fondle 'Em singles. Initially, he thought they sounded sloppy and haphazard, but DOOM grew on him—especially after hearing *Operation: Doomsday*, which he describes as having something earthy, organic, and honest about it.

A painter by trade, Lawrence also dabbled in production on his MPC3000. His musical tastes ran the gamut from hip-hop to punk rock, house, and electronic music, which was experiencing a breakout moment at the turn of the millennium. In 2000, he and several like-minded friends in New York decided to start their own independent record label, Sound-Ink, as an outlet for releasing their own music. Taking a page from progressive UK labels like Warp, they combined hip-hop, electronic, and more avant-garde sounds to create a unique brand of fusion. Two of the label partners, Nat Gosman and Matt McDonald, also produced music, while the third, Alex Threadgold, was about to enter law school. Pooling what limited resources they had, they started putting together a compilation that reflected their cutting-edge, eclectic tastes.

Working as a short-order cook to support himself, Lawrence caught a huge break when fellow RISD grad Shepard Fairey, of OBEY fame, introduced him to street promotions. Fairey had shot to notoriety as a street artist, making former pro wrestler Andre the Giant a cult figure by plastering his image everywhere. Street promotions involved wheat-pasting, a nineties grassroots style of marketing, as well as distributing posters, stickers, and flyers to advertise new albums or club nights. The new gig put Lawrence in contact with many record labels, and he soon worked his way up to becoming a main rep for Philly.

"So Sub Verse was sending us street team stuff," Lawrence says. "We're hitting up the old-fashioned record stores, postering, doing sniping, that whole kind of thing. And then I was like, Hey, why don't you guys have DOOM come up, do a couple in-stores and I'll set up a show for him." Through deejaying, he already knew Cosmo Baker, who along with Rich Medina, promoted a popular night at the club, Fluid. Medina had previously partnered with Bobbito Garcia in setting up a short-lived Footworks boutique in Philly. Since both he and Baker were fans of DOOM, they offered to pay him a $1,000 fee to perform.

DOOM's introduction to Philly was Space 1026, where he met Lawrence on the day of the show. "Everybody who I was associated with, we were just obsessed with him, you know what I mean?" he says. "So, he comes to our art co-op, and everybody was just kind of, like, dumbfounded." Being in a new environment around people he didn't know, DOOM acted a bit standoffish at first. His initial reaction was, *Like, dude, this shit is weird*. But it didn't take long for him to come around.

"I just think that like, everything was so goofy that was going on, and everybody was such a weirdo that I think he kind of felt like, oh, OK," says Lawrence, suggesting that the oddball MC probably felt right at home. In fact, he liked it so much he ended up coming back several more times. "I think in Philly he was able to see that it wasn't just hip hop and indie hip-hop culture that had fallen in love with him," Lawrence observes, "It was punk rock, it was DIY, it was rock 'n' roll. Everybody had, you know." DOOM's ever-widening exposure was apparently turning him into something of a freak magnet.

After checking out the space, they convened upstairs in Lawrence's studio, where DOOM's interest was instantly piqued by the sight of an MPC. "He's like, 'You make music?' And I was like, Yeah, but it's not good, dude, like, I was just very honest," says Lawrence. "But I played him this beat and he's like, 'Dude, that's dope!' This is what DOOM said to me, he's like, 'If you keep making beats like this, let's do an album together.' And I was like, OK, funny that you should mention this. I'm involved with a record label up in New York." But they didn't get too deeply into the subject as the Villain had to go and get ready for his show.

The day after his memorable Monday night performance at Fluid, DOOM and his crew returned to Space 1026 to pick up his fee. Lawrence ended up chipping in an extra $500 of his own money for the Villain to drop some lyrics on that beat he was feeling. But, first, the MC needed a little more inspiration. Though he had demolished his host's liquor stash the previous night, Lawrence went out and bought him a fifth of Grey Goose vodka and orange juice. Properly lubricated, DOOM started writing:

> *You need to be careful.*
> *Safety first.*
> *The streets ain't no joke like that.*
> *You might see him with a small attaché case.*
> *Come out cha neck,*
> *Get caught like . . . Klaow! Well then, there now.*
> *Blaow, outta nowhere, the dunce couldn't prepare for how.*

Using the previous night's events as a jump-off, he and Lawrence (aka King Honey) began their first collaboration. A couple of weeks later, DOOM returned with Kurious to add a guest verse, while recording another verse as King Ghidra to complete the track, appropriately titled "Monday Night at Fluid."

Meanwhile, a skeptical but excited Lawrence couldn't wait to drop DOOM's random proposal on his partners at Sound Ink. "I can't produce enough good stuff," he told them. "So, I'm like, we need to pull in other producers."

Childhood friend and label partner Nat Gosman, who taught audio engineering at Manhattan's Institute of Audio Research, was already involved in the production duo known as Heat Sensor (with partner Matt Schmitz). "I mean, basically, when we heard he was interested in doing an album we jumped on it because we loved him," says Gosman. "But I think at that point he was just looking for as much work as possible. And he knew that the people who loved him were like, you know, underground heads and we were making those kinds of beats and were tied into that community. So, I think it was like a smart business choice from his perspective, 'cause he saw it as a way to kind of build out his listenership."

But it wasn't all about strategic thinking, as Gosman adds, "There was like an artistic thing to it, too. I think he sensed that we were kind of doing something a little different and with Viktor Vaughn he could take some risks and get out of the kind of more traditional scope of hip-hop that he had been in. Having said that, I mean, he's always been really experimental, but he knew that he was gonna get some weird shit from us and we threw a lot of weird shit at him." With the rest of the Sound Ink team on board—Alex Threadgold, the business guy, and Matt McDonald, who produced under the alias Max Bill—they quickly came to terms with DOOM.

"I just remember him saying like, you know, for this amount, I'll do an album for you. And we were like, all right, let's see if we can get that," says Gosman. "And then we came back to him. We were like, we can do it. We paid him what he asked, and I will say that at the time it seemed reasonable. But like, in retrospect when I look at what a master he was, it was nothing." DOOM probably understood exactly who he was dealing with and adjusted his expectations accordingly. In any case, the album was never meant to be a proper MF DOOM release, since he produced and rhymed over his own beats and was already working on the follow-up to *Operation: Doomsday*.

"We really established from the beginning, what was this album, and what was he not willing to give up," says Lawrence. "And we worked within those confines. There was a clear delineation—DOOM has hooks, Viktor Vaughn does not." Up front, they also established that the record was to be fully collaborative. "And it was clear to DOOM that everybody who was involved was very much invested in him and we're not going to just let him sit at home with his Roland VS-880 and send us verses," Lawrence adds. "It was important that we were all together on these recording sessions." The fact that he wasn't toiling alone but had a whole support structure in place—unlike the Geedorah album—obviously appealed to DOOM, who sometimes found it challenging to bring projects over the finish line by himself.

Early on, Threadgold, who was tasked with securing financing for the album, had a chance to see DOOM in action at Lawrence's studio. "It was DOOM, Benn [Klingon], me, and King Honey," he says, "and Max was just playing him beats out of the MPC. And he [DOOM] said, 'I like that one. I like that one. I like that one.' And he was writing in his notebook. And, so, you can hear like studio banter in there. That whole thing happened in like a four or five-hour window."

Lawrence spliced together four different instrumentals, including one that sounded like a double-time polka beat, as DOOM worked his lyrical magic: "Rappers be on some you, you, you / Forgot who they talking to, too much pork stew / They need to not come out with nothing new / Blew the whole shit up on some, 'What this button do?'" According to Threadgold, "I just remember being in the studio with them being like, oh my God, this track is amazing, you know? And like literally watching them put it together organically." Eventually titled "Change the Beat," it became a bonus track on the Viktor Vaughn album. Meanwhile, their previous collabo, "Monday Night at Fluid," became a last-minute addition to the inaugural Sound Ink compilation, *Colapsus*, released in the summer of 2001.

"We just went into mad beat-making mode. I don't think I've ever made as many beats in [such] a short period of time," says Gosman. "We were just all so inspired by the prospect of making an album with him." According to Threadgold, "We would compile beats from Max Bill, King Honey, and Heat Sensor, and we would mail CDs to Georgia to DOOM's place. And he would pick the ones he liked and write to them. And then we would schedule him to come [to NYC]. It was not long after 9/11, so DOOM was too spooked to fly. He wouldn't fly. So, we would book him on the train, and we would pay for a rental car and Ben would drive him around.

"He had the Viktor Vaughn concept in mind already, but the way it developed, especially the science and science fiction part, was because our guys' beats were more electronic," says Threadgold. "He was like, 'Oh this is some crazy shit.' This isn't your nineties hip hop vibe, right, so that lent itself style-wise to this high concept sci-fi stuff. He was like, 'All right, this fits' because this is the sound, you know."

Despite its futuristic beats and sci-fi motifs, the album's title, *Vaudeville Villain*, had a nostalgic ring to it—apropos as a prequel to MF DOOM. Though the popular form of entertainment known as vaudeville originated in nineteenth century France, where it connoted musical farce or comedy, on export to America, it gained an association with burlesque and minstrelsy. Any performer from that era was referred to as a "vaudevillian," a term DOOM obviously corrupted to suit his own needs. Explaining his new alter ego to NPR, DOOM said, "His whole thing is tearing up the MC circuit. Where's the open mics at? Where's the little, like, down-low hip-hop clubs. That way, yunno, it ties into the whole title of the album, the *Vaudeville Villain*, similar to the vaudeville era with burlesque acts, and I kind of made it to where like it's similar to hip-hop now."[8]

As the sole member of Sound Ink who didn't produce beats, Threadgold settled into the role of helping enable DOOM's vision. "For Alex, it was like directing a movie," says Lawrence. "It was DOOM's plot, you know what I'm saying, but Alex knew how to assist. And the thing that Alex and DOOM had together was comics."

One of the first things Threadgold did was buy everyone a 1999 Marvel collection called *The Villainy of Doctor DOOM*, which compiled DOOM's origin story and his first encounters with the Fantastic Four into graphic novel form. "He builds a suit of armor, but then the last thing, that made no sense that I was dying when I read, was he used special herbs to finish the armor," says Threadgold. "And, like, a special blend of herbs and armor—that doesn't make any sense, right? All in this one panel. And I scanned it, and I sent it to everybody. I said, this is amazing. And then that became the *Special Herbs* concept."

DOOM, in fact, used several panels from the *Villainy of Doctor DOOM* as covers for the *Special Herbs* series.

But Threadgold is quick to add, "DOOM brought in all these like comic book, TV show samples that bled into the comic book stuff, you know, he came up with as much comic stuff as we did." He is referring to old episodes of *Spider-Man* and *Fantastic Four* that DOOM compiled on VHS, from which many vocal snippets from the album were sourced.

After the initial sessions in Philly, the focus shifted to Gosman's Inkonkeysta Studios, located in his Bergen Street apartment in Brooklyn's Carroll Gardens. He worked with a simple setup, running the computer-based Cubase program through a digital board, and recording directly onto hard drive. Though he owned some decent microphones, he improvised a vocal booth, hanging heavy army surplus blankets around a small nook in his spare room to create isolation. Over the course of six or seven trips to New York, DOOM would stay for several days at a stretch, allowing him to work on multiple songs while taking care of other business he had in the city.

They usually started sessions in the early afternoon and worked late into the night. "There was a combination of him coming in prepared and then writing rhymes on the spot, too," recalls Gosman. "Like he was just a prolific writer." Though DOOM mostly showed up solo, sometimes Benn Klingon or another friend would accompany him. He even brought his son once. "Occasionally, it would just make sense for them to stay over at my place 'cause like, it was big enough that there was space in our living room," Gosman adds. "We would record, party a little bit, and then record the next day. But I will say that he was like, all business."

The Sound Ink crew matched DOOM's commitment to the project every step of the way. Gosman and Schmitz, for example, went to the trouble of recording ambient sounds on the subway for songs like "Lickupon," to represent Viktor moving through the city. "I felt like we dedicated our lives to that record while we were making it, 'cause we felt we had something special there," says Threadgold.

Unlike DOOM's other projects up until then, a real flow of information and ideas characterized this collaboration. "We would like be passing around comic books and like *Scientific American* magazine," says Threadgold. "And, like, the way he would sponge ideas out of just our conversations and shit that was lying around was so inspiring. 'Cause there was so many references that were like, you would only get if you were in this space."

One day, they came across an article about a hypothetical Doomsday scenario involving "grey goo," a term that referred to self-replicating molecular nanotechnology that could eat everything on Earth if it ever escaped from its holding container and went rogue. DOOM couldn't resist using it as a double entendre for his preferred brand of vodka. "Keep a liter of vodka inside my locker / Use it like a book on the Grey Goo Scenario," he says on "Never Dead," turning an allusion to teen drinking into a heady scientific concept—provided you caught it. Such was the brilliance of DOOM's wordplay as he stacked levels of deeper meaning into the most innocuous lines, while dropping references that often sailed over everyone's heads.

In "A Dead Mouse," he says, "V catch the beat too ridiculously / People think he study levitation's true mystery / Had a pal named Ed Leedskalin, until he got him for his sweet 16." The friend in question was a real-life Latvian immigrant (with Latvia probably the basis for Viktor's fictional homeland of Latveria), who built a castle out of coral in Florida in the 1920s, dedicating it to his lost love, whom he referred to as his "Sweet Sixteen." When asked how he was able to single-handedly lift and move thousands of tons of material, Leedskalin claimed to be privy to the secrets of the pyramid builders. In just a few lines, then, DOOM was able to give us a peek inside the mind of Vik Vaughn, whose preoccupation with esoteric knowledge mirrored his own interest in the topic.

In addition to giving nerds endless hours of debating the meaning behind his lyrics, and geek out on his obscure references, DOOM's off-beat flow sounded just as inscrutable. His warped cadence modulated slightly ahead of or just behind the beat in a conversational, almost confessional tone executed with perfect elocution. As if riding a mechanical bull, however, this rhinestone cowboy always managed to maintain control.

"DOOM had this crazy way of recording tracks," says Threadgold. "He would punch in, like sometimes up to seventeen times in one verse. He didn't spit the whole verse in a row. He would spit like a couple of bars. And I don't know if it was like a breath control thing or what, but the thing that was crazy was that it didn't sound like [he was doing] it. You can't hear that. It's very hard to make your voice sound the same when you're punching in that many times." DOOM's monotone may have helped mask the punch-in points, but his real skill was hitting certain pockets that married his vocal to the beat. Unfortunately, this technique also made remixing his stuff very difficult, as the label eventually found out.

"We tried to get some remixes made of the tracks and almost all of them came back and they sounded like shit. And we were like, what's going on? Why can't we get a good remix? Everything just sounded off," says Threadgold. "And my theory was from punching [in] so much, each of those little punches would hit a different pocket on the beat. So even if you were like in the same BPM and theoretically you could take the acapella and line it up, it just didn't work because he was catching a different pocket every time in the beat." So, not only was the content of his lyrics unique, but his whole flow sounded incredibly distinctive.

What originally started out as a lark gelled into a powerful piece of conceptual art that bucked convention. Though an excuse for DOOM to revisit his youth and spit the usual shit that other rappers were spouting—albeit with his own eccentric twist—the album probably exceeded his own expectations, thanks, in part, to production that kept him on his toes. Lawrence, as King Honey, produced the more hip-hop-oriented tracks such as "Vaudeville Villain," "Mr. Clean," and the bonus track, "Change the Beat." Gosman and Schmitz, otherwise known as Heat Sensor, were responsible for introducing more electronic elements, as on tracks like "Raedawn" and one of the album's bangers, "Modern Day Mugging." Meanwhile, Matt McDonald (aka Max Bill) was credited with some of the more experimental jams like "Popsnot" and "G.M.C." that proved that DOOM could rhyme over just about anything. In addition, they reached out to RJD2 (Ramble Jon Krohn), a friend of some residents of Space 1026, who was fast making a name for himself in indie hip-hop. He supplied the most conventional beat for the horn-fanfare-driven "Saliva," which was released as a promo seven-inch on HipHopSite.com. All in all, however, *Vaudeville Villain* proved an impressive outing for these first-time producers.

Inspired by their futuristic beats, DOOM could focus on his writing, stepping up his pen game. "Viktor the director, flip a script like Rob Reiner," he says on the title track, capping it with the punchline, "The way a lot of dudes rhyme, their name should be knob shiner." On that same track he flexed similes like "Hit him straight to the head like Reggie Denny," referencing the unfortunate white trucker who was dragged from his vehicle and badly beaten up during the 1992 LA riots. But most of the time, DOOM was making hay out of the mundane like Larry David. On "Saliva," he delivered laugh-out-loud one-liners like "Leave him hangin', like I ain't know where his hand's been." He also expanded his vocabulary, co-opting one of Joe Biden's favorites—"malarkey"—and even throwing in a little Spanish at one point, exclaiming, "Ay, caramba."

But, for a solo outing, *Vaudeville Villain* also featured no shortage of guests. "We were sitting around and talking about, like, how funny it was when you go [to these open mic events] and MCs are battling," says Lawrence of a conversation that inspired the album's two biggest skits. "Open Mic Nite, Parts 1 & 2," nods at the Nuyorican, where DOOM reintroduced himself to the public, offered a medley of beats and humor—an underground version of the Def Comedy Jams of the nineties. The first part featured host Lord Sear, a regular from Stretch and Bobbito's radio show, introducing such acts as a fictional, Last Poets–style, conga-playing bard by the name of Brother Sambuca, hilariously played by Benn Klingon. He was followed by real MCs Louis Logic and Rodan (as Dr. Moreau), who ripped the mic over two different King Honey beats.

In "Pt. 2," Lawrence's buddy Andrew Jeffrey Wright, a fellow resident at Space 1026, played a stoner poet for comic effect. Underground rapper Creature added some freestyle flavor before DOOM killed it over a soaring Iron Butterfly loop (from "In the Time of Our Lives"). "Local bartenders called him barfly V / He used they CDs as coasters / Harassed their street team and graffitied up their posters," he says with a nod to his producer's previous gig. He even evoked legendary Philly rapper Schoolly D (of "Gucci Time" fame), saying, "Lookin' at my Seiko, it's about to be Waco / And it won't be televised, you can make sure." Both live-action skits—complete with crowd noise and applause—contrasted with DOOM's usual audio collages that were constructed over months, and in solitude, using found sources. But to illustrate Viktor's back story, he obviously couldn't resist mining his VHS archives for snippets from Spider-Man cartoons from the early eighties—specifically the episodes "Cannon of DOOM" and the "Origins of DOOM."

In addition to these skits, two other tracks featured collaborations. The first, "Let Me Watch," featuring Queens MC Apani B. (Apani Smith), provided one of the album's more memorable moments. The poignant piano and guitar loop, sampled from the breakdown in "Sara Lee" (MGM, 1971), by an obscure southern rock band called 6680 Lexington, lent itself perfectly to this relatable tale of love gone sour. Unlike some of DOOM's more challenging rhymes, it was also possible to follow in real time. What starts off as a promising relationship deteriorates after Viktor disrespects the object of his desire. It's also an example of DOOM's self-deprecation at its best, proving he dared go where most rappers wouldn't.

"We knew he wanted to do a kind of vocal pair up with a female MC," says Gosman. "And so we made the suggestion, and he was into it." Lawrence reached out to Apani through Louis Logic, and she was good to go. Though the track played like an intimate conversation between her and Viktor, the two were never actually in the same room during its making, and, in fact, recorded their verses weeks apart.

"It would basically work verse by verse," says Lawrence, who produced the track. "And then what we ended up doing is, we would leave like 16 bars. We'd be like, all right. So, here's 16 bars, 16 bars. So, he would record two verses. Then she would record two verses. Then he came back and was like, 'Oh, hell no!' You could tell by each verse that got written and then recorded, [that] they keep one upping each other and it took multiple recordings." All that effort paid off, however, as the song provided not only a clear insight into Vik Vaughn's motivations, but a unique perspective on the male/female dynamic, not often expressed in the boys' club of rap.

The label was also working with M. Sayyid (Maurice Greene) of the left-field rap group Antipop Consortium and saw a dream pairing of him and DOOM. After getting the Villain's go-ahead, Gosman, who produced "Never Dead," says, "I think maybe DOOM recorded his verse and then I handed it over to Sayyid and then he wrote to it." Vibing off the eerie strings, DOOM delved into some of his favorite subjects—science and mysticism—as he talked about time travel, weird spells, resurrection, and transfiguration. There's hardly an album where he didn't pay homage to his deceased brother, and here he said, "To your health, we rock Chinese slippers / Me and King Gilizwe and two Guyanese strippers" (utilizing the couplet that John Robinson had spied on a sticky note on his studio wall). The lines that follow, "I watched him freeze roaches and bring 'em straight back to life / He used a different approach than I ever read / The only thing he ever said was, 'The roach is never dead,'" also referenced Subroc, who sometimes referred to himself as the Great Roach.

"DOOM was not just a brilliant artist, but like a really good person in my experience. Like I just enjoyed hanging out with him," says Threadgold. "He was a genuine guy who you could be real with, you know. I wouldn't say I became close with him, but there was something about him that to me was special. It was a special experience collaborating with him. 'Cause he was just a good guy who I think cared about people and you know, super observant and like had a heart, you know?"

Following more than two years in production, the *Vaudeville Villain* album was finally released in September 2003. Threadgold was able to strike a deal with Traffic distribution in Massachusetts to press it up and get it into stores. He also forged a relationship with Biz 3, a publicity firm in Chicago, to help promote the record. Since the King Geedorah album had only recently been released, Sound Ink and Big Dada ended up splitting the costs of the publicist—an unconventional partnership that in the long range worked for both projects and DOOM's benefit. In his glowing *Pitchfork* review, Rollie Pemberton wrote, "Despite its admittedly slight flaws, *Vaudeville Villain* goes head-to-head with DOOM's other 2003 project, King Geedorah's *Take Me to Your Leader*, for what stands as the hip-hop album of the year thus far."[9] Forget the year's chartbusters like 50 Cent, Dipset, or Chingy—the DOOMiverse had supplanted them all, ushering in a parallel dimension of hip-hop.

As an independent release with decent promotion, it sold a respectable twenty to thirty thousand copies, becoming the biggest seller on Sound Ink "by miles," according to Threadgold. It earned enough to pay back the label's debts and cover DOOM's advance and even some additional royalties. The record might have done even better had it not been overshadowed by another one of DOOM's releases shortly afterward.

Incidentally, unlike Geedorah, DOOM did reprise the Viktor Vaughn character again on *VV:2 Venomous Villain* (Insomniac, 2004), an album very different from the first. Insomniac, the brainchild of Israel Vasquetelle, a hip-hop deejay from the Bronx who relocated to Orlando, Florida, originally started off as a hip-hop magazine. In an effort to expand into music, Vasquetelle, an MC himself, was able to secure the financing to entice DOOM to do a record.

Produced largely by a crew of unknowns (though Diplo also contributes a track) that included the Analears, DiViNCi, DJ I.N.C., Dub-L, Session 31, Swamburger, and System D-128, the beats are solid head-nodders, featuring scratching by Kut Masta Kurt. DOOM doesn't exactly phone it in, but only raps for a total of fifteen minutes—half the running time of this short release—giving the impression of an unapologetic money grab. The album's second track, "Back End," seems to support this notion as he warns, "Dub it off your man, don't spend the ten bucks / I did it for the advance, the back end sucks." Despite the record's brevity and the fact that it's hard to find, *VV:2* is worth listening to if only to hear the collaboration between DOOM and his spiritual predecessor and doppelganger, Kool Keith, on "Doper Skiller." This follow-up also put the original Viktor Vaughn album in perspective, highlighting how DOOM, leading a committed cast of misfits, could produce one of his best and most fully realized collaborations.

17

MADVILLAIN/*MADVILLAINY*

The rest is empty with no brain, but the clever nerd,
The best MC without no chain ya ever heard.

—MF DOOM, "FIGARO"

In the canon of DOOM, *Madvillainy*, far and away, ranks as his magnum opus—an album that transformed a hungry underground upstart, struggling for a second chance, into a serious contender. As seldom as critical and popular tastes overlap, the stars were definitely aligned for this one, as the overwhelmingly glowing response greeting its March 2004 release suggested. *Pitchfork* called it "inexhaustibly brilliant," adding, "Good luck finding a better hip-hop album this year, mainstream, indie, or otherwise."[1] The *Village Voice* hailed "an outlandishly imaginative collaboration."[2] Already divining the future, the site Hip-Hop DX said, "Classic albums generally need some time to marinate and gain that status, but fuck it; they didn't follow any guidelines so why should I? Classic. Yes, I said it. Classic."[3] They were even dazzled across the pond. "The wily creativity on display here is astonishing,"[4] marveled *Mojo*, while *Q* magazine simply called it "one utterly badass album."[5]

Such effusive praise wasn't bought and paid for by some well-funded hype machine bolstered by the usual avenues of radio play and big-budget videos, but rather came from the buzz bubbling up from chat rooms and file-sharing sites, making it all the more amazing. The album reviewing site The Needle Drop called it "a defining record for abstract hip-hop,"[6] for good reason, as its popularity rode the crest of a wave of "backpacker rap," before that became a pejorative term. But, regardless, this small, independent record—one of the first to go viral before it was even released—lived up to all the hype.

At a time when CD sales and the music industry, in general, were experiencing a precipitous decline, the album managed to ship about 50,000 copies on its way to selling upward of 150,000.[7] Though these numbers pale in comparison to the gold and platinum records of the previous decade, the phenomenon that was *Madvillainy* could be quantified by other metrics—such as how many people obsessed about it and for how long. In the intervening years since its release, the record has grown into the stuff of legend, largely thanks to those behind the scenes, who witnessed its creation.

With 20/20 hindsight, however, we discover that as much as *Madvillainy* achieved, success came at the expense of broken friendships, unleashing a Pandora's box of bitterness and resentment. The resulting drama—largely involving label head Chris Manak (aka Peanut Butter Wolf); Eothen "Egon" Alapatt, label manager; and Walasia Shabazz (formerly Miranda Jane Neidlinger), DOOM's manager at the time—figured prominently in Will Hagle's recent 33 1/3 book on *Madvillainy* (Bloomsbury Academic, 2023). The irony of this situation being that the project's two prime movers, DOOM and Madlib (Otis Jackson Jr.), played no part in the politics and managed to stay above the fray. On the contrary, while maintaining the superhuman focus it took to get the work done in the face of many setbacks, their relationship blossomed. Perhaps the fact that they were both so reticent by nature allowed others to take over the narrative. But regardless, the basic details behind the making of the album are pretty much indisputable.

The idea for the collaboration originated with Madlib, sometime in 2001. During an interview with *Mass Appeal* magazine, the typically reserved producer revealed as much, stating that he wanted to work with J Dilla as well. The article was credited to Miranda Jane (aka Walasia), who happened to be a friend of DOOM's. She not only relayed the request to him but lobbied to make it happen, since DOOM had never heard of the then underground producer from Oxnard, California. In early 2002, in an unrelated effort to make Madlib's wishes a reality, Alapatt sent a package of material to his friend, DJ and rapper Jon Doe

(Jon Foster), who, coincidentally, lived only five minutes away from DOOM in Kennesaw, Georgia. Introduced by a mutual friend, Dwight Conroy Farrell (aka Count Bass D), they sometimes hung out. Doe passed Madlib's records on to DOOM.

The Villain was notoriously picky when it came to whom he worked with. He kept an even tighter inner circle of friends, who served as a kind of buffer between himself and the outside world. Farrell managed to gain entry into this exclusive club after contributing a couple tracks to MF Grimm's *Downfall of Ibliys* album, on which DOOM served as executive producer. They also shared a common lineage in the industry, as he had been one of the first artists—along with Kurious—signed to Pete Nice's Hoppoh imprint. Since they both currently lived in the Atlanta area, they began to see more of each other. DOOM had once paid Farrell the ultimate compliment, telling him that he reminded him of his deceased brother.

"So, he came to the crib, and I remember, at one point he pulled me to the side," recalls Farrell. "He was like, 'So, I got contacted by these people out on the West Coast. And they were talking about making an album and whatnot with this guy named Madlib.' I was like Madlib from Stones Throw? He's like, 'I think that's it.' 'Cause at that time DOOM, you know, when I tell you he was checked out, he was checked out, you know what I mean? He was making his music and you could have asked him, [but] he didn't know who anybody was. You know what I mean? You can't just take it personally. He wasn't paying attention to anything or anybody."[8]

Despite prodding from Walasia and the package of material from Alapatt (that he apparently liked), DOOM, doing his due diligence, had approached a friend and fellow artist for a second opinion. "So, he asked me like, you know, 'What's up with that?' just looking for a little bit of insight," Farrell elaborates. "And I gave him the green light. I'm like, 'Look, man, I think that that could be something that you should definitely do.' And he was like, 'Word?' I was like, 'Yeah, you should definitely do that.'"[9] At the time, Madlib, obviously, did not have the huge reputation he has today. Though DOOM might have liked what he heard, he was also probably fielding offers from any number of labels. Farrell helped him cut through the noise and make a momentous decision that would be a game-changer, not only for his career, but for independent hip-hop.

In May 2002, following long-distance negotiations, DOOM and Neidlinger, now going as Walasia, and acting as his manager, arrived in LA at the Stones Throw mini mansion, where the label guys lived with Madlib. DOOM beelined straight for the studio, the Bomb Shelter, tucked away in a real Cold War–era concrete bunker, while Walasia went to handle business with Alapatt. The Villain had predetermined the conditions for his involvement—a flat fee of $1,500 to rap on three tracks, plus flights and hotel—deploying Walasia as his mouthpiece/enforcer. A deal was hastily scrawled on the back of a paper plate and later signed by all parties.[10]

Meanwhile, down in the Bomb Shelter, two eccentrics were meeting for the first time. The awkwardness was likely cut by a genuine expression of admiration for each other. Then, ganja was ritually burned—some of that kind Cali Sour Diesel—and beats started bumping. "We clicked immediately," DOOM recalled. "You know how children automatically click? You wanna go, let's play!"[11] Apropos to the occasion, the first selection Madlib threw on was a beat that would become "America's Most Blunted." According to DOOM, "We connected so good on it—we did that shit in like a day. After that, we was like, 'No, we should just take this shit and do a whole album.'"[12] Each had obviously found his ideal playmate.

DOOM ended up lingering in LA for almost two weeks, forgoing a Beverly Hills hotel room to just crash on a couch with his new Cali crew. He spent most days up on the rooftop deck, in that peaceful, somewhat secluded environment, filling his composition book with chicken scratch that only his eyes could decipher. Sucking on beers and bong hits for inspiration, he OD'd on Thai food to fill his belly. Madlib floated him dozens of tracks—fifty beats per CD-R, to be exact—and they made early versions of two more songs, "Figaro" and "Meat Grinder" (formerly titled "Just for Kicks"). The Villain worked as expeditiously as possible so he could head back to Georgia, where his second child had just recently been born.

Describing the creative process, DOOM said, "He's always in the Bomb Shelter and I'm always on the deck writing, and then he would give me another CD. I get the CD and I'm writing, and he's back in the Bomb Shelter."[13] Despite living under the same roof, sometimes days would pass without them even seeing each other. On the rare occasions they did commune, it was usually while sharing a blunt and listening to some finished tracks or recording. "I mean we hardly spoke, really," said DOOM. "It's more through telepathy and like we spoke really through the music."[14] Despite exchanging few words, Madlib and DOOM shared that rare spiritual connection that bound together advanced souls. "Felt like I knew him all my life," said DOOM. "That's my brother, yo! My long-lost brother."[15] Their unique relationship proved an asset when they switched to working remotely and Madlib kept the beat CDs coming via mail.

Everything was humming along quite nicely before he left to take part in some events surrounding the annual Red Bull Music Academy, held in São Paulo, Brazil, in November 2002. He burned two CD-Rs to listen to on the plane—one of rough *Madvillainy* tracks and the other of unfinished mixes from his dream project with J Dilla, which would be released under the name Jaylib. With working titles like "peeyano keys" ("Great Day"), "jack off" ("America's Most Blunted"), "brain melt" ("Supervillain Theme"), and "horny" ("All Caps"), these *Madvillainy* songs were far from finished. But Madlib was eager to share dubs of them among his Stones Throw crew along with the new material he was currently working on.

The trip, documented in the film *Brasilintime* (2003), expanded the young producer's horizons in many ways. Exposed to a whole new body of music with which he was unfamiliar, Madlib splurged on vintage Brazilian vinyl. Wearing a floppy rope hat, he spent his days in the hotel suite equipped with a portable turntable, an MPC, a BOSS SP-303 drum machine/sampler, and a tape deck, borrowed from reception, transforming this sonic booty into sixty-minute beat tapes (on actual cassettes). In fact, he claimed to have made the entire *Madvillainy* album on this same minimal setup. At night the rail-thin producer found himself jamming at clubs with legendary local musicians. His whole attitude had changed since that 2001 *Mass Appeal* piece, in which he admitted, "I don't like rap at all. I don't know why I'm doing it."¹⁶ Here he was, only a year later, working on highly anticipated projects with two of the biggest names in the underground—Dilla and DOOM—and he couldn't wait to finish and release them.

All of this progress and momentum came to a screeching halt, however, when the unthinkable occurred. Returning from his trip, he discovered that the entire *Madvillainy* track list he had taken to Brazil—thirty-six minutes of music in total—had been leaked on the internet (the same thing happened with his Dilla tracks as well). It was a heavy blow to everyone involved in the project, but Madlib remained defiant and unphased, apparently claiming, *I'll just make a new record*. Since DOOM was already elbows deep in three other records, this one was pushed to the back burner for a minute. But they kept the vibe alive via more beat CDs.

Finally, in the summer of 2003, with some slack in their respective schedules, they reconvened in person to finish up the album at the Bomb Shelter. In addition to recording additional tracks, DOOM made the unprecedented decision to re-record all his vocals. On the pre-leaked version, most of his performances had been delivered in an upbeat, energetic style—reminiscent of Viktor Vaughn (whose album he was working on simultaneously). He decided to dial it down a notch, however, assuming the slower, lower conversational tone that was his signature. It was a pivotal artistic choice that made all the difference.

"We all got 'demo-itis' because we were so used to him rapping the whole album with a hype tone, and then to hear it with the relaxed tone, we didn't like it at first," says Stones Throw head honcho Chris Manak. "I was thinking to myself, 'No, no, no, we can't let this happen.' But I was just thankful he was finishing the album."[17]

Quite unexpectedly, the leak, which could have killed the record, had the opposite effect, ratcheting up anticipation to new heights. In fact, they could not have devised a better marketing strategy. The precedent of giving away free download tracks to entice customers to purchase physical product had only been recently established, so the leaked tracks functioned as a teaser. The first single, featuring the album's two most accessible songs, "Money Folder" b/w "America's Most Blunted," dropped in the fall of 2003, proving that all the hype was real. When the album finally saw light in March 2004, it became DOOM's first release to chart, peaking at number eighty on the Billboard album charts. In addition to setting a benchmark for underground hip-hop, it catapulted both artists to a whole new level of exposure and recognition, and remains, to this day, the best-selling album on Stones Throw.

The real story of *Madvillainy*, then, is not about the politics or personal rivalries that played out on the sidelines, but the chemistry between Madlib and DOOM, and the magic they conjured in their secret lair. Each artist could have found no better foil to bring out their respective strengths. Entering a new phase in their creative lives, they needed this collaboration to supercharge their careers, and, in retrospect, such a breakthrough seemed preordained. Taking the setbacks in stride, they worked diligently and patiently to bring the project to fruition, knowing, perhaps better than anybody, that the sum of their parts was more powerful than each acting alone. No amount of money (which was scarce) or prodding (which was plentiful) ultimately mattered because these artists understood that the world needed to hear what they were doing.

Both loners, who shared a rigorous work ethic, the similarities between DOOM and Madlib didn't end there. Born October 24, 1973, the same year as Subroc, Madlib, like his counterpart, also grew up in a coastal city—Oxnard, a part of greater Los Angeles—and started a group, Lootpack, with friends Jack Brown (aka Wildchild) and Romeo Jimenez (aka DJ Romes), while in high school. He even had an early brush with a major label that probably influenced his decision to go indie as well. In the late nineties and early aughts, after having amassed a few different projects under various aliases, he seemed as prolific and driven as DOOM.

But two years younger than his collaborator, Madlib, the more disciplined and regimented of the two, treated beat-making as a nine-to-five job, applying himself daily and churning out tracks at a breakneck pace. DOOM, on the other hand, preferred his time, like his rhyme style, unstructured. For him, creativity wasn't a faucet you could turn on at will. Yet working at his own pace, he still managed to stack up a surplus of material.

Unlike DOOM, Madlib hailed from a musical family, where he was exposed to a variety of music from an early age. "I started listening to jazz when I was real young—my grandparents were into jazz—I've always listened to soul, old rock. My pops used to bump European stuff," he said. "I listened to disco and funk, too. I listened to everything."[18] It helped to have an uncle, Jon Faddis, who was a jazz trumpeter, while his father, Otis Jackson Sr., worked as a band leader, and session musician. Otis Sr., in fact, helped him press up his first project—Lootpack's *Psyche Move* EP—released on Madlib's own Crate Digga's Palace imprint in 1995.

Only two years earlier, Madlib had produced "Mary Jane," his first ode to weed, off Tha Alkaholiks' debut, *21 & Over* (Loud/RCA, 1993). Lootpack also appeared on the follow-up, *Coast II Coast* (Loud/RCA, 1995), but when a proposed deal with Loud failed to materialize, he decided to take the independent route and never looked back. Lootpack's EP happened to catch the attention of Manak, who was trying to take the Stones Throw imprint he started in 1996 to the next level. Recognizing the latent talent before him, he practically restructured the label around Madlib and his many aliases and side projects, relocating from San Jose to establish a headquarters in LA in 1999.

Manak eventually rented a large house on a hill in the quiet neighborhood of Mount Washington, with commanding views of the surrounding area. He brought in Alapatt, a former college radio DJ from Connecticut, and artist/designer Jeff Jank, a friend from San Jose, as the creative team who helped him release Lootpack's debut album, *Soundpieces: Da Antidote!* (1999), Quasimoto's *The Unseen* (2000), and Yesterdays New Quintet's *Angles Without Edges* (2001). Quasimoto, depicted as a quirky little furry character who rapped with a pitched-up voice, was none other than Madlib—not to mention the entire fictional quintet, his answer to a jazz band. "I just make music I want to hear," said Madlib. "Hopefully, other people will like what I do."[19] Like DOOM, that apparently required being somewhat schizophrenic. But as innovative and ambitious as his projects were, they failed to give him the broader recognition and exposure he felt he deserved.

DOOM recalled Madlib's declaration at their first meeting: *Let's get ill with it. Let's bring it to the edge of gangster, but still it's going to be artistic, of course, dealing with us.*[20] Today, those words ring like a mission statement for the album that would become *Madvillainy*. They wanted to keep it "ill" and "gangster," meaning still based within the accepted parameters of hip-hop, but, at the same time, "artistic," or staying true to their own progressive nature. It was the kind of concept that recalled the best of hip-hop's golden era, guided by the tenets of creativity, originality, and innovation.

"I don't have an idea of what the album is gonna sound like until I hear the beat. So, music is what drives the idea," said DOOM. "The music is what guides it, and I'm coming in with the idea after I hear what the music is telling me."[21] In other words, he didn't like to preconceive lyrics or concepts, but derived inspiration directly from the track. The same kind of openness and spontaneity characterized Madlib's production style. "I don't think so much about it going into it. It just happens,"[22] said the man, whose credo was, "Always be different. Challenge yourself. Don't be scared to try new things. Once you get bored, challenge yourself to do something you wouldn't think you would do."[23] Their similar approaches to creativity put them on the same page and helped seal a successful partnership.

"Shit usually works out when you're with the like-minded," Madlib said. "DOOM's like my super-smart cousin. We trade books and records: Sun Ra equations, biographies of Charlie Parker. Some people are born off that same energy."[24]

"As quick as I was coming up with ideas, he would have more music for me to listen to," said DOOM. "As I'm doing the writing, he's in the other room finishing up more instrumentals."[25] Out of every fifty beats he received from his partner, DOOM estimated he probably wrote four or five new songs.

"The most important part of their process is simply that DOOM understood Madlib right off the bat," said Jeff Jank. "He understood where he was coming from with the music, how it connected with the records they listened to from the '60s–'90s, and Madlib's inclination to work on his own in privacy. DOOM was all for it."[26] In turn, Madlib respected the way DOOM approached his art, supplying mostly beats without hooks. The standard structure of a rap track—sixteen-bar verses alternating with a catchy hook—had become so formulaic that the Villain felt compelled to mess with people's expectations.

"I like to do what other people are not doing, so what I do stands out a little more," he explained. "I cut out all the unnecessary shit. Hooks is good, you know, for certain motherfuckers who need 'em. To me, when I write, every lyric is as strong as a hook would be. So, kill 'em with the verses, and you won't need a hook. It makes a more intense experience."[27]

In addition to hooks, they tossed aside traditional song structure entirely. Some tracks, in fact, were so short that DOOM had to extend them to allow himself enough room to rhyme. But plenty of one- or two-minute tracks also made the final selection. With the addition of instrumental interludes and the requisite skits, the album plays more like an eclectic mixtape, often segued together with the use of DJ cuts and spin backs. It's constantly moving in unpredictable ways, with hardly a moment of silence and an amazing attention to detail. Madlib might have stepped up his game for DOOM, but the Villain, in turn, rose to the challenge with some of his most quotable lines.

In a 2019 interview with *Spin*, he went uncharacteristically deep into his writing process. "When you're looking at quality wordplay, you're looking at how many words rhyme in a bar or two bars. How many syllables can you use that still make sense in a song?" said DOOM. "What I be looking at is the quality of the rhyming word: phonetically, how the tone is in the pronunciation of the word."[28] He compared choosing the appropriate word to getting a triple word score in Scrabble. "It's similar to getting points like that, if you really take it to the next level," he said. "The more complex the subject matter and wordplay is, that's where you get your points. I'm a rhymer, so I go for points."[29]

He even went so far as to explain what differentiated *Madvillainy* from the typical DOOM record. "The whole DOOM persona and idea and how we approach those records, is like, I'm thinking of my own mind. I'm not speaking to anyone," he said. "You're hearing my thoughts, what I'm thinking about when

I'm walking, random thoughts, as if you're in the mind of a writer. Now, Madvillain, the approach I took on that one is like, I'm talking to Otis. Like, 'Yo, O, check it out, ha, ha!' Making jokes at somebody, like I'm speaking to somebody audibly, out loud. So that's the difference."[30] Though the contrast may be subtle, the fusion of Madlib's music and DOOM's musings sounded like nothing less than the Holy Grail for a new generation of hip-hoppers.

> *Two historical figures, outlaws, and desperadoes at that,*
> *The villainous pair of really nice boys, who just happened*
> *To be on the wrong side of the law . . .*
> *Villains who possess supernatural abilities,*
> *Villains who were the personification of carnage,*
> *Madvillain, more accurately, the dark side of our beings.*
> *Perhaps it is due to this seminal connection that audiences*
> *Can relate their experiences in life with the villains and*
> *Their dastardly doings.*
>
> —FROM "THE ILLEST VILLAINS"

More an adventure than an album, *Madvillainy* ushers the listener through an epic masterclass in sampling and linguistics. Fast-paced, eclectic, and unpredictable, it's an enjoyable ride, but for those who bother to fully engage and pay attention, many jewels await. The album begins, auspiciously enough, with a spooky keyboard vamp from one of Madlib's spiritual mentors, Sun Ra. He reappropriates what was originally the closing section of "Contrast" (Evidence, 1972), which segues perfectly into a bass interlude from "Beach Trip," off the *Hawaii Five-O* soundtrack (Capitol, 1968), to become the album intro, "The Illest Villains."

In his only co-production on the album, DOOM finds the ideal vocal snippets to bring to life the album's concept via an old VHS tape titled *The Documented History of the Fabulous Villains* (Burbank Video, 1989). Utilizing the cut-and-paste style he has perfected over the course of several albums, he paints the protagonists of this story as over-the-top bad guys. But in a brilliant flash of insight—a nod to Carl Jung's concept of the Shadow—his narrator also suggests that the listener is interested in the villains because they are a reflection of the dark side in everyone. And how much of a coincidence is it that this narrator uses the term "madvillain," a compound word that incorporates both artists' identities? Snippets from the same film, used in tracks like "Money Folder," "Rainbows," and "Rhinestone Cowboy," help tie the record together conceptually.

As this intro abruptly cuts off, the staccato beat of "Accordion" kicks in with its clock-like syncopation. Despite the track's title, the "accordion" sound is actually a Magnus 391 Electric Chord Organ, as played by the artist Daedelus on a track called "Experience." Madlib, who had done a remix of that song from their debut release *Invention* (Plug Research, 2002), appropriated the whole melancholic melody, adding only a kick drum and bassline that drops in and out.[31]

DOOM opens with one of his more memorable lines, "Living on borrowed time, the clock ticks faster," which many have come to interpret as an acknowledgement of his impending mortality. But that might be reaching a bit considering he wrote this in 2002 or 2003 and did not pass away until 2020. He also says, "Nice to be old," a few lines later. At a hair short of two minutes, the track only has enough time for a single verse and an outro, but DOOM maximizes even short appearances like this one with his steady conversational flow—as if he's addressing you from the next barstool. Dropping catchy one-liners like "And gets more cheese than Doritos, Fritos, and Cheetos," he doesn't need hooks.

As the song fades out, Madlib scratches in the intro to the next track, a Mothers of Invention loop from "Sleeping in a Jar" from their album *Uncle Meat* (Bizarre, 1969). Helmed by Frank Zappa, the band was known for their sonic experimentation, and this piece provides an appropriate slice of weirdness. After a few bars, Madlib spins back the loop, letting it start over, a popular deejay technique used to build anticipation. Meanwhile, a voice chants, "The jar is under the bed," over a cacophonous drum roll and electric guitar. But this busy intro suddenly subsides, giving way to a bouncy bass groove courtesy of Lew Howard and the All Stars. Their song "Hula Rock" (Bosworth, 1975) also supplies the lap steel that languorously twangs atop the bubbling beat.

As he does for much of the album, DOOM free associates his lyrics, packing in references to cartoons (Destro from G.I. Joe) beside two, no-longer fashionable sneaker brands (Adidas' Rod Lavers and Ellesse). He rhymes seventies fitness guru Jack Lalane with "Wrath of Kane" (the Big Daddy Kane classic)—all heavily nostalgic fodder for his fellow Gen X-ers. If the album were a high-end tasting menu, this course would be one that demanded seconds. But just as quickly as it appears, this delicious nugget is gone.

Butting up next to it is "Bistro," a shout-out track made after the album's leak. Right up DOOM's alley, it samples an eighties R&B, slap-bass groove from Atlantic Starr's "Second to None" (A&M, 1983). Unlike the album intro, which establishes the Madvillain concept, this track acknowledges all the individual players involved—including Madlib, King Geedorah, Yesterdays New Quintet, Viktor Vaughn, Quasimoto, and The Supervillain—the joke, of course, being that all these aliases simply represent DOOM and Madlib, who are essentially thanking themselves. DOOM also manages to fit in a little inside joke—a shout-out to Big Hookie and Baba from the laundromat, who are cartoon characters created by designer Jeff Jank.

The fifth track in the selection, "Raid," also marks the first one suitable for radio play, clocking in at two and a half minutes. The intro, taken from a live recording at the 1968 Montreux Jazz Festival, features Bill Evans tinkling the ivories. It segues perfectly into a swinging piano loop from the song "América Latina" (Som Livre, 1972) by Brazilian artists Osmar Milito and Quarteto Forma. Madlib made this track in his hotel room in Brazil, performing some loop alchemy in the 303 by repeating a note so it plays in 4/4 time. DOOM spits a faster-than-usual verse before turning over the mic to rapper M.E.D. (Nick Rodriguez), another member of the Stones Throw stable. As the instrumental fades out, we hear probably the only millisecond of silence to be found on the whole album.

But that void is soon filled by "America's Most Blunted," featuring Madlib's first vocal appearance on the album (as both himself and pitched-up alter ego Lord Quas). Contrasting with the album's more innovative material, this song adheres to conventional song structure with the usual alternation of hook and verse. At almost four minutes, it also runs twice as long as most of the other selections. Since this tune kicked off their collaboration, perhaps it made sense to begin with an ode to weed. But frankly, the subject matter feels as clichéd as rapping about guns or hoes. Thankfully, DOOM offers a new spin with his effortless, often self-deprecating sense of humor, rapping, "DOOM nominated for best rolled L's / And they wondered why he dealt with stress so well / Wild guess? You could say he stay sedated / Some say Buddha-ed, some say faded / Someday, pray that he will grow a farm barn full / Recent research shows it's not so darn harmful."

Though Madlib's verse can't compete, he went to town on the production, sampling a staggering nineteen songs for this track. A fan of the Dust Brothers, who produced the Beastie Boys' sampledelic *Paul's Boutique* (Capitol, 1989), the Beat Konducta combines such disparate elements as Steve Reich, Sun Ra, the Dramatics, a Disneyland children's record, and, of course, Fever Tree, whose 1968 cover of Wilson Pickett's "Ninety-Nine and a Half" (Atlantic, 1966) makes up the main guitar loop. He also cuts in lines from rappers like Prodigy, Redman, Phil da Agony, Ed O.G, and Pharaohe Monch for the hook. But the best sampled vocals come from Jack Margolis, who narrates a pro-weed counterculture comedy album, *A Child's Garden of Grass* (Elektra, 1971). In the song's outro he says, "It's a known fact that grass increases creativity from eight to eleven times. In fact, everyone finds that they're more creative stoned, than straight," before spelling out "marijuana" to the accompaniment of a xylophone. As much as a paean to their favorite high, the song also seems to be giving a nod to the playful subversiveness of *Mr. Hood*.

Following some canned laughter, Madlib scratches in the beat to the next selection, "Sickfit," the first of three instrumentals. Based on a loop from the Generation Gap's cover of "Family Affair" (RCA/Camden, 1972), Madlib added a bassline and an unknown string sample that he manipulates so well, it sounds like he's playing it. Before the album leak, DOOM had rhymed on this track—originally titled "Winter and Spring"—but apparently, he felt his performance was rushed. Since his vocal only ran for forty-seven seconds, anyway, they decided to scrap it and keep the instrumental. With DOOM's lyrical performances on the album often being so dense and wordy, instrumental tracks like this one give the listener a break and helps with the overall pacing of the album.

"Sickfit" gets swallowed whole by the next track, "Rainbows," one of the album's stranger selections. Here, Madlib sources samples from the soundtracks to two different Russ Meyer films—*Finders Keepers, Lovers Weepers* (1968) and *Motor Psycho* (1965). In fact, the track's meandering melody uses almost a minute from the first film, while employing a horn fanfare from the second as its closeout, repeating this pattern twice. Behind its slow, creeping tempo, the Villain takes the opportunity to rap in a sing-songy style that he uses on occasion. In another departure, he also uses ad-libs for the first time. At 2:52, "Rainbows" clocks in as one of the longer songs on the album. It concludes with another line from *The Documented History of the Fabulous Villains*: "This Villain was a ruthless mass conqueror with aspirations to dominate the universe."

Next up is an album highlight, "Curls," another one of Madlib's Brazilian creations. Its cartoonish backing track is constructed from two different parts of the "Airport Love Theme" (Copacabana, 1970) by Brasilian pianist, composer, bandleader, and arranger, Waldir Calmon. The Hammond organ, guitar, and horn arrangements also contribute to the nostalgic feel. Typical of DOOM's performances on this album, he delivers a nonstop verse sans hook, only mentioning the song's title in the opening line, "Villain get the money like curls." One gets the impression that titles are an afterthought for DOOM. Neither is a clear narrative important, though fragments materialize when he raps, "Yup, you know it, growin' up too fast / Showin' up to class with Moet in the flask / He ask the teacher if he leave will he pass / His girl is home alone, he tryin' to get the . . ." DOOM, who barely curses in his rhymes, invites the listener to supply the missing word. But check out how the cheeky Madlib fills in the blank with a guiro, which produces a sharp rasping sound when scraped—suspiciously, like a fart. It's a good bet that he picked up that instrument in Brazil along with the record he samples here.

After a quick fade-out and more canned laughter, the next instrumental, "Do Not Fire," adds some exotic appeal to an already eclectic mix. Madlib's raw materials for this track include vintage Bollywood soundtracks—namely music from the films *Maha Chor* (1976) and *Suraj Aur Chanda* (1973)—as well as random sound effects from the *Street Fighter II* soundtrack. Indian music presented another novel genre for the producer, who enjoyed sampling it so much that he dedicated a whole project to it—*Beat Konducta, Vol. 3–4: Beat Konducta in India* (Madlib Invasion, 2007). It's also interesting to note that since this track and "Shadows of Tomorrow" are probably the album's most experimental joints, they are separated by the album's most accessible track, "Money Folder," the first single.

It begins abruptly after another brief vocal interlude from the villain's documentary—"The Villain took on many forms." Over a slamming back beat, courtesy of drummer Babatunde Lea, and a simple keyboard melody, DOOM demonstrates why he is the undisputed master of alliteration and internal rhymes: "The underhanded ranted, planned it, and left 'em stranded / The best, any who profess, will be remanded / Yessir, request permission to be candid. Granted / I don't think we can handle a style so rancid / He flipped it like Madlib did an old jazz standard." As if on cue, the beat drops, replaced by a heavily manipulated snippet of Freddie Hubbard's "Soul Turn Around" (Atlantic, 1969) that runs longer than expected (twelve seconds to be exact) before the main beat returns. "Money Folder" ends as it started—with another vocal collage from the villain doc.

If "All Caps" is considered DOOM's calling card on this album, "Shadows of Tomorrow" serves as Madlib's, doubling as a homage to his spiritual mentor, Sun Ra, the avant-garde composer and band leader born Herman Poole Blount. The track title is based off a rare, hand-painted seven-inch he released called "The Shadows Cast by Tomorrow." In addition to sampling Ra's own voice, the lyrics that Madlib recites in his first verse, via alter ego Lord Quas, quote his mentor's as well: "Today is the shadow of tomorrow / Today is the present future of yesterday / Yesterday is the shadow of today / The darkness of the past is yesterday." These words come from a poem that Sun Ra wrote on the back cover of his album *Angels and Demons at Play* (Impulse!, 1974). If sampling and quoting the maestro isn't enough, Madlib also invokes his name, twice, later in the song, before ending the track with dialogue from the Sun Ra film *Space Is the Place* (1974): "Equation-wise, the first thing to do is to consider time as officially ended / We work on the other side of time."

A dramatic keyboard riff suddenly interrupts this declaration. The Beat Konducta unearths another incredible break, 3:34 deep into George Duke's "Prepare Yourself" (MPS, 1975). Dripping with emotion, it demands a story, but DOOM responds with the last thing you'd expect. "Operation Lifesaver AKA Mint Test" is a quick ditty about meeting girls in the club who have bad breath. It takes a minute to gauge what he's saying, but he sums up the song in the following verse: "It don't matter if she's slim or dressed to impress / I won't rest, fellas don't fess / Some of 'em just need to eat the whole thing of Crest." The Villain strikes again with another laugh-out-loud moment in an album chock-full of them.

The organ vamp that announces the next song, "Figaro," sounds like the introduction to a cheesy game show, but that intro and the guitar loop that drives the track are both from Lonnie Smith's album *Finger Lickin' Good* (Columbia, 1966). Madlib simply lashes them to a shuffling beat. It's just another day at the office for DOOM, who indulges in some of his most free associative wordplay of the album while never slacking on the internal rhymes. "A shot of Jack, got her back, it's not an act stack / Forget about the cackalack, Hollaback clack clack," he says in a voice as thick and juicy as prime rib. DOOM's booming delivery and the way he enunciates his words sound good no matter what he's saying, so comprehension isn't even an issue. It is this speculative quality that allows fans to endlessly debate the meaning of his lyrics while also attempting to impose their own interpretations on them.

As "Figaro" fades out, we hear a new voice on the album for the first time. The appearance of Wildchild (of Lootpack) on "Hardcore Hustle" may seem a bit puzzling at first—as in, what does this song have to do with Madvillain— but Madlib was probably just looking out for his people. The song is based on a loop from Diana Ross and the Supremes and the Temptations' cover of Sly Stone's "Sing a Simple Song," which might be the most recognizable piece of music used on the album. But with a running time of only 1:22, the track serves as a kind of palate cleanser for the ears and a suitable intro for "Strange Ways." Even the transition is weird, as Wildchild ends with the couplet, "And just when you got caught up in cynical thought / Intervals in the shape of a mic get pushed through your heart like...." With his usual attention to detail, Madlib slips in horror soundtrack sounds of a man screaming in agony.

Though DOOM is not known for wading into politics, he makes an exception on "Strange Ways." Keep in mind, however, that it was written during the wall-to-wall cable news coverage that accompanied the run-up to the US invasion of Iraq in March 2003. When he raps, "They pray four times a day, they pray five / Who ways is strange when it's time to survive / Some will go of their own free will to die / Others take them with you when they blow sky high," there's absolutely no mincing of words. The track serves as a condemnation of Islamophobia and the hypocrisy of war. Madlib mines a brilliant string sample from the British prog-rock band Gentle Giant, chopping the chorus of "Funny Ways" (Vertigo, 1970) into two parts to create one of the album's highlights. The track ends with a snippet from a cartoon soundtrack, "that Mary was going around with an old flame," which sets up "Fancy Clown."

DOOM maintains that he always includes something in his albums for the ladies, and both "Fancy Clown" and "Eye," which follows, check that box on *Madvillainy*. On the former track, DOOM returns as his younger self, Vik Vaughn, to accuse his girlfriend, played by Walasia (and credited as "Allah's Reflection"), of cheating on him. It's not until the last lines, however, that we discover the hilarious twist—that poor Vik has been cuckolded by DOOM. "Ain't enough room in this—ing town/When you see tin head, tell him be ducking down," he threatens. Only someone with DOOM's chutzpah could pull off such a brilliant lyrical conceit. Madlib helps bring the drama to life chopping up Z. Z. Hill's "That Ain't the Way You Make Love" (United Artists, 1975), for its main piano loop and chorus, "You've been trippin' around, uptown/Wooing some fancy clown."

Meanwhile, "Eye" which immediately follows, sounds like something DOOM might have produced. Updating some syrupy R&B from the Whispers' "So Good" (Solar, 1984), Madlib adds a bouncy bassline and shuffling percussion to create a riff-ready soundtrack for singer Stacey Epps. Again, while the track may have nothing to do with the Madvillain concept, sometimes DOOM likes to hook up a friend. Epps never collaborated with the Villain on any other music, but after eventually earning her law degree, she became one of the lawyers representing his estate.

Moving into the album's last quarter, the third instrumental, "Supervillain Theme," ramps up the energy following a brief sampled intro from Just-Ice classic "Cold Gettin' Dumb." Another beat made in Brazil, Madlib uses two different parts—a guitar and drum fill—from "Adormeceu" (Continental, 1973) by O Terço. At only fifty-three seconds, the song plays more like an intro, as the guitar helps ratchet up the tension.

The payoff is "All Caps," not only one of the defining tracks on *Madvillainy* but also DOOM's theme song. The concluding line of his first verse, "Just remember, all caps when you spell the man's name," has transformed into a battle cry of sorts among his hardcore fan base, who deride those that don't adhere to the Villain's wishes. Once again, Madlib delivers the fire, chopping up the opening credits of the popular sixties and seventies detective show *Ironside*, starring Raymond Burr, for its diabolical minor chord progression, horns, and string intro, which he turns into an extro. The mellifluous intro to "All Caps" comes from another popular seventies show, *The Streets of San Francisco*. Even DOOM has to give it up to his partner, observing that "The beat is so butter." But no slack himself he also says: "Spot hot tracks like spot a pair of fat asses / Shot of scotch from out the square shot glasses / And he won't stop til he got the masses / And show 'em what they know not through flows of hot molasses." What other MC would use an expression like "know not," which sounds downright Shakespearean?

The climactic "All Caps" flows breezily into "Great Day," another amorphous composition based on Stevie Wonder's "How Can You Believe" (Gordy, 1968). The musicality of this track prompts Madlib to add some live flavor on his Rhodes electric piano. Meanwhile, DOOM returns to the sing-songy style that he debuted earlier on "Rainbows."

That brings us to *Madvillainy*'s grand finale, which also happens to be the last track they recorded for the album. Apparently, the label wanted something a little stronger than "Great Day" to end this incredible set, so they booked studio time and DOOM chose to rock another one of Madlib's Brazil creations. Made from only a few seconds of "Mariana, Mariana" (Philips, 1971) by singer Maria Bethânia, "Rhinestone Cowboy" ends up being the longest track on the album because of a series of stops and starts that give it the feel of a live performance. It's also one of his most quotable songs as he drops memorable one-liners like "Known as the grimy slimy limey—try me, blimey!"

But DOOM's real brilliance is displayed in self-referential rhymes about the making of the album:

> *It speaks well of the hyper base,*
> *Wasn't even tweaked and it leaked into cyberspace,*
> *Couldn't wait for the snipes to place,*
> *At least a track list in bold print typeface.*
> *Stopped for a year,*
> *Come back with thumb tacks, pop full of beer.*

As applause showers the end of his first verse, he seems to mess up, rhyming "Leaving your mind blown" with his last word, "rhinestone." He only adds "cowboy" as an afterthought as the applause track gets louder. But he shrugs it all off with "No, no, no, enough," before beginning the second verse with more triple word scores. "Goony goo-goo, looney cuckoo / Like Gary Gnu off New Zoo Revue, but who knew? / The mask had a loose screw," he raps, an admission that he's crazy and he knows it. Bringing the album full circle, we hear a final commentary from the Villain's documentary before the beat reprises and finally fades out.

These twenty-two songs with a running time of forty-six minutes challenged the established orthodoxy of rap at a time when it desperately needed some pushback. Though the record might not have fomented the kind of grassroots revolution that Wu-Tang had unleashed a decade earlier, it nonetheless influenced a whole new generation of MCs coming up—including Tyler, the Creator, Earl Sweatshirt, and Joey Badass. "Madvillain redeems the pretensions of independent hip-hop,"[32] stated a review in the esteemed *New Yorker*, the highbrow literary publication not typically known for its coverage of hip-hop. They definitely took DOOM seriously, though, commissioning two features on him over the years. While long a fixture in the underground, *Madvillainy* turned DOOM into a certified star and no longer simply your favorite rapper's favorite rapper.

18

MF DOOM/*MM . . FOOD*

> *I, personally, think there is a real danger of taking food too seriously. Food should be part of the bigger picture.*
>
> —ANTHONY BOURDAIN

Minneapolis seems an unlikely place to launch a rap dynasty, but, against all odds, that's exactly what Rhymesayers Entertainment was able to pull off. In 1995, a close circle of friends, formerly known as the Headshots crew, who had come of age in hip-hop's heyday of the late eighties/early nineties, decided to form their own label to release the music that they and their friends were making. They included rappers Sean "Slug" Daley and Musab "Sab the Artist" Saad, producer Anthony "Ant" Davis, and Brent "Siddiq" Sayers, who promoted parties. Aside from a healthy dose of ambition, and a determined, DIY mentality, Daley and Sayers already had the benefit of retail experience, the former working at the well-known mom-and-pop shop Electric Fetus, and the latter at Best Buy. These day jobs offered a vital, behind-the-scenes education into the mechanics of how music was distributed and sold.

"I gained a lot of experience just in the sense of what happens to records once they're made and put on the shelf," says Sayers. "I sat and watched a lot of records collect dust. I learned right away that building a demand is something that's important. Just the fact that you've got a record isn't going to matter."[1]

According to Daley, "I was able to pay attention to what worked in what markets, in this state at least," adding, "I was able to push Rhymesayers music onto people who I thought were already fucking with that box. And in that regard, I would say working at that store mostly was good for promotional purposes, on a local level."[2] Eventually, the crew took the bold step of opening their own record store, Fifth Element, running the label from the back room. While able to successfully nurture a loyal local following, they always kept an eye on expansion.

To that end, Atmosphere, the label's flagship act, composed of Daley and Davis, began relentlessly crisscrossing the country to promote their early releases. In the late nineties, a touring circuit for independent rap groups was nonexistent, so they blazed their own trail playing indie rock venues and quietly making a name for themselves. In 2001 alone, they completed three tours of the US. By the time of their second full-length, *God Loves Ugly* (Rhymesayers, 2002), they had added Europe and Japan to their touring schedule. After that album, distributed by Fat Beats, sold a staggering 130,000 copies, major labels like Sony, Warner Bros., and Interscope came knocking on their door.

Sayers, who had stepped back from the music to focus more on business concerns, diligently followed up on all the interest, taking meetings in LA and hearing everyone out. But having just built their own thriving independent enterprise from the ground up, he didn't understand what these labels could do for Rhymesayers that they hadn't already done for themselves. "It didn't seem like they really got it," he recalls. "It seemed like, at that moment in time, they were trying to cherry-pick Atmosphere. I don't think they got the big picture of Rhymesayers."[3] Needless to say, not only did the label rebuff all offers and stay independent, but they have since grown into one of the most lauded success stories in indie rap.

It was only inevitable, then, that Rhymesayers would eventually cross paths with the reigning underground champ, who was busy doing one-offs for any indie imprint who could meet his fairly modest demands. The Villain found an in through his Sub Verse labelmates Micranots, who had originally formed in Minneapolis and knew the Rhymesayers crew. He then deployed acting manager Big Benn Klingon to negotiate a deal on his behalf. Not only was said mission accomplished, but Klingon ended up finding a home for the Monsta Island Czars debut, *Escape from Monsta Island!* (Metal Face/Ben Grimm Entertainment, 2002), as well. Since that record was practically done, it made sense to release it first. Meanwhile DOOM's long-anticipated *Operation:*

Doomsday follow-up, *Mm..Food*, which he had been working on simultaneously, had to wait in line for a release date.

Since his partner Grimm was away serving a bid, DOOM figured heavily into bringing the Monsta Island Czars project to fruition. He brought in his old friend Web D (Ray Davis), at whose studio he had made some of the Fondle 'Em singles, to help carry some of the weight. "In Long Beach, he asked me, did I wanna be down to start a group and help him with that shit?" says Davis. "I was like, yeah, what the fuck. I'll do it. I was already in a group, which was Darc Mind on Loud [Records], but I was like, yeah, I'm down, you know what I'm saying? And he wanted me to create an MC name and all this other shit." For his Monsta Island alias, Davis chose King Cesar, a half-lion, half-lizard who first appeared in *Godzilla vs. Mechagodzilla* (Toho Studios, 1974).

The other members of the group were recruited from among people they already knew. Davis was working with a rapper named KD from the group Dirt Nation. After running into him at several sessions, DOOM asked him if he wanted to be down. "That's Kamackeris," says Davis, referring to KD's alter ego. "And then Kong was already down. Spiega got down 'cause he was Kong's cousin, and then, Gigan, you know. Everybody just started running with that shit." M.I.C grew to nine members, including Megalon, Rodan, DOOM, and Grimm, who does not even appear on the group's debut due to his incarceration.

In 2000, Davis moved to Jamaica Estates in Queens, where he set up his new studio, Island Digital, shortly before DOOM moved to Georgia. "I bought some more equipment, and I built the studio out here and I started just bringing everybody in recording, you know what I'm saying?" he recalls. "And DOOM had hit me up and said, 'Yo, I got a deal on Rhymesayers.' And he said, he's doing a solo record with them, and he also wants to do the Monsta Island shit. So, I said, let's go." Davis adds, "I'm kind of a little bit of a perfectionist. So, once I get involved with a project I'm trying to go deep. So, once I co-signed to do it, I'm buying like mad monster movies. I'm looking for samples, you know what I'm saying?"

He, in fact, supplied most of the music for the twenty-track album, of which DOOM produced only six songs. Four of those tracks—"Scientific Civilization (skit)"; "MIC Line," the only track he raps on; "Make it Squash!"; and "Escape from Monsta Isle"—were taken from existing *Special Herbs* instrumentals. Another track, "1,2 . . . 1,2," subsequently showed up on Ghostface's 2006 *Fishscale* (Def Jam) album as "9 Milli Bros." While not averse to double dealing, which inevitably caused problems down the line, DOOM's villainy didn't end there.

"The budget was a little shaky because it was revealed to us that it was only gonna be $10,000. But, then again, the actual deal was for $20,000. So, there was some fucked up shit that went on on the money side," according to Davis. "So that's why he [DOOM] got into a lot of arguments with them after that. Because he kind of did them wrong. But I'm not gonna lie. He paid me what he told me he would." While Davis received $2,000 for his involvement in the project and each of the MCs, who appear on multiple tracks, earned $1,000, that accounts for only $8,000 of the advance. Big Benn Klingon benefited from a broker's fee, but it's not even clear if Percy Carey (aka Grimm), who is credited as an executive producer of the album along with DOOM and his wife, received a cut at all. Even before the Rhymesayers deal, he had given DOOM money to help with the production of *Operation: Doomsday*, which the Villain had invested in new equipment. But, according to Grimm, he had never been repaid, which might explain why he and DOOM had a falling out following his release from prison.

To add insult to injury, DOOM, after blowing up, went on to apparently diss the group. In the song "El Chupa Nibre," he jokingly says he once joined a rap clique called "Midgets into Crunk," obviously a veiled reference to Monsta Island Czars. Grimm, however, was not amused, and, in response, recorded one of the harshest diss tracks of all time, called "The Book of Daniel," from his self-released album *American Hunger* (Day by Day Entertainment, 2006). But they eventually called a truce and came to an understanding, according to Grimm.

"He was always a good dude to me. I can't front, you know," says Davis. "Me and him had a pretty decent relationship, but at one time he just cut everybody off, you know what I'm saying? When he really got into his persona. This is probably after *Mm . . Food* I would say."

One of rap's biggest trends to be turbocharged in the new millennium were "collabs," which saw artists padding their releases with any number of high-profile cameos. DOOM, in fact, would become very much in demand as a featured artist on other rapper's records—as he did on De La's "Rock Co.Kane Flow" and the Gorillaz track "November Has Come" (both 2004). However, being notoriously picky about whom he worked with, he hardly ever reciprocated when it came to his own albums. One artist who managed to capture his attention and respect, though, was the Atlanta-based Empress Stahhr tha Femcee (Kimberly Richardson), who earned guest features on three different DOOM releases, beginning with *Mm . . Food*—the only person to enjoy such an honor.

The two initially met in January 2000 at Atlanta hot spot MJQ, where Micranots were throwing a release party for their sophomore effort, *Obelisk Movements* (Sub Verse Music, 2000). As the group performed, their friend and associate, Stahhr, joined them on stage for a raucous freestyle session. Afterward, DOOM popped backstage and introduced himself, telling her, *Yo, you dope!* But it wasn't until almost two years later, on Halloween of 2001, that they connected again at another Sub Verse showcase at Club Kaya. This time, when DOOM told her, *Yo, I wanna work with you*, she found herself at his house the following week.[4]

The first song they collaborated on was "Next Levels," also featuring Lil' Sci and ID 4 Windz, of Scienz of Life. DOOM was busy cobbling together tracks for his King Geedorah album, so that's where it landed. But more than simply a straight work-for-hire situation, he ended up taking Stahhr under his wing because he recognized something special in her. According to Stahhr, he told her, *You're dope, you're like a female version of me, I don't even think you know how ill you are*.[5] They also bonded over shared interests—such as following the teachings of Dr. Malachi York, who had, at this point, relocated his Nuwaubian community to Georgia. In fact, they attended Dr. York's final class at the Eatonton compound together before the government raid in May 2002 that sent him to prison. "We bonded more personally than musically," she says, "But the personal bond is what helped with the music. That made it all come together."⁶

In addition to accompanying DOOM on the road when he opened for Talib Kweli's Beautiful Struggle Tour in 2004, she absorbed a lot by virtue of being in his presence. "He told me not to date my music," she says. "When you are writing [or rapping] don't say the year. He said when you are approaching something, you are a writer. You should be able to write about anything. That was why he had all the different personalities." DOOM told her, *That is your creative license, use it. You don't have to personalize everything and that will give you more freedom.*⁷

DOOM even encouraged her to assume different aliases and personalities, pointing her in the direction of the *Spider-Man and His Amazing Friends* animated series from the 80s. That show and its one-off comic book introduced a superhero called "Firestar," formerly a member of the X-Men, who could control any form of heat or fire. In her normal life she was known as Angelica Jones, a love interest of Peter Parker's. "I went to the comic bookstore, I bought all the comics about Firestar, and I read them," she says. "Like, this is exactly me."⁸

When DOOM was finally able to focus his attention on his next solo album, he made sure to include Stahhr in his plans, telling her, *You're the secret weapon.*⁹ He gave her a beat CD to choose from along with some words of guidance: *I want you to do whatever you want to do on this beat. I want you to bring a feminine perspective to this album. You're gonna be the balance.*¹⁰ She even initiated her new persona, Angelika, for the track that would eventually be called "Guinnesses." Though they discussed doing a full-length Angelika album for DOOM's Metal Face imprint, it was one of many ideas that never materialized. "Here is the thing about DOOM," she says. "You can be in touch with him and then not be in touch with him for like years, and then be back in touch."¹¹ So, even with close collaborators, the Villain was known to work in mysterious ways.

Released in November 2004, only eight months after *Madvillainy*, the *Mm.. Food* album, titled after an anagram for DOOM's name as well as the record's unifying theme, provided the one-two punch that made for a banner year. While the mainstream offered plenty of distractions for the masses—including Kanye West's *College Dropout* (Def Jam/Rocafella), a debut that sold 441,000 copies in its first week on its way to quadruple platinum, or Lil Wayne's *Tha Carter* (Cash Money/Universal), another platinum seller with sales of 116,000 in its first week—no one could keep up with the prolific DOOM, who dropped a trifecta of albums (including *VV:2 Venomous Villain*) on three different labels that year. Considering he commanded nowhere near the same budget or promotional power as his major label rivals, it was an astounding feat, and a small triumph of art over commerce. In further defiance of industry standards, he enjoyed full ownership over his art, a claim that no other high-profile rapper could make.

A fitting follow-up to *Operation: Doomsday*, *Mm . . Food* finds Metal Fingers back behind the boards, with a few production assists from his friends, whipping up the kind of bizarre concoctions that only his twisted imagination could conjure (e.g., a track called "Vomitspit"). Per his signature style, he skillfully strings together his food-themed menu with carefully sourced morsels from Spider-Man and Fantastic Four cartoons from the seventies and eighties that further flesh out his character's back story. But if you're already on board the DOOM train, these lengthy aural collages, while injecting some humor into the mix, are almost an overindulgence on the Villain's part. It's the screenwriter's equivalent of hitting us over the head with exposition, and on repeated listening, tends to mire the album's momentum—especially the extended skit that he places smack dab in the middle of the selection. But apparently, DOOM, proud of the work he put into these collages—watching hours of cable TV, cartoons, and films for just the right parts—wants to make you listen to them whether you like it or not.

The first words of dialogue we hear on the album come from Charlie Ahearn's classic *Wild Style* (Music Box Films, 1983), a film that captured the rawness and creativity of the budding hip-hop revolution in the Bronx from the point of view of its main character, graffiti writer Lee Quiñones. Nas begins his masterful debut, *Illmatic* (Columbia, 1994), with the theme music from that same film, evoking the kind of old-school nostalgia for which ex–graf writer DOOM also aims. Adhering to the album's concept, the Villain finds a throwaway scene in which the characters are talking about food. But DOOM employs food in a metaphorical sense. "It's all analogies between food and life,"[12] he explained. On another level, too, he is feeding heads, alienated by the mainstream, who hunger for some good old-fashioned boom bap.

After weaving in food-related fragments from the sci-fi film *Logan's Run* (MGM, 1976) and even Frank Zappa asking "Would you like a snack?" he mines his biggest source of material, cartoons. The animated *Spider-Man* TV series—particularly season one, episode seven ("Cannon of DOOM")—produced by Marvel in 1982 provides not only the bulk of Doctor Doom's back story, but also some choice loops from its soundtrack. After his minions declare Operation Doomsday complete, and the good Doctor himself speaks, a dramatic horn fanfare, sampled as the foundation for "Beef Rap," announces the Villain's triumphant return.

"The challenge is what it's about with me—the challenge of being such a picky topic to handle," DOOM explained about this track. "Also, the double entendre with the word 'beef,' the way it's perceived in the street world, and it's a food—a so-called food—so how it's perceived in the nutritional realm. The fact that there's two things that correlate there gave me enough metaphors to play with. But it's all fun. I always do it with something that's fun. Anger is something I don't deal with."[13] Despite this admission, the song seems to revolve around rivalry, feuds, and conflict in the rap game, in what has become one of the album's most eminently quotable tracks.

From the first verse, he already displays a skillful knack for mixing metaphors: "Beef rap, could lead to getting your teeth capped / Or even a wreath from mom dukes on some grief crap / I suggest you change your diet / It can lead to high blood pressure if you fry it / Or even a stroke, heart attack, heart disease / It ain't no startin' back when arteries start to squeeze." Recited in his typical husky-voiced, conversational tone, DOOM sounds more like an MD than an MC, as he conveys a simple message: Beef is not healthy for you. As far as rap rivalries go, how many rappers have lost their lives over a diss? The same goes for red meat, cited as a leading cause of death behind heart disease, hypertension, and high cholesterol.

But DOOM is obviously determined to take on everybody, taunting the competition with laugh-out-loud lines like, "What up? To all rappers: Shut up with your shutting up / And keep a shirt on, at least a button up / Yuck! Is they rhymers or stripping males? / Out of work jerks since they shut down Chippendales." With more jokes than Redd Foxx or Richard Pryor, he indulges in a little self-aggrandizement as well: "Whether animal, vegetable or mineral / It's a miracle how he gets so lyrical / And proceed to move the crowd like an old negro spiritual." The rapper Mos Def later gushed with admiration for DOOM on a YouTube video, reciting these exact lines. A song like "Beef Rap" finds the Villain at the top of his game as both an MC and producer.

On the following track, "Hoe Cakes," DOOM dips into his usual bag of tricks, the blending of eighties R&B with hip-hop beats. His starting point is a snippet of beatboxing from "Supersonic" (Ruthless, 1987) by all-female Cali rappers J.J. Fad. At the time of its release, this one-hit wonder, produced by Arabian Prince, broke the top-ten dance charts before garnering a Grammy nomination in 1989. But in the fast-changing world of beats, the song didn't age well, and to even consider sampling it would have been considered ludicrous by most.

Enter DOOM, who upends our preconceived notions and biases. Using the beatboxing as a rhythm track, he also places a snippet of the chorus—the word "Super"—at the end of certain lines to function as a kind of call and response to his rhymes. For example, he says, "On the microphone, he flossed the ring, *Super* / Average MCs is like a TV blooper." In the same verse, DOOM also manages to work in rhyming references to King Koopa, the antagonist from Nintendo's Super Mario franchise, and daring hijacker D. B. Cooper, who disappeared with $200,000 in ransom money after parachuting from a commercial airliner in 1971. In a completely inspiring, yet left field move, DOOM marries the beatboxing to the opening of Anita Baker's smooth R&B classic, "Sweet Love" (Elektra, 1986), making the two disparate elements sound completely compatible. Originally appearing on a volume of *Special Herbs* as "Jasmine Blossoms," this track is one of several from the series that gets a vocal treatment on this album.

As for the song's title, "Hoe Cakes" refer to a meal made in slavery days, usually consisting of a cornmeal mixture cooked over an open fire via the business end of a garden hoe. In this case DOOM's double meaning becomes fairly obvious, as he flexes his pimp game. "Whether a bougie broad, nerd ho, street chick / Don't call her wifey if you met her at Freaknik," he says, referencing the black version of spring break in Atlanta, discontinued in 1998 over lewd activity, violence, and sexual assaults.

The album's first collaboration arrives next—the Count Bass D produced "Potholderz," on which he also rhymes. Though, technically, not about food, he explains, "It was a complete song of mine before I knew [DOOM] was working on *Mm... Food*. I gave the song to him because he asked for it and it belonged on *Mm... Food*."[14] That probably explains why he spits two verses compared to DOOM's one. The breezy beat owes its effervescence to a guitar loop off Billy Butler's "400 Girls Ago" (Kilmarnock, 1973), supplemented by some scratching and the alternating vocals of Dr. Dre (saying "Hot shit") and Big Daddy Kane (saying "Aw, shit"). Though this is the first time DOOM and the Count have gone head-to-head with each other on a track, they complement each other perfectly, sounding very much in sync.

What follows is an outtake from *Madvillainy* called "One Beer," which begins as an ode to DOOM's favorite beverage. In the intro, he even interpolates the lyrics to Cole Porter's "I Get a Kick Out of You" (1934), originally sung by Ethel Merman: "I get no kick from champagne / Mere alcohol doesn't thrill me at all / So tell me why it should be true / That I get a kick out of you." But DOOM sneakily substitutes "brew" for the last word before romping through the track with his usual no-holds-barred, free-associative wordplay. He's gunning for the heights of hilarity with verses like: "He went to go laugh and get some head by the side road / She asked him to autograph her derriere, it read: / 'To Wide Load, this yard bird taste like fried toad turd / Love, Villain'—take pride in code words."

Madlib creates a hard-hitting foundation for DOOM's comedic ravings, sampling two parts of the song "Huit octobre 1971" (Esperance, 1973), by an obscure French band called Cortex. The five-piece ensemble that fused jazz, rock, funk, and soul was formed in 1974 by producer Alain Mion, who, according to Whosampled.com, holds the distinction of being one of the most sampled French producers (his compositions have been used in works by Rick Ross, Tyler, the Creator, and Wiz Khalifa). But the band's lead singer, Mireille Dalbray, whose ethereal vocals soar atop a drum roll and harmonica, is what catches Madlib's fancy. She appears to be singing the words "A Oui" (Ah, yes), which almost sounds like a chipmunk's rendition of "one beer," perhaps explaining how that track received its title.

The next track, "Deep Fried Frenz," is instantly recognizable as a piece of Whodini's "Friends" (Jive, 1984)—originally sampled from Ronnie Laws's "Friends and Strangers" (EMI, 1977). Already released as the instrumental "Myrhh," from *Special Herbs, Volumes 1&2*, this track puts a pause on the album's humorous content to address a topic that's obviously heavy on DOOM's mind—fake friends. Lyrically, it's one of the few songs in which he uses the word "I" instead of the third person as per usual. So, you know he's speaking from the heart when he raps, "I found a way to get peace of mind for years and left the hell alone / Turn a deaf ear to the cellular phone / Send me a letter or better, we could see each other in real life / Just so you could feel me like a steel knife." Ouch!

As the track devolves into more Fantastic Four material, DOOM makes a somewhat questionable move. The next four selections—"Poo-Putt Platter," "Fillet-O-Rapper," "Gumbo," and "Fig Leaf Bi-Carbonate"—segue into each other to make up one extended audio collage, about 6:26 in length, that, unfortunately, disrupts the album's flow. Accompanied by various musical samples from the *Fat Albert Halloween Special*, Hubert Laws, Frank Zappa, and the soundtrack to the animated *Spider-Man* TV series, the running gag essentially centers around a spoof taken from the seventies children's show *The Electric Company*. The joke involves actor Skip Hinnant playing outdoorsman, forager, and early health food advocate Euell Gibbons, who, unfortunately, passed away at only sixty-four due to an aortic aneurysm. He delivers choice lines like, "I tripped a lot out here in the woods lately," that function as the double entendre that DOOM intended. But any joke told repeatedly loses its luster, and after a couple listens, this extended skit section becomes fast-forward material.

Following this intermission of sorts, DOOM returns to the mic on "Kon Karne," a touching tribute to Subroc. Using his patented blend technique, he again samples two different parts of the sultry piano/bass groove of Sade's "Is It a Crime" (Epic, 1985), placing them atop the beatbox rhythm from Just-Ice's

"Latoya" (Fresh, 1986). "Me and Sub is like the brown Smothers Brothers," he says, comparing them to the famed comedy duo of the fifties and sixties who started off as singers. He ends his tribute with: "Dog-gone it—do the statistics / How he bust lyrics, it's too futuristic for ballistics / And far too eccentric for forensics / I dedicate this mix to Subroc / The hip-hop Hendrix."

As with most songs on the album, it ends with more of Doctor Doom's back story, which he leaves open for interpretation:

> As years passed, he became even more bitter and angry,
> Burning with a vengeance against the world,
> Finally, amidst hidden scrolls he found what he had been seeking.
> Then clothed in a suit of invulnerable armor and possessing
> The world's greatest secrets of science and magic,
> He returned to his homeland, and there he remained.
> Scheming, dreaming, planning,
> Plotting his mad campaign to conquer the entire world.

DOOM has always maintained that he does not act out of anger, despite having more than enough to be angry about in his life, so he is feeding his own mythology here, and creating the brand, as it were. The character's preoccupation with science and magic, however, does reflect DOOM's own interest in esoteric knowledge, which he constantly hints at but never explores in any depth in his music. He reserved that realm for his own research and experimentation, but anyone who knew the Villain more than casually was aware of where his head was really at.

Stahhr makes her appearance on the only vocal track on which DOOM does not appear, "Guinnesses," originally titled "Purple Heart Love." This time around, however, she plays her alter ego, Angelika, detailing the experience of a relationship gone awry, which forces her to drink away the pain. Not many people have earned the distinction of getting their own solo track on a DOOM album, and she does not disappoint, presenting a strong female voice and perspective. The Villain fully approved, asking her to change only one thing.

"It needed to have a food title because we had gotten to where everything was going to be named after a food," says Stahhr. "I thought about what happens when you break up with somebody. You're bitter, you're heartbroken, you're drinking away the pain. There's this anger, and that's where "Guinnesses" came from."[15] The instrumental, titled "Lovage," originally appeared on the second volume of *Special Herbs*.

"Kon Queso," which follows, is the second of two songs that DOOM did not produce. After previously appearing on a twelve-inch titled "Yee Haw" (2003), by Chicago underground group Molemen, DOOM tapped their producer, PNS, for a remix to include on *Mm..Food*. He samples a bass and keyboard part from "Newscast One" (Coloursound, 1983) by Christian Chevallier and John Tender, a loop that may have appealed to the Villain for its borderline-cheesy keyboard sounds. Perhaps that's also why the track is called "Kon Queso" or "with cheese" in Spanish.

Lyrically, DOOM smashes it, lacing his internal rhyme scheme with spot-on observations: "Have no fear, the ninja here / Feel him like a tinge in your ear / From drinking ginger beer." He also displays a keen sense of his audience and how people perceive him when he says, "We have the Supervillain in his own defense to speak / It's all part of my mental techniques / Available to freaks and pencil neck geeks / Train a sane brain to an insane train of thought / On a campaign trail to gain your support." He follows that last line with the usual drop-dead humor: "Charge cash for an autograph / Say some shit to make your daughter laugh / Then slaughter that ass."

Moving toward the album's finale, DOOM saves some of his finest work for last. "Rapp Snitch Knishes," the second of two collaborations with the equally shadowy Mr. Fantastik (the first, "Anti-Matter," appeared on the King Geedorah album), is one of the few DOOM songs that boasts a hook, and it's a doozy: "Rap snitches, tellin' all their business, see 'em in court, they be their own star witness / Do you see the perpetrator? Yeah, I'm right here / Fuck around, get the whole label sent up for years." DOOM and Fantastik are essentially poking fun at rappers who admit to committing crimes in their rhymes and are taken to task for it in court. Unfortunately, too many instances of art imitating life made this song both relevant as well as funny—just ask rappers such as Bobby

Shmurda (Ackquille Jean Pollard), Tekashi 6ix9ine (Daniel Hernandez), or Young Thug (Jeffrey Williams).

It's also noteworthy that this track is probably the only rap song in history to use the Yiddish word *knish*. "I grew up in New York, so knishes were a part of life," DOOM explained. "It's a funny sounding word, too. Knish. Words that rhyme with knish, any aspect of that, how it sounds, how it can match with something in society. So 'rap snitch' and 'knishes' go together, so it was easy to find a title. The challenge was coming up with good enough references to make the song."[16] Both MCs, however, rise to that challenge, complementing each other's effortless styles. For the backing track, DOOM flips another borderline-cheesy loop—David Matthews's cover of "Space Oddity" (CTI, 1977)—simply speeding it up. The instrumental originally appeared as "Coffin Nails" from *Special Herbs, Volumes 5&6*.

The album's penultimate track, "Vomitspit," falls into another definite type that DOOM likes to rock, as its main loop, sampled from Canadian rockers Mashmakhan's "Happy You Should Be" (Columbia, 1970), evokes a children's song. One can picture the Villain riding a merry-go-round, sipping on a spiked Slurpee, as he casually rhymes, "Plead the fifth, sip wine stiffly / Patiently come up and be spiffy in a jiffy / Gift for the grind, criminal mind shifty / Swift with the nine through a fifty-nine fifty." This song is also one of the few in which DOOM simply lets the instrumental ride out.

The selection ends with a track called "Kookies," whose subject matter one might never discern from its title. "Kookies is ill, totally on some Internet porn shit," DOOM explained. "I notice when you online on some porn shit, the word 'cookies' comes up. Oh, I guess that's the picture as it saves to your hard drive. They call those cookies. So, I got a fever for them cookies. I'm a cookie monster, trying to go into the cookie jar."[17] That explains DOOM's metaphorical use of the term in his rhymes, as he references such brands as Girl Scout Cookies and the English brand Peek Freans. As it relates to computers, cookies comprise small packets of data that a computer receives and sends, for authentication or tracking, while browsing a website. But after hearing DOOM's musings on the topic, it's impossible to look at the term in the same way. Following some sloppy scratching and a final word from the *Spiderman* cartoons, DOOM ends the fifteen-song, forty-nine-minute romp that is *Mm .. Food* with a reprise of the theme from "Beef Rap," which started it off.

It is difficult to wrap one's head around the fact that while working on four albums simultaneously (five if you include *Special Herbs*) during the early part of the new millennium, he still managed to make each a unique piece of art—an unprecedented feat in rap. The closest comparison might be the RZA, who hardly left his basement between 1993 and 1997, producing that first round of game-changing Wu-Tang Clan solo albums. In a similar manner, DOOM, through sheer hard work, perseverance, commitment, and a boundless enthusiasm for his craft, attained a creative zenith during these years, easily explaining his surge in popularity. Though mainstream recognition still eluded him, that, too, would change in the upcoming years as he finally emerged from the underground to become an international icon.

To promote the new album, he embarked on his first national tour, The *Mm .. Food* Drive Tour, with dates in Chicago, Minneapolis, San Francisco, LA, Fort Collins (Colorado), Boulder (Colorado), Philly, and New York. Since the tour ended just before Thanksgiving, DOOM and the label designed a raffle to encourage fans to donate canned goods at the shows in exchange for prizes. Coordinating with local food banks, they were, apparently, able to raise over one thousand pounds of food. Rappers weren't generally known for being so generous, and only someone who had experienced hunger himself knew the power of a free meal. On "Kon Karne," DOOM even said, "He came to feed the children like Sally Struthers," referencing the former *All in the Family* actress who became a spokesperson for the Christian Children's Fund. Unlike his more villainous posturing, this was no idle boast.

19

DANGER DOOM/
THE MOUSE AND THE MASK

This is the real secret of life—to be completely engaged in what you are doing.... And instead of calling it work, realize it is play.

—ALAN WATTS

DOOM wasn't the only underground artist to enjoy a breakout year in 2004. In March, the same month *Madvillainy* dropped, a little-known DJ by the name of Brian Burton (aka Danger Mouse) was already whipping up quite a frenzy in the music world with a totally illegal, unlicensed project that almost broke the internet. *The Grey Album*, his mash-up of Jay Z's *The Black Album* (Def Jam/Rocafella, 2003) and the Beatles' classic *White Album* (Apple, 1968)—so nicknamed for its plain cover—could be considered the first viral sensation of the millennium. In an era that saw computers beginning to reshape the consumption of music, hundreds of thousands of people downloaded the album for free, in flagrant violation of copyright and intellectual property laws. While Jay-Z may have been flattered to hear the Fab Four backing him, EMI, owner of the Beatles catalog, took the issue a bit more seriously, sending Burton a cease-and-desist letter. Though the naïve and unassuming deejay had never foreseen this donnybrook, his provocative actions nevertheless amounted to a straight-up gangsta move, bound to make any villain blush. It also transformed "Danger Mouse" into a household name overnight.

Prior to his entry on the world stage, the current six-time Grammy winner, who is spoken of in the same breath as the likes of Phil Spector and Brian Eno, seemed an unlikely candidate for super-producer status. Burton had only started dabbling in production while a telecommunications major at the University of Georgia in Athens. Though he had grown up listening to rap, his big revelation in college was sixties rock—bands like the Beatles and Pink Floyd, who had somehow eluded his youth. "Hip-hop was what I knew really well, but it's not what inspired me to make music," says Burton. "It was really the older rock stuff I started to hear."[1]

A serendipitous encounter with CeeLo Green (Thomas DeCarlo Calloway) at a concert at the university led to his first big break. After passing the Goodie Mob rapper a tape of his beats, which veered more toward trip-hop than rap, they, surprisingly, bonded over a mutual love of Portishead. In fact, Green, who had diverse tastes when it came to music, was at a point in his career where he was branching out beyond rap and contemplating a solo move. He saw something in the untested kid worth taking a chance on, offering him the opportunity to produce his forthcoming album.

What would have been a coup for most unknown artists proved just the beginning for Burton, who agreed to work on Green's solo project as the rapper's schedule permitted. In the meantime, however, he made the bold decision to relocate to the UK, since so much of the music he loved originated there. To help support himself, he spent his days bartending at a pub near London Bridge, while working on music at night. Before leaving Georgia, he had started a relationship with the Atlanta-based Cartoon Network, who licensed some of his beats as incidental music between shows. To help supplement his meager income, he maintained this side hustle. While living abroad, the ambitious Burton took full advantage of the opportunity to network, dropping his demos off at different British labels. One eventually bit.

Lex Records was then operating as an offshoot of Warp, the British independent known for its futuristic techno and electronic releases by such boundary-breaking acts as Aphex Twin, Autechre, and Squarepusher. The subimprint was the brainchild of Tom Brown, a Warp employee and hip-hop head, who initially ran the label's mail-order and online store, Bleep.com. He had been instrumental in getting New York alterna-rappers Antipop Consortium signed to Warp in 2000, before his bosses gave him the go-ahead to do a series of twelve-inches that they would finance in exchange for half ownership of his start-up. Burton dropped off a bunch of his CDs at Lex. A mash-up that paired the rapping of Brooklyn's Audio Two with the music of French electronic duo Air was enough to get his foot in the door.

Offered a twelve-inch release, the young deejay originally proposed doing a collaboration with underground Brooklyn MC Jemini the Gifted One (Thomas Smith), of whom he was a fan. A mutual friend, New York rapper J-Zone (Jarret A. Mumford), promised to connect them. Using his small advance, Burton flew to New York to record Jemini, making three tracks together. Released in 2002, the twelve-inch was fairly-well received, leading to an entire album called *Ghetto Pop Life* the following year. Produced entirely by Burton, it featured cameos by Tha Alkaholiks, J-Zone, the Pharcyde, and Prince Po of Organized Konfusion.

That record marked Danger Mouse's signing to Lex as a solo artist, for an exclusive five-album deal. It was only fitting that he had borrowed his alias from a popular British animated TV series that ran from 1981 to 1992. Following a two-year stint in England, Burton eventually moved to California, where, serious about pursuing a career in music, he was able to secure the services of a manager. Lex subsequently used Burton's connections to build up their catalog. They signed Prince Po to do a whole album called *The Slickness* (2004) on which the deejay acted as executive producer and contributed three tracks. One of those tracks, "Social Distortion," marked his first collaboration with DOOM. J-Zone, once again, provided the introduction.

"He was like, 'DOOM's amazing. You should get DOOM on a track.' And, you know, we were like, 'Yeah, but how do we get hold of him?' He was like, 'Gimme the money,' you know, this kinda thing," says Brown. DOOM had been on the radar of Lex's head honcho since *Operation: Doomsday*, and he was eager to work with the mysterious MC. So, the label coughed up their usual fee of $2,000 to $3,000 for his cameo on the album. Burton subsequently tapped DOOM for a verse on a remix of "Somersault" that he did for British trip-hop duo Zero 7.

Meanwhile, Danger Mouse and Jemini's *Ghetto Pop Life*, released in September 2003, was moving slowly. "We came up with a kind of plan to keep it going, to kind of try and blow it up," according to Brown. "And there were like a few points on the plan. And one of them was get a kind of A-list rapper to do a guest verse. And then another was go on tour with a big band. And then another was do a mixtape, and the mixtape we used for an example was *NastraDOOMas*." That unofficial release, a mash-up of Nas acapellas over DOOM *Special Herbs* beats, had been released via HipHopSite.com, run by DJ Mike Pizzo.

Burton, in fact, had already been in touch with Pizzo, who provided him with acapellas from what was billed as Jay-Z's retirement album, *The Black Album*. In December 2003, while cleaning his room he came across a copy of *The Beatles* (aka *The White Album*), when sudden inspiration struck. For his entire life, the racially ambiguous Burton, both light-skinned and sporting a reddish afro, felt plagued by a nagging dilemma: Black kids weren't supposed to listen to rock (even though Black artists originally created the music). Yet he knew in his heart that music was colorless, possessing the transcendent power to bring people together. What if he were to combine these two popular albums—made by totally unique artists, eras apart, and aimed at different audiences—to create something that everyone could relate to and enjoy? He considered it both an art project and a personal challenge, but certainly not something he could sell due to the obvious copyright issues. Therefore, he planned to work quickly and not devote too much time to it, though, in the end, *The Grey Album* took him about two weeks of serious toiling. In February 2004, Lex paid for a pressing of three thousand promo CDs, circulating them among press and media to help jump-start interest in Danger Mouse's official release. The music was also posted online for free, where it didn't take long to register a reaction.

"I remember flying to New York to go and see people, probably to go and see Prince Po," says Brown. "And I had flu, and I was in the Grammercy Park Hotel before they'd done it up. It was still like a big scruffy old shithole. I got to the hotel, and I was feeling really ill, so I stopped to get some flu medicine. I had never had American flu medicine. So, when I sat there like shivering and watching TV, on the news ticker on the bottom of the screen, it was like, 'DJ Danger Mouse takes Jay-Z's *Black Album* and the Beatles' *White Album*,' you know, it was on CNN somehow. And, like, I thought I was tripping on the flu medicine 'cause it was so strong." That Danger Mouse had just become the beneficiary of the best viral marketing campaign on the planet, however, proved to be no hallucination.

The caricature of a Jazz Age flapper, Betty Boop may have broken the seal on adult-oriented animation in the thirties. But it took Fox TV's *The Simpsons*, first airing in 1989, to create a viable audience for it. Since that time, no other entity has done more to nurture the crucial teen/young adult demographic than Cartoon Network's Adult Swim, a late-night block of original programming for insomniacs. In 1994, *Space Ghost Coast to Coast* debuted as their first original show, featuring the Hanna-Barbera superhero from the sixties as host of his own late-night comedy/talk show. Then, in late 2000, the network's head programmer, Mike Lazzo, premiered an entire slate of late-night original shows that could only be described as irreverent, sarcastic, surrealist, and just plain weird. These not-ready-for-prime-time cartoons, including *Sealab 2021*; *Harvey Birdman, Attorney at Law*; *Aqua Teen Hunger Force*, and *The Brak Show*, started winning over a cult audience of dedicated fans.

Jason DeMarco, who had created a block of action cartoons and Japanese anime called Toonami, was senior vice president of Adult Swim on-air when he first met Burton, then a university student. "We were buying songs from people to use in our commercials and promos and packaging. We didn't have a lot of money, so we were trying to find up and coming beat-makers," he says. "He would make mixtapes as DJ Danger Mouse, but he also released instrumental hip-hop albums under the title Pelican City that were very Portishead-inspired. And I found one of those CDs at a local record store. And, so, when I was trying to find people to make beats for us, I reached out to him. So, from that point on, he became somebody we worked with a lot," says DeMarco.

After returning from England, Burton stopped by the Williams Street offices in Atlanta, where Adult Swim was produced, to catch up and discuss some projects. Having just completed *The Grey Album*, which was not out yet, he was excited to preview it for DeMarco and his boss, Lazzo. "We were blown away,"

DeMarco recalls. Burton, then, broached the topic of doing an album with DOOM, using the cartoons from Toonami as a sample source. "And I said, OK, well I don't know that a Toonami record would make sense, but maybe an Adult Swim one since we have so many Hanna-Barbera characters we've repurposed and I know DOOM loves to sample those old Hanna-Barbera, Fantastic Four cartoons," says DeMarco. "And, so, they were like, 'How do we do it?' I said, well, first tell me how much money you need and then let me go to my boss and see if I can somehow convince him this is good marketing for us to be associated with this."

The idea wasn't so much of a stretch considering Adult Swim, since its inception, had always featured rap in its shows and commercials. Philly legend Schoolly D had even created the opening theme for *Aqua Teen Hunger Force*, which revolved around a talking hamburger patty named Meatwad, and his sidekicks, Frylock, an order of fries, and Master Shake, who joined forces to solve various asinine capers. A fan of both DOOM and Danger Mouse, Lazzo gave the green light. But releasing an album proved to be an entirely novel proposition for a TV production company.

"Danger Mouse's manager, Jeff Antebi, said, 'Well, I think I can set it up with Epitaph. They seem really excited about what an unusual project this is. They'll promote it. And if you guys will promote it, too, this could be something,'" says DeMarco, referring to the punk/post-punk label out of LA. "So that's kind of how it happened, was really Lazzo being a fan and allowing me the space to say, OK, let's spend this money and we don't know what the return is gonna be other than a cool thing. And then Epitaph saying, 'Okay, yeah, we'll put it out.' And they gave us the shittiest record deal ever. We didn't know any better, and they made tons of money and we didn't make a dime because we didn't make a good deal." DOOM and Danger Mouse made out like villains, however, scoring a $150,000 advance as well as the unique opportunity to collaborate with a popular, rap-friendly cable network.

While the artists had to deduct studio expenses from that fee, the network covered all clearances for cartoons, paying the voice actors, designing the original artwork, and funding the production of two music videos—not to mention free TV advertising. Epitaph handled the manufacture of CDs and LPs and paid for all the regular promotion, including radio. They eventually had to cede world rights (outside of the US) to Lex, who had signed Burton to an exclusive deal. Considering the huge underground buzz behind DOOM and Danger Mouse, the release had strong potential, but, at the same time, nobody knew for sure what the reception would be.

Both artists came to the DangerDOOM project with their own motivation and agendas. "I kind of had the idea of taking like the coolest most underground kind of MC that's basically kind of out right now—credibility-wise—and just kinda seeing what would happen if we did the most silly pop thing that we could do," says Burton. "And we got mixed reactions out of the whole thing and never really told people we were approaching it that way."[2] DOOM, on the other hand, admitted, "The one thing that really made me do that project was basically because of the bread. It had nothing to do with the music really. I know [Danger Mouse] is a good dude, everybody got beats and shit, but what about the bread? He had a good strategy for getting bread and we made bread, so it was a good thing."[3]

But DeMarco, who acted as a kind of A&R on the project, had broader concerns. "The whole question was, can we do this album and not have it be corny because, essentially, it's a commercial for a TV network, you know? It could be looked at that way," he says. "And I knew that DOOM was a real cartoon fan and so was Brian so that it came from a place of actual appreciation. And, so, it wasn't a money thing, although DOOM, in later years, did talk shit that it was for money. But I think he was just bitter 'cause we weren't talking."

The Adult Swim exec recalls his first encounter with DOOM—soon after the deal was completed—when the rapper was singing a different tune. The meeting took place at an apartment DOOM rented in the U-Haul Lofts in Midtown Atlanta—incidentally, the same building where DeMarco's boss lived, but two floors below. Apparently, the Villain, whose main residence was in Kennesaw, only stayed there when he had business in town, as evidenced by the ratty, secondhand couch that comprised the apartment's sole piece of furniture. Curiously, the only thing adorning the walls was a periodic table of elements, while DOOM's preferred reading material—*Merriam-Webster's Dictionary of Allusions*, *The Dictionary of Clichés*, and *Depraved and Insulting English*—lay stacked on the floor.

"We sat down, and he just talked about how excited he was about the project," says DeMarco. "But really beyond that, he just wanted to talk about cartoons. He talked mostly about Scooby-Doo, Fantastic Four. He talked about his favorite Adult Swim shows. He wasn't really like let's sit down and I'll tell you all my ideas about the album. It was literally just like wanting to talk about cartoons as a fellow person who loves cartoons. He just was very sweet. And you could tell, he was genuinely a person who was madly in love with cartoons and that they had meant a lot to him, his whole life." They also shared a bonding moment over a mutual love of Pink Panther cartoons.

While DOOM may have been conducting a charm offensive for the guy writing the checks, he also ended up putting in his fair share of work for this album. "Usually, I wasn't up all-night watching cartoons and shit until that project came into view," he said later. "I had to really watch the shows and get the *Adult Swim* thing and get current references and see what the viewers of the show liked, get a feel for it. A lot of research was done."[4]

The next time they met, it was so DeMarco could take him to the studio for his first recording session with Danger Mouse and another voice actor. Arriving at nine in the morning, he had been instructed to bring along a six-pack of Heineken. But DOOM, on rap time, only bothered answering the door an hour later. Then they headed over to an audio-post facility called BAIR Tracks. "When you hung out with him, you felt weirdly like both, you didn't know him, but you also knew him for twenty years at the same time—it's hard to explain," says DeMarco. "When he felt comfortable with a group of people, when he felt understood, and was doing something he was interested in, he was relaxed. He was just drinking his beer, making jokes, telling stories about growing up in New York, you know, whatever wild stories, and laughing with Danger Mouse. It was, like, very relaxing. And then he was only there for like four hours, 'cause you could never keep him anywhere for very long." During that first session he laid down vocals for two or three songs.

The two artists completed their initial push on the album after only three weeks before going their separate ways. Burton continued to work on it back in California, while DOOM returned to whatever was on his plat du jour. "Then the longest part was actually like five months because we had to get Talib Kweli, we had to get CeeLo. Like, all those guest verses were not planned out," according to DeMarco. "And then DOOM needed to come back in and tweak his verse based on what the other person did. So, it was kind of a decent amount of back and forth. Everything else, the sampling, the clearing of the samples, the deals with all the guests, recording them, Brian was in charge of all that. DOOM was gone once he did his [vocal] part."

Talib Kweli, with whom DOOM had just completed a US tour, appeared on "Old School," an up-tempo track driven by the horn fanfare from Keith Mansfield's "Funky Fanfare" (KPM, 1968). Keeping with the album's cartoon theme, he raps, "Maybe I'm trippin' and it's just a cartoon to you / But I got chills when I heard how DOOM flipped the Scooby-Doo / And I might be buggin' but it seem to me / That cartoons be realer than reality TV."

Burton brought in his other collaborator, CeeLo Green, to sing the hook on "Benzie Box," a straight up pop rap, in which he name-drops DOOM again. Trading some of his instrumental beats for verses, DOOM was able to wrangle a guest appearance from Ghostface on the track "The Mask." This initial collaboration would not be their last, fueling feverish anticipation of a DOOM-Starks project that, unfortunately, would never materialize during DOOM's lifetime (and has yet to be released).

While originally dangling access to the Hanna-Barbera catalog before the artists, Cartoon Network had to walk that back since they were not authorized to do so. They ended up focusing on Adult Swim shows instead. "Mostly, they used a lot of existing samples, but then they said, 'We'd love Brak to do an intro to the album. We have an idea about Master Shake being mad—he wasn't called to be on the album,' but they didn't tell them what to say," says DeMarco. "And, so, the actors would go in and I directed them, and they would just ad-lib, you know, they would just riff and see what would come up. And then we gave all of that to Brian and let him figure out what he wanted to use."

While many Adult Swim characters showed up on the album's interstitial skits, three songs in particular—"Perfect Hair," "A.T.H.F." (Aqua Teen Hunger Force), and "Space Ho's"—were dedicated to actual shows. In fact, DOOM subsequently scored a recurring voice-actor role as Sherman the giraffe on the show *Perfect Hair Forever*, about a young boy on a quest to address his premature balding (incidentally, a perfect match for DOOM, who constantly made light of his own hair loss). "Space Ho's" was a riff on Adult Swim's first superhero star, Space Ghost, whom DOOM tried to displace as the host of his show *Coast to Coast*. The hilarious crime-fighting trio from *Aqua Teen Hunger Force*— Meatwad, Frylock, and Master Shake—probably made the most appearances, but unless one was a regular viewer of these shows, which aired during the wee hours, a lot of the puerile humor felt like in-jokes. A perfect example was the song "Sofa King," based on a gag from *Aqua Teen Hunger Force*, where the characters instruct the listener to say "I am Sofa King, We Todd Ed," really fast. As novel an idea as the record may have been, it still seemed like its appeal might be limited to a very niche audience.

Meanwhile, back in London, Tom Brown was managing the tremendous response to *The Grey Album*. He sent a copy to Damon Albarn, the former lead singer of Britpop superstars Blur, who had recently struck gold with his new outfit, Gorillaz. This virtual band, made up of characters drawn by cartoonist Jamie Hewlett of *Tank Girl* fame, sold a staggering seven million copies of their self-titled debut in 2001. Using a revolving cast of real musicians, Albarn co-produced the album with Dan "the Automator" Nakamura of Dr. Octagon fame, combining dub, trip-hop, Latin, alternative rock, and pop into the perfect cocktail for mass appeal.

Immediately impressed by Burton's unlikely mash-up of rap and vintage rock, Albarn wasted no time drafting him to help him write and produce seven tracks for the upcoming Gorillaz record, *Demon Days* (Parlophone, 2005). The former rocker's influence also helped defuse the situation with EMI, who had originally disapproved of his new collaborator. Though Burton already had his hands full with DangerDOOM and CeeLo's project, he could not turn down such an amazing opportunity. He, in turn, brought DOOM in to do a guest verse on the track "November Has Come." Upon its May release, *Demon Days* cracked the top ten in twenty-two countries on its way to selling eight million copies worldwide.

"Danger Mouse by 2005 was easily one of the hottest artists in the world, in terms of everybody wanted to work with him," says Brown. "He did *The Grey Album* and got a huge amount of profile from that, you know, *GQ* Man of the Year and all sorts of stuff, and then he produced the Gorillaz album, which is still the biggest Gorillaz album. I think 2005, his manager also leaked the demo for 'Crazy,' and the demos got picked up on UK radio and got a bunch of plays and, you know, it all became exceedingly hot."

The aforementioned track, from his pending release with CeeLo, did not officially see light until March 2006, but it became the first song in the UK to go number one based solely on downloads, according to the BBC. Since Burton had blown up in the interim, the proposed solo CeeLo project morphed into a collaboration called Gnarls Barkley. Their album, *St. Elsewhere* (Downtown/Atlantic/Warner Bros., 2006), three years in the making, became a worldwide smash thanks to the hit "Crazy" and was quickly certified platinum following its release.

Where did all of this leave the DangerDOOM project, which was still in production while all of the above was happening? Obviously, both artists were exceedingly entrenched in building illustrious solo careers, with hardly a timeout to catch some air. But when *The Mouse and the Mask* dropped on October 11, 2005, it charted at number forty-one on *Billboard's* Top 200 albums. Sales-wise, it upstaged *Madvillainy*, DOOM's previous top-seller, moving 350,000 units. The Villain had finally broken into the mainstream, but in the strangest of ways. Clinging to the coattails of a previous unknown, he was suddenly catapulted into being the flavor of the moment.

Cartoon Network could not have been happier with their beginner's luck. "When I heard it, I was like, oh my God, I think they've actually done it," says DeMarco. "This feels like Adult Swim, but it feels like DOOM. It feels like a synthesis of those two things, and it works, like, it makes sense. It's DOOM, stretching himself to fit what we do. And it's us coming to meet him where he is. And it doesn't feel like any other DOOM record. And it also doesn't necessarily feel just like Adult Swim. It was a synthesis of the two things. So, I was shocked that they pulled it off."

Yet, despite the encouraging numbers, the record didn't remotely approach the response to *The Grey Album* or Gorillaz, and reviews for it were mixed. Mainstream outlets like *Entertainment Weekly*, which had never reviewed a DOOM record, and, therefore, had no context for it, were wowed by the novelty and humor, calling it a "hip-hop tour de farce."[5] Usually a bit more critical, *Pitchfork* gave it the benefit of the doubt, saying, "DOOM and Danger go all out, calling in the Aqua Teen Hunger Force to help craft the best funhouse hip-hop since *De La Soul Is Dead*. It may not move the critical masses like *Madvillainy*, but if nothing else, DangerDOOM will get Comic-Con going nuts."[6] *Spin*, most likely, captured how many hardcore DOOM fans felt about the record: "If expectations are just disappointments waiting to happen, DangerDOOM is a white-hot flame of anticipation fated to sizzle your rap lovin' heart to a bitter char."[7] An "ouch" moment, to say the least.

In fact, it's fair to say that all three publications were in the ballpark. *The Mouse and the Mask* might not be considered a bad album by any stretch, but coming on the heels of records like *Madvillainy* and *Mm . . Food*, it sounded more like hip-hop lite. Staying close to its cartoony concept, the music was much more whimsical, with much of DOOM's inner darkness excised. After all, Burton had no pretensions of being a Miles, but rather more mainstream like Kenny G. As he told filmmaker Steven Soderbergh, "I suppose I could try to be some avant-garde artist if I wanted to, but that doesn't interest me as much."[8] His collection of Grammys attests to that assertion.

DOOM, on the other hand, couldn't be mainstream if he wanted to. But as reigning champ of the underground, he had no place left to go but up. This collaboration gave him the boost he needed to finally break the surface and garner recognition that was long overdue. Yet he seemed to somehow resent the attention this record, and Danger Mouse, received, privately complaining to friends about why and how it had been so successful compared to his other material. His response was to step back for a minute and not release another album until 2009. Though one might have expected a follow-up, he and Danger

Mouse did collect outtakes from the project, along with a Madlib remix, to release an EP called *Occult Hymn* (Adult Swim, 2006).

The Villain received more than just mainstream recognition from the Danger-DOOM project. An unforeseen windfall turned out to be the rapper's continued association with Cartoon Network, who approached him with further opportunities over the next several years. "So, then we came back to DOOM and said, 'Yeah, we want to do another record with you,'" says DeMarco. "Because Brian was at that point, he was working with CeeLo on Gnarls Barkley and Broken Bells and he was already starting to blow up. So, we knew that Brian couldn't be involved, but I said, DOOM makes his own beats. So, we made a deal with him for another album." DeMarco's plan was to legally acquire access to the Hanna-Barbera catalog. This time, however, the network only coughed up a $45,000 advance.

DOOM also approached them for other work. According to DeMarco, "He always said, 'If you ever need a voiceover, don't hesitate to call me.' So, when *Perfect Hair Forever* was like, 'We need a rapper, we need a character. Who's a rapper? Who's got a great voice?' I said, Well, we should try calling DOOM. He might be into it. And I gave them DOOM's number. They got him in, and he was a recurring character." For someone so obsessed with cartoons since his youth, it was undoubtedly a benchmark of his creative career when he made his TV debut as Sherman the giraffe.

Pretty soon, DOOM started cropping up all over the network. When *The Boondocks*, a show about a black family living in the burbs, premiered on Adult Swim at the end of 2005, they licensed four tracks from *Madvillainy*. Then, when the network was looking for someone to host its Christmas programming block in 2006, DeMarco recommended DOOM as well, since he knew the rapper needed money. "DOOM said, 'I'm down,' because we had to shoot it at night," says DeMarco. "He said, 'That works great for me. I stay up all night, anyway.' He's like, 'As long as there's beer, I'll come down and do whatever you want.' So, we had a bunch of beer, filmed it at Williams Street [studios] and he got paid for that and he had a blast. We just basically let the camera roll and shot him for six hours.

"And then I think the only other thing we had DOOM do was 'The Star-Spangled Banner,'" DeMarco adds. "We had him do a version of 'The Star-Spangled Banner' that we signed off the network with every night. That was Lazzo's idea. He was like, 'We should get DOOM to do the Star-Spangled Banner.' And I was like, I'll ask him. And he said, 'Yeah, gimme ten grand and I'll do it.' So, we paid him and got a version of 'The Star-Spangled Banner' that we ran for about a year."

When it came time for the 2006 upfronts, the annual preview party of new network shows staged for advertisers, DeMarco thought it made sense to have DangerDOOM perform, since their well-received album had only been released the previous year. Both artists agreed to do it. "And then Danger Mouse called me and said, 'Well, DOOM's got this idea. It's kind of crazy, but he wants us to give him money to make like a DangerDOOM outfit and he's gonna wear the actual outfit to perform in.'" Though an odd request, for sure, DeMarco signed off on it, and DOOM worked on the design with a costume maker in New York. After a fitting, he sent photos to DeMarco, who described him as looking like a "team mascot"—basically a giant mouse with his own version of the metal mask.

The day before the event, which was held in New York, DOOM didn't show for rehearsal. "Brian's like, 'He never shows for rehearsal, he'll be here,'" says DeMarco. "And then a couple hours before the show, the day of, Brian's like DOOM has some idea that he wants to have his friend—he didn't say who his friend is gonna be—in the costume, but he knows all the songs and DOOM's gonna be backstage rapping live and his friend is gonna be pantomiming. It's gonna look like it's DangerDOOM." As if to underscore that this last-minute plan was not up for negotiation, he also mentioned that DOOM was feeling a little under the weather and didn't want to be jumping around onstage in a hot, furry suit. "I remember them saying, 'When we get there, he needs to have orange juice and aspirin.' Probably he was just hung over," says DeMarco. "So, he gets there, and they did a song or two before everyone got there, just to see. And I remember thinking, like, maybe it'll work. I remember I was trying to be hopeful, like, maybe they'll pull it off. It's a cool, weird idea, you know? It's a little bit of a performance-art type approach, but maybe he'll pull it off."

That evening the place was packed with twenty-something ad buyers, who were getting loose at the open bar, and enjoying themselves. Familiar with the popular album, they were excited to be privy to what would be the first-ever performance by DangerDOOM. "And then he comes out, or his friend comes out, and it goes off the way he wanted it to. But literally the show ends, and I remember thinking, well, that wasn't so bad. That was kind of cool," says DeMarco. "But right next to me was a guy who was like, 'That wasn't fuckin' DOOM.' And, like, I knew right then and there. . . . I was just telling myself it was okay. And then all my bosses were like, 'What the fuck was that? All the ad buyers are talking about that wasn't DOOM. What the hell was that?' And, so, I got in trouble, a decent amount of trouble." But it wasn't the last time DeMarco would stick his neck out for DOOM, and it was only the beginning of the notorious DOOMbot saga.

20

DOOM/*BORN LIKE THIS*

You have to know how to accept rejection and reject acceptance.

—RAY BRADBURY

By the end of 2005, DOOM had surpassed even himself—orchestrating not only his reinvention as an MC, but affecting a full-scale transformation. Like his larger-than-life namesake, he no longer seemed mortal. Following a near exile from the rap game, he had rebuilt himself like the Six Million Dollar Man, returning better, stronger, and more popular than ever, thanks to an incredible run of releases in the early aughts. But after attaining a level of peak exposure, he also felt like he had earned a break. Reflecting on this juncture of his career, he told the Red Bull Music Academy:

> *I just kinda took some time off, really for family, and like just to get away from it for a second. It started being where, yunno, I don't necessarily want to be doing one thing for too long. It gets to where it gets boring and overwhelming. You want to take a step back and just reflect, so it was really like that kind of thing. I didn't think it was noticeable from the outside, though. I figured there was enough work out there for people to still absorb, yunno, and it comes to a point where I need to get more information to study. To give out information, I need information, so I would do things like leave it alone for a second and just observe the world, so I have more things to say. I think a lot of times people expect us to be constantly talking and I'm the kind of cat, I'll lay back, you know*

what I mean? And the conversation ain't always about what I gotta say. Sometimes it's time to listen. So that was more like the listening time.[1]

Though he may have taken a step back from writing and production, this period of self-imposed obsolescence did not apply to getting money, a perpetual driving force—especially as his family was expanding with a new son and daughter. Once again, Danger Mouse came through for him.

In the wake of his unprecedented success co-producing the second Gorillaz album, the label Lex, to which he was signed as a solo artist, suddenly lost their deal with parent company Warp. In an additional twist, EMI, who had initially gone after the creator of *The Grey Album*, ended up releasing Gorillaz in the UK, and was now trying to sign Gnarls Barkley, his collaboration with CeeLo. Lex boss Tom Brown, who was doing his best to make sure his label didn't get lost in the shuffle, was understandably vexed that a major was trying to poach one of his artists. He immediately got on the phone to set up a meeting with the head of EMI, Keith Wozencroft, the man responsible for signing Radiohead.

"He was like, 'Look, we are gonna help market the Gnarls Barkley record for you and we'll pay your overhead. And in return, we're the first label that you come to when you've got a big record,'" recalls Brown. "So, what they're trying to do was like, you know, 'This guy, Tom Brown, found one Danger Mouse, if he finds another one, we're all gonna be rich kinda thing.' And, so yeah, I was like, cool, you can pay my overhead. And I didn't really have any intention to licensing much stuff to anyone anyway." At the very least, he had saved his label.

Though Gnarls Barkley eventually got picked up by Warner Bros., Burton, who had caught wind of Lex's new arrangement with EMI, phoned up Brown to see about getting a deal on behalf of DOOM. It made perfect sense to Brown, who went back to Wozencroft and made his pitch, citing the banner sales of *The Mouse and the Mask* and DOOM's involvement with Gorillaz. "I was like, 'Look, I really wanna sign this guy DOOM. He's got the potential to be a really huge artist if EMI gets behind him,'" he says. "And they're like, 'Yeah, let's do it.' Back then, you know, I mean, I dunno what their finances were like, but obviously not great 'cause they got bought and sold and flipped and shut down and torn to pieces at the end. But they certainly were acting like they had shitloads of money."

Negotiations proceeded between lawyers for both parties. According to Brown, "So, you know, we'd get a message back from DOOM's lawyer going, 'Yeah, that's not gonna cut it we need more money,' and then I'd go, 'Oh, they need more money.' And then they'd [EMI] go, 'Okay, we'll beat that.' And they just kept on going until it was a really substantial deal." While not quoting a precise number, he says the deal ended up in the "large six figures." DOOM, who officially joined the Lex roster in early 2006, was finally pulling in the kind of money he deserved.

Brown didn't even meet his new signing until sometime in 2008 during a trip to Georgia, when DOOM's first record for Lex, *Born Like This* (2009), was almost done. He had also come to see Khujo from Goodie Mob, who was working on another project for Lex with producer Jneiro Jarel. Both meetings, coincidentally, took place at sports bars, only a day apart, but they could not have been more different. When Brown showed up for the first, he found Khujo, his large frame covered in tattoos, with a braided head and mouthful of gold fronts, holding court among a crowd of twenty to thirty patrons, looking every bit the local superstar and relishing all the attention.

"And then the next day I went to another sports bar to meet DOOM," says Brown. "And I walked in and him and Jasmine were sitting like eating shrimp with just rows of vodka shots—I think it was vodka—like some of them drunk, some of them not, and watching sports on TV, you know, like one o'clock in the afternoon or something." Despite selling hundreds of thousands of records and appearing on Adult Swim and magazine covers, none of the other patrons were the wiser, and the Villain clearly appreciated the anonymity. Brown only knew he had found his man by DOOM's shit-eating grin, which he said reminded him of another popular villain, Tony Soprano.

"DOOM was like an incredibly intelligent, really charming, funny, super talented guy, and he also had other qualities that were, um, less appealing," says Brown, who managed to develop a good rapport with the rapper over the years. "I think he would justify things in ways that were often, you know, seemingly hard to understand. But I sometimes think some of those things were like post rationalizations. I think the 'robots' as he called them, you know, like sending out imposters at shows, that was not designed as part of an elaborate art project that he was masterminding that would all fall into place for his audience eventually. That was DOOM not wanting to do live shows, but still get paid for them."

Prince Paul, who had always maintained a close relationship with DOOM, fulfilling the role of mentor/confidante, adds confirmation. "When he did the DOOMposter thing, he called me up," he recalls. "He's like, 'Yo, Unc, I can't do these gigs, but there's all this money out there. So, I'm thinking about, you know, putting out like somebody in the mask so I could get paid.' I'm like, Yo, you buggin'. He was like, 'Yo, yo, yo! But, you know what I'm saying? 'Cause I can't be at these places.' I was like, good luck. And then next thing you know, it became a thing."

As doing live shows became more lucrative, the Villain was looking for ways to exploit the many offers that came his way. But to even dare sending out imposters was a totally unprecedented and next-level scheme. As he told *Rolling Stone* later on, in his defense, "Everything that we do is villain style. Everybody has the right to get it or not. Once I throw it out it's open for interpretation. It might've seemed like it didn't go well, but how do you know that wasn't just pre-orchestrated so that we're talking about it now? I'll tell you one thing: People are asking more now for live shows and I'm charging more, so it must've worked somehow."[2] After all, he had always maintained that *Anybody in here could wear the mask and be the Villain.*[3] But as DOOM obsessively cultivated a mystique around his assumed persona, in many ways, he morphed into that character, often blurring the distinction between truth and propaganda.

"I think that my understanding is that DOOM was quite ill when he first did it and had committed to a bunch of shows," says Brown. "But I think that was quite a big problem and it defined a lot of the later years of his career where, you know, he'd kind of burned a lot of fans and turned a lot of people off him and kinda squandered a lot of goodwill."

Whether art project or shameless money grab, DOOM can't assume full credit for the infamous DOOMbots, which initially started proliferating concert stages around 2006 to 2007. According to the website Comic Book Resources:

> *First introduced in 1962's Fantastic Four #5 (by Stan Lee and Jack Kirby), the Doombot is the standard in terms of henchmen for Doctor Doom. While his first prototype was more akin to a Life Model Decoy than anything else, various iterations over the years have culminated in the quintessential killer robot. Doombots are also more than just super strong steel cans—they are also capable of fooling most telepaths into believing they are genuine human beings at first glance. This coupled with their ability to disguise themselves as needed makes them the perfect choice for almost any scenario Doctor Doom might find himself in.[4]*

Since only a dedicated Marvel fan would be familiar with the arcane Doombots, DOOM had stumbled upon another brilliant conceit. Even when the issue became a lightning rod of controversy, he didn't try to shirk responsibility, but owned it, doubling down on his position in defiance of critics and upset fans. His willingness to do so was totally consistent with his desire to always define the narrative when it came to himself as an artist.

Even before the controversy erupted, DOOM had flirted with such hijinks as sending a masked Big Benn Klingon in his stead for photoshoots, such as the infamous 2005 cover shoot for *Elemental Magazine*. In that same issue, he taunted readers with a letter to the editor: "Question: Is that the real MF DOOM on the cover photo? Answer: Yes. The part of DOOM was played by Big Benn Klingon, Don King. Still confused? Well you needn't be. It's rather simple, actually the legendary MC MetalFace DOOM, The SUPERVILLAIN, is one of many characters invented by myself, Daniel Dumile, author. If you will, think of each record as a book with different chapters often made for words expressed for a whole host of characters."[5] He drew a fitting analogy to the Batman film franchise in which various actors had portrayed the Caped Crusader over the years. But sending in a proxy for a photoshoot was a far cry from trying to fool a live audience of paying customers, which for a DOOM show, usually numbered in the thousands by then.

The DOOMbots seemed to show up with increasing frequency during the summer of 2007 at shows that DOOM performed as part of the Rock the Bells festival. Some attendees of his July 29 performance at Randall's Island in New

York accused him of lip-synching, though he clearly wasn't (with the mic pressed up to his mask, it's near impossible to see his mouth moving, but the sound confirmed that the mic was live). This criticism, however, followed him to the West Coast when he performed in San Bernadino on August 11, LA on August 12, and San Francisco on August 15. The lip-synching claims persisted, but, at this last date, at a club called the Independent, fans claimed that the person who showed up onstage wearing the mask was thirty to forty pounds lighter than DOOM, recognizable by his distended belly. Apparently, he performed only a handful of songs before abruptly ending his set, exiting to boos and bottles of water flung after him. Though booked for the following night, as well, that show was canceled along with the rest of the dates of his tour. The Independent's owner, Allen Scott, later said that DOOM's booking agent had told him that "it was some sort of circulatory problem where his feet were swollen."[6] Such symptoms would be consistent with gout, diabetes, or heart or kidney disease, and if that were the case, it proved to be the first indication of DOOM's mounting health issues, also confirming Brown's explanation for the rise of the DOOMbots.

There were other occasions, however, where DOOM seemed to be testing the limits of what he could get away with. Later that year, at a December 13 show in Atlanta's MJQ Concourse, a club where he had previously performed, a masked figure took the stage with his entourage and proceeded to lip-synch through a twenty-minute set. The crowd, who had paid the thirty-dollar admission fee, could instantly see through the obvious charade, and booed him offstage. But not before the imposter and his crew absconded with all the door receipts. Promoter Randy Castello was so incensed that he posted DOOM's phone number and address in a MySpace bulletin, encouraging people to contact the rapper directly if they wanted a refund of their money. He also posted pictures of local DJ WESU next to photos of the masked pretender, and the identical birthmark they had on their hands seemed to confirm that the suspicions were true. Despite the lost income and his frustration at having been hoodwinked, Castello could not help but be somewhat impressed by the caper, saying, "I think it's brilliant that he's going so far as to send out impersonators to do his dirty work. I just don't like being on the receiving end of a joke."[7] Many fans would concur, and have continued the debate on YouTube and Reddit, thus contributing to the Villain's legend.

The DOOMbot scandal, as anyone who paid to see a DOOM show would frame it, came to a head during his tour with Mos Def, years later. At a show at Chicago's Congress Theater on February 13, 2010, documented by several videos on YouTube, it was clearly apparent that whoever was wearing the mask was lip-synching to a CD (since the sound, including DOOM's voice, had a very canned quality). While the controversy clearly downgraded the rapper's soaring stock, DOOM, in a weird way, seemed not to care—even deriving some bizarre thrill out of it. Perhaps it was his way of rebelling against the newfound attention coming his way. Ever since the KMD days, he had never felt comfortable with fame, so hiding his face offered a solution. But, in an ironic twist, the mask had taken on an identity of its own. In this respect, DOOM obviously felt justified deploying his bots—especially since he never left money on the table.

Impressed by his execution of the daring ploy, Prince Paul called DOOM up to offer his congratulations. "They say there's no such thing as bad publicity, which I think there is in some ways," he says. "But in his case, even though you had some people complaining, it made other people want to go out to see if it would ever be him." DOOM's calculated risk actually paid off, then, as attendance to his shows thrived during this period. It's as if the Metal Face was made of Teflon.

His first major release in four years, *Born Like This* represents a real departure from DOOM's previous solo efforts, while tracking his growth and maturity as an artist. Flush with funds and no other competing projects on his plate (aside from, maybe, his ongoing collaboration with Ghostface and the almost mythical *Madvillainy* sequel), he was able to really dive in and devote his full attention to it like no other project before or since. At the same time, he had attained a level where he could draw on all kinds of assistance from collaborators old and new. On production, for example, he gets help from Dilla, who provides two tracks (arranged via Stones Throw); newcomer Jake One, who contributes four (arranged via Rhymesayers); as well as another one from Madlib. Unlike DOOM's usual gritty fare, these songs sound polished and radio friendly, signaling a definite upgrade in his overall aesthetic. To get around paying for samples, several songs are also supplemented by live instrumentation courtesy of G Koop (Robert Mandell) and Mr. Chop (Coz Littler), who gets several co-production credits.

But DOOM doesn't abandon the old playbook entirely. He recycles three previously released beats from the *Special Herbs* series, leaving the total number of new songs at just seven. Of these, "Bumpy's Message" is not even a track, but an answering machine message from rapper Bumpy Knuckles (aka Freddie Foxxx) backed by a live bassline—a recurring motif, played by Mr. Chop. "Thank Yah," the album sign-off, also reprises the same "Coca Leaf" beat (from *Special Herbs 9&0*) as the "Supervillain Intro," based on an uplifting gospel loop from Bishop Eric McDaniel and The Lord's Church Cathedral Choir.

Lyrically, too, DOOM features more cameos on this album, tapping some big names, including Wu-Tang's Ghostface and Raekwon. "Angelz," his duet with Ghost, had previously appeared on the Nature Sounds compilation *Natural Selection* (2006), but he adds a drum track to it for the album version. DOOM had traded beats for verses with Ghost. Then in February 2006, he announced on MySpace that an entire project with Ghost, tentatively titled *Swift & Changeable*, was in the works, though the project's release date kept being pushed back.

Raekwon gets a solo feature on "Yessir!," based on the old-school break from ESG's "U.F.O." (99 Records, 1981). So does longtime DOOM contributor Empress Stahhr, on "Still Dope," a vocal treatment of the "Passion Flower" instrumental (from *Special Herbs 9&0*), which is based on elements from Arthur Verocai's "Seriado" (Continental, 1972). The posse cut, "Supervillainz," reunites DOOM with his old buddy Kurious, featuring as well Slug from the Rhymesayers crew; Mobonix, a member of DOOM's Metal Face Akademy, a short-lived side project involving several Atlanta-area MCs; and a special appearance by Posdnuos of De La, credited as P-Pain, since he ad-libs his lines through the auto-tune function popularized by singer T-Pain. Popular British singer Paloma Faith makes a cameo as Cat Girl on several tracks, but probably the album's biggest surprise guest is the late writer Charles Bukowski, who appears at the beginning of "Cellz." The recitation of his apocalyptic poem, "Dinosaura, We," taken from the documentary *Bukowski: Born into This* (Redolent, 2004), not only serves as the album's centerpiece, but provides its title as well:

> *We are born like this, into this*
> *Into hospitals which are so expensive that it's cheaper to die*
> *Into lawyers who charge so much, it's cheaper to plead guilty*
> *Into a country where the jails are full and the madhouses closed*
> *Into a place where the masses elevate fools into rich heroes*

"*Born Like This*, that's why I chose that as the title," DOOM explained. "Writers are born and we're not doing it like, 'Yeah, I think I'll be a writer today.' We can't help it. If I had another job, if I was a gardener or a city worker, I would still be writing rhymes and doing my little thing. I'm just blessed to be able to do it for a living."[8] He found a kindred spirit in the iconoclastic scribe, known for documenting the lives of the down and out, as well as being an unapologetic lush. Henry Chinaski, Bukowski's literary alter ego, a lover of art, women, alcohol, solitude, and nihilistic behavior—though not necessarily in that order—could not have provided a better doppelganger for the eccentric MC.

"I'm totally inspired by that dude. Him as a writer blows me away," said DOOM of Bukowski. "His writing style would always catch me off guard. I'd be reading and think I know where he's going, and he'll just pull a left and spin everything up. Time after time, each story was so different in its own right. Even now, when I feel stuck and wanna relax, I'll pick up Bukowski and read a short story. His stuff can be so weird it makes me feel normal. I can't be weirder than this guy, which is cool because once you realize what the extremes are, you can do anything."[9] Whereas most rappers typically glorified crime figures, real-life or otherwise, it's quite telling that DOOM lavishes the same attention on a fellow writer.

He also matches Bukowski's incendiary verses with some of his hardest and most technically challenging wordplay, highlighting his command of language:

> *Rancid rants having rambling savages scavenging*
> *For scraps, perhaps roadkill, if that*

Gift of gab, and he flowed ill, chrome stiff hat
Known for writing lightning tight lines, chiefin'
Beefin', being off deep ends, divine bright shines even
Dimes quiet as mimes by design mighty fine
Slightly rewind, tightly bind, blind lead blind.

By now, DOOM fans have surrendered hopes for a linear narrative, but that doesn't mean they haven't given up on imposing some kind of order by attempting to parse these lyrical abstractions, which ends up being a futile task. One might get the gist of it, but only DOOM truly knows what he's really talking about. He chides his listeners, later, "Metal face Finster, playin' with the dirty money / Sinister, don't know what he sayin' but the words be funny." Sometimes, as in "More Rhyming," it's better to just sit back, relax, and enjoy the euphonic wordplay, "More rhymin' / Pure diamond / Tore hymen / Poor timin' / Paul Simon tourin.'"

On this album, gone are the long interstitial audio collages for which DOOM is famous, along with the ubiquitous cartoon dialogue. But he does sample a fair amount of cartoon soundtracks—particularly Hanna-Barbera's animated *Super Friends* series from the seventies and eighties, as well as some obscure Japanese anime. Who would have guessed, for example, that the chilling music behind "Cellz," one of the album's darker turns, would have come from a popular Saturday morning children's cartoon? But DOOM was already hip to such sources way back on "Hey!" from the first album, which samples the Scooby-Doo soundtrack.

Following his experience working with actual voice actors on *The Mouse and the Mask,* he is also inspired to use custom dialogue this time around, tapping Prince Paul's acting chops. "He gave me this thing that he wanted to use as an intro, but it was just too obvious," says Paul. "So, he's like, 'Yeah, you're good at doing voices, can you record this for me. This is the sentiment of what I need.' And, so, I just sat in my studio and recorded a bunch of things, and I sent it to him, and he's like, 'Oh, this is perfect.' But I didn't know what he really was gonna use it for. I thought it was like a song. I didn't realize it would be the introduction to the album." In addition to the intro, Paul's faux tough-guy voice peppers the record, dropping silly phrases like "Time to get the feta" and "Murderizing Sucker MCs."

While DOOM made several deliberate changes on this album, one element that remains consistent is his ridiculous flow, which, like wine, only seems to improve with age. Though his deep baritone sounds a little raspier for the wear, his ability to daisy-chain internal rhymes into denser verses that pack more syllables per measure seems supercharged. Take "Gazzillion Ear," which begins with: "Villain man never ran with krills in his hand and / Won't stop rockin' til he clocked a gazillion grand / Tillin' the wasteland sands / Raps on backs of treasure maps, stacks to the ceiling fan." In the same song the erudite MC crams together a lifetime's worth of Gen-X references, mentioning Worf (from *Star Trek*), pro wrestler Chief Jay Strongbow, the unknown comic from the *Gong Show*, and J.J. from *Good Times*. And out of the blue, he also throws in the Hadron Collider for good measure. Those scrambling to keep track on lyric websites like Genius.com know that listening to DOOM has been proven to make you smarter.

"As I'm writing it, I'm also thinking of it from a listener point of view. So, I try to make it to where I can catch myself off-guard," he explained. "You want to keep the story interesting, like, soon as somebody thinks they know what you gonna say—that's part of the essence of rhyming is to kinda keep everybody off-guard a little—so I take that, and I stretch it with these different things. Leave one word blank, yunno, knowing that the listener is following along and will fill in that blank. But always put the word that you would least expect. It keeps the story interesting like where you can match wits with the listener."[10]

DOOM often employs this technique to delete obvious curse words or foul language, which he rarely uses. A perfect example appears on the song "Batty Boyz," where he raps, "Hit him with a kryptonite brick / Children come and prick his body with a dead stick / Wrote this lyric in bed with a chick / She had the tightest grip on the head of my . . ." before an abstract break interrupts, in a completely different time signature than the rest of the song. Resuming with the second verse, he fills in that blank with "Bic," not the word you were expecting. It's one of DOOM's patented head fakes that works time and time again.

Incidentally, this song's homophobic lyrics and subject matter—about Batman and Robin being gay—ended up fueling some controversy that DOOM summarily dismissed. "It's not about homos. It's about Batman and them. They just happen to be homos," he said. "The character DOOM is just in the realm of cartoons and comics, so his competition is Batman and these guys."[11] The ultimate value of his alter egos seems to be that he can always claim to be in character and talking shit—even in a most politically incorrect manner. Underscoring the point, he defiantly added, "I don't give a shit. I'm a writer. I touch on all topics. DOOM happens to talk shit about everyone—regular street niggas, punks, fat niggas, queens, and kings. I talk shit about every facet of life."[12] The real story behind that song, however, makes DOOM's intentions appear fairly innocuous. Apparently, his younger son made him buy him a Batman outfit and then taunted his dad, saying, *Batman is better than you!* DOOM's response was "Word? Batman's better than me? I'm spending $24 at the store and Batman's better than me? All right I got some shit for Batman."[13]

As he told journalist David Ma, "This record is DOOM's most personal record. This is where you get to the center of his character, so I decided to drop the MF for this album only. I didn't think it was a big deal or nothing. Then everyone's asking me why I changed the name."[14] But, of course, anything related to DOOM gained oversized import among his fans.

Putting this album into context with his other records, he explained, "*Operation: Doomsday*, the way I presented it was an introduction to the character from an outside point of view—way outside, OK. There's this guy that everybody's calling the Supervillain. You hardly know anything about him, so you're hearing things, and you gradually get introduced to him through what he puts out as propaganda."[15] Regarding *Mm.. Food*, he added, "Then you get the 'Oh, he's not such a bad guy.' They call him the Villain, but now we get to know him, and he seems cool. What's so villainous about this guy? Right? So with this record, the third installment in the trilogy, there's even a closer, more [candid] look."[16]

After a couple false starts, *Born Like This* (Lex), one of his boldest statements to date, finally hit stores on March 24, 2009. A year represents an eternity in the fast-paced music industry, which was in the process of collapsing due to declining sales of physical product and the incursion of digital downloading. Out of the spotlight for several years, DOOM might as well have been Rip Van Winkle to the fans who eagerly followed him in the early part of the decade. He had spoiled them with multiple releases at a time when hip-hop desperately needed an intervention, but also gaslit them with his DOOMbots and other villainous behavior. As the main arbiter of taste, *Pitchfork* begrudgingly gave him his props, saying, "I don't know if *Born Like This* arose from disillusionment or fatigue or something else, but whatever caused DOOM to scale back his output and go off the grid, he's only come back from it sharper, stronger, and more powerful than before. Villains don't really die; they just emerge from the rubble even more determined to make the world see their way."[17]

"*Born Like This* was a big deal," recalls the former graffiti writer and visual artist Vaseem Bhatti (aka EHQuestionmark). "It was a long-awaited [DOOM] solo album and Lex Records were super excited to have bagged such a project." While an inordinate amount of praise has been lavished on the cover of *Madvillainy*, a simple black-and-white photo of the Villain, snapped in haste, picturing his world-weary gaze barely visible from behind the mask, his latest record strikes a much more compelling and mysterious look that merits further attention. As if out of a museum catalog, the cover features a golden effigy of the mask, rendered in stone, beside a rustic slate tablet carved with characters resembling Sumerian cuneiform. Inside, three versions of the mask—in stone, chrome, and what resembles fur—are photographed against a black background. There is also a sonogram of a baby in utero wearing a mask, a literal translation of the album title. Designed by Bhatti, who, at that point, had been defining Lex's elaborate visual aesthetic for the last eight years, he describes it as, "Something archaic, ephemeral and harking from a long-lost civilization, something spanning different civilizations so as to merge and blur time and context, something timeless, mythological and vague, something geology based as a metaphor for our blip of an existence in geological terms."

Obviously, a lot of thought went into the artwork, but equal amounts of time, trouble, expense, and cajoling as well. Underwritten by Warp and later EMI,

Lex had a reputation for plowing big budgets into packaging that really popped. But, this time, apparently, DOOM came prepared with an illustration of his own in mind. Bhatti describes it as, "A colorful self-portrait drawn in pencil crayon, rendered in a naïve, child-like, subversive, and kitsch style of himself as a chimpanzee in a green room, [sitting] in front of a big light-bulb-framed mirror with a mic and a banana. Something modest, low fi, and very anti-design." As this was such a hugely anticipated release, however, the artist responsible for Lex's Rorschach-inspired version of *The Mouse and the Mask* was given the unenviable task of convincing DOOM to forgo using his own illustration. "I knew it wasn't going to be easy," he admits. "I set to work and presented ten or so written concepts, which were all initially rejected. He was adamant his artwork was to be used." Finally, however, DOOM relented and came around to what Bhatti describes as the "antiquated museum object vibe." Though his own artwork was not used, he remained very involved every step of the way, offering tons of feedback.

"'Cellz' was a massive influence on the artwork," says Bhatti. "I always got an apocalyptic and prophetic vibe from DOOM's various projects. Even in its more jovial moments, it always came from a dark place." After obtaining a mask from DOOM, he set about replicating it using different materials. "DOOM had a relationship to food so I thought of making a mask using bread, an ancient foodstuff that has helped us evolve, allowed us to exponentially grow as a species, and could be seen as one of the possible reasons for our eventual apocalyptic downfall," he says. Not only do grain shortages contribute to starvation in many underdeveloped nations, but the overconsumption of grains (and complex carbohydrates in general) has also contributed to skyrocketing rates of diabetes in the developed world. Using the ancient grain spelt to fashion a mask out of dough, Bhatti popped it in the oven, but didn't like what came out, calling it "globular and bulbous—there was nothing armor-like about it at all." He says, "It sat in the studio and began to rot into a beautiful green hairy mold-covered mask."

Next, he cast another replica of the mask, pouring plaster into a sand mold to create a faux relic from some fallen empire of antiquity. According to Bhatti, the sandstone mask felt "solid and powerful, a sacred artifact of a divine omnipotent superhuman, and photographed with harsh chiaroscuro lighting in the blackness of a museum space it felt ominous and mysterious." Indeed, its golden hue and rough-hewn features make it appear like the head of some ancient statue unearthed in modern times. Taking inspiration from Bukowski, who talks about the poisoning of our food system, Bhatti threw his rotting bread mask in a blender, added water, and liquified it to create a spore paint, which he ingeniously applied to another sand cast mask. After placing it overnight in a box next to the heater, the smell was overpowering, but he had achieved the desired effect: "A DOOM mask blooming with hairy green mold, which was then photographed for the inner sleeve images."

For the front-cover text, Bhatti designed a wildstyle font based on cuneiform, the most ancient written language, developed by the Sumerians. "I used the negative space between letters to confuse the reader," he says. "To create something obscure and mythological, referencing the notion of prophetically 'reading between the lines.' DOOM was a fellow Sumerian enthusiast, so he loved the idea, but then demanded it was carved in stone." Obviously, this one task alone would have required a major effort, but they were running out of time. Bhatti solved the problem by photographing an old slate headstone at his local cemetery and carefully photoshopping in the custom-designed lettering to make it look hand-carved. Nonetheless, it still appears completely cryptic and strange—like a remnant of some lost civilization—and, unless you are accustomed to reading graffiti, illegible as well.

Other elements of the artwork include the stylized DOOM graffiti, inspired by crumbling pyramids and obelisks, as rendered by TORS (aka David Oates), and the clear, glossy hieroglyphics overprinted on the cover (and on the actual CD) that were hand-drawn by EKO (aka Matthew Moran). One last-minute detail that almost got scrapped was the sonogram image of a fetus, in utero, wearing the mask. Bhatti tried to recreate the image with an adult model wearing a mask, but says, "This was rejected as too effeminate, so this idea appeared as two versions, initially in adult form on a limited number of copies and the other as a sampled baby sonogram with a doctored mask." Considering how much of a control freak DOOM was, it's amazing that Bhatti was able to accommodate him in the end, delivering one of his most memorable album covers. In hindsight, he says, "The whole process reeked of time—living bread mold from an ancient wheat born in the Cradle of Civilization, the Fertile Crescent, morphing into an inanimate artifact carved from sedimentary Sumerian sandstone."

In March 2010, DOOM, who traveled with a British passport, completed his first tour of Europe in support of the new album with dates in Paris, Amsterdam, London, Zurich, and Brussels. Returning to the US he was admitted back into the country under a tourist visa. Later that year, in October, he left again for a longer nineteen-date tour that would take him around the UK, Ireland, France, the Netherlands, Germany and, finally, a swing through Scandinavia. After performing his last show at the Hornstull Strand Etablissement in Stockholm, Sweden, on Saturday, November 6, 2010, he and Big Benn Klingon stopped in London on their way back to the US. They spent the night at the posh four-star K West Hotel and Spa in Shepherd's Bush, a popular spot for music-industry clientele.

When Tom Brown stopped by briefly to say hi, he found them near the mezzanine bar, where they were relaxing at a long banquet table, big enough to seat ten. With their nineteen-date tour concluded, the fellas, in celebratory mood, had splurged. The remnants of a lavish meal covered the table—empty champagne bottles bobbing, bottoms up, in ice buckets, and the rosy carcasses of several half-eaten lobsters. Content and satiated, they were looking forward to flying home.

"I think it was the morning, not the next morning, but the morning after that, I start getting text messages from Ben," Brown recalls. "It was just like, 'Yo, Tom, go meet D at K West.' And I was like, OK, Ben, but DOOM flew back forty-eight hours ago kind of thing. And he was like, 'No, he's at K West now.'" When Brown arrived at the hotel this time, it was a different story. "It was kind of like a mirror image of what I'd just seen: DOOM sitting in the lobby during the daytime, downstairs at the K West Hotel, just looking totally dejected and shriveled," he says. "He just gave me the kind of headlines that he'd been refused entry back into the States. It was weird."

It was probably even weirder for DOOM, who had spent his entire life in the US, and never called any other place home. But born in London, his immigration status had never been properly sorted out—first by his mother and then later by himself, as an adult. Though he had been allowed back into the country in March, US Customs and Border Protection subsequently said they had made that decision in error. This time, when DOOM arrived with wads of cash from all the shows and a mysterious metal mask, they pulled the rapper aside. While questioning him, they discovered his arrest record, which led to further scrutiny of his immigration status. Determining that he was not eligible for entry into the country, they put him on the first flight back to the UK. Brown says, "And he's like, 'You know, I think I'm gonna be here for a while.'"

21

JJDOOM/*KEY TO THE KUFFS*

The Supervillain got kicked out your country,
And said the Pledge of Allegiance six times monthly.
—MF DOOM, "BORIN CONVO"

I can't understand why people are frightened of new ideas.
I'm frightened of the old ones.
—JOHN CAGE

In the middle of the song "Breathin," from one of his early releases, *Three Piece Puzzle* (Ropeadope, 2005), Brooklyn-born producer Jneiro Jarel (Omar Jarel Gilyard) laments, "To me, in this modern-day music, everybody's doing the same thing. It's like, claustrophobic. . . . I need some space to breathe, man." His desire to be different would ultimately guide a career characterized by genre-defying, boundary-breaking music that challenged the status quo while still garnering the respect of an ever-expanding, loyal following. Having spent time in New York, Philly, Atlanta, Houston, New Orleans, and LA, the nomadic army brat displayed a preternatural knack for absorbing the influences of his environment and synthesizing various styles into his music—from hip-hop, jazz, soul, funk, and rock, to drum and bass, electronica, and even Brazilian sounds. Refusing to be associated with any scene, he simultaneously embraced experimentation, forging a sound that lay beyond classification.

Beat Journey (2006), his first release on Lex, credited to Dr. Who Dat?, demonstrated his wide range and versatility as he fused laid-back jazz and loping funk over the bedrock of head-nodding beats. He pushed this eclecticism even further on the follow-up, *Craft of the Lost Art* (2007), assuming various alter egos to create a one-man band like Madlib's fictional supergroup, Yesterdays New Quintet. Joining beat-master Dr. Who Dat? were his alter ego Rocque Wun, the psychedelic vocalist, and multi-instrumentalist Jawaad, who composed the imaginary outfit, Shape of Broad Minds. But the album also featured contributions from the likes of Count Bass D, John Robinson, and Stacey Epps—all associates of DOOM—as well as an appearance by the Villain himself (on "Let's Go"). Unlike DOOM's many one-offs and cameos for other producers, this unorthodox track proved to be a primer for things to come.

As like-minded left-field artists, he and Jarel forged a friendship that eventually blossomed into a working relationship when DOOM drafted him as his tour deejay. Later, while working on *Born Like This*, Jarel invited the Villain to spend some time in LA, where he was renting a house in the Hollywood Hills next door to Dave Sitek. With his band on hiatus, the TV on the Radio guitarist was branching out and making a name for himself as a producer for hire. He tapped his neighbor to program drums on several remixes, and, in turn, Jarel began to involve Sitek on some of his own projects.

These sessions produced the Sitek remix of "Gazzillion Ear" from *Born Like This*, as well as an electro version of a track called "Rhymin Slang" that Jarel had done with DOOM. On December 16, 2011, that remix appeared on the *Pitchfork* site beneath a photo of DOOM, Jarel, and Sitek, presumably all in the studio together. It was the public's first taste of DOOM's recently announced collaboration with Jarel, known as JJ DOOM. Created well before the Villain's deportation, the track had an eerily prescient hook, delivered by Jarel:

> All the way to UK to BK,
> Hear the echo of the bang
> And the Cockney rhyming slang.

The celebrated, working-class dialect of London's East End, cockney used rhyming words to connote an alternative meaning. For example, the expression "apples and pears" meant going up the stairs. Similarly, "frog and toad" meant up the road. It might have been pure coincidence that they referenced cockneys and the UK on this track, if not for the fact that DOOM didn't believe in such things.

"Hey, why don't you move into my house?" asked Will Skeaping, Lex's label manager at the time. The question was addressed to DOOM, whom Tom Brown had just fetched from the K West Hotel, following his whole imbroglio with US Customs. "At least get yourself settled. Come for a few weeks, come for a month, see how you feel," said Skeaping, who lived alone in a tiny flat in Camden equipped with a spare room. "And then DOOM turned up and it was like something out of a movie. I mean, he just turned up with like a couple of bags, the mask, you know. He came in, sat on the sofa, and DOOM was my housemate."

Though hardly strangers, the young Brit and the displaced American didn't know each other very well at that point. But Skeaping felt an almost familial obligation toward DOOM, saying, "He's one of our artists, and I really respected him. I think he's obviously a really smart, interesting guy. And we had an album coming [out] with him and I wanted to make sure that he was as comfy as possible and had someone that he could rely on." In an act of pure selflessness, he even offered to vacate his own bedroom for his guest, making do with the couch in the spare room.

At first, DOOM couldn't conceal his anger over his deportation. "He was really pissed off with the system. He was pissed off with the way that he'd been handled, the way that he'd been approached," says Skeaping. But soon enough, his attitude morphed into one of acceptance as he became pragmatic about the whole situation. "He was really like, 'Fine. Fuck it. Fuck the US,' you know. 'Like if they don't want me, fuck the US, I don't wanna go back there anyway, I'm bringing my family over,'" Skeaping says. "Looking back, I think he could have handled that situation very differently, and I'm really glad that he did end up in the UK as a result of various health issues he had later in which he was able to get absolute grade A healthcare. And I suspect we would've actually seen him probably die a lot earlier if he hadn't had that." Considering the sorry state of health care access in the US, he makes a valid point. "But there were certain times where he was stressed about not seeing his family and he was stressed about his situation, and we talked about it," he adds.

Though a decade younger than DOOM, and thrust together by circumstances beyond their control, Skeaping and his new housemate got along marvelously during the ten-week period they lived together. "I felt very much that he was somebody who was looking to be exposed to new ideas and make the most of the kind of exchange of thinking and practices that were kind of available in London," he says. "And that's kind of what I could do as a friend is introduce him to new things that I'd seen, and thought were cool and interesting. And it turned out, we had a lot of stuff in common."

A lover of painting and the fine arts, Skeaping introduced DOOM to galleries like White Cube and the Tate, where they checked out the latest in contemporary art. He fed his roommate books by Malian photographer Malick Sidibé and Rupert Sheldrake, a parapsychology researcher. They, in fact, bonded over Sheldrake's theory of morphic resonance, which posited that all living things inherited a collective memory from members of their species that preceded them. The two went apartment hunting around London and on boat trips up the Thames. During this time, Skeaping witnessed a side of DOOM to which few others were privy, gaining some valuable insights into the Villain's mysterious ways.

"So, he was interested in ideas and esoteric thinking. And, at this point, by the time I met him, I felt very strongly that he was probably no longer considering himself a musician," he says. "The reason it was so difficult to get music out of DOOM was because, actually, he was far more interested in exploring science, esoteric ideas—not perhaps in the way of like developing his own practical research—but in kind of, joining the dots and using that as a framework to imagine new rhymes and new ideas and to share them with his audience. Like that was very much the trajectory he was on and the way it felt to me was that in many ways he was being held back by this kind of, 'When's *Madvillainy* two coming out?'" In other words, Skeaping firmly believes that the pull of DOOM's core fan base impeded his exploration of the creative paths that he wanted to pursue.

"It's like trying to move on and do a new album and everyone would keep going like, 'Oh, go on, then. Do that funny song you did like 20 years ago.' That was like a big theme I'd say," he posits. "And he'd certainly considered himself like some kind of journeyer and researcher. And I think as much within that, he was really interested in psychedelics. And I think that's massively underplayed, like the extent to which psychedelics played a role in all his music. It wasn't like booze and weed. It was like, this is a guy who was doing acid a lot, apparently for several years at a time with his brother and hanging out in Central Park. And from what I gather from DOOM—he didn't go into much detail—but it sounded to me like the incident with his brother [Subroc] would have been directly related to, you know, being on acid."

While DOOM, no doubt, had a history with psychedelics, his everyday escape remained alcohol. For breakfast, a can of liquid pumpernickel—i.e., Guinness Stout—would often suffice. Empty bottles of harder stuff would also turn up now and then around the flat. "He'd disappear off on walks," says Skeaping. "I think he was really hiding the drinking. I'm gonna be honest, like looking back now sort of 10, 11 years later, I think he must have been drinking like a shitload more than anyone noticed." After all, the hip Camden area that they called home was buzzing with bars and pubs. Instead of buying groceries and eating in, DOOM would also take most of his meals outside the flat. "He was going out to bars for dinner, and he was frequently out with friends and people that he knew," says Skeaping. "So, I think Damon Albarn and those guys, there were a few people in that circle who I think he was seeing for drinks and stuff quite a bit. And he had his cousins around who began to turn up a lot more."

One activity that Skeaping did not see DOOM doing much of was making music, even though, early on, he had arranged for his MPC and rhyme books to be shipped over. Apparently not hurting for cash, he also went out and purchased whatever he needed—including a pair of Genelec speakers and a top-of-the-line MacBook. But he ended up spending much of his time at the flat doing research. "He'd be on his headphones, and he'd mainly be in his room watching YouTube videos," says Skeaping. "I mean, that was literally how I remember him was just constantly having YouTube lectures and videos. Sometimes ones where I would very clearly feel that it was, you know, garbage, and he was watching like weird conspiracy theory stuff, and others where it was really interesting things. But there was a sort of real mix and, obviously, like, again, he was looking for inspiration. He was looking for new ideas and new ways of imagining life."

In addition to his insatiable appetite for learning, DOOM didn't believe in coincidence, according to Skeaping, but rather quantum patterns that shaped reality. Viewing everything as part of a grand plan, he readily accepted his fate of ending up in England, and focused on bringing his family over permanently. The only other person with whom he shared his thoughts was, obviously, his wife, Jasmine. "They'd frequently be talking in quite sort of candid terms about like esoteric beliefs as if he was perhaps in some kind of like, I don't wanna say cult or religion, but he'd been cherry picking the bits of religions that he found compelling and interesting, and they would talk about stuff like that," he says. Most likely he is referring to the eclectic teachings of Dr. York, which provided the foundation for DOOM's esoteric belief system.

For someone who had lived his entire life in the US, and still had a home and family there, it must have been a huge adjustment for DOOM to be "banished" as he expressed in song. "Therefore, the best I could do was to like, make sure he was supported and happy, or, at least as happy as he could be," says Skeaping, who never asked him to contribute to the rent or any other expenses. "And, you know, he was with a WIFI connection and on his own and not being hassled, I think those were like the things that got him through." Eventually, after almost two and a half months, DOOM moved into a spacious loft apartment in Bermondsey on the south bank of the river Thames. He stayed there for about a year before moving into an even more spacious (and expensive) converted church when Jasmine and his brood, which had grown to five children, finally joined him in England the following year.

I'm gonna have to work. I just need to fill out my time. And, so, I want you to get in touch with everybody, DOOM told his label head. His priority was getting money, according to Brown, who says, "At first maybe there were a handful of people that he'd promised verses to, or, you know, that had inquired about doing stuff." The Lex boss reconnected him with Damon Albarn from Gorillaz, as well as the Australian band the Avalanches, for whom DOOM did a remix of "Tonight May Have to Last Me All My Life" (released posthumously in 2021). "Then he was like, 'Oh, let's record a project. You can pay me a track at a time, a verse at a time and I'll just start knocking them out,'" says Brown, who put out a call for beats.

"He'd been working quite a lot with JJ [Jneiro Jarel]. They'd been on tour together. Jneiro had remixed him twice. So, they'd known each other for a long time and they're both friends with Count Bass D. And so out of all the beats that we were sending DOOM's way, he was only recording over the Jneiro Jarel beats," he explains. "And I think at the time, you know, he was talking a lot about how he always gets the same kind of beats, same kind of samples, same kind of sound. And he just really wanted to do something different." This desire to take a creative swerve, then, figured prominently into the JJ DOOM project. Brown, who was psyched to have DOOM in town and working again, started strategizing with him as they hatched an ambitious plan for the new album.

They decided to feature four prominent guests—two from the UK and two from the US. On the British side, Damon Albarn, with whom DOOM had already worked, was a no-brainer. But Beth Gibbons, the enigmatic and reclusive chanteuse from Portishead, seemed like the ultimate bucket list choice. As for possible American contributors, they settled on Kanye West and Nas, both of whom DOOM had hung out with on the West Coast and considered friends. Courtney Brown, who served as DOOM's personal assistant for several years beginning in 2005, and was a friend of Kelis, Nas's wife at the time, even recalled an episode in *The Source* when the two MCs freestyled over some *Special Herbs* beats after having dinner together in LA.

The Lex boss delivered on the two Brits. Albarn appeared on "Bite the Thong," a manic electronic track on which he performs the hook, "I know / You go / We all go / POP!" in a heavily effected vocal that barely cut through the noise. Ironically, the track's staccato beat and swirling textures represented one of the album's more experimental offerings, whose subject matter revolved around rappers compromising themselves for fame. "We the wrong ones, so don't even ask / It's hard enough tryna breathe up in the mask," DOOM rapped, as if feeling the heat from his own notoriety.

After sending Gibbons's manager the music for a mellower, more conventional track called "GMO," Brown received a positive response from them as well. "I think she just genuinely really liked MF DOOM, thought he was an artist that she wanted to work with, and liked the music, so it was just a really genuine thing," he says. Unfortunately, her delicate, lilting vocals barely register above the track's pounding kick drums. Meanwhile, we get a dose of the activist DOOM, as he dishes about so-called "Franken food," rapping "Uh, I get what you're sellin' / Swellin' from alien microfilaments its Morgellons / Even if you're gellin', what's that in your melon? / And what the hell is they sprayin'? No tellin'." Sharp-tongued as ever, his prodigious skills are burnished by research—this time into the bizarre condition known as Morgellons, which causes mysterious fibers to sprout from under the skin. "Sometimes I do have to hit the books real hard," he later confirmed. "I'm taking information in and gathering data to look at a certain subject."[1]

Brown also forwarded music to Noah Goldstein and Che Pope, of Kanye's GOOD Music label. "They said he was recording on stuff and then we never got it, but we sent them probably every track on the album at some point," he says. The perpetually busy Nas, who had grown into quite a mogul, diversifying his portfolio beyond music, turned out to be a no-show as well. Instead, it fell on Jarel to sort out two replacements—former collaborator Khujo Goodie, who dropped a short verse on "Still Kaps," and singer Boston Fielder, featured on "Bout the Shoes." Unfortunately, both solo turns, along with the only instrumental track, "Viberian Sun Pt. II," seemed somewhat out of place and superfluous on the taut forty-two-minute album, encroaching upon DOOM's limited rhyme time as well.

"With all DOOM's stuff, it's a lot easier for him to get it across the [finish] line when he's not the producer," Brown acknowledges. But unlike his other collaborations that only involved writing and recording verses, he remained fully engaged with this project until the end. "JJ was sending him like rough beats, DOOM was arranging them and then they'd go back to JJ and then back to DOOM," he says. "Sometimes they'd changed the whole beat over the course of messing around."

Take "Banished," one of their early efforts, which wasn't even meant to be a song. Jarel had originally sent DOOM a short piece of music that he planned to use as an interlude. But the Villain took it upon himself to loop the noisy, futuristic rock-meets-crunk snippet, adding vocals to make it a proper song. In a departure from his usual laid-back delivery, he also rapped double-time, leading fans to believe his vocal had been sped up. "It wasn't at all. It was just like, you know, DOOM liberated, showing off that he can rhyme over [a fast track]," according to Brown. "The weird thing about DOOM fans is that they'd rather have something like Czarface where he's rapping over some kind of super regular beat rhyming about Captain Crunch cereal, than see him grow as an artist." Sadly, that was probably true, as fandom clings to the familiar. But in London, DOOM was completely untethered—from friends, family, and any expectations—providing a perfect opportunity to shed his skin.

One afternoon during the summer of 2011, after DOOM had moved out, Skeaping received a panicked phone call from him. "He called me and was like, 'Will, I'm having trouble. I can't breathe. I'm outside my apartment.' And like I was in between meetings, and it was a complete fluke that I picked up the phone. Luckily, I knew exactly where he was because I'd taken him to the apartment and was then able to call an ambulance for him and direct them to where he was, because he was like passing out." When he and Brown subsequently visited him in the intensive care ward, after DOOM's condition had stabilized, they discovered that he had had a massive heart attack. "It was like a pretty intense situation," says Skeaping. "And I think from what I gathered, it was a touch-and-go, life-saving moment because he was, you know, essentially dying."

Following this close call, DOOM remained in the hospital for several days while he slowly regained his strength. When friends popped by for daily visits, they found him in good spirits, and incredibly thankful to be alive. As to what could have landed him there, Skeaping says, "I suspect at this point he'd been doing various amounts of cocaine. And I don't know if that had, you know. . . .

On top of everything else, he was obviously not in good shape physically. He was like robust and active, but, you know, he had a substantial beer belly. I think you could say that he did not look like a healthy guy.

"Whenever he went to a bar, he must have been doing, like, a lot of spirits and he was drinking Grey Goose and bottles of champagne," he adds. "And I guess in some ways that must have made him feel like he wasn't drinking vodka behind a park bench, you know, but it was still booze in vast quantities. Anyway, it caught up with him." Whether booze or something more sinister, practically everyone who dealt with DOOM or knew him well would regard him as a functioning alcoholic. Considering his addictive personality, flirting with harder substances certainly did not bode favorably for his general health and well-being.

As DOOM lay recovering in the hospital on a restricted, low-sodium diet, he started complaining about the food to his wife. Skeaping remembers a phone call with Jasmine where she asked him to get DOOM some McDonald's. "And I remember thinking to myself, like, what the fuck is going on? This is bonkers," he says. "So, as far as I can remember, she said, 'Well, if you don't do this, I'm going to, you know, you're not gonna put the album out. That's the last time you're gonna work with DOOM.'" Upon receiving such a blunt ultimatum, Skeaping figured he had no other choice but to smuggle in some McDonald's, but not before a surreal negotiation with DOOM over his order. "The most exciting thing he could do was, like, pull one over on someone or do a little prank and get something extra," he says. "That was his modus operandi, always. Like, it wasn't even about the thing. It was just doing a little move that managed to get the extra thing he wanted." That behavior, according to Skeaping, extended to more than just quarter-pounders.

On February 21, 2012, DOOM had been booked to appear at the Boiler Room, an online streaming platform known for hosting DJ sets by cutting-edge artists. "I went to pick him up to DJ and to take him to the venue," he says, "And he was like, 'I'm not doing it.' He wasn't ready. He didn't wanna do it. And I was like, come on. This is starting in like an hour, you've gotta do it. It's not a big deal. He's like, 'I don't wanna do it. I don't feel comfortable doing it.'" Skeaping suspects he hadn't prepared a set. But, luckily, Jarel, who happened to be in town, had accompanied them. "We dressed him up in all of DOOM's clothes, gave him DOOM's watch, you know, put the mask on, the cap on, did the facial hair, put a pillow under his sweatshirt so that he looked like DOOM with a big beer belly. And it was entirely convincing, amazingly," he recalls.

Even hardcore fans who attended that night were none the wiser until the story eventually came out. "He loved that 'cause it was like a heist," says Skeaping. "And we were all in on it together, and we had a little secret, and he still got the loot at the end. Like he got paid several thousand pounds. And it was, you know, it was like a real bonding moment. I think that's when he realized that I was prepared to help out on a scam." But such episodes also put the label manager in a difficult position, ultimately influencing his decision to quit the music industry. (He currently works as a climate activist for Extinction Rebellion.)

Though DOOM had dodged a major bullet regarding his health, lingering issues still dogged him. "I was really worried about his cocaine consumption, you know, I just wanted to make sure that he wasn't doing cocaine or if he was, it was in some way rationed," says Skeaping, who felt somewhat complicit. "I think I even took a bag away from him, and said like, please don't do this. It's gonna kill you. And he's going, 'No, I'm as fit as an ox. I'm fine. I'm good.' Anyway, I think, at this point, he had quite a lot of facilitators around him. But he was actually in better health [when] he came out of this, and we definitely went out of our way to limit what he was doing as much as we could." At the same time, however, no one in the UK was in a position to tell a grown man how to conduct himself.

Living in London, where he was detached from his past, offered DOOM the ultimate anonymity, which had always been a major concern. After settling into his own place, he also gained a measure of autonomy not enjoyed since his bachelor days since it was much more difficult for the label, or even his wife, to keep tabs on him (though Jasmine and their five children eventually joined him). For their part, Lex respected his privacy and left him alone, allowing him the space to work. But, once, after trying to contact him and receiving no response for a couple of days, Brown started to worry. So, one summer evening, he drove down to DOOM's loft. "And I got there and, you know, still couldn't get hold of him, ringing on the door and ringing on the buzzer of the gate," he recalls. Eventually, when somebody let him into the courtyard of the property, he proceeded to DOOM's ground-floor flat, where he found an open window. Not comfortable entering on his own, he called the landlady, and after explaining the situation, she suggested calling the cops.

When a male and female officer responded to the call, Brown relayed his concerns regarding DOOM's sudden disappearance and his previous health issues. The policeman then climbed through the open window and let Brown and the other officer in through the front door. Littered with used takeaway cartons, beer cans, and empty bottles of liquor, the place, at first glance, appeared to have been ransacked. "There was a big flat table that was covered with like models that you glue together, like plastic Airfix models, kinda thing, and little constructions with crystals hanging on them and kinda mystical crystal things," according to Brown. "And then the biggest bag of weed and just piles of scrunched up bank notes, just a mountain of them." Though the police initially suspected a burglary, they couldn't figure out why so much money had been left lying around. They didn't even bother about the weed, to Brown's great relief, as DOOM's bad housekeeping most probably saved the day.

"The police locked the door, and gave me a number to follow up, you know, that kind of thing," he says. "I can't remember the exact series of events, but like maybe the next day or that night or something, somebody got a message from DOOM, and he was OK." But when he returned to his flat, he discovered that the policeman had dropped the key to his handcuffs. "And when I spoke to him," says Brown, "I was like, man, there was quite a lot of drama, you know, are you okay? And he was like, 'Oh yeah, sometimes you just gotta check out and get away from things, you know? But I was working, don't worry.' But for him that key to the cuffs is obviously symbolic to name the album."

In addition to its clever title, *Key to the Kuffs* (Lex, 2012) stands out as DOOM's most experimental album, and one that finds him really stretching himself as an artist. Stranded far from home like a modern-day Ulysses, he obviously has plenty to get off his chest, and offers more personal insights this time around. The album landed three years after his last project—par for the course for DOOM—but not soon enough for those spoiled by his fertile period, for whom it seemed like he had been on hiatus forever. But it's amazing he was able to pull together such a strong showing considering everything he was dealing with at the time.

Songs like "Banished" and "Guv'nor" expressly deal with his forced immigration. "Villain got banished / Refused out the US, he ain't even Spanish," he says on the former, clarifying, "No not deported / Be a little minute before things get sorted." Though he didn't know it at the time, that would never happen. Meanwhile, on "Guv'nor," cockney slang for someone in a position of authority, he references his new surroundings, saying, "Vocals spill over like the rolling hills of Dover." The fact that they are actually cliffs would have, obviously, ruined his rhyme scheme. Speaking of which, in the same song, he tackles the utterly unpronounceable Icelandic volcano, whose eruption during the spring of 2010 played havoc with air traffic across Europe: "Catch a throatful from the fire vocal / With ash and molten glass like Eyjafjallajökull." Triple word score for the Villain!

Some of his most quotable verses appear on "Rhymin Slang," the track that officially launched the album. "Got to do it, snottily putrid, true grit / Came to spew spit like bodily fluid with mucus," says DOOM, boasting an internal rhyme game that is as tight as ever. In the second verse he unleashes one of his patented tongue-tying tornados: "Rarely scarcely scary glaring stare / Let's be very clear, MC's is derriere / As well as aware, wearily, just don't be nearly near, you hear me? *Yeah*." Aside from such an awesome display of alliteration, he shows his clever sophistication, dissing the competition in French.

Although this album lacks a feminine perspective, he still aims one at the ladies with a mature love song directed at his wife. The weeping strings of "Winter Blues" convey the pain of his separation as he raps, "Each and every day making cash with Satan / Can't eat, can't sleep, it's exasperatin' / Mad light burning off / All he needs is one warm hug to keep from turning off." On the same track he deftly weaves in a reference to Henrietta Lacks, a Black cancer patient whose cells were preserved for use in medical research without her permission. The track's finale includes a long vocal snippet by Dr. Jewell Pookrum, who speaks about the benefits of the natural pigment, melanin.

Of his latest collaborator, the Villain said, "Usually when I write to another producer's work it brings out other elements, and with this dude, the way his production is, these songs are on a different level."[2] Not since *Vaudeville Villain* had he written to such unconventional material. Jarel displays a knack for totally changing up his sonic palette from one song to the next, making the album's progression interesting and unpredictable. No stranger to the mic either, he holds his own on the solo "Dawg Friendly," on which he raps, "Ayo, D, what the dealy? You know me / Dropping all these beats to slap these cats silly / Feeling 90% of these dudes? Not really / So many wack cats that I'm more dog friendly."

While Jarel also contributes all the musical interludes between tracks, DOOM, as usual, handles all the skit material, which, for the first time, are not exclusively culled from cartoons. Aside from snippets of *Spider-Man*, which find their way into the opening skit, "Waterlogged," and "Ello Guv'nor," whose title as well as dialogue come from an episode of Cartoon Network's *Regular Show*, most of the other voices come straight out of DOOM's YouTube research, manipulated for comic effect. It's especially entertaining how he chops up outtakes from esoteric teacher Bobby Hemmitt, known for his stream-of-consciousness monologues delivered in Ebonics with a South Carolina twang, who never gets boring.

While sharing the mixing duties with his partner, DOOM always reserved the right to EQ (equalize) his own voice and to get it to sound how he wanted. When it came time to master the album in London, he also insisted on being present, and went through the process no less than five times. "We ended up picking up the bill for a whole day session, you know, and it was like 150, 250 quid an hour for DOOM to sit there with an engineer," according to Brown. "He was super persnickety and really aware that anything he dropped was gonna be, like, analyzed and torn to bits." As always, DOOM was right.

While reviews for the album were mostly positive, an influential outlet like *Pitchfork* only gave it a 7.3 rating on top of a very mixed review, which Brown blames for hampering the marketing campaign. But this was no longer the early aughts, which saw sales of the dominant format, CDs, peaking. In the decade before downloading and streaming finally eclipsed sales of physical product, the bottom fell out of the music industry, affecting independent labels especially hard. The JJ DOOM album and its accompanying collection of remixes, *Bookhead EP*, suffered as a result. Brown quotes sales of between 35,000 to 40,000 copies, a far cry from even *Born Like This*, which sold at least double that amount. For most of his second incarnation as an MC, DOOM had practically defied gravity, but he was swiftly heading back to Earth.

In August 2011, a full year before *Key to the Kuffs* dropped, Nature Sounds released the twelve-inch of "Victory Laps," thought to herald the beginning of the long-anticipated collaboration between DOOM and Ghostface. First announced back in 2005, when both artists appeared together on the cover of *Mass Appeal*, the proposed project—alternately known as Iron Man vs. Metal-Face, DOOMStarks, and *Swift & Changeable*—seemed plagued by problems from the outset. "DOOMStarks were signed by Nature Sounds," says Brown. "I'm not sure what their deal looked like, but they licensed it to Lex for the world outside of North America in 2005 and so I picked it up and we picked up the publishing, and then I think tracks just started getting cannibalized, you know, like, ending up on other projects."

After hearing one of the *Special Herbs* releases, Ghost had contacted DOOM about using selected tracks on the *Fishscale* and *More Fish* albums, both released in 2006. (Incidentally, later in 2012, Masta Ace released an entire album based on *Special Herbs* instrumentals, called *MA DOOM: Son of Yvonne*.) In return, Ghost made cameos on *The Mouth and the Mask* and *Born Like This*, as the two announced their own collaborative project. "He [DOOM] actually tried to stick two tracks from DOOMStarks onto JJ DOOM," according to Brown. "But it just seemed so pointless to have them on there. DOOMStarks is all themed around *Charlie's Angels*, so all the tracks kind of fit together thematically."

In interviews from July 2009 and late 2011 regarding the status of their collaboration, Ghost repeatedly claimed to be waiting on DOOM, who, when asked, claimed the opposite. But the Villain was known for taking his time and never rushing the work—especially when it came to something as important as his dream project with Ghost, whom he obviously held in high regard. In a concerted attempt to finish the album, Nature Sounds arranged for a recording session in Amsterdam that took place sometime between 2012 and 2014, where DOOM and Ghostface apparently met face-to-face. "DOOM sent me the recordings from that stuff from those sessions," says Brown. "But I don't think it was as productive as they hoped 'cause I think, you know, both DOOM and Ghostface were pretty smashed."

By the time the two MCs shared the same bill at London's storied 100 Club, on April 18, 2013, their long-anticipated collaboration had become somewhat of a chimera. Who knows if they even saw each other that night, considering DOOM's penchant for disappearing in a taxi following his hasty exit from stage. But he definitely ran into another MC from upstate New York, an up-and-comer known as Bishop Nehru (Markel Ni'Jee Scott), the night's opening act. At the tender age of fifteen, he had won a talent contest sponsored by WorldStar-HipHop that he parlayed into appearances on Hot 97 and Power 105.1, New York's top rap stations. The following year, he released his first mixtape, *Nehruvia*, a throwback to the nineties boom-bap sound, featuring production from the likes of DJ Premier along with Madlib and DOOM. Riding a huge buzz at the time, he had been invited to come to Europe to open for Wu-Tang Clan's 20th Anniversary Tour.

According to Nehru, "DOOM's people reached out to me and said they were interested in working with me. I played the Converse 'Get Dirty Show' at the 100 Club in London recently. We spoke there and DOOM was mad chill. A real cool dude. It is a dream come true to be honest. Seems like it was just yesterday when I first discovered his music."[3] Though they didn't talk business that night, they hung out and got to know each other better over burgers. Subsequently, they announced a collaboration titled *NehruvianDOOM*, produced by the Villain, in which Nehru handled most of the vocal duties.

Unlike DOOMStarks, this project came to fruition not long after its inception. Lex released *NehruvianDOOM (Sound of the Son)* on October 7, 2014, to mostly positive reviews, even though the nine-track, thirty-two-minute album seemed lacking or unfinished. While Metal Fingers produced most of it (with an assist from Madlib, who contributed "Disastrous"), he only rhymed on four tracks, usually just popping in for a quick verse or hook. Either he wanted to give his younger partner a chance to shine, or was attempting to get away with doing the least amount of work possible. As far as DOOM was concerned, both were probably true. Lyrically, though their styles complemented each other, as much hype as followed Nehru at the time, he was hardly in a position to carry an album on his own—even despite its brevity. After being signed to Nas's Mass Appeal label in 2014, Nehru left a couple years later, and despite releasing new music in the interim, has yet to materialize another full album.

NehruvianDOOM happened to be DOOM's last major contribution behind the boards. But of the eight tracks he produced, two were previously released instrumentals from the *Special Herbs* series and one was a recycled beat. These included "Darkness," a vocal version of "Bergamont" (from *Special Herbs 9&0*), which sampled the horn fanfare from "Black Man's March" (Now Again, 2003) by L.A. Carnival, and "Coming for You," originally "Fo Ti" (from *Special Herbs, Volumes 7&8*), which sourced a suspenseful snippet from the soundtrack of the seventies children's show *The Electric Company*. On "Great Things" he also used the same Waltel Branco sample from "Zoraia" (CBS, 1975) as he did for the track "Devastator" (Unicron, 2008), featuring Trunks. On the remaining five joints, one of which was the opening skit, "First Day of Class," DOOM pulled samples as well as vocal snippets from his usual sources—cartoons or children's records, TV shows, movie soundtracks, and jazz. After releasing back-to-back experimental albums, however, he covered no new ground here.

Despite pocketing a $45,000 advance for an album that he never delivered and going AWOL for several years, DOOM eventually found his way back to Adult Swim. At first, Jason DeMarco wasn't returning his calls, until he learned from Jasmine that one of their daughters had been in desperate need of medical attention at the time. "I can't be mad at him. It's like he was a super villain," he says. "He was a nice guy, but at the same time, he wasn't afraid to fuck someone over if it helped him out and he needed some shit. Like he wasn't gonna worry about it, right? I mean, you're talking about a guy who had an apartment and didn't live with his wife 'cause he wanted to have affairs and his wife was like, 'Fine then stay in your apartment.' He was a complicated man. I don't think anyone really knew DOOM. I don't even think Jasmine really knew DOOM."

The reason he kept forgiving him and giving him further opportunities, according to DeMarco, was because "I understood to some degree that this is just his nature and it's the gamble you take when you work with him. When you work with DOOM, you're not working with an equal partner. You're working with somebody—at least, unless you're an artist—who you are helping fund something they want to do. And you either accept that and go, 'I hope whatever comes of it is good for him and for his art' or you say, 'I can't risk any more of this because I might lose my job or get in trouble or whatever.' And I basically rode that line for twenty years."

After the two finally spoke and settled their differences, DOOM offered up some new music. Instead of doing a regular album, however, they came up with the concept of serializing the fifteen rare or unreleased tracks, which would be called *The Missing Notebook Rhymes*. They would release one track per week, for free, on Adult Swim's website. As DeMarco told *Mass Appeal*, "They're tracks that [DOOM] either doesn't have a home for, or they are part of other projects which aren't necessarily complete, but we can sort of tease them. It's sort of a peek at everything he has going on right now."[4]

Released on August 7, 2017, the first track, "Notebook 00—Negus," was a collaboration with Sean Price that DOOM had recorded before that rapper's untimely death in 2015. Featuring two underground legends, it was an ideal way to kick off the series. Unfortunately, DOOM hadn't produced the track, nor did he have the right to release it. Crummie Beats, the producer, demanded compensation from Adult Swim, who had no recourse but to pay him. In fact, over the ensuing weeks, the company was besieged by other such claims and realized that DOOM had not paid any of the outside producers or artists involved. There was also the small matter of DOOM's exclusive deal with Lex, who had no qualms about protecting their rights and going after other labels that put out their artist's material.

On September 26, following the release of "Notebook 06—Pause Tape (Remix)," Adult Swim had no choice but to remove all the *Missing Notebook*

Rhymes material from their website, issuing a statement that they had terminated their relationship with DOOM. An explanation would only come after DOOM's passing in a series of tweets sent by DeMarco. "I think part of the *Missing Notebook Rhymes* was him trying to get money from someone that wasn't Lex, with beats he had no rights to, and he thought, 'I can get away with this.' I don't even think he really cared if he got away with it," he says. It appeared to be just another ruthless money grab on the Villain's part, though he clearly had his own reasons for doing so.

For someone who had gone out on a limb for DOOM time and time again, it was the final straw, but, surprisingly, their relationship didn't end on a sour note. "We bonded over our love for the Pink Panther cartoon," says DeMarco. "And, so, he painted me a big painting, of course, a bandit from the Pink Panther cartoon robbing a safe. And that hangs in Adult Swim." He also painted one for DeMarco's boss, Mike Lazzo, of a guy holding a cosmic cube in his hand. "He gave me those just out of the blue and it was kind of his way of saying, 'I'm sorry,' you know, without really having to say, I'm sorry," he says. "They just delivered them to work one day. Jasmine was like, 'Hey, these are paintings DOOM made for you.'"

In hindsight, 2017 turned out to be one of the toughest years in recent memory for DOOM. Though he had made unprecedented progress as an artist and huge strides toward healing since the twin tragedies that had rocked him years earlier, the hands of fate delivered a crushing blow. On Monday, December 18, he sadly posted news of his fourteen-year-old son's passing on Instagram. "King Malachi Ezekiel Dumile 2/22/03–12/18/17 the greatest son one could ask for," he wrote, holding a picture of the deceased. "Safe journey and may all our ancestors greet you with open arms. One of our greatest inspirations. Thank you for allowing us to be your parents. Love you Mali." Losing a loved one was tragic enough, but losing a child was unimaginable. It delivered a jolt from which the Villain probably never recovered.

Like a circle completed, DOOM's last recorded albums were collaborations with the group Czarface, composed of rappers Esoteric (Seamus Ryan) and

Wu-Tang's Inspectah Deck (Jason Hunter) along with DJ/producer 7L (George Andrinopoulos). A decade before forming their comic-book-inspired supergroup, the Boston duo of 7L & Esoteric had witnessed the birth of MF DOOM at the Nuyorican Poets Café, as he rocked the crowd with only a sheer stocking covering his face. "It was probably one of the first times an actual idol had been humanized to me," says Esoteric. "This was an artist I'd see rocking on *Yo! MTV Raps* as Zev Love X from KMD in the early '90s, and that level was something that just wasn't tangible for me. . . . He was like a superhero." Though traveling in the same indie rap circles, they never had the opportunity to link up at the time. But 7L & Esoteric did end up collaborating with the Wu-Tang wordsmith for a track called "Speaking Real Words" (Direct Records, 1999), released as an EP.

Fast forward to 2013, when the group Czarface announced themselves with a self-titled debut on Boston's Brick Records. Street artist L'Amour Supreme (who incidentally illustrated the cover of this book) helped the group realize their comic-book-inspired mascot, who graced the cover, resembling the Terminator. Combining a return to the boom bap sound of the nineties with pop-culture comic-book references and a whole host of high-profile cameos—from Ghostface Killah, Roc Marciano, Cappadonna, and Action Bronson—the album was well received, debuting at number thirty-four on *Billboard*'s Top R&B/Hip-Hop chart. For the follow-up, *Every Hero Needs a Villain* (Brick, 2015), it was almost a no-brainer to ask DOOM for a guest verse on the track, "Ka-bang!" According to Esoteric, "The collaboration for 'Ka-bang!' came about pretty easily, just reaching out through a mutual friend and the collaborative relationship started from there."

After burnishing their indie credentials with two more successful albums, the group wanted to try something different. "We liked the idea of a 'versus' type of collaborative record, and when I threw out the title 'Czarface vs. Metalface' to 7L and Deck, it really inspired us to try and make an LP happen," says Esoteric. "DOOM was down, but he suggested that we call it 'Czarface *meets* Metalface,' so it was more us working together as a team than as rivals clashing and competing." Even though DOOM was living abroad by this point, working remotely did not pose a problem. 7L would send beats to Deck and Esoteric, who recorded their parts first. "I'd send them to DOOM, and he'd playfully rename the beats when sending over ideas," says Esoteric. "For instance, I sent him the 'Nautical Depth' track, but the working title was 'Meet in the Subway,' and he'd send it back with a verse, and a file renamed 'MEAT IN THE SUBWAY,' stylized in all caps." Working assiduously, they knocked out the album's sixteen tracks in about a year.

When *Czarface Meets Metal Face* (Get on Down/Silver Age) dropped on March 30, 2018, it immediately shot to the top of *Billboard*'s Heatseekers chart, also peaking at number 5 on the Independent chart and at 134 on the Top 200. It had obviously been a while since the public had heard DOOM on a full album's worth of material, though he had been busy doing one-offs with the likes of Flying Lotus, Cannibal Ox, Earl Sweatshirt, and Danny Brown. So, the interest and curiosity were there, but for all its golden-era nostalgia, the album seemed somewhat tired and DOOM uninspired. After constantly challenging the listener with his technical flows and proving that he could spit to any kind of rhythm, he seemed content to simply coast this time around. Considering the painful loss of his son the previous year, such a lackluster performance was not at all surprising.

The idea for a follow-up came from their distributor at Traffic Entertainment, Joe Mansfield. This time they also released an accompanying comic book, written by Esoteric, on which DOOM, a control freak to the end, revised some of his lines. Though they completed the ten-track album by April of 2020, COVID had struck by then, so they took the summer to fine-tune the record. Then, the announcement of DOOM's passing on December 31, 2020, further stalled the album, which finally saw light on May 7, 2021. As Esoteric said, on its release, "I speak for everyone involved when I say we were incredibly fortunate to have collaborated with DOOM. . . . He was a one-of-a-kind, never-to-be-duplicated emcee, producer, and visionary. We wish peace and healing to his family, friends and everyone touched by the gifts he shared with the planet. MF DOOM FOREVER."[5] Such a simple but fitting eulogy, no doubt, resonated across the DOOMiverse, soon to be followed by many more.

THE LEGEND

His life is like a folklore legend.

—MF DOOM, "CURLS"

22

NEVER DEAD

The only way to deal with an unfree world is to become so absolutely free that your very existence is an act of rebellion.

—ALBERT CAMUS

Superlatives like "legend" and "genius" get tossed around very loosely these days—especially in the hyperbolic realm of rap, where ego and a gladiatorial mentality predominate. Even the expression "G.O.A.T." (greatest of all time), credited to and most associated with the undisputed heavyweight champ, Muhammed Ali, has found its way into colloquial (over)use. But rap bears greater comparison to pro wrestling than boxing, with many spirited pretenders to the throne among its diverse and colorful ranks. Run-DMC called out these so-called "Sucker MCs" in song, highlighting the art form's preoccupation with lyrical combat and taking out the competition. But as far as continuing that legacy, none has displayed as much consistency, creativity, or pure dedication to the craft as DOOM.

"DOOM is at the top. He's one of the top people up there," says Posdnuos of De La Soul, of his friend and fellow rhymer's place in the pantheon of hip-hop. "And he did it his way." Among the many incredible talents to have grabbed the mic and advanced the art form over the last fifty years, mainstream or otherwise, DOOM managed to distinguish himself from the rest by all measures, forging a singular path on his own terms. So remarkable is his story, in fact, that it rings even stranger than fiction. The same goes for his passing, reported two months after the fact with little or no accompanying details. While death often confers legendary status on the well-known and famous, or those who have distinguished themselves in some way, DOOM had already attained such a benchmark in life, though never aspiring to it. To that point, he actively resisted such a characterization and sometimes sabotaged his own success. Yet, without peer among his fellow MCs, he remains one of the few rap artists to transcend hip-hop.

In DOOM, who bucks comparisons to his contemporaries, we see echoes of bluesman Robert Johnson, whom the Rock and Roll Hall of Fame dubbed "the first ever rock star." The Mississippi-born guitarist and songwriter had an even shorter life and career than the Villain, dying at the age of twenty-seven while having never enjoyed much commercial success or recognition in his lifetime. But remembered today as "King of the Delta Blues," he is hailed as a huge influence by such latter-day rock stars as Bob Dylan, Keith Richards, and Robert Plant.

Poor documentation during the Jim Crow era, when he plied his trade as an itinerant musician, may have contributed to the lack of information about Johnson, but it also helped fuel the mystery surrounding him, including the popular rumor that he had made a Faustian deal with the Devil. That narrative arose after he disappeared from the scene of juke joints and Saturday night dances, where he was considered just another mediocre player, only to re-emerge several years later as a guitar virtuoso. Apparently, the best place to practice your chops all night without disturbing anyone was at the local cemetery, which might account for the intrigue. Like DOOM, complete dedication to his craft fueled his virtuosity, which, in turn, became the driving force behind his resurgence and ultimate veneration.

Despite said deal, Johnson was considered charismatic and friendly, demonstrating a real knack for establishing a rapport with audiences—traits that DOOM also shared. Those lucky enough to call the Supervillain a friend described him as a good-natured, gentle soul, while fans claimed to share a close personal relationship with him through his lyrics. Johnson's weaknesses—whiskey and women—were DOOM's as well, not to mention the way each treated music as both a moneymaking hustle and the ultimate source of happiness and fulfillment. The similarities between these two artists appear clearly more than superficial, suggesting that great minds—even across time—did, indeed, think alike, and legends are likely cut from the same cloth.

News of DOOM's passing had barely hit Instagram when an avalanche of responses descended from all corners of social media. "RIP to another Giant your favorite MC's MC . . . MF DOOM! crushing news . . . ," tweeted Q-Tip, who had coined the expression widely associated with his fellow abstract poet. But scores of similar testimonials backed him up. Mos Def (aka Yasiin Bey), who had been previously seen gushing over DOOM lyrics on YouTube, presented a video homage to his fallen comrade on Instagram. He literally gave DOOM his flowers, performing a cover of "All Caps," with face partially obscured, accompanied by the words, "Inspiration Information. Thank you and thank you again. Peace," followed by rows of rose emojis.

Odd Future's Tyler, the Creator and Earl Sweatshirt had similarly been captured on video as unapologetic fanboys meeting DOOM for the first time backstage at a music festival. Both registered their reactions on Twitter. "Safe travels villain," said Tyler, while Earl wrote, "humbled to b thought of in the same sentence as dumile. I've been crying and listening to his music since I found out. Made a shrine and drank some beer." They were among the next generation of rappers upon whom DOOM had left his mark, along with Joey Badass, who tweeted "RIP MF DOOM THE SUPER MF VILLAIN."

Brainfeeder label boss Flying Lotus, who divulged that he had been working on an EP with DOOM, only offered, "My soul is crushed." Meanwhile, Lupe Fiasco, who had never met him, said, "Thanx DOOM. . . . I learned so much about the art of rapping. Studied and analyzed you for years as recently as a few days ago. I wish I could have met you to tell you that . . . here's some raps . . . rest easy . . . Amin." The respect DOOM engendered among these younger artists was unequivocal and rare—especially considering rap's intergenerational rivalries.

One of the most poignant tributes came from his old friend, Busta Rhymes, formerly of Leaders of the New School, one of KMD's labelmates at Elektra.

Posting a video of "In the Streets," their 2016 collab with BJ The Chicago Kid, he wrote, "It has taken me days to come to terms with this enough to type about it and I still can't believe it or come to terms with it. I'm completely fucked up by the loss of this God MC & incredible human being!! Over 30 years of friendship & brotherhood almighty!! I wanted to believe this was another elaborate scheme by the great Whodini [sic] MF DOOM himself but this time I have received the confirmation that it wasn't."[1] He went on to add that DOOM, "meant something to our culture that no other MC has because he figured out something that none of us before him [had] and that was to be completely free!!!"[2] Having full control over their art as well as their business was purely aspirational for most artists, but something DOOM had actually attained. More than anyone else in the game, he was beholden only to himself, and managed to truly operate on his own terms.

And the rap world was not alone in its grief. Those mourning DOOM's passing came from all corners, including jazz bassist Thundercat, who tweeted, "Thanks for everything DOOM." On the same platform, Radiohead's Thom Yorke, who had remixed "Gazzillion Ear" and "Retarded Fren," wrote, "I am so sad to hear of MF DOOM's passing. He was a massive inspiration to so many of us, changed things . . . for me the way he put words [together] was often shocking in [its] genius using stream of consciousness in a way I'd never heard before." Tributes even came from outside the music industry. Cord Jefferson, a writer for HBO's *Succession* and *Watchmen* (who went on to win an Academy Award for his 2024 directorial debut, *American Fiction*), tweeted, "It felt special for one of the greatest artists alive to actively avoid the spotlight in a media landscape that's increasingly reliant on endless self-promotion via as many channels as possible. RIP to MF DOOM."[3] In paying their respects, all of these people verbalized what made DOOM so unique, outlining, as well, how his legacy would be defined.

An enigma in life, DOOM managed to maintain much of that mystique after leaving the planet. Even close friends, associates, and family found out about his passing like everyone else—two months after the fact on Instagram. Only those in his inner circle, including people like Big Benn Klingon, Blake Lethem, Kurious, and Devin Horwitz, had any inkling of how he spent his final years, much less days. The rest of us, fans and supporters, were left to speculate—if only for some kind of closure and to suspend disbelief after such a sudden and tragic loss. Certainly, more than a few have allowed for the outside hope that DOOM faked his own death and was living his best life on some exotic island hideout like a Bond villain.

Though no posthumous sightings of him, like Tupac, have emerged, a YouTube video released by Nature Sounds in 2016, called "A Villainous Adventure . . . ," seemed to give credence to such a possibility. Set to the suitably suspenseful instrumental for "Lively Hood," one of the DOOMStarks tracks, it featured scenes of a cigar-puffing DOOM surveying dramatic views from his mountain retreat in Saint Lucia, or behind the wheel of a luxury sailboat sporting a New York Islanders hockey jersey. Of course, he's wearing the mask—even while taking a dip in the pool—along with his "Metal Face Villain" New Era cap, for which a purchase link appears at the end of the video. Besides the low-budget marketing opportunity, the purpose of the video seemed to suggest that DOOM had not disappeared without a trace but was alive and well and working on his next devious scheme. But it was shot four years before he passed, and much had transpired in the interim.

While DOOM had, indeed, left England to relocate to the Caribbean for several years—most probably one of the British Virgin Islands, where he would not have needed a visa to live—he eventually returned to the place of his birth. No one can confirm exactly when, or whether it had anything to do with the passing of his son Malachi in December 2017. But Will Skeaping recalled a curious encounter with his former roommate around October 2018 in London. It was their first meeting since DOOM's departure as well as the last time they would see each other. "So, he'd gone to some island place and just because he hadn't played ball, he'd pissed off the locals, or they'd realized that he had some money or somebody had found him on the internet or something," he says. "And I didn't ask what had happened, but he was like, 'Oh, we are in deep shit, and we have to be on the run and these guys are trying to kill us and stuff.' But the way he made it sound, I literally was like, I can't tell if he's not making this up."

Well-acquainted with DOOM's penchant for tall tales and exaggeration, Skeaping compares the story to the nature of his lyrics, saying, "The thing about DOOM is he gave you certain things, but he didn't articulate everything. What he gave you was access points to understand and bring your own interpretation of what he was saying onto his work. So, everyone projects onto DOOM, whatever they want, and that's part of the magic." It's an astute observation, corroborated by the comments section of Genius.com, which offers all manner of interpretation of his lyrics by devout fans and armchair critics. Certainly, DOOM was famous for operating on a need-to-know basis, which obviously helped cultivate his mystique. But he wasn't against fabrication—especially if it helped him control the narrative and obscured the reality of the situation.

One of the more surprising reactions to DOOM's passing came from Geoff Barrow, the producer of Portishead, who also fronts the band Beak. On his Instagram page, he declared, "So gutted and flattened by the news of the passing of MF DOOM. . . . Someone extremely special has been taken away from us tonight. After this fuckin' year it's [sic] just dosnt [sic] seem fair considering his age and influence on the world of music." Crossing paths at a couple of the same festivals, they were probably more acquaintances than friends, yet the MC had obviously left an indelible impression. In that same post, Barrow relayed a curious story about the last time they had met:

> He had bought a ticket to see us Beak at the Brudenell club in Leeds. I was selling merch at the table when a dude (not him) asked me to sign a poster for him (as we sign anything for anyone). I asked if there was a name he wanted it to [say] he replied MF DOOM. I was like "What.. Who..Why?" As I did I looked up and there was DOOM Stood there smiling I'm like FUCK MATE LEEDS??? Whaaaaaa? What the fuck you doing here? We chatted and he was so lovely. I felt amazingly honoured that he had come to see us but still utterly confused that he was there? We chatted after we played and he seemed to dig it. As his music was a huge inspiration to me it was a night I'll never forget and treasure.

Beak last played the Brudenell Club in Leeds on December 8, 2019, which would have been just short of a year before DOOM passed away. Barrow was obviously caught off guard—not simply because DOOM showed up at his band's concert, but for the fact that it happened in Leeds, of all places.

Located roughly two hundred miles north of London, in the county of West Yorkshire, Leeds was a working-class, industrial town—population about half a million—well past its prime. Why the Villain was slumming, off-the-radar, in that random corner of the world was anyone's guess. But it somehow made sense that a person preoccupied with privacy might choose a quieter, more remote place to live than London—especially if dealing with health issues. Following up on Barrow's story and other rumors, local journalist Rob Conlon took it upon himself to do some snooping around, and actually uncovered some persuasive evidence that DOOM had spent some time in his town.

Various patrons and employees of the Brudenell club recalled seeing an unmasked DOOM nonchalantly sipping a Guinness at the back during a show. The owner of a store selling remote-controlled cars, one of DOOM's hobbies, claimed he was a regular customer, and even asked not to print the name of the business in deference to his privacy. A local DJ posted on Facebook that he knew the person who had just purchased DOOM's house. "Someone told me he was living in [nearby] Shadwell with his wife, someone else said he was living with two guys who worked either as managers or promoters," Conlon wrote. "It's typical of the universe DOOM created. Fact and fiction are rarely distinguishable."[4]

Following the announcement of his death, graffiti murals in his honor started appearing around the city. The Leeds art collective Two Times, both hardcore fans, were commissioned to cover an entire wall of the Belgrave Music Hall with DOOM's masked image along with the lyrics (from "Lickupon"), "There are four sides to every story, if these walls could talk, they'd probably ignore me." Little did they know, at the time, that they may have even crossed paths with their subject at some point. While offering no conclusive proof, Conlon summed up the feelings of many in his northern outpost when he concluded, "Daniel Dumile lived his life playing with the most tantalizing aspects of myth and mystery. Nobody will know for sure if they ever casually chatted to a supervillain in the Belgrave on a Saturday night, but now we all hope we might. Whether it's true that he lived here or not, the myth is stronger. It gives Leeds a unique place in the universe he created and left behind for everyone else to explore."[5] The article, published in February 2022, offered an interesting postscript to DOOM's secret life, but raised more questions than answers.

Then, in a surprising twist, as America celebrated another birthday, on July 4, 2023, the online site Leeds Live broke a story titled "Heartbroken Wife of Famous Musician Has Unanswered Question after Sudden Death in Leeds." In it, they reported that an inquest into DOOM's death had determined that a rare and severe reaction to blood pressure medication had been the cause. After two doses of a newly prescribed medication, he experienced angioedema, or swelling of the tongue and throat, that restricted his breathing and was rushed to St. James Hospital in Leeds. According to the article, "The inquest heard that on October 21 Daniel had complained that he couldn't breathe and tried to get off his hospital trolley before he collapsed and suffered respiratory arrest."[6] After being placed on a respirator, his condition stabilized, even improving to the point where he was able to take food and water and speak to the doctors, who explained what had happened to him.

At some point during his ten-day stay, however, his condition took a rapid turn for the worse. COVID restrictions, apparently, prevented Jasmine from visiting her husband in hospital, but she kept in constant contact via phone, even alerting the nurses when he needed assistance. The article went on to report, "She said: 'I was not able to see him until the 31st (of October)—that's when the respirator was turned off that was helping him breathe.'"[7] Following his death, however, she raised several concerns about DOOM's treatment at St. James, leading to the inquest.

A follow-up piece in the same publication noted that DOOM already suffered from a slew of health issues including kidney and heart failure, Type 2 diabetes, and hepatitis B, a viral infection of the liver. According to the coroner, severe reactions to the blood pressure drug were rare, but more common in smokers and people of Afro-Caribbean descent, of which he checked both boxes. Even so, the hospital did not try to shirk responsibility. "Following the inquest's conclusion, the Leeds Teaching Hospitals NHS Trust apologised for the care Daniel received which it said was 'not to the standard we would expect,'"[8] according to the piece.

Knowing the truth about DOOM's last days may not make his passing any less painful, but it does go a long way toward finally humanizing him again. The man who reveled in the realms of the imagination, developing a larger-than-life persona that appealed to so many, took us all along for a memorable and incredible ride. In the process, he ascended to almost mythical status, reaching a point where he was considered capable of almost anything, except, maybe, dying. From DOOM we learned that villains, like his Marvel namesake, were never truly vanquished, but always returned to disrupt the program. In fact, by challenging the status quo, perhaps they weren't so bad in the first place. He offered us the fresh perspective of stepping into someone else's shoes, while displaying an empathy and understanding of the other that revealed his true humanity.

Suffering, too, ranks as the most universal human trait, and one to which no one is immune. Knowing that DOOM had to deal with more than his fair share of pain—physical and otherwise—makes him even more real and relatable. His response to the constant struggle of life was to endure and fight to the end, qualities of which we are all capable as humans. Whether or not he knew his time was limited, as the opening lines of "Accordion" suggested ("Living off borrowed time, the clock ticks faster"), in the very least, he contemplated his own mortality, which is a very human thing to do.

Despite all that we may have discovered about DOOM, he remains an enduring mystery like the Sphinx. An anachronism in rap's contemporary pop era, he was like Don Quixote gallantly staving off the decline of this once-mighty grassroots art form by refocusing on the basics of dope beats and clever rhymes. Through an impressive command of language, he wielded humor like a cudgel and metaphors like missiles, drawing from a seemingly bottomless well of creativity. His casual, laid-back delivery belied highly technical rhyme schemes and dense verses that demanded one's intellect to decipher—kind of like a crossword puzzle. He challenged his audience, like any good artist should, rewarding the most engaged listeners with his understated brilliance.

Part of his appeal was old school and nostalgic, as he reclaimed rap for the rebels, misfits, renegades, and nonconformists who originally started it. But his love for comic books and cartoons elevated nerd culture in the process, appealing, as well, to a broader and weirder fan base. He ceded the spotlight to the in crowd, who flossed in expensive jewelry and fashionable gear or duked it out for fame, while gleefully enjoying himself and his anonymity. In short, in an age when hip-hop's assimilation into the mainstream was a done deal, DOOM brought it back to its original essence. As MC, producer, and performance artist, he delivered the whole package—a one-man renaissance without rival. By ultimately transcending hip-hop, he defied such classifications as G.O.A.T., evolving instead into a universal artist for the ages.

EPILOGUE

Who the fuck wanna be an MC, If you can't get paid, to be a fuckin' MC?

—OL' DIRTY BASTARD

Artistically speaking, there's little debate about DOOM's dominance. He earned his accolades fair and square with highly technical flows, a superb command of language, and an acerbic wit that helped distinguish himself from the crowd. But what usually gets lost in a discussion of his craft is his knack for selling himself without selling out—a feat made all the more impressive since he operated on the fringes of the music industry. Sure, DOOM enjoyed making art, but he liked making money, too. Unlike his more privileged major-label counterparts, who benefitted from a huge promotional infrastructure and widespread distribution of their work, he navigated a network of smaller, independent labels, relying on a much more creative approach to market his music. Regardless, he effectively harnessed this underground ecosystem to his advantage, exploiting any opportunities that came his way, and eventually parlaying himself into a brand—albeit one that was cool and with which people wanted to be associated. DOOM's unorthodox approach to presenting and promoting his work, in fact, demonstrates a low-key mastery of marketing that has everything to do with preserving his legacy.

On that count, the underground champ has more in common with eighties and nineties pop icons like Madonna, Prince, or David Bowie than he does with most rappers. As unique and different as these superstars may appear, what they all had shared was the ability to constantly reinvent themselves. Bowie was even an early pioneer of alternative personas. While never relying on a formulaic approach to their music, they also exhibited the will and agility to adapt with the times and stay ahead of the pack—as visionaries did. Meanwhile, rap, like much of the music industry, remained stuck in reactive mode, mimicking the proven sellers, or chasing the flavor of the moment.

Gangsta rap provided a blueprint for success in the nineties in the same way that regional styles like crunk and trap ushered in the Dirty South's dominance in the new millennium. But as a veteran of rap's golden era, which valued creativity, originality, and innovation above all else, DOOM didn't feel the need to follow trends. By sticking to his own idiosyncratic ideals and maintaining his independence, he was able to create his own exclusive lane within rap's superhighway. Like a latter-day Pied Piper, he enticed legions to follow him down this path less traveled. DOOM certainly wasn't the first MC to claim multiple aliases, but he went one further, releasing albums by these alter egos, who each assumed a life of their own. This schizophrenic approach represented his successful exercise in reinvention.

Another key factor contributing to his marketability was the aura of mystique he created around himself. In an era when artists were becoming increasingly more accessible, sharing the minutiae of their lives on social media, DOOM went in the opposite direction, retreating from the spotlight. While caught up with his creative endeavors, it was his wife who maintained his presence on Instagram, Twitter, and Facebook. Covering his face in public, remaining purposely hard to find, and playing his cards close to his chest, DOOM clearly did not want to be bothered. But, at the same time, by making himself inaccessible, he also provoked people's curiosity, effectively adding to his allure. His initial bout with celebrity had taught him a precious lesson. "Fame never helped the situation," he told journalist Ta-Nehisi Coates. "Fame in the streets is something you don't want."[1] DOOM knew that being famous was like having a target on your back, with everyone else wielding a laser scope. His response, then, was to become as enigmatic as possible.

He took this obsession with privacy to such lengths that he hardly ever rapped about himself, instead employing the third person, which really set him apart from other MCs. Such a singular approach opened greater avenues of freedom for DOOM. It distinguished him as a writer and storyteller, who employed his fertile imagination to keep it unreal, further obscuring the real Daniel Dumile. While cultivating this mystique may have started as a form of self-preservation, it evolved into a superpower for DOOM. He became such an unpredictable quantity that nobody knew what to expect from him next. Operating beneath that veil of mystery contributed to an imbalance of power—advantage DOOM.

The mystery was, of course, personified by the mask, in which he always presented himself in public. Initially designed to deflect from the person wearing it, the metal face grew into an iconic symbol that drew much attention, assuming a life of its own like the individual characters DOOM created. In this respect, this physical object became one of his most potent marketing tools. While attempting to justify the whole DOOMbot controversy, he even maintained that it didn't matter who wore the mask, thereby acknowledging that it represented something bigger than himself. Just as protestors from 2011's Occupy Wall Street movement adopted the stylized Guy Fawkes mask, worn in the movie *V for Vendetta* as a symbol of rebellion, DOOM's mask also became associated with an idea. In an age of commercial rap, it represented an outlier or disruptor trying to save the game from mediocrity and, ultimately, itself. Today, that familiar metallic visage that adorns T-shirts, buttons, rings, and all manner of merchandise, has proven its potency and transcendent power, even outliving its creator.

Limitations foster creativity, and DOOM made the most out of what he had to get what he needed. In this light, his marketing savvy may be seen as a natural extension of his charisma and the ability to mobilize people to do his bidding. Whether the succession of superfans or close friends who voluntarily signed on as his manager, or the independent labels that released his music, everyone involved with DOOM attempted to do good by him because they felt like they were dealing with an uncommon talent. But the Villain, in his affable but self-serving manner, had no qualms about taking full advantage of them. People who worked with DOOM talk about being routinely fucked over by him—with a smile on their face—as if that were simply the price of doing business. Labels, too, often dealt with his villainous behavior.

DOOM made double deals for music he had already sold—as in the case of tracks from the *Special Herbs* series. Sometimes he went as far as bootlegging his own records, as he did with *The Mouse and the Mask*, or not paying collaborators, as on *The Missing Notebook Rhymes*. Even disappearing with an entire album advance was not out of bounds for him, as he demonstrated with Adult Swim. After being fucked over by the industry himself, breaking the rules, artistically or otherwise, simply seemed part of his Machiavellian worldview, neatly intersecting with his concept of the Supervillain. Like any creative looking for the means to manifest his ambitious ideas, he was forced to think outside the box. But, in so doing, he attracted novel opportunities to generate an income and promote his work beyond simply releasing records and touring.

Back in 1986, when Run-DMC played to a sold-out Madison Square Garden for the first time, they were already massive. *Raising Hell* (Profile, 1986), their third record, was on its way to selling platinum, and they had become the first rap group to appear on MTV and the cover of *Rolling Stone*. Before performing the album's first single, "My Adidas," they asked everyone in the audience to hold up their footwear, knowing full well that Adidas executive Angelo Anastasio was a guest of their manager Lyor Cohen. Seeing the crowd of twenty-thousand proudly displaying thousands of pairs of his company's shoes proved to be a eureka moment that led to the first major endorsement deal between a rap group and a major brand. Valued at a million dollars, that deal paved the way for all manner of brand collaborations since, giving rappers, like athletes and other celebrities, a piece of the endorsements pie.

But Run-DMC, in their heyday, represented a phenomenon. In addition to their many firsts, they also held the distinction of being the only rap group to step on stage at the historic Live Aid benefit for the famine in Ethiopia. Contrast their superstar status and high visibility to that of DOOM. Despite the breakout success of *The Mouse and the Mask*, which helped expand his fan base, he was still largely considered an underground icon. Nevertheless, the Villain was approached about doing a collaboration with Nike in 2006, becoming only the second rap act after De La Soul to get his own Nike SB Dunk.

Unlike the Kings from Queens, DOOM had done nothing to engineer this opportunity, but stumbled onto it, much like De La did. After the group made an unscheduled appearance at the Action Sports Retailers Show in San Diego in 2003, Nike SB, the company's skateboarding division, who had a booth there, offered the quirky Native Tongues trio a sneaker collaboration on the spot. Two years later, De La's Nike SB Dunk, a tribute to their groundbreaking debut, *3 Feet High and Rising* (Tommy Boy/ Warner, 1989), hit stores and promptly sold out. As a follow-up to that successful collab, Nike's Rob Sissi enlisted the group's aid to contact DOOM to see if he would be interested in doing one as well. The shoe exec received his answer one day while driving through the mountains of Utah, when the Villain phoned out of the blue, catching him off guard.[2]

That conversation led to the development of the DOOM Nike SB Dunk, which debuted in July 2007. Like most anything DOOM touched, it was understated but unique, chock-full of the kind of exquisite detailing that sneaker enthusiasts loved, while also capturing the essence of the Villain. While its predominant color scheme of gunmetal gray/midnight fog symbolized the mask, illustrations from *Mm.. Food* adorned the translucent soles and sock liner. The metal face logo peered out from the top of the tongue, while two metal lace guards spelled out his nickname, "SPR VLN." If that wasn't enough customization, DOOM's name in bubble-lettering embroidery graced the ankle. Further details included the ostrich-textured leather on the toe box, reflective piping across the whole shoe, and red leather laces, completing a design that DOOM and associates (e.g. Frenel Morris) obviously put much work into. Originally retailing for $150, the shoes initially sold poorly. For their sheer exclusivity, they commanded a price of around $400 on resale sites, but since DOOM's passing, the asking price has skyrocketed to upward of $3,000 a pair. Though the financials of the deal remain unknown, Nike stood to gain the most from the "cool quotient" that their association with the Villain had bought them.

It was previously unheard of for an artist without national name recognition to score such a significant deal with a major brand, but DOOM had a reputation for making the impossible happen. In fact, during the latter part of his career, as his recording output diminished, he increasingly committed to such deals, ensuring an alternative income stream, while keeping his name out there. He entered a similar sneaker collab with the trendy Japanese street fashion label A Bathing Ape. But the resulting Bapesta's pale in comparison to the Nikes, only containing an embroidered DOOM logo on the ankle. Sneakers were only the tip of the iceberg.

DOOM's next big collaboration, with English shoe company Clarks, was negotiated via Lex, while living in London. Clarks Wallabees, a style icon associated with the old school era of hip-hop, had experienced a resurgence of popularity thanks to the Wu-Tang Clan, especially Ghostface, the self-professed "Wally Champ," who started wearing his own custom designs. In 2015, DOOM was invited to add his own personal touches to both a Wallabees shoe and boot. He chose to keep them as simple and understated as possible, adding only an embroidered image of the mask on the heel, duplicated as "wallpaper" on the inner lining. A hangtag featuring a stylized "DOOM" in graf-style, bubble-lettering appeared on the laces as well.

The low-cut version came in textured, brown leather uppers, with the signature gum sole, and 3M material in the stitching and laces, while the high-tops altered the color scheme to New York Knicks colors—blue leather uppers with orange gum soles and laces. DOOM even designed the boxes that the shoes came in, once again, emblazoning it with his name in bubble letters. Staying close to the original design, he described them as "classy yet casual."[3] Though the original runs of both shoes quickly sold out, resale sites still offered a few pairs for upward of $500. Just like his sneaker collab, DOOM seemed to cut the line, getting a deal before more higher-profile contemporaries, thereby demonstrating the kind of cultural cachet he commanded. Even though Wu-Tang had revived an interest in Clarks, they didn't do an official Wallabees collab until 2019.

As more opportunities came his way, DOOM reached a point where he could pick and choose the ones he took advantage of—like a real boss. In 2015, New Era gave him his own "Metal Face Villain" 59Fifty cap as well as a limited-edition Yankees cap featuring a profile image of the mask intertwined with the NY logo. Both designs, which retailed for $35.99, sold out immediately. Adidas didn't engage in any product collaborations with him, but featured DOOM in a video doing an exclusive graffiti piece, for which they paid him in gear. Pumas went one better, gifting DOOM an exclusive pair of sneaker speakers made from an oversize pair of Clydes, three feet in length. Nash Money, a well-known sneaker customizer in the UK, built the custom-made one-offs in collaboration with *Sneaker Freaker* magazine, who had approached Puma with the brilliant idea. Of course, he received input from DOOM as well.

After receiving a demonstration of the final product, which exceeded his wildest dreams, the Villain could hardly contain himself, saying, "Oh man, check it out! With the metal wires coming out and the overall specs, I mean it just looks bonkers! Based on the woofer and the tweeters and the mid-range speakers in there, it's out of control. Then there's separate controls for everything, there's volume control, crazy lights, you can also bypass the amp, so based on that, this thing can thump! It's dope!"[4] While he received a one-of-a-kind pair of speakers out of the deal, it's unclear how Puma benefitted, considering that a lot of people were unaware of this unique collaboration.

Out of all the creative marketing opportunities that DOOM exploited during his career, perhaps none was more foresighted or higher-yielding than his involvement with NFTs. Non-fungible tokens, for which the abbreviation stands, were defined as one-of-a-kind digital representations that could be bought and sold like any other physical, collectible object, though existing only virtually. As Bitcoin was touted as the digital equivalent of hard currency, NFTs were being hailed as a digital proxy for fine art—their speculative value lying at the heart of both. Once again, Wu-Tang, a group known for the myriad ways in which they have successfully marketed themselves, became the first rappers to be associated with this new digital frontier, after their one-off album *Once Upon a Time in Shaolin* was acquired by the NFT investor group known as PleasrDAO. Though a physical copy of the album existed, the way its sale was handled by auction resembled that of an NFT.

On October 19, 2020, DOOM and Rhymesayers Entertainment announced a partnership with the digital art platform Illust Space, to auction off a series of eleven custom-designed virtual masks in time for Halloween, the day he passed away. Though *Mm . . Food* was the last project he released via the Minnesota-based imprint, label head honcho Brent "Siddiq" Sayers, who had become his official manager by this time, negotiated the deal. Two different drops, on October 23 and 28, introduced the virtual mask designs, which came in a variety of styles including a "Mummy" style and a "Sludge" style, each selling for between $15,000 and $75,000. In addition to receiving 10 percent of the proceeds, DOOM also stood to gain 10 percent from any resale, for perpetuity.

NFTs, according to Illust Space CCO Tim Prochak, "should allow musicians to take back control, it should allow artists to create in this new zone and actually be able to illustrate upon the world."[5] In fact, the initial auctions were so successful that DOOM's widow, Jasmine, offered another round of augmented-reality NFT masks in March 2021, with one going for almost $800,000. Since control of his art as well as his business proved to be a major priority for DOOM in life, it was not surprising to see him at the forefront of such new developments as NFTs—even in death.

While pursuing such opportunities for financial gain, DOOM also enhanced his creative profile in the process, truly demonstrating his marketing prowess. The path to fame usually requires endless exposure, and not everyone who's famous necessarily evolves into a brand. But DOOM was able to become both without putting himself out there like that, successfully selling himself without selling out. Today, his wife, Jasmine, continues that work, helping preserve his legacy by reviving the official DOOM website (gasdrawls.com). Here, his entire musical catalog, as well as new branded products such as hoodies, sweatpants, socks, and slides, pay homage to the man in the mask. As someone dedicated to his family, who knew him as "Old Dad," DOOM would have had it no other way.

THE CATALOG: A DOOMOGRAPHY

Solo Albums:
MF DOOM/*Operation: Doomsday* (Fondle 'Em)—October 19, 1999
(Sub Verse)—May 1, 2000
MF DOOM/*Mm.. Food* (Rhymesayers Entertainment)—November 16, 2004
DOOM/*Born Like This* (Lex)—March 24, 2009

Collaborative Albums:
KMD/*Mr. Hood* (Elektra)—May 14, 1991
KMD/*Black Bastards* (Sub Verse/Metal Face)—May 15, 2001
Monsta Island Czars/*Escape from Monsta Island!* (Rhymesayers Entertainment/Metal Face)—2002
King Geedorah/*Take Me to your Leader* (Big Dada)—June 17, 2003
Viktor Vaughn/*Vaudeville Villain* (Sound Ink)—September 16, 2003
Madvillain/*Madvillainy* (Stones Throw)—March 24, 2004
MF DOOM and MF Grimm/*Special Herbs & Spices Vol. 1* (Day by Day Entertainment)—May 11, 2004
Viktor Vaughn/*VV:2* (Insomniac)—August 3, 2004
DangerDOOM/*The Mouse and the Mask* (Epitaph/Lex/Metal Face)—October 11, 2005
JJ DOOM/*Key to the Kuffs* (Lex)—August 20, 2012
NehruvianDOOM/*NehruvianDOOM (Sound of the Son)* (Lex)—October 7, 2014
Czarface Meets Metal Face (7L)—March 30, 2018
Czarface and MF DOOM/*Super What?* (Silver Age)—May 7, 2021

Live Albums:
Live from Planet X (Nature Sounds)—March 8, 2005
Expektoration (Gold Dust Media)—September 14, 2010

Instrumental Albums:
Special Herbs, Volume 1 (Female Fun)—2001

Special Herbs, Volume 2 (High Times)—January 1, 2002
Special Herbs, Volume 3 (Female Fun: CD) (Nature Sounds: LP)—2002
Special Herbs, Volume 4 (Nature Sounds)—September 23, 2003
Special Herbs, Volumes 4, 5, 6 (Shaman Works)—November 24, 2003
Special Herbs, Volumes 5&6 (Nature Sounds)—March 23, 2004
Special Herbs, Volumes 7&8 (Shaman Works)—September 24, 2004
Special Herbs: The Box Set, Volumes 0–9 (Nature Sounds)—January 24, 2006

Compilation Albums:
Special Blends Volume 1 (Metal Face)—2005
Special Blends Volume 2 (Metal Face)—2005
Unexpected Guests (Gold Dust Media)—October 27, 2009
The Missing Notebook Rhymes (Adult Swim: digital download)—August 2017

EPs:
KMD/*Black Bastards Ruffs + Rares* (Fondle 'Em)—1998
MF DOOM/MF Grimm/*MF EP* (Brick)—November 28, 2000
DangerDOOM/*Occult Hymn* (Adultswim.com)—May 30, 2006
MF DOOM and Trunks/*Unicron* (label unknown)—January 2008
DOOM/*Gazzillion Ear* (Lex)—2010
DOOMStarks/*Victory Laps* (Nature Sounds)—2011
JJ DOOM/*Bookhead* (Lex)—May 27, 2017
WestsideGunn and MF DOOM/*Westside DOOM* (Griselda)—October 13, 2017

Singles:
"Dead Bent"/"Gas Drawls/Hey" (Fondle 'Em)—1997
"Greenbacks"/"Go with the Flow" (Fondle 'Em)—1997
"The M.I.C."/"Red & Gold" (Fondle 'Em)—1998
"I Hear Voices" (Sub Verse Music)—2001
"My Favorite Ladies"/"All Outta Ale" (Nature Sounds)—2002
"Raedawn"/"Change the Beat" (Sound Ink Records)—2003
"Yee Haw"/"Is He Ill?" (Molemen)—2003
"Anti-Matter" w/ Mr. Fantastik (Big Dada)—2003
"Mr. Clean"/"Modern Day Mugging" (Sound Ink)—2004
"Money Folder"/"America's Most Blunted" (Stones Throw)—2004
"All Caps"/"Curls" (Stones Throw)—2004
"Hoe Cakes" /"Potholderz" (Rhymesayers Entertainment)—2004

"Project Jazz" (7-inch) (Impose Records)—2007
"One Beer" (7-inch) (Drunk Version) (Stones Throw)—2008
"Sniper Elite" w/ "Murder Goons" w/ Ghostface (Stones Throw)—2008
"Gazzillion Ear" (Lex)—2010
"Papermill" w/ Madvillain (Adult Swim)—2010
"Lively Hood" w/ Ghostface Killah (Nature Sounds)—2015
"Avalanche" w/ Madlib (Stones Throw)—2016
"Chocolate Conquistadors" (prod. by Badbadnotgood) (XL)—2020
"Nautical Depth" w/ Czarface (Silver Age)—2022

Guest Appearances:

3rd Bass featuring Zev Love X—"The Gas Face" from *The Cactus Album* (Def Jam/Columbia)—1989

3rd Bass feat. KMD—"Ace in the Hole" from *Derelicts of Dialect* (Def Jam/Columbia)—1991

Molemen feat. Slug, Aesop Rock & MF DOOM—"Put Your Quarter Up" from *Ritual of the Molemen* (Molemen)—2001

Prefuse 73 feat. Aesop Rock & MF DOOM—"Black List" from *Vocal Studies & Uprock Narratives* (Warp)—2001

MF Grimm feat. Megalon, MF DOOM—"Foolish," "Voices, Pt.1" from *The Downfall of Ibliys: A Ghetto Opera* (Day By Day Ent.)—2001

King Honey feat. MF DOOM and Kurious—"Monday Night at Fluid" from *Colapsus* (Sound Ink)—2001

Q-Unique feat. Breeze Brewin', Godfather Don, J-Treds, MF DOOM—"Fondle 'Em Fossils" from *Farewell Fondle 'Em* (Def Jux)—2002

Count Bass D feat. MF DOOM—"Quite Buttery," "Make a Buck" from *Dwight Spitz* (Day By Day Entertainment)—2002

Fog feat. MF DOOM—"A Word of Advice" from *Fog* (Ninja Tune)—2002

The Herbaliser feat. MF DOOM, Blade, and Phi-Life Cypher—"It Ain't Nuttin'"/"Time to Build" from *Something Wicked This Way Comes* (Ninja Tune)—2002

The Herbaliser feat. Rakaa Iriescience & MF DOOM—"Verbal Anime"/ "It Ain't Nuttin'" from *Something Wicked This Way Comes* (Ninja Tune)—2002

Scienz of Life feat. MF DOOM—"Yikes" from *Project Overground: The Scienz Experiment* (Sub Verse Music)—2002

Non Phixion feat. MF DOOM—"Strange Universe" from *The Future is Now* (Uncle Howie/Landspeed)—2002

THE CATALOG: A DOOMOGRAPHY

C-Rayz Walz feat. Wordsworth, Thirstin Howl III, J-Treds, Breeze Brewin', Vast Aire, MF DOOM—"The Line Up" from *Ravi Pops (The Substance)* (Def Jux)—2003

Semi-Official feat. MF DOOM—"Songs in the Key of Tryfe" from *The Anti-Album* (Rhymesayers)—2003

Prince Paul feat. Chubb Rock, Wordsworth, MF DOOM—"Chubb Rock Please Pay Paul the $2200 You Owe Him (People, Places and Things)" from *Politics of the Business* (Tommy Boy/Warner)—2003

Madlib feat. MF DOOM—"Stepping into Tomorrow" from *Shades of Blue* (Blue Note)—2003

Science Fiction feat. MF DOOM—"Hold On" (Third Earth Music)—2003

Babbletron—"Space Tech Banana Clip" (prod. By MF DOOM)—2003

Prince Po feat. MF DOOM—"Social Distortion" from *The Slickness* (Lex)—2004

Zero 7 feat. Sia and MF DOOM—"Somersault" from *When it Falls* (East West)—2004

De La Soul feat. MF DOOM—"Rock Co.Kane Flow" from *The Grind Date* (Seven Heads)—2004

Vast Aire feat. MF DOOM—"Da Superfriends" from *Look Mom . . . No Hands* (Chocolate Industries)—2004

Klub des Loosers feat. MF DOOM—"Depuis que j'etais enfant" from *Vive La Vie* (Record Makers)—2004

Wale Oyejide feat. MF DOOM—"This is dedicated to" from *One Day . . . Everything Changed* (Shaman Work)—2004

Cipher feat. MF DOOM—"Verse Vs. the Virus" from *Children of God's Fire* (Uprising)—2005

Gorillaz feat. MF DOOM—"November Has Come" from *Demon Days* (Virgin)—2005

Talib Kweli feat. MF DOOM—"Fly That Knot" from *Right About Now: The Official Sucka Free Mixtape*—2005

Daedelus feat. MF DOOM—"Impending DOOM" from *Exquisite Corpse* (Mush)—2005

RZA and MF DOOM—"Biochemical Equation" from *Wu-Tang Meets the Indie Culture* (Babygrande/Think Differently Music)—2005

Moka Only feat. Wizwon and MF DOOM—"More Soup" from *The Desired Effect* (Nettwerk)—2005

Jonathan Toth from Hoth feat. MF DOOM—"Ghostwhirl" (HipHopSite.com)—2005

Quasimoto feat. MF DOOM—"Closer" from *The Further Adventures of Lord Quas* (Stones Throw)—2005

Blend Crafters feat. MF DOOM—"Melody" (Up Above)—2005

Substance Abuse feat. MF DOOM—"Profitless Thoughts" from *Overproof* (Threshold)—2006

Drum and Knowledge of Parallel Thought present MF DOOM—"Vomit" (Super Bro)—2006

Dabrye feat. MF DOOM—"Air" from *Two/Three* (Ghostly International)—2006

Hell Razah feat. Talib Kweli and MF DOOM—"Project Jazz" from *Renaissance Child* (Nature Sounds)—2007

Shape of Broad Minds feat. MF DOOM—"Let's Go" from *Craft of the Lost Art* (Lex)—2007

The Heliocentrics feat. Percee P and MF DOOM—"Distant Star" from *Out There* (Now Again Records)—2008

C Rayz Walz and Parallel Thought feat. MF DOOM—"Vomit Chorus" from *Chorus Rhyme* (Super Bro)—2008

Jake One feat. MF DOOM—"Trap Door," "Get 'Er Done" from *White Van Music* (Rhymesayers Entertainment)—2008

The Mighty Underdogs feat. MF DOOM—"Gun Fight" from *Droppin Science Fiction* (Def Jux)—2008

DJ Babu feat. Sean Price and MF DOOM—"The Unexpected" from *Duck Season, Vol. 3* (Nature Sounds)—2008

Kurious feat. MC Serch and MF DOOM—"Benetton" (Amalalm Digital)—2009

J Dilla feat. MF DOOM—"Firewood Drumsticks" from *Jay Stay Paid* (Nature Sounds)—2009

DJ Rob A feat. MF DOOM—"She Still Got Dimples" from *The New Mortal Sin* (Rugged Soul Records)—2009

Paul Barman feat. MF DOOM—"Hot Guacamole" from *Thought Balloon Mushroom Cloud* (Househusband Records)—2009.

CX Kidtronik & King Geedorah—"Wild Kingdom" (Stones Throw)—2010

Bk-One feat. MF DOOM—"Exile Mind the Gap Remix" (Rhymesayers)—2011

Oh No feat. DOOM—"3 Dollars" from *Ohnomite* (Five Day Weekend)—2012

Masta Ace feat. Big Daddy Kane and MF DOOM—"Think I Am" from *MA_DOOM: Son of Yvonne*—2012

MF DOOM & The Child of Lov—"Owl" from *The Child of Love* (Double Six)—2013

Captain Murphy feat. Viktor Vaughn and Earl Sweatshirt—"Between Villains" (Adult Swim)—2013

CXKidtronik feat. King Geedorah and Mobonix—"Ghidra Got It" from *Krak Attak 2: Ballad of Elli Skiff* (Stones Throw)—2013

Also Known As feat. MF DOOM—"Action Reaction"

BadBadNotGood feat. Ghostface Killah and MF DOOM—"Ray Gun" from *Sour Soul* (Lex)—2015

Cannibal Ox feat. MF DOOM—"Iron Rose" from *Blade of the Ronin* (IGC Records)—2015

Czarface feat. MF DOOM—"Kabang" from *Every Hero Needs a Villain* (Brick Records)—2015

Med/Blu/Madlib feat. MF DOOM—"Knock Knock" from *Bad Neighbor* (Bang Ya Head)—2015

Pryhme feat. MF DOOM and Phonte—"Highs and Lows"—2015

ASM feat. MF DOOM—"Masking" (7-inch) (HHV.DE)—2016

The Avalanches feat. MF DOOM and Danny Brown—"Frankie Sinatra" from *Wildflower* (Astralwerks)—2016

Busta Rhymes feat. MF DOOM & BJ The Chicago Kid—"In the Streets" from *Return of the Dragon* (The Conglomerate Entertainment)—2016

Atmosphere feat. Kool Keith and MF DOOM—"When the Lights Go Out" from *Fishing Blues* (Rhymesayers)—2016

Kool Keith feat. MF DOOM—"Super Hero" (Mello Music Group)—2016

Omegah Red feat. RZA and MF DOOM—"Books of War"—2016

Sean Price feat. MF DOOM and Ike Eyez—"Negus" from *Imperius Rex* (Duck Down)—2017

KMD feat. Jay Electronica and MF DOOM—"True Lightyears" (Adult Swim)—2017

IDK feat. Young Gleesh, MF DOOM and Del the Funky Homosapien—"Pizza Shop Extended"—2017

J Dilla/MF DOOM/Guilty Simpson—"Mash's Revenge" from *Peanut Butter Wolf's B Ball Zombie War* (Stones Throw)—2017

Dabrye feat. MF DOOM—"Lil Mufukaz" from *Three/Three* (Ghostly International)—2018

Youth of the Apocalypse feat. MF DOOM—"Drop the Bomb" (Fader)—2018

DJ Muggs & MF DOOM—"Death Wish" (Soul Assassins)—2018

Your Old Droog feat. MF DOOM and Mach Hommy—"BDE" from *Jewelry* (Mongoloid Banks)—2019

Your Old Droog feat. MF DOOM and Mach Hommy—"RST" from *It Wasn't Even Close* (Green Streets Entertainment)—2019

Open Mike Eagle and MF DOOM—"Police Myself" from *The New Negroes (Season 1)*—2019

DOOM/Damu—"Coco Mango" from *Analogtronics* (Redefinition Records)—2019

Danger Mouse and Sparklehorse feat. MF DOOM—"Ninjarous"—2019

Tuxedo feat. MF DOOM—"Dreaming in the Daytime" from *Tuxedo III* (Funk On Sight)—2019

Wilma Archer feat. MF DOOM—"Last Sniff" from *A Western Circular* (Weird World)—2020

Bishop Nehru feat. MF DOOM—"Meathead" from *Nehruvia: My Disregarded Thoughts* (2020)

Rejjie Snow feat. MF DOOM—"Cookie Chips" from *Baw Baw Black Sheep* (Honeymoon)—2020

Sa-Roc feat. MF DOOM—"The Rebirth" from *The Sharecropper's Daughter* (Rhymesayers)—2021

Your Old Droog and MF DOOM—"Dropout Boogie" (Mongoloid Banks)—2021

IDK feat. MF DOOM, Westside Gun, Jay Electronica—"Red (Visualizer)" from *USEE4Yourself* (No Clue/Warner)—2021

Atmosphere feat. Aesop Rock and MF DOOM—"Barcade" (Rhymesayers)—2021

Justin Time feat. Canibus, Kool Keith, MF DOOM—"Chase"

Chris Craft feat. MF DOOM—"Hooks is Extra"—2021

Kool Keith and MF DOOM—"Doper Skiller"—2021

DangerMouse and Black Thought feat. MF DOOM—"Belize" from *Cheat Codes* (BMG)—2022

White Girl Wasted feat. MF DOOM and Jay Electronica—"Barz Simpson"—2022

Sean Price feat. MF DOOM—"Straight Music"—2022

Outside Production:

"9 Milli Bros.," "Clipse of DOOM," "Jellyfish," "Underwater," from Ghostface Killah/*Fishscale* (Def Jam)—2006

"Guns N' Razors," "Alex (Stolen Script)" from Ghostface Killah/*More Fish* (Def Jam)—2006

Masta Ace/*MA_DOOM: Son on Yvonne* (M3/Fat Beats)—2012

Soundtracks:

MF DOOM & Scott Free—"New Beginning" from *On the Ropes* OST—1999

Ghostface Killah & DOOM—"Chinatown Wars" from *Grand Theft Auto* OST (Rockstar Games)—2009

Flying Lotus feat. MF DOOM—"Masquatch" from *Grand Theft Auto V* OST (Rockstar)—2014

Flying Lotus feat. MF DOOM—"Lunch Break" from *Grand Theft Auto: Cayo Perico Heist* (Rockstar)—2020

BadBadNotGood feat. MF DOOM—"The Chocolate Conquistadors" from *Grand Theft Auto: Cayo Perico Heist* (Rockstar)—2020

BIBLIOGRAPHY

Books:

Brown, Cecil. *Stagolee Shot Billy*. Cambridge, MA: Harvard University Press, 2003.

Campbell, Joseph with Bill Moyers. *The Power of Myth*. New York: Doubleday, 1988.

Carey, Percy and Ronald Wimberly. *Sentences: The Life of MF Grimm*. New York: Vertigo/DC Comics, 2007.

Coleman, Brian. *Check the Technique Volume 2: More Liner Notes for Hip-Hop Junkies*. Everett, MA: Wax Facts Press, 2014.

Frank151. *Chapter 48: DOOM*. Frank151 Media Group LLC, 2012.

Hagle, Will. *Madvillainy*. New York: Bloomsbury Academic, 2023.

Kalat, David. *A Critical History and Filmography of Toho's Godzilla Series*, 2nd ed. Jefferson, NC: McFarland & Company, 2010.

Ro, Ronin. *Tales to Astonish: Jack Kirby, Stan Lee, and the American Comic Book Revolution*. New York: Bloomsbury Publishing, 2004.

Roberts, John W. *From Trickster to Badman: The Black Folk Hero in Slavery and Freedom*. Philadelphia: University of Pennsylvania Press, 1989.

Wolk, Douglas. *All of the Marvels*. New York: Penguin Press, 2021.

Wright, Bradford. *Comic Book Nation: The Transformation of Youth Culture in America*. Baltimore: Johns Hopkins University Press, 2001.

Articles:

Alapatt, Egon. "Blunted on Beats: Madvillain Interview." *Wax Poetics*, February 8, 2004. stonesthrow.com/news/blunted-on-beats.

Brown, Courtney. "Remembering MF DOOM: A Personal Story." *The Source*, February 5, 2021. thesource.com/2021/02/05/remembering-mf-DOOM-a-personal-story.

Caramanica, Jon. "An Appraisal MF DOOM, Magician of Memory." *New York Times*, January 14, 2021. nytimes.com/2021/01/14/arts/music/mf-DOOM-operation-DOOMsday.html.

Caramanica, Jon. "The New York Times Popcast: MF DOOM." *New York Times*, January 23, 2022.

Chick, Stevie. "MF DOOM: A Hip-Hop Genius Who Built His Own Universe of Poetry." *The Guardian*, January 1, 2021. theguardian.com/music/2021/jan/01/mf-DOOM-a-hip-hop-genius-who-built-his-own-universe-of-poetry.

Coates, Ta-Nehisi. "The Mask of DOOM: A Nonconformist Rapper's Second Act." *New Yorker*, September 14, 2009.

Conlon, Rob. "Supervillains in Leeds Operation: DOOMsday." *Square Ball* (blog), February 25, 2022. thesquareball.net/leeds-united/operation-DOOMsday.

Conti, Chris. "MF DOOM (Interview)." *No Ripcord*, May 2, 2004. noripcord.com/features/mf-DOOM-interview.

Davidson, Adam. "In Memoriam: MF DOOM, the Closest Companion I Never Met." *Atwood Magazine*, February 18, 2021. atwoodmagazine.com/mfdm-mf-DOOM-tribute-2021.

Dodge, John. "The Fantastic Four Just Gave Hope to Doctor DOOM's Most Devious Creations." *CBR*, December 11, 2022. cbr.com/fantastic-four-DOOMbot-doctor-DOOM-marvel.

Downs, David. "Reclusive Rapper DOOM Talks New LP 'Born Like This' and Responds to Fan Rage." *Rolling Stone*, March 23, 2009. rollingstone.com/music/music-news/reclusive-rapper-DOOM-talks-new-lp-born-like-this-and-responds-to-fan-rage-249971.

Drumming, Neil. "The Nerd Behind the Mask." *Village Voice*, August 7, 2001. villagevoice.com/2001/08/07/the-nerd-behind-the-mask.

Dunne, Brendan. "MF DOOM and the SB Dunk: How Nike Captured the Supervillain." *Complex*, February 1, 2021. complex.com/sneakers/a/brendan-dunne/mf-DOOM-nike-sb-dunk-high-history.

Fortune, Drew. "The Unknowable MF DOOM." *Vulture*, January 28, 2021. vulture.com/article/mf-DOOM-wake.html.

Fox, Luke. "Mask Off with MF DOOM." *Exclaim!*, January 5, 2021. exclaim.ca/music/article/mf_DOOM_2004_interview_madvillainy.

Gottsegen, Will. "Madvillainy at 15: MF DOOM on the Legacy of His Classic Madlib Collaboration." *Spin*, March 25, 2019. spin.com/2019/03/mf-DOOM-madvillain-interview-madvillainy-anniversary.

Green, Dylan. "2004: MF DOOM, Madvillainy." *SixtyEight2OhFive* (blog), January 22, 2020. 68to05.com/essays/2004-mf-DOOM-madvillain.

Green, Dylan, and Donna-Claire Chesman. "MF DOOM's 'Operation: DOOMsday' is the Blueprint for Independent Hip-Hop Celebrating 20 Years of Greatness." *Tidal*, April 20, 2019. tidal.com/magazine/article/mf-DOOMs-operation-20/1-54901.

Hakki, Tim. "MF DOOM: Enigmatic Rapper Leaves Behind Crypto Art Legacy." *Decrypt*, January 1, 2021. decrypt.co/53019/mf-DOOM-enigmatic-rapper-leaves-behind-crypto-art-legacy.

Hamilton, Jack. "MF DOOM Will Never Really Die." *Slate*, January 5, 2021. slate.com/culture/2021/01/mf-DOOM-dead-rapper-producer-madvillain.html.

Heimlich, Adam. "Black Egypt: A Visit to Tama-Re." *NY Press*, November 8, 2000. nypress.com/news/black-egypt-a-visit-to-tama-re-JXNP1020001114311149983.

Herbert, Conor. "Shadows of Tomorrow I: MF DOOM and the KMD Origin Story." *Central Sauce* (blog), January 5, 2021. centralsauce.com/mf-DOOM-kmd-origin-story-part-one.

Herbert, Conor. "Shadows of Tomorrow II: Positive Kauses and Constipated Monkeys." *Central Sauce* (blog), January 7, 2021. centralsauce.com/shadows-of-tomorrow-ii-positive-kauses-and-constipated-monkeys.

Herbert, Conor. "Shadows of Tomorrow III: Long Live Kingilizwe." *Central Sauce* (blog), January 9, 2021. centralsauce.com/shadows-of-tomorrow-iii-long-live-kingilizwe.

Herbert, Conor. "Shadows of Tomorrow IV: Ice-T, KMD & Hip-Hop Cops." *Central Sauce* (blog), January 11, 2021. centralsauce.com/shadows-of-tomorrow-iv-ice-t-kmd-hip-hop-cops.

Herbert, Conor. "Shadows of Tomorrow V: Zev Love X-ile & MF, The Supervillain." *Central Sauce* (blog), January 13, 2021. centralsauce.com/shadows-of-tomorrow-v-zev-love-x-ile-mf-the-supervillain.

Hevesi, Dennis. "Muslims Leave Bushwick: The Neighbors Ask Why." *New York Times*, April 24, 1994. nytimes.com/1994/04/24/nyregion/muslims-leave-bushwick-the-neighbors-ask-why.html.

Horowitz, Matt. "Shadows of Tomorrow: Nice & Nasty Vaz Speaks About M.F. DOOM's Early Career & Booking His First "Secret" Show (The Witzard Interview)." *The Witzard* (blog), January 20, 2021. thewitzard.blogspot.com/2021/01/shadows-of-tomorrow-nice-nasty-vaz.html.

Hsu, Hua. "The Mask of Sorrow." *The Wire*, March 1, 2005.

Hsu, Hua. "The Wondrous Rhymes of MF DOOM." *New Yorker*, January 4, 2021. newyorker.com/culture/postscript/the-wondrous-rhymes-of-mf-DOOM.

Illust Space. "MF DOOM Announces Augmented Reality Blockchain Auction." *PRNewswire*, October 19, 2020. prnewswire.com/news-releases/mf-DOOM-announces-augmented-reality-blockchain-auction-301155011.html.

Jockey Slut. "The Man in the Iron Mask." *Jockey Slut*, June 8, 2004. stonesthrow.com/news/the-man-in-the-iron-mask.

Josephs, Brian. "KMD's 'What a Nigga Know?' Was Ahead of Its Time." *Spin*, August 18, 2017. spin.com/2017/08/kmd-what-a-nigga-know-stream.

Kane, David. "DOOM Interview. *Bonafide* (Issue 6), 2012. bonafidemag.com/DOOM-interview.

Lasseter, Tom. "Tensions Simmer Around a Black Sect in Georgia." *New York Times*, June 29, 1999. nytimes.com/1999/06/29/us/tensions-simmer-around-a-black-sect-in-georgia.html.

Lough, Adam Bhala. "The Making Of MF DOOM's '?' and 'Dead Bent' Videos." *Passion of the Weiss* (blog), January 3, 2021. passionweiss.com/2021/01/03/mf-DOOM-dead-bent-video.

LSD. "MF DOOM Interview." *LSD Magazine*, 1999. mfDOOM.50webs.org/LSDMagazine5.html.

Lunny, Hugo. "MF DOOM Interview." *MVRemix*, April 29, 2002. mvremix.com/urban/interviews/mfDOOM.shtml.

Ma, David. "Solid Gold Telephone: An Interview With MF DOOM." *Passion of the Weiss* (blog), January 9, 2019. passionweiss.com/2019/01/09/mf-DOOM-interview.

MacManus, Darragh. "The Sneakers of MF DOOM." (blog), Sep 21, 2021. welcomejpeg.com/blog/post/mf-DOOM-and-his-sneakers.

Mason, Andrew. "Behind the Mask." *Wax Poetics*, December 8, 2020. waxpoetics.com/article/mf-DOOM-interview-behind-the-mask.

Matheolane, Mpho Moshe. "The Man Behind the DOOM Mask." *Mail & Guardian* (South Africa), April 17, 2013mg.co.za/article/2013-04-17-the-man-behind-the-DOOM-mask.

McNally, James. "Confessions of a Mask." *Hip-Hop Connection*, June 10, 2004.stonesthrow.com/news/confessions-of-a-mask.

Moreau, Jordan, and Andrew Barker. "Rapper MF DOOM Dies at 49." *Variety*, Dec 31, 2020. variety.com/2020/music/obituaries/people-news/mf-DOOM-dead-rapper-1234877295.

Newman, Jason. "Madvillain Exec Egon Remembers MF DOOM: 'He Was Such a Master of His Craft.'" *Rolling Stone*, March 17, 2021. rollingstone.com/music/music-news/mf-DOOM-madlib-madvillain-egon-1142507.

Noz, Andrew. "DOOM: Shadows on the Sun." *Hip-Hop DX*, April 13, 2009. hiphopdx.com/interviews/id.1331/title.DOOM-shadows-on-the-sun.

O'Connor, Ryan. "MF DOOM: Raps Greatest Comic Book Villain." *Medium*, January 3, 2021. medium.com/clocked-in-magazine/mf-DOOM-raps-greatest-comic-book-villain-ac1bb97a8b37.

Paine, Jake. "This 2003 Conversation with MF DOOM Is the Interview of His Career." *Ambrosia for Heads*, November 27, 2018. ambrosiaforheads.com/2018/11/mf-DOOM-interview-audio-metalface.

Pappademas, Alex. "MF DOOM: Our 2004 Profile." *Spin*, November 15, 2019. spin.com/2019/11/mf-DOOM-interview-mm-food.

Pemberton, Rollie, and Nick Sylvester. "Madvillainy/Madvillain." *Pitchfork*, March 25, 2004. pitchfork.com/reviews/albums/5579-madvillainy.

Phoenix New Times. "Beyond Good and Evil: Rapper MF DOOM's New Works of Hip-Hop Fiction Reinvent the Hero Principle for the Modern Age." *Phoenix New Times*, July 24, 2003. mfDOOM.50webs.org/PhoenixNewTimes.html.

Prefix. "Unconventional Weaponry." *Prefix Magazine*, January 1, 2000. mfDOOM.50webs.org/PrefixMag.html.

Richardson, Nick. "Reviews: Born Like This—DOOM." *Impose Magazine*. imposemagazine.com/reviews/born-like-this-DOOM.

Ringer Staff, "The MF DOOM Syllabus." *The Ringer*, Jan 4, 2021. theringer.com/2021/1/4/22212562/mf-DOOM-daniel-dumile-madvillain-syllabus-kmd-dunks.

Rollins, Brent. "News Uncovered: The Story Behind Madvillain's Madvillainy (2004) with Jeff Jank." *Egotripland*, December 11, 2011. stonesthrow.com/news/uncovered-madvillainy.

Rosado, Alex. "The Many Face of MF DOOM." *Impose Magazine*. imposemagazine.com/features/mf-DOOM.

Saleh, Oumar. "Hero Vs. Villain: Retracing MF DOOM's Ties to Comic Book Culture." *Crack Magazine*, August 8, 2021. crackmagazine.net/article/long-reads/hero-vs-villain-retracing-mf-DOOMs-ties-ties-to-comic-book-culture.

Sorcinelli, Gino. "'I Don't Remember the Samples I Use. Hell No.'—The Story of 'Madvillainy.'" *Micro Chop* (blog), July 21, 2018. medium.com/micro-chop/i-dont-remember-the-samples-i-use-hell-no-the-story-of-madvillainy-e6b378d4689c.

Sosibo, Kwanele. "Forever Dope: Stahhr on Lessons from DOOM." *Mail & Guardian*, January 8, 2021. mg.co.za/friday/2021-01-08-forever-dope-stahhr-on-lessons-from-DOOM.

StrausMedia. "Interview with MF DOOM: The Supervillain." *NY Press*, November 11, 2014. nypress.com/news/interview-with-mf-DOOM-the-supervillain-DANP1020010605306059971.

Tayneicangetinto, "DOOMSTARKS: A History of Ghostface Killah / DOOM Collaborations." Reddit, 2015. reddit.com/r/hiphopheads/comments/468z67/DOOMstarks_a_history_of_ghostface_killah_DOOM.

Thompson, Paul. "Strange Days: Remembering MF DOOM." *GQ*, January 1, 2021. gq.com/story/mf-DOOM-obituary.

Turner-Williams, Jaelani. "Impending DOOM: 'MM . . . FOOD' Warned You 15 Years Ago." *Complex*, November 15, 2019. complex.com/pigeons-and-planes/2019/11/mf-DOOM-mm-food-anniversary.

Watson, Elijah. "Without Stan Lee MF DOOM—One of the Greatest Rappers of All Time—Wouldn't Exist." *OkayPlayer*, 2022. okayplayer.com/originals/stan-lee-mf-DOOM-marvel-villain.html.

Weiss, Jeff. "Searching for Tomorrow: The Story of Madlib and DOOM's Madvillainy." *Pitchfork*, August 12, 2014. pitchfork.com/features/article/9478-searching-for-tomorrow-the-story-of-madlib-and-DOOMs-madvillainy.

Westhoff, Ben. "From Madvillain to Milli Vanilli." *Village Voice*, August 28, 2007. villagevoice.com/2007/08/28/from-madvillain-to-milli-vanilli.

Westhoff, Ben. "Private Enemy." *Village Voice*, October 31, 2006. villagevoice.com/2006/10/31/private-enemy.

Westhoff, Ben. "Suspended disbelief dissed: MF DOOM." *Creative Loafing*, January 9, 2008. creativeloafing.com/content-160845-suspended-disbelief-dissed-mf-DOOM.

XXL Staff. "DOOM Shares The Stories Behind Ten Of His Best Verses." *XXL*, October 13, 2013. xxlmag.com/DOOM-shares-the-stories-behind-ten-of-his-best-verses.

Yoo, Noah. "Untangling MF DOOM's Lifelong Struggle With the U.S. Immigration System." *Pitchfork*, June 22, 2021. pitchfork.com/features/article/untangling-mf-DOOMs-lifelong-struggle-with-the-us-immigration-system.

NOTES

Introduction

1. Jasmine Dumile (@MFDOOM), "Begin all things by giving thanks to THE ALL!," Instagram caption, December 31, 2020, accessed December 31, 2020, instagram.com/p/CJefkDalNYo/?igshid=jojfrkanfmdb.
2. Jordan Moreau and Andrew Barker, "Rapper MF DOOM Dies at 49," *Variety*, December 31, 2020.
3. Ryan O'Connor, "MF DOOM: Rap's Greatest Comic Book Villain" *Clocked In Magazine*, Medium, January 4, 2021.
4. Adam Davidson, "In Memoriam: MF DOOM, the Closest Companion I Never Met," in *Atwood Magazine*, February 18, 2021.
5. Metal Fist Terrorist, "MF DOOM—In depth interview with Benji B," YouTube video, January 20, 2014, youtu.be/JkIBbC9-MPM?si=lkG1-_T8MH3_b7qn.
6. Jockey Slut, "The Man in the Iron Mask," in *Jockey Slut*, June 8, 2004.
7. David Ma, "Solid Gold Telephone: An Interview with MF DOOM," *Passion of the Weiss*, January 9, 2019.
8. Ma, "Solid Gold Telephone."
9. Ta-Nehisi Coates, "The Mask of DOOM: A Nonconformist Rapper's Second Act," *New Yorker*, September 14, 2009.
10. Metal Fist Terrorist, "MF DOOM" video.
11. Ediction UK, "MF DOOM Interview," YouTube video, September 8, 2014, youtu.be/b6En7HoD94s.
12. Ediction UK, "MF DOOM Interview" video.

Chapter 1: Back in the Days

1. DOCtAKH, "KMD-MF DOOM Way: Ceremony and Celebration," YouTube video, August 3, 2021, 0:00–1:00, youtu.be/1h-ziPSMUQ8.
2. DOCtAKH, "KMD-MF DOOM."
3. Noah Yoo, "Untangling MF DOOM's Lifelong Struggle with the US Immigration System," *Pitchfork*, June 22, 2021.

4. Yoo, "Untangling MF DOOM's."
5. Ta-Nehisi Coates, "The Mask of DOOM: A Nonconformist Rapper's Second Act," *New Yorker*, September 14, 2009.
6. Red Bull Music Academy, "MF DOOM: Interview with the Masked Villain," YouTube video, May 14, 2015, youtu.be/JGu0ao_rdAk.
7. Red Bull Music Academy, "MF DOOM: Interview" video.
8. Peter Agoston, "Episode 100—DOOM," May 16, 2003, in *The House List*, podcast.
9. Red Bull Music Academy, "MF DOOM: Interview" video.
10. Red Bull Music Academy, "MF DOOM: Interview" video.
11. Luke Fox, "The Mask of DOOM," *Exclaim!*, January 5, 2021.
12. Hua Hsu, "Mask of Sorrow," *The Wire*, March 1, 2005.

Chapter 2: The Gas Face

1. Red Bull Music Academy, "MF DOOM: Interview with the Masked Villain," YouTube video, May 14, 2015, youtu.be/JGu0ao_rdAk.
2. MC Serch, "Gas Face Genesis," 2021, in *Did I Ever Tell You the One About . . . MF DOOM*, podcast.
3. Serch, "Gas Face Genesis."

Chapter 3: Peachfuzz

1. Luke Fox, "Mask Off with MF DOOM," *Exclaim!*, January 4, 2021.
2. Fox, "Mask Off."
3. Brian Coleman, *Check the Technique, Volume 2: More Liner Notes for Hip-Hop Junkies* (Everett, MA: Wax Facts Press, 2014), 282.
4. Coleman, *Check the Technique*, 283–284.
5. KMD interview, *Hip-Hop Connection*, October 1, 1991.
6. Red Bull Music Academy, "MF DOOM: Interview with the Masked Villain," YouTube video, May 14, 2015, youtu.be/JGu0ao_rdAk.
7. Chris Wilder, "I'm Is God," *The Source*, August 1991.

Chapter 4: Black Bastards

1. Brian Coleman, *Check the Technique, Volume 2: More Liner Notes for Hip-Hop Junkies* (Everett, MA: Wax Facts Press, 2014), 285.
2. Hugo Lunny, MF DOOM interview, *MVRemix*, April 29, 2002.
3. Red Bull Music Academy, "MF DOOM: Interview with the Masked Villain," YouTube video, May 14, 2015, youtu.be/JGu0ao_rdAk.
4. Andrew Mason, "Behind the Mask," *Wax Poetics*, December 8, 2020.

5. Andrew Nosnitsky, "CM Fam," in *Frank 151: Chapter 48—DOOM*, January 2012.
6. Nosnitsky, "CM Fam."
7. 24/7HH, "Del the Funky Homosapien—Meeting KMD and Relationship with MF DOOM (24/7HH Exclusive)," YouTube video, August 10, 2016, youtu.be/-bOUikKFlJI.
8. Coleman, *Check the Technique*, 286–287.
9. Coleman, *Check the Technique*, 297.
10. Coleman, *Check the Technique*, 287.

Chapter 5: The Time We Faced DOOM

1. Jerry M. Levin, op-ed, *Wall Street Journal*, July 3, 1992.
2. Mike Heck, "Ice-T Speaks Out on Censorship, Cop Killer, Leaving Warner Bros., and More," *The ROC*, October 13, 2007.
3. Cage interview, Rap Worlds Forum, March 22, 2007.
4. Cage interview, Rap Worlds Forum.
5. Kinetta Powell-Dumile, "In Memory of Subroc," *The Source*, July 1993.
6. Kurious Jorge, "Everything's Changed," 2021, in *Did I Ever Tell You the One About . . . MF DOOM*, podcast.
7. Jorge, "Everything's Changed."
8. Brian Coleman, *Check the Technique, Volume 2: More Liner Notes for Hip-Hop Junkies* (Everett, MA: Wax Facts Press, 2014), 288–289.
9. 24/7HH, "Del the Funky Homosapien, Meeting KMD and Relationship with MF DOOM (24/7HH Exclusive)," YouTube video, August 10, 2016, youtu.be/bOUikKFlJI.
10. Big Benn Klingon, "Everything's Changed," 2021, in *Did I Ever Tell You the One About . . . MF DOOM*, podcast.
11. Red Bull Music Academy, "MF DOOM: Interview with the Masked Villain," YouTube video, May 14, 2015, youtu.be/JGu0ao_rdAk.
12. Coleman, *Check the Technique*, 291–292.
13. Jon Shecter, "Corporate Hysteria," editorial, *The Source*, June 1994.
14. Coleman, *Check the Technique*, 291.
15. Shecter, "Corporate Hysteria."
16. Havelock Nelson, *Billboard*, April 16, 1994.
17. Coleman, *Check the Technique*, 289–290.
18. Coleman, *Check the Technique*, 293.
19. Shecter, "Corporate Hysteria."
20. Coleman, *Check the Technique*, 292.
21. Ronin Ro, "Life After Death," *The Source*, June 1994.
22. Ro, "Life After Death."

Chapter 6: Hero vs. Villain

1. Cecil Brown, *Stagolee Shot Billy* (Cambridge, MA: Harvard University Press, 2003), 24.
2. "Beyond Good and Evil: Rapper MF DOOM's New Works of Hip-Hop Fiction Reinvent the Hero Principle for the Modern Age," *Phoenix New Times*, July 24, 2003.
3. "Beyond Good," *Phoenix New Times*.
4. Hua Hsu, "Mask of Sorrow," *The Wire*, March 1, 2005.
5. Hsu, "Mask of Sorrow."
6. Joseph Campbell with Bill Moyers, *The Power of Myth* (New York: Doubleday Books, 1988), 99.
7. Bradford W. Wright, *Comic Book Nation: The Transformation of Youth Culture in America* (Baltimore: Johns Hopkins University Press, 2001), 28.
8. Wright, *Comic Book Nation*, 203.
9. Douglas Wolk, *All of the Marvels: A Journey to the Ends of the Biggest Story Ever Told* (New York: Penguin Press, 2021), 55.
10. Wolk, *All of the Marvels*, 56.
11. Neil Drumming, "The Nerd Behind the Mask" *Village Voice*, August 21, 2001.

Chapter 7: Monster Zero

1. David Kalat, *A Critical History and Filmography of Toho's Godzilla Series* (Jefferson, NC: McFarland & Company, 2010), 4–5.
2. Kalat, *A Critical History*, 81.
3. "Beyond Good and Evil: Rapper MF DOOM's New Works of Hip-Hop Fiction Reinvent the Hero Principle for the Modern Age," *Phoenix New Times*, July 24, 2003.
4. "Beyond Good," *Phoenix New Times*.
5. "Beyond Good," *Phoenix New Times*.
6. Hua Hsu, "Mask of Sorrow," *The Wire*, March 1, 2005.
7. Andrew Mason, "Behind the Mask," *Wax Poetics*, December 8, 2020.
8. Hugo Lunny, MF DOOM interview, *MVRemix*, April 29, 2002.
9. Mason, "Behind the Mask."
10. Mason, "Behind the Mask."
11. Alex Rosado, "The Many Face of DOOM," *Impose Magazine*, September 2003.
12. Christopher R. Weingarten, "Three Faces of DOOM," *College Music Journal*, September 2003.

Chapter 8: Take Me to Your Leader

1. Susan J. Palmer, "The Ansaaru Allah Community," in *The Handbook of Islamic Sects and Movements* (Boston: Brill Publishers, 2021), 700.

2. Adam Heimlich, "Black Egypt: A Visit to Tama-Re," *NY Press*, November 8, 2000.
3. James McNally, "Confessions of a Mask," *Hip-Hop Connection UK*, June 10, 2004.
4. Gabriel Warburg, *Islam, Sectarianism, and Politics in Sudan since the Mahdiyya*, (University of Wisconsin Press, 2003), 171–175.
5. Ruby S. Garnett, *Soul Sacrifice: One Story of Many* (Bloomington, IN: Author House, 2011), 112.
6. Palmer, "Ansaaru Allah Community," 718.
7. Garnett, *Soul Sacrifice*, 19.
8. Palmer, "Ansaaru Allah Community," 719.
9. Heimlich, "Black Egypt."
10. Garnett, *Soul Sacrifice*, 129.

Chapter 9: Suspended Animation
1. "The Man in the Iron Mask," *Jockey Slut*, June 8, 2004.
2. Peter Agoston, "Episode 100—DOOM," May 16, 2003, in *The House List*, podcast.
3. Agoston, "Episode 100—DOOM."
4. Agoston, "Episode 100—DOOM."
5. Agoston, "Episode 100—DOOM."
6. Agoston, "Episode 100—DOOM."

Chapter 10: Deep Fried Frenz
1. Andrew Nosnitsky, "CM Fam," in *Frank 151: Chapter 48—DOOM*, January 2012.
2. Kurious Jorge, "Everything's Changed," 2021, in *Did I Ever Tell You the One About... MF DOOM*, podcast.
3. Kurious Jorge, "Everything's Changed."
4. Jon Caramanica, "How Zev Love X Became MF Doom," January 23, 2021, in *Popcast*, podcast, *New York Times*.
5. Caramanica, "How Zev."
6. Caramanica, "How Zev."
7. Caramanica, "How Zev."

Chapter 11: Who You Think I Am?
1. Bobbito Garcia, "How Zev Love X Became MF Doom," January 7, 2021, in *Popcast*, podcast, *New York Times*.
2. Peter Agoston, "Episode 100—DOOM," May 16, 2003, in *The House List*, podcast.
3. Alex Pappademus, "Imminent DOOM," *Spin*, December 1, 2004.

4. Peter Agoston, "Episode 75—Lord Scotch 79/KEO X-Men," 2018, in *The House List*, podcast.
5. Blake Lethem, "Everything's Changed," January 2021, in *Did I Ever Tell You the One About… MF DOOM*, podcast.
6. Lethem, "Everything's Changed."
7. Lethem, "Everything's Changed."
8. Andrew Mason, "Behind the Mask," *Wax Poetics*, December 8, 2020.
9. David Ma, "Solid Gold Telephone: An Interview with MF DOOM," Nerdtorious.com, January 2, 2019.
10. Mason, "Behind the Mask."
11. Luke Fox, "Mask Off with MF DOOM," *Exclaim!*, January 4, 2021.
12. Ta-Nehisi Coates, "The Mask of DOOM: A Nonconformist Rapper's Second Act," *New Yorker*, September 14, 2009.
13. Mason, "Behind the Mask."

Chapter 12: The Mic

1. Matt Horowitz, "Shadows of Tomorrow: Nice & Nasty Vaz Speaks about MF DOOM's Early Career & Booking His First 'Secret' Show (The Witzard Interview)," *The Witzard*, January 20, 2021, thewitzard.blogspot.com/2021/01/shadows-of-tomorrow-nice-nasty-vaz.html.
2. Drew Fortune, "The Unknowable MF DOOM," *Vulture*, January 28, 2021.
3. Fortune, "Unknowable MF DOOM."
4. Phillip Mlynar, "The Nuyorcan Poets Club, A DIY Hip-Hop Incubator," Red Bull Music Academy, November 7, 2018, daily.redbullmusicacademy.com/2018/11/nuyorican-poets-cafe-feature.

Chapter 13: MF DOOM/*Operation: Doomsday*

1. Robert Greene, *The 48 Laws of Power* (New York: Penguin Books, 2000).
2. Red Bull Music Academy, "MF DOOM: Interview with the Masked Villain," YouTube video, May 14, 2015, youtu.be/JGu0ao_rdAk.
3. Red Bull Music Academy, "MF DOOM: Interview" video.
4. Red Bull Music Academy, "MF DOOM: Interview" video.
5. Peter Agoston, "Episode 100—DOOM," May 16, 2003, in *The House List*, podcast.
6. Robert Christgau, "Consumer Guide," *Village Voice*, August 7, 2001.
7. Christgau, "Consumer Guide."
8. Bobbito Garcia, "How Zev Love X Became MF Doom," January 7, 2021, in *Popcast*, podcast, *New York Times*.

9. Adam Bhala Lough, "Adventures with the Supervillain," in *Frank 151: Chapter 48—DOOM*, January 2012.

Chapter 14: Metal Fingers/*Special Herbs*
1. Stan Lee and Jack Kirby, *The Villainy of Doctor Doom* (Marvel Enterprises, 1999), 11.

Chapter 15: King Geedorah/*Take Me to Your Leader*
1. Red Bull Music Academy, "MF DOOM: Interview with the Masked Villain," YouTube video, May 14, 2015, youtu.be/JGu0ao_rdAk.
2. Red Bull Music Academy, "MF DOOM: Interview" video.
3. Peter Agoston, "Episode 100—DOOM," May 16, 2003, in *The House List*, podcast.
4. Agoston, "Episode 100—DOOM."
5. Red Bull Music Academy, "MF DOOM: Interview" video.

Chapter 16: Viktor Vaughn/*Vaudeville Villain*
1. Red Bull Music Academy, "MF DOOM: Interview with the Masked Villain," YouTube video, May 14, 2015, youtu.be/JGu0ao_rdAk.
2. Ediction UK, "MF DOOM Interview," YouTube video, September 8, 2014, youtu.be/b6En7HoD94s.
3. Alex Rosado, "The Many Face of DOOM," *Impose Magazine*, September 2003.
4. Rosado, "The Many Face."
5. Rosado, "The Many Face."
6. Red Bull Music Academy, "MF DOOM: Interview" video.
7. Rosado, "The Many Face."
8. MF DOOM interview, "MF DOOM Becomes the Vaudeville Villain," *Day to Day*, NPR, October 1, 2003.
9. Rollie Pemberton, "Vaudeville Villain/Viktor Vaughn Review," *Pitchfork*, September 15, 2003.

Chapter 17: Madvillain/*Madvillainy*
1. Rollie Pemberton and Nick Sylvester, "Madvillain/Madvillainy Review," *Pitchfork*, March 25, 2004.
2. *Village Voice*.
3. J-23, "Madvillain-Madvillainy," *Hip-Hop DX*, March 15, 2004.
4. Madvillain review, *Mojo*, June 2004, 114.
5. Madvillain review, *Q Magazine*, July 2004, 116.
6. The Needle Drop, March 2004.

7. Jeff Weiss, "Searching for Tomorrow: The Story of Madlib and DOOM's Madvillainy," *Pitchfork*, August 12, 2014.
8. Peter Agoston, "Episode 69—Count Bass D," 2018, in *The House List*, podcast.
9. Agoston, "Episode 69—Count Bass D."
10. Jason Newman, "Madvillain Exec Egon Remembers MF DOOM," *Rolling Stone*, March 17, 2021.
11. "The Man in the Iron Mask," *Jockey Slut*, June 8, 2004.
12. Luke Fox, "Mask Off with MF DOOM," *Exclaim!*, January 4, 2021.
13. Red Bull Music Academy, "MF DOOM: Interview with the Masked Villain," YouTube video, May 14, 2015, youtu.be/JGu0ao_rdAk.
14. Red Bull Music Academy, "MF DOOM: Interview" video.
15. Fox, "Mask Off."
16. Miranda Jane, "Mad Lib," *Mass Appeal*, 2001.
17. Will Hagle, *Madvillainy* (New York: Bloomsbury Publishing Inc, 2023), 111.
18. Egon Alapatt, "Blunted on Beats: Madvillain Interview," *Wax Poetics*, February 8, 2004.
19. Alapatt, "Blunted on Beats."
20. Fox, "Mask Off."
21. Will Gottsegen, "Madvillainy at 15: MF DOOM on the Legacy of His Classic Collaboration," *Spin*, March 25, 2019.
22. Gottsegen, "Madvillainy at 15."
23. Alapatt, "Blunted on Beats."
24. Weiss, "Searching for Tomorrow."
25. Gottsegen, "Madvillainy at 15."
26. Brett Rollins, "The Story Behind Madvillain's Madvillainy (2004) with Jeff Jank," *Ego Trip*, December 11, 2011, archived at stonesthrow.com/news/uncovered-madvillainy.
27. Fox, "Mask Off."
28. Gottsegen, "Madvillainy at 15."
29. Gottsegen, "Madvillainy at 15."
30. Gottsegen, "Madvillainy at 15."
31. Hagle, *Madvillainy*, 116.
32. Weiss, "Searching for Tomorrow."

Chapter 18: MF DOOM/*Mm . . Food*

1. Shawn Setaro, "Rhymesayers at 20: An Oral History," *Forbes*, November 30, 2015.
2. Setaro, "Rhymesayers at 20."
3. Victoria Hernandez, "Rhymesayers CEO Brent 'Siddiq' Sayers Details Turning Down Interscope Offer from Jimmy Iovine," *Hip-Hop DX*, December 4, 2015.

4. Kwanele Sosibo, "Forever Dope: Stahhr on Lessons from DOOM," *Mail & Guardian* (South Africa), January 8, 2021.
5. Jaelani Turner-Williams, "Impending DOOM: 'Mm . . Food' Warned You 15 Years Ago," Complex.com, November 15, 2019, complex.com/pigeons-and-planes/a/jaelanitw/mf-doom-mm-food-anniversary.
6. Sosibo, "Forever Dope."
7. Sosibo, "Forever Dope."
8. Turner-Williams, "Impending DOOM."
9. Turner-Williams, "Impending DOOM."
10. Sosibo, "Forever Dope."
11. Sosibo, "Forever Dope."
12. Luke Fox, "Mask Off with MF DOOM," *Exclaim!*, January 4, 2021.
13. XXL Staff, "DOOM Shares the Stories Behind Ten of His Best Verses," *XXL*, October 13, 2013.
14. Turner-Williams, "Impending DOOM."
15. Turner-Williams, "Impending DOOM."
16. *XXL* Staff, "DOOM Shares."
17. Fox, "Mask Off."

Chapter 19: Danger DOOM/*The Mouse and the Mask*

1. Brian Hiatt, "Danger Mouse," *Rolling Stone*, May 1, 2008.
2. "Danger Mouse Interview, Pt. 1," *UCLA Magazine*, August 11, 2009.
3. *XXL* Staff, "DOOM Shares the Stories Behind Ten of His Best Verses," *XXL*, October 13, 2013.
4. *XXL* Staff, "DOOM Shares."
5. "Review of The Mouse and the Mask," *Entertainment Weekly*, October 14, 2005, p. 152.
6. Peter Macia, "The Mouse and the Mask: Review," *Pitchfork*, October 11, 2005.
7. Keith Harris, "DangerDOOM: The Mouse and The Mask," *Spin*, October 6, 2005.
8. Danger Mouse, interviewed by Steven Soderbergh, in *Interview*, November 29, 2008.

Chapter 20: DOOM/*Born Like This*

1. Red Bull Music Academy, "MF DOOM: Interview with the Masked Villain," YouTube video, May 14, 2015, youtu.be/JGu0ao_rdAk.
2. David Downs, "Reclusive Rapper DOOM Talks New LP 'Born Like This' and Responds to Fan Rage," *Rolling Stone*, March 23, 2009.

3. Red Bull Music Academy, "MF DOOM: Interview" video.
4. John Dodge, "The Fantastic Four Just Gave Hope to Doctor DOOM's Most Devious Creations," CBR, December 11, 2022, cbr.com/fantastic-four-doombot-doctor-doom-marvel.
5. Courtney Brown, "Remembering MF DOOM: A Personal Story," *The Source*, February 5, 2021.
6. Ben Westhoff, "From Madvillain to Milli Vanilli," *The Village Voice*, August 28, 2007.
7. Ben Westhoff, "Suspended Disbelief Dissed: MF DOOM," *Creative Loafing*, January 8, 2008.
8. Andrew Noz, "DOOM: Shadows on the Sun," *Hip-Hop DX*, April 13, 2009.
9. David Ma, "Solid Gold Telephone: An Interview with MF DOOM," Nerdtorious.com, January 2, 2019.
10. Red Bull Music Academy, "MF DOOM: Interview" video.
11. Noz, "DOOM: Shadows."
12. Ma, "Solid Gold Telephone."
13. Noz, "DOOM: Shadows."
14. Ma, "Solid Gold Telephone."
15. Noz, "DOOM: Shadows."
16. Noz, "DOOM: Shadows."
17. Nate Patrin, "Born Like This Review," *Pitchfork*, April 6, 2009.

Chapter 21: JJ DOOM/*Key to the Kuffs*
1. XXL Staff, "DOOM Shares the Stories Behind Ten of His Best Verses," *XXL*, October 13, 2013.
2. David Kane, "DOOM Interview," *Bonafide*, issue 6, 2012.
3. Kidd Future, "The Futurist: Bishop Nehru's Got the Juice," *The Boombox*, August 16, 2013.
4. Jaap van der Doelen, "Behind the Scenes of MF DOOM's New Adult Swim Project," *Mass Appeal*, August 14, 2017.
5. Rob Hakimian, "Czarface Reveals New DOOM Collab Album, Super What?," *Beats Per Minute*, May 5, 2021.

Chapter 22: Never Dead
1. Rhian Daly, "Busta Rhymes Pays Tribute to MF DOOM," *NME*, January 3, 2021.
2. Daly, "Busta Rhymes Pays."
3. Janet Lee, "Rapper MF DOOM Remembered by Musicians, 'May Your Sound Inspire Music Forever,'" *Variety*, December 31, 2020.

4. Rob Conlon, "Supervillain in Leeds, Operation: DOOMSDAY," *Square Ball Magazine*, February 25, 2022.
5. Conlon, "Supervillain in Leeds."
6. Andrew Robinson, "Heartbroken Wife of Famous Musician Has Unanswered Question after Sudden Death in Leeds," *LeedsLive*, July 4, 2023.
7. Robinson, "Heartbroken Wife."
8. Andrew Robinson, "Leeds Hospital Says Sorry after Famous Musician Died from 'Rare' Reaction to Drug," LeedsLive, July 6, 2023.

Epilogue

1. Ta-Nehisi Coates, "The Mask of DOOM: A Nonconformist Rapper's Second Act," *New Yorker*, September 14, 2009.
2. Brendan Dunne, "MF DOOM and the SB Dunk: How Nike Captured the Supervillain," *Complex*, February 1, 2021.
3. Darragh MacManus, "The Sneakers of MF DOOM," *Welcome Blog*, September 21, 2021.
4. Simon Woods, "RIP MF DOOM: Remembering the Nash Money Sneaker Speakers," *Sneaker Freaker*, June 1, 2021.
5. Will Gottsegen, "Just in Time for Halloween: Rapper MF DOOM Auctioning NFT Masks," *Decrypt*, October 19, 2020.

ACKNOWLEDGMENTS

Thanks to my brother, Sid, for the inspiration. Thanks to my agent, William Loturco, for his unequivocal support. Thanks to my editors, Ben Schrank and Rola Harb, and everyone at Astra House—especially Alexis Nowicki, Tiffany Gonzalez, Rachael Small, Alissa Theodor, Olivia Dontsov, and Joseph Gunther. Respect to Danny Vazquez for acquiring the book. Thanks to Chandra Fernando for her encouragement and support. Thanks to my colleagues: Michael Gonzales, Vikki Tobak, Rob Kenner, Andrew Mason, and David Ma. Thanks to everyone who contributed their time and insights: Dimbaza Dumile, Michelle Mitchell, Lystra Rice, Courtney Brown, Ray "Web D" Davis, Uncle E, Mr. Hood, Prince Paul, Posdnuos, Pete Nice, Rich Keller, MC Serch, Stretch Armstrong, Rob Swift Aguilar, John Robinson, Big Juss, Beans, Esoteric, Havelock Nelson, Peter Agoston, Fiona Bloom, Peter Lupoff, OP Miller, Kevin Hutchinson, Adam DeFalco, Alex Threadgold, Max Lawrence, Nat Gosman, Michael Bull, Mark Murphy, Carol Bobolts, Adam Bala Lough, Rocky Montagne, Will Ashon, Tom Brown, Will Skeaping, Jason DeMarco, Mister Zechariah Wise, Jason Fragala, Morgan Garcia. Special salute to the late, great Daniel Dumile aka MF DOOM, who dedicated his whole being to this art form and culture that we love so much. All praises due to The Mighty Unseen Force that makes all things possible.

ABOUT THE AUTHOR

S.H. Fernando Jr. is a writer/journalist whose byline has appeared in national publications from the *New York Times* and *Rolling Stone* to *The Source*. He currently lives in Baltimore, Maryland.

"A BEST MUSIC BOOK OF 2024 — *VARIETY, FLOOD, CLASH, & MOTHER JONES*"